WORLD WAR II AND ITS CONSEQUENCES

A note for the general reader

War, Peace and Social Change: Europe 1900–1955 is the latest honours-level history course to be produced by the Open University. War and Society has always been a subject of special interest and expertise in the Open University's History Department. The appeal for the general reader is that the five books in the series, taken together or singly, consist of authoritative, up-to-date discussions of the various aspects of war and society in the twentieth century.

The books provide insights into the modes of teaching and communication, including the use of audio-visual material, which have been pioneered at the Open University. Readers will find that they are encouraged to participate in a series of 'tutorials in print', an effective way to achieve a complete command of the material. As in any serious study of a historical topic, there are many suggestions for further reading, including references to a Course Reader, set book and to two collections of primary documents which accompany the series. It is possible to grasp the basic outlines of the topics discussed without turning to these books, but obviously serious students will wish to follow up what is, in effect, a very carefully designed course of guided reading, and discussion and analysis of that reading. The first unit in Book I sets out the aims and scope of the course.

Open University students are provided with supplementary material, including a *Course Guide* which gives information on student assignments, summer school, the use of video-cassettes, and so on.

A318 War, Peace and Social Change: Europe 1900–1955

Book I   *Europe on the Eve of War 1900–1914*

Book II   *World War I and Its Consequences*

Book III   *Between Two Wars*

Book IV   *World War II and Its Consequences*

Book V   *War and Change in Twentieth-Century Europe*

Prepared by the course team and published by the Open University Press, 1990

Other material associated with the course

Documents 1: 1900–1929, eds Arthur Marwick and Wendy Simpson, Open University Press, 1990

Documents 2: 1925–1959, eds Arthur Marwick and Wendy Simpson, Open University Press, 1990

War, Peace and Social Change in Twentieth-Century Europe, eds Clive Emsley, Arthur Marwick and Wendy Simpson, Open University Press, 1990 (Course Reader)

Europe 1880–1945, J. M. Roberts, Longman, 1989 (second edition) (set book)

If you are interested in studying the course, contact the Student Enquiries Office, The Open University, PO Box 71, Walton Hall, Milton Keynes MK7 6AG.

Cover illustration: 'Der Feind Sieht Dein Licht. Verdunkeln!' ('The Enemy Can See Your Light. Black Out!' (Trustees of the Imperial War Museum).

WAR, PEACE AND SOCIAL CHANGE: EUROPE 1900–1955
BOOK IV

WORLD WAR II AND ITS CONSEQUENCES

*Clive Emsley, Arthur Marwick,
Bill Purdue and Tony Aldgate*

**OPEN
UNIVERSITY
PRESS**

Open University Press
in association with
The Open University

The Open
University

A318 Course team

Tony Aldgate   *Author*
Kate Clements   *Editor*
Charles Cooper   *BBC Producer*
Henry Cowper   *Author*
Ian Donnachie   *Author*
Nigel Draper   *Editor*
Clive Emsley   *Author*
David Englander   *Author*
John Golby   *Author*
John Greenwood   *Liaison Librarian*

Tony Lentin   *Author*
Arthur Marwick   *Author and Course Team Chair*
Ray Munns   *Cartographer*
Bill Purdue   *Author*
Wendy Simpson   *Course Manager*
Tag Taylor   *Designer*
Bernard Waites   *Author*
Geoffrey Warner   *Author*

Open University Press
Celtic Court
22 Ballmoor
Buckingham MK18 1XW
England

and
1900 Frost Road, Suite 101
Bristol, PA 19007, USA

First published in 1990

© 1990 The Open University

British Library Cataloguing in Publication Data

War, peace and social change: Europe 1900–1955.
  World War II and its consequences.
  1. Europe, history
  I. Open University, *A318 War, Peace and Social change course Team*
  II. Open University   III. Emsley, Clive
  940

  ISBN 0-335-09311-6   ISBN 0-335-09310-8 (pbk)

Library of Congress Cataloging in Publication Data

World War II and its consequences / Clive Emsley . . . [et al.].
    p. cm. – (War, peace, and social change; bk. 4)
  ISBN 0-335-09311-5. – ISBN 0-335-09310-8 (pbk.)
  1. World War, 1939–1945 – Influence – Sources.   2. Civilization, Modern – 20th century – Sources.   3. Social change – History – 20th century – Sources.   I. Emsley, Clive.   II. Title: World War Two and its consequences.   III. Title: World War 2 and its consequences.
IV. Series.   D735.W64   1990
940.53'142–dc20   90-7057   CIP

Designed by the Graphic Design Group of the Open University
This book is set in 10/12pt Palatino by Rowland Phototypesetting Ltd, Bury St Edmunds, Suffolk
Printed and bound in Great Britain by Butler and Tanner Ltd, Frome, Somerset

1.1

CONTENTS

Acknowledgements

Grateful acknowledgement is made to the following sources for permission to reproduce material in this book:

Text

Bédarida, F. 'World War II and social change in France', in Marwick, A. (ed.) *Total War and Social Change*, 1988, Macmillan; Maier, C. S., 'The two post-war eras and the conditions for stability in twentieth-century Western Europe', *American Historical Review Forum*, vol. 86, no. 2, April 1982, American Historical Association; Dahrendorf, R., *Society and Democracy in Germany*, 1968, Weidenfeld and Nicolson.

Tables

Table 21.1: Overy, R. J., 'Hitler's war and the German economy: a reinterpretation', *Economic History Review*, no. xxxv, 1982, Basil Blackwell, Ltd.; *Tables 21.2 and 21.3*: Costello, J. and Hughes, T., *The Battle of the Atlantic*, 1977, Collins; *Table 22–25.1*: Kennedy, P., *The Rise and Fall of the Great Powers*, 1988, Unwin Hyman; *Table 22–25.2*: Ellwood, D., *Italy 1943–45*, 1985, Leicester University Press.

Figures

Figure 22–25.1: Kosinski, L. *The Population of Europe: A Geographical Perspective*, 1970, Longman.

UNIT 21 THE NATURE OF WORLD WAR II

Clive Emsley

Open University students will need to refer to:

Set book: J. M. Roberts, *Europe 1880–1945*, Longman, 1989

Course Reader: *War, Peace and Social Change in Twentieth-Century Europe*, eds Clive Emsley, Arthur Marwick and Wendy Simpson, Open University Press, 1990

Documents 2: 1925–1959, eds Arthur Marwick and Wendy Simpson, Open University Press, 1990

Offprints Booklet

Maps Booklet

Video-cassette 2

INTRODUCTION

This unit is concerned with the conduct and nature of the Second World War in Europe. By the end of the unit you should be able to recognize:

1 the different ways in which the war was waged on land, sea and in the air; and

2 the contrast between the conduct of the war in the west and in the east of Europe.

In Britain, probably the immediate impression that people have of the contrast between the First and Second World Wars is that the former was essentially static, with the two sides entrenched in positions which hardly moved for four years, and that the latter was one of rapid movement typified by the *Blitzkrieg* ('lightning war') tactics of the Germans. This, like many first impressions or traditional views, requires qualification. As you will have learned from Book II, Units 7 and 11–13, the First World War, including the revolutionary conflicts which followed it, was not static in the east; moreover, while there was considerable movement in North Africa involving British, German and Italian armies between 1939 and 1943, nothing could have been more static than the western front involving Britain and occupied Europe from the summer of 1940 to the summer of 1944. On the eastern front, following the German invasion of the USSR in June 1941, the combatant armies swept backwards and forwards over enormous tracts of territory; this was a war of movement, but in no sense was it a 'lightning war'. Before we address ourselves to the detail of *Blitzkrieg* and the war on the western and eastern fronts, it is worth noting the sheer variety of European theatres of war between 1939 and 1945.

The final chapter of Roberts (set book, pp.553–80) gives a broad survey of the war and will provide an introduction to many of the issues that we will be studying in this unit. Read those pages now.

The following table omits the detail of the German-Soviet war and the reconquest of Western Europe following the landings of 1944; instead it lists the beginning, end, and some of the key events of World War II in the other European theatres. Study it now, as it will help you when I refer to these theatres later in the unit.

The European Theatres of World War II

The Polish war of 1939

1939

23 August: Nazi-Soviet pact, with a secret protocol assigning Estonia, Finland, Latvia and eastern Poland to the Soviet orbit.

1 September: German invasion of Poland. Polish army virtually destroyed by 18 September.

17 September: Red Army invades eastern Poland.

27 September: Warsaw surrenders.

28 September: Nazi-Soviet pact revised; Lithuania included in the secret protocol concerning the Soviet orbit. In October the USSR imposes treaties on Estonia, Latvia and Lithuania requiring Red Army garrisons on their territory; the following summer the three countries are incorporated into the USSR. Finland is asked to exchange territory with the USSR (particularly to assist the defence of Leningrad) but refuses.

The Russo-Finnish war, 1939–40

1939

30 November: USSR attacks Finland.

1940

12 March: Peace of Moscow. Finns cede Karelian Islands, Eastern Karelia, and lease Hangö to USSR.

Hitler's successful war in the west, 1939–40

1939

3 September: British and French ultimatums to Germany over Polish invasion expire, leading to war.

September 1939–April 1940: 'The phoney war'; little action on the fronts between British and French and German armies.

1940

9 April: Germany occupies Denmark.

9 April–10 June: Germany occupies Norway.

10–15 May: Germany occupies Belgium.

26 May–3 June: British troops evacuated at Dunkirk.

10 June: Italy declares war on Britain and France.

22 June: French sign armistice.

With the French surrender the war in Western Europe was largely over until the summer of 1944, except for limited resistance activity, strategic bombing and occasional pinprick raids by British commando or parachute units.

The war in the Balkans, 1939–41

1939

April: Italy occupies Albania.

1940

June: USSR occupies north-eastern Romania.

August: Hungary occupies north-western Romania; Bulgaria occupies south-eastern Romania.

28 October: Italians invade Greece from Albania.

1941

March: British troops land in Greece.

6 April: Germany invades Yugoslavia.

11 April: Bulgaria, Hungary and Italy invade Yugoslavia.

17 April: Yugoslav army capitulates.

27 April: Germans occupy Athens.

May–June: Germans occupy Crete and the Greek islands.

With the defeat of Greece the conventional war in the Balkans was over, although partisan warfare, and in some instances civil war, continued. Hungarian and Romanian troops fought alongside Germans in the invasion of the USSR; Bulgaria declared war on Britain (and subsequently on the USA) but, fearful of the pro-Russian sympathies of the population, the Bulgarian government declined to join the war against the USSR.

The war in Italy, 1943–45

On 13 May 1943 'Army Group Africa' capitulated: 252,000 German and Italian troops became prisoners-of-war and the Allies turned their attention to Italy.

1943

10 July: Allied troops land in Sicily.

25 July: Italian King dismisses Mussolini.

17 August: Allies capture Messina; the campaign in Sicily ends.

3 September: Italy signs armistice; first Allied landings on the Italian mainland.

12 September: German paratroops free Mussolini, who assumes leadership of the Fascist Republic of Salò in the north of Italy.

3 October: Kingdom of Italy declares war on Germany.

There followed eighteen months of hard fighting as the Allies pushed up the Italian peninsula; there were also bursts of occasional fierce fighting in the rear of the German front between Italian partisans, Germans and Italian Fascists.

1945

28 April: Mussolini captured by partisans and shot.

2 May: German troops in Italy surrender.

The war in the Balkans, 1944–45

1944

March: The Red Army begins an advance into the Balkans.

23 August: Coup in Romania; Romania declares war on Germany. Red Army occupies Romania.

25 August: German troops begin evacuation of Greece.

5 September: USSR declares war on Bulgaria.

8 September: Bulgaria declares war on Germany followed by pro-Soviet coup; Red Army occupies Bulgaria.

9 September: Yugoslav Partisans link up with Red Army.

11 October: Hungary makes secret armistice with USSR, but German army in Hungary forces its revocation.

18 October: Yugoslav Partisans enter Belgrade. Greek government returns to Athens supported by British troops. Civil war in Greece between communists and British-backed monarchists.

23 December: Counter-government in Hungary declares war on Germany.

1945

13 February: Budapest falls to Red Army.

1 *THE 'LESSONS' OF WORLD WAR I, AND THE* BLITZKRIEG

Exercise   I want you to turn now to your *Offprints Booklet* and read Hew Strachan's essay entitled 'Blitzkrieg'. As you read the essay, note down answers to the following questions:

1   What significant technological developments were made in military hardware during World War I?

2   To what extent did these developments, and other 'lessons' of the war, figure in the consideration of the conduct of a future war?

3   How far was *Blitzkrieg* a coherent plan for conducting war? ■

Specimen answers   1   The two principal developments discussed by Strachan are the aeroplane and the tank.

2   Trench warfare during World War I had prompted much of the discussion of military tactics to concentrate on defence and had led to the construction of sophisticated fortified lines, most notably the Maginot line. Some military experts were keen to develop armoured warfare, but only in the USSR did generals, drawing on their experience of mobility in World War I and the civil war, develop advanced offensive tactics combining the use of artillery, tanks and aircraft; the disappointing performance of tanks in the Spanish Civil War and Stalin's purges effectively silenced the advocates of these tactics. In Germany tanks were seen as providing mobile defence. Especially after the re-introduction of conscription in 1935, German military planners still thought in terms similar to Schlieffen, with large bodies of infantry as the primary instruments for the battlefield.

Most military planners contemplated linking airpower with ground forces, but in Britain, with a unique airforce separate from the army and the navy, the notion of strategic bombing was developed in the belief that this could be deployed to undermine both the morale of an enemy population and an enemy's economy. The principal theorist of strategic bombing, however, was not British but the Italian General Guilio Douhet.

3   Strachan shows that while *Blitzkrieg* may have had a meaning at 'a purely operational level', it was not perceived as a military doctrine until after the victories of 1939 and 1940. Moreover, although the German army was successful in these short campaigns, it believed (rightly as it turned out) that it should be planning for a long war and not a succession of short ones. □

The success of the *Blitzkrieg* campaigns, especially that against France, can blind us to the true nature of the way that the bulk of Hitler's armies were deployed, fought, and received supplies. Most of the German combat troops, indeed most of the combat troops of all nations engaged in World War II, were infantrymen. Panzer tanks could spearhead an attack; railways could transport troops to Germany's frontiers; but after that, for much of the time during campaigns, the infantry walked – and they did not walk any faster than their fathers had done in 1914. Hitler had decreed that his armies should be mechanized; this concentration on providing motor transport for the army in fact led to a decline in railway rolling stock so that, even though it worked out cheaper to use internal railway communications for journeys over 200 miles, there was less railway stock available in

1939 than there had been in 1914. A further problem was that the German motor industry was not sufficiently developed to provide the vehicles that Hitler wanted; and motor vehicles require oil and rubber, both of which had to be imported to Germany – something which was to create serious wartime problems, as considerable funds were syphoned off for the research and development of synthetic oil and rubber. Only sixteen of Germany's 103 divisions were fully mechanized in 1939, and a considerable amount of German transport remained horse-drawn. A lack of marching discipline led to congestion and jams as infantry, lorries and horse-drawn transport shared the same roads; in retrospect, perhaps, this makes the success of the German army's early campaigns even more remarkable.

These successes encouraged the popular impression in Germany that the war was over in the summer of 1940 and again in October 1941; indeed, Hitler himself contemplated running down arms production in both years. German economic production for war did not show a massive increase until after 1942, and this has led some economic historians to develop the idea of the *Blitzkrieg* economy. The most sophisticated version of this has been put forward by Professor Alan Milward in a series of studies of the Nazi war economy. He has argued that the Nazi Party wanted a system that would enable them to wage war without a drastic reduction in civilian consumer standards. Accordingly German rearmament was geared for producing armaments in 'width' rather than in 'depth'; this enabled the Nazis to fight short, relatively limited wars and not to risk internal disorder by inflicting too much privation on the German population. Only with growing pressure on the eastern front and the entry of the USA into the war were the Nazis compelled to organize Germany wholly for total war, the key shift being indicated by Goebbels' speech in February 1943 threatening the Allies with '*totalen Krieg*'.

Exercise Study Table 21.1 and answer the following questions:

1   When was the greatest percentage increase in German military expenditure?

2   Do the figures in the table raise any questions about the idea of the *Blitzkrieg* economy? ■

Specimen answers 1   The greatest percentage increases in military expenditure are to be found in the years 1939–40 and 1940–41. These are, respectively, 120.9 per cent and 46 per cent. Military expenditure became a much greater percentage of state expenditure between the years 1938–39 and 1939–40, rising from 43.6 per cent to 65.5 per cent; this is a much larger jump than in later years.

2   Since there is no qualitative leap in military expenditure after 1941 and 1942, the figures suggest that the reasons for the increase in war production after 1942 need to be sought in something other than the idea of the *Blitzkrieg* economy. □

Discussion As the figures presented in the table are annual estimates, you might have considered that monthly fluctuations could still add weight to the theory of the *Blitzkrieg* economy. However, if the expenditure went up during the campaigning months to produce those overall annual figures, then surely emergency production for the periods of *Blitzkrieg* must have been far in excess of the steady, continuous production achieved in the period of total war.

Exercise You will have noticed that Table 21.1 was taken from an article by Richard Overy which is in the Course Reader and which you have already read in conjunction

Table 21.1   *Military expenditure, state expenditure and national income in Germany, 1938–39 to 1943–44 (milliard Reichmarks, current prices)*

Year	Military expenditure	State expenditure	National income
1938–39	17.2	39.4	98
1939–40	38	58	109
1940–41	55.9	80	120
1941–42	72.3	100.5[1]	125
1942–43	86.2	124[1]	134
1943–44	99.4	130[1]	130

[1]based on revenue from occupied Europe and the *Reich*

Source: R. J. Overy, 'Hitler's war and the German economy: a re-interpretation', *Economic History Review*, no.xxxv, 1982, p.283.

with Book III, Unit 18. Turn to that article again now. What is Overy's criticism of the concept of the *Blitzkrieg* economy? ■

Specimen answer   Overy maintains that Hitler was planning for total war during the 1930s, and that his economic planning got out of phase with the events of his foreign policy; in particular, Hitler did not expect war to develop with Britain and France as a result of his Polish adventure. In sum, Overy maintains that Hitler was planning for a long war, not a *Blitzkrieg*. □

Discussion   Overy has developed these arguments in subsequent essays, notably 'Mobiliz-ation for total war in Germany, 1939–41' (*English Historical Review*, vol. ciii, no. 408 1988, pp. 613–39). He argues that while there were plans for total war, for the mass mobilization of the labour force and all of Germany's resources – plans which were technically put into operation in 1939 – they were undermined by poor and diffused leadership. Goering, for example, was not up to the task of the economic management of total war, and though he tried to centralize the war economy in his office whenever and wherever he could, both the civilian and the military economic leadership tried, often successfully, to circumvent his jurisdiction.

Much of the early military expenditure went towards the construction of an industrial substructure of factories and airfields which, as a result of the Treaty of Versailles, scarcely existed for a war economy. Here too there was mismanage-ment of resources: in 1942 it was reported that 1.8 million construction workers were employed in building new factories, while firms producing for the war effort could not mount second shifts because they were short of 500,000 workers. Additional problems were to be found in the kinds of weaponry produced and how they were produced. The German military demanded a high standard of finish in its equipment and insisted on a flexible, highly trained workforce to achieve this. Such insistence did indeed get very high-quality weaponry, but such expensive equipment was not necessarily the best option; the mass-produced, much cheaper equipment that was more speedily produced by the war economies of Britain and, later, the United States did the job just as well, and was more readily replaced. In 1940, for example, Germany and Britain spent, respectively, an estimated $6 billion and $3.5 billion on armaments, yet Britain produced twice as many vehicles, over 50 per cent more aircraft, and almost as many tanks.

Overy's research adds weight to the thrust of Strachan's argument: *Blitzkrieg* was not a planned tactic for quick, limited wars; it became elevated to such only after a succession of victories which were achieved by the imagination of German field commanders, the courage and initiative of their men, together with a degree of luck and a greater number of errors on the part of their enemies.

Overy's research cannot be taken as the last word on the subject, however. David Kaiser has stressed that we still know little about exactly how the German government made decisions on the day-to-day management of economic policy. Both he and Hans-Erich Volkmann have suggested that by 1939, because of labour shortages, a foreign exchange crisis and competing domestic priorities, the Nazis could not have continued peacetime rearmament at the existing pace. The economic clauses of the Nazi–Soviet pact eased the situation, while the victories of 1939 and 1940 gave the Nazis fresh economic resources, and additional labour supplies to tap. The war against Russia can be seen, in turn, as an attempt to carve out a self-sufficient empire in Central Europe which would enable Germany to fight a long war against Britain supported by the USA.

> Each new war, in short, grew at least partly out of the need to secure additional resources to continue and expand rearmament, and production did expand dramatically from 1940 until 1942 . . . the bulk of the existing evidence seems to show that [Hitler] found himself obliged to proceed at least to limited war in 1939 or else to abandon the existing pace of rearmament. Driven by his ideology, he refused even to consider the latter alternative and chose the former. One may also discern an element of self-fulfilling prophecy in Hitler's economic thought. The rearmament which he undertook ultimately to free Germany from dependence upon the world market in itself made it harder and harder for Germany to draw sustenance from the world market, and impelled him to begin the conquest of *Lebensraum* . . . sooner than he had anticipated. (David Kaiser, from Kaiser *et al.*, 'Debate: Germany, domestic crisis and war in 1939', *Past and Present*, no.122, 1989, pp.204 and 205)

2 THE NATURE OF THE WAR IN THE WEST, 1940–45

With the fall of France in the summer of 1940 the British were effectively barred from engaging German and Italian troops in Western Europe. However, both sides maintained armies in North Africa, and British troops were sent to assist Greece against invasion in 1941.

Exercise   1   Using your common sense and general knowledge, what main problem do you think is created by having an army hundreds or even thousands of miles from home?

2   How is this problem to be solved in general? How do you suppose it was solved during the Second World War? ∎

Specimen answers   1   The principal problem is that the army has to be supplied with food, fuel, munitions, replacements, etc.

2   This can only be overcome by keeping supply lines open. For Britain, Germany and Italy, the maintenance of armies in North Africa required the use of merchant shipping; aircraft simply could not carry the volume of supplies

necessary. However, aircraft, together with warships, could be deployed to protect merchant shipping and to disrupt the supply lines of the enemy. □

Exercise   Thinking back to the conduct of World War I, what other crucial supply routes were likely to witness major fighting? ■

Specimen answer   Britain was still an important trading nation and relied on other countries (including the territories of its far-flung empire) for supplies of oil, raw materials and much of its food. During World War I the Germans had sought to cripple Britain by unrestricted submarine warfare. □

Discussion   Of course, unrestricted submarine warfare had contributed significantly to American involvement in World War I. Admiral Erich Raeder, the commander-in-chief of the *Kriegsmarine* (the German navy) recognized the danger of American involvement. Nevertheless, he concluded in October 1939:

> no threat by other countries, especially the United States, to come into the war – which can certainly be expected if the conflict continues for a long time – must lead to a relaxation of economic warfare once it is begun. The more ruthlessly economic warfare is waged, the earlier it will show results and the sooner the war will end. (Quoted in John Costello and Terry Hughes, *The Battle of the Atlantic*, 1977, p.42)

Exercise   Thinking back to the Treaty of Versailles, can you suggest any reason, besides the principal German desire to starve Britain of supplies and therefore to concentrate on attacking its merchant fleet, for there not being any great fleet action similar to Jutland? ■

Specimen answer   The Treaty of Versailles forbade the Germans from having large warships (specifically ships of over 10,000 tons); while Germany did circumvent the treaty in many respects, it would have been very difficult to conceal the construction of battleships. Although Germany did begin to rearm in the 1930s, it would have taken a considerable time to build a battle fleet capable of challenging the Royal Navy. □

Discussion   By agreements between Britain and Germany in 1935 and 1937 the latter was authorized to build up to 35 per cent of the British surface fleet and to achieve parity in submarines. Germany had, in fact, already begun rebuilding its fleet, laying down in particular the *Bismarck* and the *Tirpitz* – battleships more powerful than any others then afloat or contemplated. Raeder had formulated a plan for a large battle fleet, but when war broke out this was abandoned in favour of what were seen as immediate priorities – submarines and the completion of *Bismarck*, *Tirpitz* and two heavy cruisers.

British naval strategy had three key aims in the war against Germany: ensuring the safe arrival of supplies to the United Kingdom; the prevention of enemy landings; and facilitating landings by British forces and supplying them on foreign territory. The Royal Navy considered that the best way of achieving these aims was to seek out and destroy enemy ships whenever they took to sea. The German surface fleet was involved in the seizure of Denmark and Norway in 1940, but after this the principal aim of the *Kriegsmarine*, as noted above, was to cut Britain's supply lines using surface raiders, aircraft and, above all, submarines. The aims of the naval war ensured that the focus of the struggle was the Atlantic Ocean. The battle of the Atlantic, while enlivened by the forays of German surface warships, notably *Graf Spee* in the autumn and winter of 1939 and *Bismarck* in May 1941, was essentially a struggle involving on the one hand convoys and their escorts and, on the other, the U-boat 'wolf-packs'.

Exercise   The Germans were greatly assisted in the battle of the Atlantic by the fall of France. Why? ■

Specimen answer   The fall of France enabled the *Kriegsmarine* to station its U-boats on the Atlantic coast, which had not been possible in World War I. It also made Atlantic convoys vulnerable to air attacks from the French coast. □

Discussion   You may find it useful to work through this discussion with your *Maps Booklet* open at map 11.

You might have suggested that the fall of France made the French fleet available to the Germans, but in fact article 8 of the armistice agreed to by the French specified that, except for those ships required for the maintenance of their empire, the remainder of the fleet was to be immobilized. The British were sceptical and set out to immobilize the French fleet in their own way. The few warships in British ports were seized, while those in North Africa were given an ultimatum: they could join in the war alongside the British, or they could surrender their ships under a promise of repatriation of the crews and the ultimate restoration of the ships; otherwise they were expected to scuttle themselves within six hours of the receipt of the ultimatum, or face attack. The French ships in port at Alexandria, alongside units of the Royal Navy, agreed to surrender and be repatriated. A much larger contingent at Mers-el-Kebir, to the west of Oran on the coast of Algeria, rejected the ultimatum and were shelled by a Royal Navy squadron; the fifteen-minute 'battle' resulted in enormous French losses, but destroyed the potential threat perceived by the British government.

The battle of the Atlantic swung to and fro for three and a half years (see Tables 21.2 and 21.3). It began with the 'happy time' for the U-boats when, in the early months of the war, they wrought havoc among the Atlantic convoys. Gradually during 1940 and 1941 the convoy escorts gained in experience, numbers and equipment: the Royal Canadian Navy was considerably increased in size, and US warships began escort duty in July 1941 as far as Iceland; air cover was developed from land bases in North America, Iceland and the British Isles, as well as from escort carriers; ship radar was improved and given a high priority for convoy escorts. In addition, the British were probably assisted, unwittingly, by Hitler's

Table 21.2   *British, Allied and neutral merchant ship losses 1939–45*

Period	Tonnage of ships lost (all causes)	Tonnage of ships lost (to U-boats)	Percentage of tonnage lost in Atlantic	Number of British merchant ships lost (all causes)	Number of British merchant ships lost (U-boats)
Sept–Dec 1939	755,392	421,156	99.9	95	50
1940	3,991,641	2,186,158	91.6	511	225
1941	4,328,558	2,171,070	76.1	568	288
1942	7,790,697	6,266,215	79.0	590	452
1943	1,218,219	804,277	37.2	266	203
1944	530,510	358,609	63.9	102	67
Jan–May 1945	411,127	270,277	89.2	45	30

Source: based on figures in Costello and Hughes, *Battle of the Atlantic*, pp.304–5.

Table 21.3   German U-boat operations 1939–45

Year	Quarter	Total Fleet	Daily average numbers		Sunk	Atlantic theatre	
			Operational	Engaged in Atlantic		New U-boats commissioned	Ships sunk by U-boats
1939	Sept–Dec	57	12	5	9	2	105
1940	Jan–Mar	51	11	5	6	4	80
	Apr–Jun	49	10	7	8	9	75
	Jul–Sep	56	10	8	5	15	150
	Oct–Dec	75	11	9	3	26	130
1941	Jan–Mar	102	20	12	5	31	100
	Apr–Jun	136	25	15	7	53	150
	Jul–Sep	182	30	17	6	70	90
	Oct–Dec	233	35	16	17	70	70
1942	Jan–Mar	272	45	13	11	49	225
	Apr–Jun	315	60	15	10	58	240
	Jul–Sep	352	95	25	32	61	290
	Oct–Dec	382	100	40	34	70	260
1943	Jan–Mar	418	110	50	40	70	200
	Apr–Jun	424	90	40	73	69	120
	Jul–Sep	408	60	20	71	68	75
	Oct–Dec	425	70	25	53	83	40
1944	Jan–Mar	445	65	30	60	62	45
	Apr–Jun	437	50	20	68	53	20
	Jul–Sep	396	40	15	79	50	35
	Oct–Dec	398	35	20	32	67	17
1945	Jan–May	349	45	20	153	93	55
				Total	782	Total 1,133	

Source: as Table 21.2.

determination to keep a sizeable U-boat presence in the Mediterranean, thus reducing the number available for the Atlantic.

When the United States entered the war formally in December 1941 the U-boats embarked on their second 'happy time' since, in spite of appalling losses, the Americans did not establish a convoy system for ships sailing on their east coast and sea lanes until May 1942. In July 1942 the U-boat packs switched to the 'Black Gap' – that stretch of the north Atlantic which could not be patrolled by the long-range, four-engine Liberator aircraft operating from land bases. The climax of the battle came in the first half of 1943; the U-boats had a particularly successful month in March, but a disastrous one in May. At the end of April the Atlantic wolf-packs targeted a slow-moving convoy of forty ships, known as ONS 5. Their initial attacks were successful, but then a thick fog came down making the convoy and its escorts invisible to the U-boats, while the latter remained vulnerable to ship radar and to the High Frequency Direction Finders (HFDF) of the escorts, which pinpointed U-boats from their radio transmissions. Twelve ships of ONS 5 were sunk, but the escorts destroyed five U-boats, two more collided and sank, and another two were destroyed by air patrols. The total U-boat losses for May 1943 came to forty-one, and they were temporarily withdrawn from the Atlantic. The U-boat war was by no means over, as is demonstrated by the statistics in Tables 21.2 and 21.3. *Schnörchel* equipment was developed which enabled U-boats to remain submerged while recharging their batteries, and acoustic torpedoes were introduced which homed in on the sound of a ship's propellers. Increasingly, however, it was the U-boats that became the hunted rather than the hunters, and in the last year of the war the average life expectancy of a U-boat was reduced to one and a half sorties.

In addition to the Atlantic, the convoy system was employed from the summer of 1941 to transport goods from Britain to the USSR. The ships were routed through Arctic waters around Scandinavia and through the Barents Sea to Murmansk or Archangel. U-boats played a role in German attempts to destroy these convoys, but the merchant ships on this route also had to run the gauntlet of naval bases and airfields in both Germany and Nazi-occupied Norway. The significant battle here was fought by surface vessels. At the end of 1942 British destroyers protecting convoy JW 51 B by a mixture of skill, luck and the last-minute arrival of a covering squadron of cruisers, beat off an attack by German warships in the battle of the Barents Sea. As a result of the battle Hitler concluded that Germany's surface fleet was not worth maintaining; Raeder resigned in disgust as Hitler decommissioned the bulk of the fleet.

The Mediterranean was the third area of significant naval operations in the European war. Mussolini had dreamed of mastery over the Mediterranean and had built up the *Regia Marina* in consequence. But this fleet was rather more impressive for its size than the weight and equipment of its ships. While the four new battleships built since 1933 were as good as, or even better than, their British counterparts, overall the Italian navy was inferior. At the outset of the war its fleet of 113 submarines was, with the probable exception of the USSR, the largest in the world; but these submarines were primitive and in particular were slow to dive and vulnerable to depth-charge attack. There were no aircraft carriers, and since co-operation between different sections of the Italian armed forces was poor, the proposed reliance on the *Regia Aeronautica* provided no real substitute, even in waters close to Italy. Italy's ship-building industry, with its limited raw materials and financial resources, was considerably less developed and less able to replace lost ships than that of Britain; and while during the inter-war period the Italian aircraft industry had seemed to be in the forefront of innovation, the lack of financial resources and raw materials meant that any such innovations were rarely transferred into military development and production. The British and Italian fleets fought a succession of engagements in the Mediterranean before the Italian fleet surrendered in 1943. British historiography has tended to speak of the Royal Navy's 'moral superiority' over the *Regia Marina*, although a recent re-appraisal by James J. Sadkovich suggests that a double standard has been applied and that it would be more just to consider the conflict as a draw ('Re-evaluating who won the Italo-British naval conflict, 1940–2', *European History Quarterly*, vol.18, no.4). First, Sadkovich stresses that the Italians succeeded in maintaining a battle fleet which continued to present a threat to the British. While this might not seem, on the face of it, a 'success', it must be remembered that the Italians could not offer battle unless sure of an advantage, since they did not have the industrial base easily to replace lost ships. Second, Sadkovich emphasizes the overall Italian success in protecting their convoys to Tunisia, Libya, the Aegean and the Balkans.

German warships constituted the first targets of RAF Bomber Command during the war when a raid was mounted on ships in the Kiel Canal on 4 September 1939. There was considerable concern about the effects of the bombing of civilian targets and, while Warsaw had been hit by the *Luftwaffe* in September 1939, there was a general avoidance of bombing civilian populations in the west until May 1940. The turning point came with two accidents. On 10 May 1940 three German bombers mistakenly bombed the German town of Freiburg-in-Breisgau instead of an airfield by the French town of Mulhouse; the British suspected a German plot to justify the future bombing of civilians and warned that they would take appropriate action. Four days later the *Luftwaffe* bombed Rotterdam, killing nearly a thousand people and starting huge fires – not because incendiary bombs were used but because the oil from a margarine factory caught fire and because the bombing destroyed the main water supply system. The raid was designed to break Dutch military resistance in the city; the Dutch in fact agreed to surrender while the German attack planes were in the air, but only just under a half of the hundred German bombers received the recall message. Technically, since Rotterdam was resisting a military ground attack and since the aircraft had been called in to neutralize Dutch artillery, the raid could not be termed a terror attack on civilians; yet it was precisely in the latter terms that the raid came to be seen, and it was for this reason that it was raised during the Nuremberg war crimes trial. On 15 May RAF Bomber Command was authorized to attack industrial targets east of the Rhine, and that night ninety-nine bombers raided oil refineries and railways in the Ruhr. This raid can be seen as the beginning of the strategic bombing offensive against Germany. (For a comparison of tonnage of bombs dropped during World War II see Table 21.4.)

The first major air 'battles' following the fall of France were fought over Britain and the English Channel. In July and August 1940, as a prelude to Operation *Seelöwe* (Sea-lion) – a seaborne invasion – the *Luftwaffe* attacked radar installations and fighter airfields in the south of England. Wrongly estimating the effects of the attacks, and in response to British bombing raids on Berlin, early in September

Table 21.4   *Comparative bombing statistics*

Target	Number of raids	Tonnage of bombs dropped
(a) German raids		
Rotterdam 14 May 1940	1	94 (high-explosive)
London (Blitz) 7 Sept 1940– 10 May 1941	86	19,141 (high-explosive) (also 36,568 incendiary cannisters each holding 72 incendiary devices)
Coventry 14 Nov 1940	1	503 (high-explosive) (also 881 incendiary cannisters)
(b) RAF raids		
Berlin (main raids only) 16 Jan 1943– 24 Mar 1944	24	49,400 (plus incendiaries)
Hamburg ('battle of') 24–29 July 1943	4	7,196 (plus incendiaries)
Dresden 13 Feb 1945	1	2,978 (plus incendiaries)

Source: compiled from Matthew Cooper, *The German Air Force*, 1981; David Irving, *The Destruction of Dresden*, 1963; Max Hastings, *Bomber Command*, 1979.

Goering switched the attack from the airfields to London. This decision, probably a mistake given the pilot losses which RAF Fighter Command had suffered (there was no similar shortage of planes), signalled the beginning of the 'Blitz' of British cities, especially London. The *Luftwaffe* attacked London incessantly from September to November 1940; there were only ten nights of the sixty-eight between 7 September and 12 November when it did not mount what it called a 'major raid' (i.e. dropping at least one hundred tons of high-explosive bombs) on the city. According to Matthew Cooper (*The German Air Force: An Anatomy of Failure*, p.165), 'This was an ordeal that, for its continuity (though not for the severity of destruction) was never to be approached by either side for the rest of the war.' The Blitz on London, as well as other cities, notably Coventry, continued less frequently until May 1941.

Exercise Turn now to video-cassette 2 and watch item 1, 'All in a Fighter's Day's Work' (7 October 1940), item 2, 'Coventry – The Martyr City' (21 November 1940), and item 3, 'Reprisal Interviews' (1941).

1 What do you consider is illustrated by the items?

2 Is there a contrast between the attitude and portrayal of the British fighter pilot in item 1 and the civilians in item 3, and might this account for the way in which the film was ultimately used?

3 What arguments can be drawn implicitly or explicitly from this film to justify the strategic bombing of Germany?

4 What other arguments could have been used to justify the bombing of Germany? ■

Specimen answers 1 In broad terms these films illustrate the war in the air over Britain between 1940 and 1941, first showing fighter pilots involved in the Battle of Britain, then one of the most notorious incidents of the Blitz – the raid on Coventry – and finally what at least some of the victims of bombing thought about it.

2 There is, I think, a significant contrast between the stiff-upper-lip fighter pilot who, having shot down a Messerchmitt, is off for a cup of tea, and the vindictiveness of the civilians in the third piece of film. The latter is, of course, understandable, but it may also explain why the film was not incorporated into a newsreel; the commentaries accompanying the first and second items are patriotic and uplifting, and with the images and interviews they contribute to a positive note and perhaps also to a positive image of English- or British-ness in the face of adversity. It would be rather difficult to create such a positive commentary to accompany the attitudes expressed in the third item, though perhaps these attitudes better reflect those of the civilian population.

3 In the heat of the war it could be, and was, argued that the strategic bombing of Germany was merely retaliation for the bombing of Britain, though politicians were not quite as blunt as the civilians interviewed in the third item here.

4 The strategic bombing could also be justified on the grounds that it would disrupt the German economy and weaken German morale (though it should be remembered with reference to this claim that the British insisted that their own morale had not been weakened by the Blitz). Also, after the fall of France, bombing was one of the few means that Britain had of striking at Germany. □

Discussion Each of the the arguments noted in questions 3 and 4 were deployed by different advocates of strategic bombing during the war, and have been re-emphasized in response to the moral condemnation of the campaign after the war. Air Vice Marshall Arthur Harris, who commanded Bomber Command from February 1942 until the end of the war, was one of the first military officers to publish justifications for his actions after the war:

> The surest way to win a war is to destroy the enemy's war potential. And all that I had seen and studied of warfare in the past had led me to believe that the bomber was the predominant weapon for this task in this war. (Sir Arthur Harris, *Bomber Offensive*, 1947, p.31)

It could also be claimed to the USSR that the strategic bombing offensive was the equivalent of a second front against Germany after the invasion of Russia in June 1941.

After the Battle of Britain and the Blitz, the forces of the air war switched to the skies of continental Europe, though the *Luftwaffe* continued to mount raids against Britain, and in 1944 the first 'V' weapons were launched (the V1 flying bomb and the V2 rocket). The strategic bombing offensive went through a series of phases and 'battles':

May–August 1940. There were attempted precision attacks on German targets largely by day; they were made under the assumption that bombers had little difficulty in finding and hitting their targets.

Autumn 1940–Summer 1941. 'Precision' attacks were continued generally by night. In August 1941 a government-commissioned report, having analysed the photos of the RAF Photographic Reconnaissance Unit, confirmed that these attacks were not precise and estimated that of 4,065 aircraft sorties which claimed to have hit their targets, only one-third had bombed within five miles of the aiming point. The government, concerned among other things with the war in the Atlantic and the threat to the Suez Canal, resolved to shelve plans for a force of 4,000 heavy bombers to win the war.

Autumn 1941–March 1943. Since precision bombing had failed, a new policy of 'area' bombing was introduced by which whole towns were to be attacked and brought to a halt. Professor F. A. Lindemann, one of the academics employed to advise on bombs and bombing, estimated that the area bombing of the working-class districts of the fifty-eight German towns with a population in excess of 100,000 could break the enemy's spirit. Lindemann reckoned that it should be possible to make a third of the German population homeless between March 1942 and the middle of 1943. Although his estimates were challenged in some quarters, the policy was adopted.

March 1943–March 1944. This was the period which Harris termed 'the main offensive'. It drew its authority from instructions drawn up by Winston Churchill, Franklin Roosevelt and their chiefs of staff; the Casablanca Directive of January 1943 declared the overall aim of the bomber offensive to be:

> the progressive destruction and dislocation of the German military, industrial and economic system, and the undermining of the morale of the German people to a point where their capacity for armed resistance is fatally weakened. (Quoted in Sir Charles Webster and Noble Frankland, *The Strategic Air Offensive against Germany 1939–1945*, vol.iv, 1961, p.153)

The offensive was now divided into two. The United States Army Air Force, operating from bases in Britain, made precision raids by day particularly on economic targets. RAF Bomber Command carried out area bombing on a massive scale by night; in particular they hit several key targets in a succession of raids which became characterized as 'battles' – the Battle of the Ruhr (March–July 1943); the Battle of Hamburg (July–August 1943); and the Battle of Berlin (August 1943–March 1944). The first two were counted as 'victories' in as much as they devastated vast areas, though they did not halt the Nazi economy. The Battle of Berlin petered out after very heavy losses inflicted on Bomber Command during a disastrous raid on Nuremberg on 30 March 1944; ninety-six of the 795 aircraft which embarked on the raid failed to return, and another twelve were damaged beyond repair.

Overall losses in aircraft and aircrew were high, especially for the USAAF on their daylight raids. Behind the scenes a sophisticated technological struggle developed as Allied researchers produced electronic equipment to blind the German defences and to find and hit targets more effectively, while German researchers sought to counter these. Bigger and 'better' bombs were developed and aircraft technology was refined. American losses were greatly reduced when a long-range fighter, the P51 Mustang, was introduced to accompany daylight bombing raids in February 1944.

March 1944–May 1945. Early in 1944 the Allies began to achieve a marked superiority in the air. Much of the spring and early summer of 1944 witnessed the bombers preparing the ground for the invasion of Europe. In mid April and late May there was very heavy bombing of the railway lines in France, particularly in the north around Lille and the Belgian border and around Paris. Attacks were also directed at communications and German oil production. However, Bomber Command continued the area bombing of German cities and this policy culminated in the devastating raid on Dresden in February 1945. This raid involved three enormous waves of bombers, the first two made by night by Bomber Command, the third in daylight by the USAAF. The full horror of the resulting fire storm, with its gale-force winds and temperatures of perhaps 1,000° celsius, was not realized by the Allies until after the war. However, what was known of the scale and impact of the raid caused considerable disquiet among ministries, legislatures and even the populations of the Allied powers.

Nine months before the raid on Dresden, Allied armies had landed in northern Europe, inaugurating the final phase of the war in the west – the liberation of the occupied countries of Western Europe and Scandinavia and the invasion of Germany from the west. The fighting in north-west Europe was not marked by any new tactics. As the Allied armies advanced, however, civilians were caught up in the fighting; its disruptive effects (there was starvation in parts of Belgium and the Netherlands in the winter of 1944–45) were on a scale unknown in 1914–18 and 1939–40. The final campaigns of the war in the west are probably most notable for the sheer volume of men and *matériel* amassed against Germany. Operation Overlord, the Allied landings in Normandy, was the largest invasion ever mounted; it was also the most thoroughly planned. For eighteen months before the first troops hit the landing grounds and the beaches in June 1944, military planners had worked on the problems and the logistics of the operation. Their answers were marked throughout by conservatism and caution, underestimating what might be achieved by determination and improvisation. Of course, men's lives and the outcome of the war were at stake, but in his important and pioneering analysis, *Supplying War: Logistics from Wallenstein to Patton* (1977), Martin van Creveld writes disparagingly of the 'war of the accountants'. When problems began to mount on the Normandy bridgehead, for example, the supply officers and planners revised all of their estimates with gloomy foreboding. One American field commander, General George Patton, ignored the planners and broke out from the bridgehead, with the armies of the American General Hodges and the British General Montgomery in his wake. The three armies crossed the Seine and had cleared its western banks on 24 August 1944, eleven days ahead of the schedule which the planners said could not be met.

3 THE NATURE OF THE WAR IN THE EAST, 1941–45

Operation Overlord was the largest seaborne invasion ever mounted; Operation Barbarossa, the German invasion of Russia in June 1941, was the largest single military operation of all time. Almost 3.5 million men were deployed by the Germans. In addition, the Finns began a second, brief 'instalment' of their war against the USSR; Romania launched two armies over the River Prut towards the Bug and Odessa; and Hungarian, Italian and Slovakian troops were also engaged on the German side. The invasion force was divided into three army groups driving respectively from East Prussia and Poland towards Leningrad (Army Group North), Moscow (Army Group Centre), and the Ukraine and Crimea with their wheat fields, coal and oil (Army Group South) (see map 9 in the *Maps Booklet*). The distances which these armies were expected to cover were enormous and made the problems of supply phenomenal, the more so because of the shortages of rubber and oil in Germany which combined with the few and generally poor roads in Russia to militate against German vehicles running at optimum efficiency. Hopes of using the Russian railway system as it was captured were complicated by German locomotives and railway stock being of a different gauge; *Eisenbahntruppen* (railway troops) were deployed with the invaders, but in insufficient numbers to solve all the difficulties of changing gauges and water stations.

Exercise   How might the concept of *Blitzkrieg* have solved the potential problems faced by the Germans in invading Russia? ■

Specimen answer   A 'lightning war' which speedily and totally destroyed the Red Army would have solved the problem of supply over long distances with bad roads and unsuitable railways, and over a long period of time. □

Discussion   In his Directive No. 21, issued on 18 December 1940, Hitler ordered his armed forces to be prepared 'to crush Soviet Russia in a quick campaign'. Of course, it is easier to issue directives of this sort than to carry them out. The plan was to push ahead with the Panzer units and envelop the Russians before they could withdraw into the east. The problem was that the distances to be covered were so much greater than in the west, where, as noted earlier, *Blitzkrieg* was as much due to accident and luck as to any forward planning or development of the concept; furthermore, there was a severe shortage of mechanized transport. Captured

British and French vehicles were brought into service and large numbers of lorries were purchased in Switzerland. Consequently the German army embarked on Barbarossa with 2,000 different kinds of vehicles, leading to nightmares for those responsible for organizing spare parts. Much of the equipment for the infantry columns behind the Panzers was horse-drawn, and seventy-five infantry divisions were each issued with 200 *panje* wagons (peasant carts) for equipment and supplies. In his discussion of the logistic preparations and assumptions underlying Barbarossa, Martin van Creveld concludes that 'the German General Staff seemed to have abandoned rational thought' (*Supplying War*, p.151).

Yet Barbarossa appeared to begin well. The Panzers of Army Group North covered 200 miles in five days; those of Army Group Centre reached Minsk after four days; and those of Army Group South, driving south of the difficult terrain of the Pripet Marshes, found themselves in ideal tank country in the Ukraine. Gradually, though, progress slowed as heavy summer rain and continual traffic turned poor roads into quagmires, and as the Panzers had to wait for the infantry. At the beginning of December, Army Group Centre was halted some fifty miles from Moscow, the furthest east that the two northern Army Groups were to penetrate. By the end of the year the Russians had suffered enormous losses: lost territory meant the loss of industry – 63 per cent of pre-war coal production, 60 per cent of aluminium, 68 per cent of steel and 71 per cent of pig iron had gone; half of the Red Army of 4.7 million men had also been lost. But the Germans had lost 830,400 men, and for them this was potentially even more serious.

Although checked in the north, the Germans did launch a new offensive in the summer of 1942. Army Group South was reorganized into Army Groups A and B, and a deep thrust was made into the Caucasus. The Germans were halted at Stalingrad, and after months of savage fighting, 90,000 German troops were taken prisoner between 31 January and 2 February 1943. An abortive advance was attempted around Kursk in July 1943, but following the surrender at Stalingrad the German armies were to be continually on the defensive in the east. Hitler insisted that they hold on to 'fortified positions'; the Russians, usually deploying far superior numbers of four or even six to one, simply encircled such positions and annihilated their defenders.

Much of the key to Soviet success was to be found in its industrial potential. The stubborn resistance of pockets of the Red Army in the summer of 1941 enabled the withdrawal of 10 million people and 1,523 plants of varying size.

Even though much of the old industrial heartland was under German occupation, fresh coal and ore deposits could be, and were, opened up in the Urals and West Siberia, and factories were relocated here or newly built. The pre-war weighting towards armaments production and the strict state supervision of industry probably facilitated the industrial reorganization, but there were other elements also working in the Russians' favour. There was a general standardization of equipment and parts in the Red Army, and while the Russians had two types of armoured fighting vehicle, the Germans had twelve. Moreover the Russians were acquainted with and equipped for their winters; when German vehicles and guns seized up because of the cold, most Russian equipment continued to function.

Exercise Thus far the struggle in the east may look similar to the land war in Western Europe, but I want you now to read documents II.1–II.3 in *Documents 2* and then answer the following questions:

1   How do these documents direct German soldiers to behave in Russia?

2   How are German troops to be punished for any offences committed against civilians?

3   How, according to Halder, did Hitler intend that Soviet Commissars were to be treated?

4   What, according to Halder, was the Generals' response to the latter (the 'Commissar Order')? ■

Specimen answers   1   The orders authorize the troops to terrorize the enemy into submission, and any enemy civilians guilty of offences against the German army are to be subject to prompt punishment without even the necessity for military courts.

2   Punishment for such offences is declared to be 'not obligatory', and Section 11.2 of the 13 May 1941 order argues that Bolshevik attacks on Germany and National Socialism should be borne in mind whenever such offences have to be judged.

3   They were to be shot.

4   The generals were outraged by the order. □

Discussion   Directives and orders such as these played a prominent part in the prosecution case at the war crimes tribunal at Nuremberg. Among the army officers who testified in those trials was Field Marshal Erich von Manstein, who had commanded an armoured corps in Army Group North during 1941. With reference to the 'Commissar Order', he told the court:

> It was the first time I found myself involved in a conflict between my soldierly conceptions and my duty to obey. Actually I ought to have obeyed, but I said to myself that as a soldier I could not possibly co-operate in a thing like that. I told the Commander of the Army Group . . . that I would not carry out such an order, which was against the honour of a soldier. (Quoted in William L. Shirer, *The Rise and Fall of the Third Reich*, 1964, p.993 note)

Similar arguments have been used by many German army veterans of the eastern front, as well as by historians. What happened, in this version, was that the *Wehrmacht* fought the war as ordinary, honest soldiers fighting for their country, but in their wake came the *Einsatzgruppen* (special forces) who rounded up Jews, gypsies, communists and other 'undesirables' or *Untermenschen* (sub-humans). Units of the *Einsatzgruppen* (*Einsatzkommando* or *Sonderkommando*) either murdered their victims then and there, or transported them to the death camps; the army was thus not involved and generaly ignored the 'Commissar Order'. However, some younger historians who have grown up since the war have challenged this version. The subtitle of Omer Bartov's book is indicative of how they interpret the conflict in the east: *The Eastern Front 1941–1945: German Troops and the Barbarisation of Warfare* (1985).

Bartov makes a detailed study of three combat divisions which served on the eastern front for the duration of the war. He suggests that the terrible physical and mental hardships – including long marches, poor food, lack of leave, battle fatigue and enormous casualties – may have contributed to the brutalization of the men and a blunting of their moral and ethical sensibilities. But he also notes that most of the officers in these divisions had grown up under the National Socialist government and appeared highly susceptible to Nazi influences. Moreover, perhaps partly because of the strain of the campaigns, it seems that the majority of the rank and file, whatever they thought of the Nazi Party, were:

> firm believers, almost in a religious sense, in their Führer and, by extension, in many of the ideological and political goals quoted in his name. It . . . seems that political indoctrination did achieve two essential purposes: it stiffened the determination of the soldiers at the front and played an important role in preventing disintegration and breakdowns among the ranks of the German army in the East; and at the same time it legitimised and enhanced the barbarisation of warfare in Russia which, coupled with the brutality emanating from the nature of the war itself . . . led to the terrible destruction of western Russia by the German army. (Bartov, *The Eastern Front*, p.149)

Whatever Manstein said at Nuremberg, many other senior officers, even non-Nazis, saw the war as ideological. General Erich Hoepner, commander of a Panzer group in Army Group North, had openly opposed Hitler in 1938 and was to be executed for his part in the July bomb plot of 1944; but in May 1941 he wrote:

> The war against Russia is an important chapter in the struggle for existence of the German nation. It is the old battle of the Germanic against the Slav peoples, of the defence of European culture against Moscovite-Asiatic inundation, and the repulse of Jewish Bolshevism. The objective of this battle must be the destruction of present-day Russia and it must therefore be conducted with unprecedented severity. Every military action must be guided in planning and execution by an iron will to exterminate the enemy mercilessly and totally. In particular, no adherents of the present Russian-Bolshevik system are to be spared. (Quoted in Jürgen Förster, 'The German army and the ideological war against the Soviet Union', in Gerhard Hirschfeld (ed.), *The Politics of Genocide*, 1986, p.18)

The documentary evidence used by Bartov, Förster and others shows that many of the troops in the field had little compunction about executing commissars or following their 'Guidelines for the Conduct of Troops in Russia' which called for 'ruthless action' (*rücksichtslos vorzugehen*) against 'Bolsheviks, agitators, guerrillas, saboteurs and Jews'. 'Ruthless action' was generally translated into shooting or hanging.

Commissars, communists and Jews were weeded out from Red Army prisoners as soon as they were taken. But even if ordinary Russian PoWs were not singled out for 'ruthless action', their chances were slim. You will have noted Halder's reference to the problem in Document II.3 above. In the early months of the war so many Russians were captured that the German army simply could not cope; in September 1941 the mortality rate in some of the prison camps was running at 1 per cent per day. Prisoners were sent to labour camps, and some were experimented upon. Ten thousand Soviet PoWs arrived in Auschwitz in September and October 1941, of whom at least 900 were gassed in experiments with Zyklon B. Of the 5.7 million Russian prisoners taken between June 1941 and February 1945, 3.3 million died or were killed. Christian Streit, in his detailed study of the treatment of Soviet prisoners (*Keine Kameraden. Die Wehrmacht and die Sowjetischen Kriegsgefangenen, 1941–1945*, 1978), concludes that the attitude of the

Wehrmacht to these prisoners, its preparedness to assist *Einsatzgruppen* by identifying Jews and communists among them, as well as its assistance in identifying and arresting civilian Jews, contributed to the Nazi decision to implement its 'final solution' policy in the summer of 1941. The Nazis, Streit argues, had been uncertain about how the army would react to the policy; there had been murmurings and even criticism by army officers when the Polish elite was exterminated after the invasion of 1939. The *Wehrmacht*'s attitude to Soviet prisoners and its preparedness to obey the Commissar Order convinced the Nazis that there would be no opposition. Of course, such an argument has not gone unchallenged. Jürgen Förster, for example, does not think it credible that the 'final solution' was unleashed because the feared opposition of the army did not materialize; he insists that the decision to exterminate the Jews of Eastern Europe was taken in conjunction with the plan for Barbarossa, and was set in motion in the early days of the invasion of Russia when early success suggested that the Soviet Union was heading for rapid defeat. But whatever the precise relationship, if any, between the systematic mass murder of millions of Jews, gypsies and others, and Barbarossa, it is clear that the Germans fought the war in the east in a different way from the war in the western theatres.

You may be wondering at this point about how the Russians fought the war; was barbarization only to be found on one side? The question has not been systematically studied with reference to the treatment of Germans in Soviet hands, but it is clear that the Soviet authorities used the opportunity created by war in a brutal and ruthless way in Poland. While the Nazis set about liquidating the Polish elite in their half of the country, so the Soviets pursued a rather similar policy in their zone (the western Ukraine and western Belorussia). Indeed, the purges were such that Nazi repatriation commissions looking for ethnic Germans to repatriate from these regions found themselves deluged with requests from non-Germans and most notably (and tragically) from Polish Jews. In April 1943 German troops found mass graves in Katyn Forest near Smolensk, an area from which they had driven the Red Army. Stalin and other Soviet leaders have insisted that the Nazis were responsible for the murder of the several thousand Polish officers in these graves, but the weight of evidence has always pointed conclusively to Soviet guilt. In addition, beginning in February 1940, the Russians deported some 1.5 million people from Poland, out of a population of 13 million, and they deliberately played on racial and social divisions in the territory they occupied. Ukrainians and Belorussians were encouraged to seek out and kill Polish settlers, described as 'gentry'; peasants were encouraged to murder landlords and seize the land.

The Soviets also conducted massive purges of their own ethnic groups at the end of the war. Thousands of Cossacks, Ukrainians and others were forcibly returned to the USSR, sometimes by those very Allied troops whom they had looked to for protection. They were either executed or disappeared into labour camps, branded as collaborators; some had fought on the German side against the Red Army, but by no means all, and many of those who were returned in this way were simply refugees. But the treatment of these people, rather than being the result of the barbarization of war, is perhaps best understood in terms of the continuation of the 'internal war' waged in Stalin's Russia and discussed in Book III, Unit 16.

4 PARTISAN WARFARE

You will have noticed that among those against whom 'ruthless action' was authorized by the 'Guidelines for the Conduct of Troops in Russia' were 'guerrillas and saboteurs'. On 3 July 1941 Stalin broadcast over Soviet radio, calling upon the people to rise up against the invaders; two weeks later instructions were issued for the organization of partisan units in Russia focused on local institutions like factories or else on villages. It took time for the Russians to organize effective partisan activity. There could sometimes be friction where the most able guerrilla leader in a district was first and foremost an army, rather than a party, man; but there were also sensible political commissars, like Nikita Krushchev in the Ukraine, who recognized the importance of the soldier over party conformity in matters of military tactics. Soviet historiography has probably overemphasized the spontaneity of the partisans; it has also played down the stupidity of the Germans, first in not seeking to build on anti-Soviet feeling in captured territory like the Ukraine, and second in alienating this feeling by savage reprisals on the civilian population after partisan raids. As the war dragged on, and as more and more men and weapons could be infiltrated behind the lines, the partisan problem became an increasing threat to the German armies in Russia. Nor was this threat only to be found in Russia; most armies of occupation commonly have difficulties with those who they are occupying, and at the peak of its power Nazi Germany and its allies occupied a considerable part of Europe (see map 8 in the *Maps Booklet*).

No country in Western Europe burst out into spontaneous resistance and partisan warfare following defeat and occupation in 1940. For one thing there was the obvious demoralization caused by defeat, and for another, potential resistance groups could not always agree politically and tactically among themselves. The political factions most used to the tight-knit, secretive organization required by resistance were the communist parties, and a few of their leaders had experience of guerrilla warfare from the Spanish Civil War. But until the German invasion of Russia the European communists remained aloof from the struggle between capitalist powers. When the communists did get involved from the summer of 1941, resistance movements generally became better organized, stronger, and more aggressive; such was the case with the *Front de l'Indépendence* in Belgium, the *Borgerlige Partisaner* in Denmark, and the *Front Nationale* in France. All of these groups had non-communists in their ranks, though the party sought to maintain overall direction. The problems of reconciling or subordinating political hostilities to a common end became still more acute when the communists joined the resistance. It took Jean Moulin, as a representative of de Gaulle's Free French in London, fifteen months of negotiation to forge resistance unity in France and to establish the *Conseil National de la Résistance* in April 1943.

Resistance in Western Europe involved collecting intelligence, aiding escaped prisoners and air-crew who had been shot down, propaganda, and, occasionally, sabotage. Most of the latter was directed from London and often carried out by SOE (Special Operations Executive) agents on the ground. Resistance in the west did not involve much in the way of guerrilla fighting until Allied troops had landed. Partisan groups began fighting in the north of Italy following Mussolini's fall in the summer of 1943; in a few instances they were joined by Allied PoWs liberated after the demise of Fascism or co-ordinated by soldiers of the British SAS

(Special Air Service) or American OSS (Office of Strategic Services). Italian partisans spanned the political spectrum from communists to royalists, with consequent internal friction and mutual suspicion; the majority of the partisans, however, were drawn from the liberal centre and the communists. In France, which until November 1942 was divided between the occupied zone in the north and west and Vichy, it was German labour policy which alienated many of the young men who took to the forested hills around the River Rhône and formed the nucleus of the *maquis*. In the summer of 1942 the Germans demanded 50,000 Frenchmen to work in Germany; the following March this number was increased to 400,000. But the *maquis* was scarcely a minor irritant to Vichy and the German army before the invasion of 1944. Even then the most successful guerrilla activities were generally those organized by SAS units of the Free French or British armies, or those directed by the uniformed Jedburgh Teams of Allied soldiers organized specifically to liaise with and co-ordinate partisan activity. About 3,000 *maquisards* attempted to fight a conventional battle with German troops on the plateau of Vercors to the west of Grenoble in June and July 1944; they were annihilated.

Exercise The biggest and most effective partisan armies were to be found in the east and south-east of Europe. Turn now to video-cassette 2 and watch item 4, an extract from the film *The Nine Hundred*. This was a short documentary made in 1944 about an airlift to Yugoslav Partisans by Allied units based in Italy; the film itself was shot by cameramen of the MAAF (Mediterranean Allied Army and Airforces). As you watch the sequences, note down what significant points it tells you about the Partisans. ■

Specimen answer Perhaps the first thing to strike you was that the Partisans contained men, women and children. Second, the film is called *The Nine Hundred*, and whether or not there are 900 partisans in these sequences, there clearly were a significant number. Third (and this point may not have occurred to you), setting up a sequence involving a large number of people zig-zagging down terraced slopes may be artistically satisfying, but it must also have taken a considerable amount of time. The fact that this could be done in broad daylight by Allied military cameramen in 'occupied' Yugoslavia, demonstrates in itself the hold which the Partisans could have over different parts of territory at different times. □

The fighting in Yugoslavia between 1941 and 1945 was not as simple, however, as a single army of Partisans against the various occupying and puppet Yugoslav forces (see Map 10). Yugoslavia remained a mixture of ethnic groups – Croats, Montenegrans, Serbs, Slovenes – and religions – Christian (Catholic, Orthodox and Protestant) and Muslim. The German conquest in 1941 gave the opportunity for right-wing Ustashi (*ustasa*) to set up, under Axis aegis, the Independent State of Croatia (usually known as the NDH after the initials of its designation *Nezavisna Drzava Hrvataskas*). The Ustashi were Croat nationalists, generally Catholics but with some Muslims. Once in power they embarked on their 'final solution' of the 'Serbian problem': about 350,000 Serbs were killed during the three and a half years of the NDH. The Serbs met violence and massacre with violence and massacre; in some instances German and Italian troops were compelled to intervene to stop the butchery. In addition to this fractricidal conflict there were two different groups of guerrilla fighters, the Chetniks and the Partisans.

The Chetniks (literally members of military companies – *ceta* – though the term also referred back to guerrilla bands in Serbia who had fought against the Turks and to a World War I veterans' association) were divided into several different groups. Some of those in the Italian district of occupation were initially armed by the Italians to fight the Partisans, but the most famous Chetnik bands were those under the leadership of Colonel Dragoljub-Draza Mihailovich. Mihailovich's aim was the creation of a 'Yugoslav Home Army', a secret body led by officers of the old royal army which would work in conjunction with the Yugoslav government in exile, and the Allies, to prepare the way for the restoration of the monarchy. The second large group of resistance fighters was the communist-led army generally known as the Partisans. Initially there appeared to be the chance of co-operation between Mihailovich and Josip Broz, better known as Tito, the Partisan leader. However, the former, conscious of his role as the representative of the exiled royal government, counselled lying low so as not to provoke German reprisals, while Tito's confrontations with the Germans were brought home to the Yugoslavs in a series of attempts by the Germans to terrorize the people into submission. On 16 September 1941 Hitler ordered that for every German soldier killed by guerillas, 100 Yugoslav hostages would die, and for every German soldier wounded, 50 Yugoslavs would die. In the following month, following a Partisan attack which left ten Germans dead and twenty-six wounded, the Germans massacred 7,000 men and boys from the town of Kraguyevats. This was only one, perhaps the most notorious, of such reprisals in Yugoslavia, but it was typical of the war in the Balkans and in Russia. There was only one equivalent massacre in the west, at Oradour-sur-Glane, near Limoges, in France in June 1944 – which might be taken as an indication of resistance performance in the west as compared with the east, but might also be taken as an indication of the Germans' racial attitudes to Western Europeans and to Slavs. The different resistance policies of Chetniks and Partisans eventually led to open warfare between the two, especially as Mihailovich's men became branded as collaborators because of the links which some Chetnik bands had with the Italians. At times the Partisans directed the bulk of their efforts towards the struggle with the Chetniks and, as the Serbian historian Veselin Djuretic revealed in a sensational book published in 1985, at one point in March 1943 this even led them into negotiations with the Germans.

Britain had begun sending aid to the Chetniks shortly after the German invasion. Rumours of the Partisan campaign and of the fighting between Chetniks and Partisans gradually filtered through to the British government, but there was uncertainty about who the Partisans actually were and about the identity of Tito.

> One school of thought refused to believe that he existed at all. The name, they said, stood for *Tajna Internacionalna Teroristicka Organizacija*, or Secret International Terrorist Organisation, and not for any individual leader . . . the more romantically inclined claimed that Tito was not a man, but a young woman of startling beauty and great force of character. (Fitzroy Maclean, *Eastern Approaches*, 1949, p.225)

In 1943 Churchill dispatched a military mission to Yugoslavia under Fitzroy Maclean 'to find out who was killing the most Germans and suggest means by which we could help to kill more' (Maclean, p.227). Maclean contacted the Partisans and was greatly impressed by them and their leader. As a result of his analysis of the situation on the ground, British aid to Mihailovich dried up and was diverted to Tito. King Peter acquiesced in the transfer of aid and accordingly changed the composition of his government in exile.

Exercise   Turn now to *Documents 2* and read document II.4. This is a series of extracts from the wartime memoirs of Milovan Djilas, one of Tito's most dependable lieutenants in the Partisan war. Djilas was editor of *Borba* (*The Struggle*), the newspaper of the Communist Party in Yugoslavia. The Partisans tried to publish *Borba* weekly when possible during the war; in addition, the editorial group under Djilas published other periodicals, directives and Marxist theoretical pamphlets. Read the extracts from his book now, and answer the following questions:

1   What were the Partisans' goals in the war?

2   What kind of appeals did the Partisans make to the peasants during the war?

3   What policies, in addition to the pursuit of the war, did the Partisans try to carry out in the field? ■

Specimen answers   1   The Partisans fought the war with both nationalist and revolutionary aims.

2   The Partisans do not seem to have appealed to the peasants in theoretical Marxist terms. Rather, with reference to the inevitability of proletarian revolution, when Djilas was called upon to address a group of peasants he appealed to Yugoslav patriotism and, in addition to the contemporary situation, he made reference back to the struggles against the Turks and to folk epics.

3   Djilas describes the Partisans as trying to neutralize the extremism that had led to massacres and reprisals among the different groups within Yugoslavia. He also describes the Partisans as trying to win over the peasants by punishing looting and recompensing victims, and as seeking to bring education and good order to the villages through which they moved. □

Discussion   You may have wanted to take all of this with a very large pinch of salt, recognizing that, as Djilas was responsible for publishing the Communist Party newspaper, he might have been painting a rather too rosy picture of the Partisans. Of course, he may have been stressing the heroism and attractiveness of the Partisans, yet neither here nor elsewhere does he deny that they shot prisoners; he reports 'requisitioning' from peasants when the Partisans were in need, and he shows considerable sympathy for the rank-and-file Chetniks as their depleted forces were hounded to destruction by the Partisans and some surviving bands of Ustashi early in 1945. The Partisans did urge ethnic and religious tolerance, often against the feelings of local Partisan groups as they moved through their lands. This tolerance seems to have helped them to survive their epic long march across Montenegro and Bosnia during the summer of 1943. The march culminated in the declaration of a provisional government at Jajce on 29 November, which divided the country into a federation of six provinces (hoping thus to eliminate ethnic hostilities), denied the authority of the royalist government in exile, forbade the return of the King, and put off a decision on the future of the monarchy until the full liberation of all territory would enable the people to decide freely. In addition, especially in those areas which the Partisans controlled for any length of time during the fighting, they set up people's committees, drawing on people of ability without reference to their political affiliation and without necessarily any previous administrative experience; these committees then ran their allotted districts, though Communist Party officials always sought a supervisory role.

Partisan fighters in Greece were divided in much the same way as those in Yugoslavia, but the outcome of the struggle there was very different. The largest guerilla army in occupied Greece was ELAS (the National Popular Liberation Army). It was the military wing of EAM (the National Liberation Front), a union of several radical and socialist groups, which became increasingly dominated by the communists. The acronym ELAS was pronounced in the same way as 'Ellas' – i.e. Greece – which made it particularly effective in focusing on the patriotic aspect of the war. ELAS was based in the mountains, and sweeps by German and Italian troops, as well as collaborating Greek gendarmes, led to villages being destroyed and executions in the search for the partisans. These punitive raids sometimes strengthened the partisans by bringing new, vengeful recruits to their ranks, but the raids appear also to have had the effect of alienating some peasants from the partisans, especially as fighting between the partisan groups at times seemed to take precedence over fighting the army of occupation. Nicholas Hammond was a British liaison officer with ELAS, and he recalled that

> [during] the first year the peasants were all in support and one was absolutely safe moving amongst peasants in Thessaly . . . In the later stages, when the five months of civil war had caused great loss of life and terrible distress to the peasant population [things were different] . . . I was in a village where the ELAS HQ was and there were executions every morning, mainly civilians – there was a great fear of all of the Resistance movements towards the end. (Discussion comment in Marion Sarafis, *Greece: From Resistance to Civil War*, 1980, p.112)

As the Germans withdrew from Greece in October 1944, ELAS claimed to control most of the countryside. The second largest guerilla group, EDES (the National Republican Greek League), had survived the onslaught of ELAS and was dominant in the remote north-west. EDES was originally republican, but increasingly it was dominated by supporters of King George II and the Greek government in exile. But what eventually tipped the balance in favour of the restoration of the monarchy was the deployment of British troops in Athens against ELAS in December 1944. The use of British troops against former allies led to disquiet in both Britain and the United States, but Winston Churchill, who seems to have felt some personal obligation towards King George for rallying to Britain in 1940–41, was determined that Greece should not 'go communist'. Tito's Partisans gave some assistance to ELAS, especially as the fighting in Greece developed into a full-scale civil war (1947–49), but a crucial blow to the communists was Stalin's refusal to become involved, acknowledging the division of Europe agreed between himself and Churchill in October 1944.

5 THE IDEOLOGICAL NATURE OF THE WAR

Diplomacy and international negotiations do not cease when war begins. The leaders of belligerent states still have to deal with neutrals and with their allies, and they commonly seek to justify the belligerence of their states by appeals to general principle. Already in this unit, and elsewhere, we have touched on the kind of ideology deployed by the Nazis to justify (and perhaps also impel) their involvement in war. Nazi ideology was intent on creating a New Order in Europe, while the looting of captured territories and the exploitation of their industrial resources would, it was believed, contribute significantly towards paying for the war and increasing German autarky. In this section I want to concentrate particularly on the anti-Axis coalition and what its leaders claimed to be fighting for.

In August 1941 Winston Churchill met the American President Roosevelt on board ship in Argentia Harbour off Newfoundland. Britain had recently enjoyed some success in North Africa, but had been driven from Greece and Crete, while war against Japan in the Far East appeared increasingly likely. The United States was not yet a belligerent, but was providing considerable military assistance to Britain under the Lend-Lease Act which had been passed by Congress in March 1941, and which authorized the lending or leasing of equipment to any nation 'whose defense the President deems vital to the defense of the United States'. Churchill and Roosevelt concluded the meeting by issuing a statement, subsequently known at the Atlantic Charter.

Exercise Read the Atlantic Charter, which is document II.5 in *Documents 2*, and then answer the following questions:

1   What do the two leaders consider to be the principal threat to the world?

2   What kind of world order do they wish to see emerge from the war?

3   Given its position as an imperial power, can you see any problems for Britain in creating this new world order? ■

Specimen answers 1   The main threat to the world is identified as military aggression, and Nazi Germany is singled out and named as an offender.

2   They seek a world order based on the abandonment of aggression and force as a means to achieving political ends, a world in which all people have the right to choose their government, and in which a liberalized world economy will bring about an end to fear and want.

3   If all people had the right to choose the form of government under which they lived, how could the British Empire survive? And was Britain's economic policy of imperial preference compatible with the proposed international economy? □

Discussion The Atlantic Charter is, as you probably noticed, a vague document. In some ways this was deliberate, as no one wished to repeat the embarrassments that had resulted from some of President Wilson's very specific Fourteen Points. Yet some things were inserted deliberately with a positive purpose in mind. The British War Cabinet, for example, persuaded Churchill to include the reference to social security specifically for home consumption. Churchill himself understood 'free peoples' to mean those European peoples who were to be liberated from Nazi and Fascist oppression: in his Mansion House speech in 1942 he pointedly declared that he had not become Prime Minister 'in order to preside over the liquidation of the British Empire'.

The continuation of European empires was just one area of disagreement between Britain and the United States, though as far as possible it was kept discreetly in the background. There were other disagreements between them over relationships with other members of the anti-Fascist, anti-Nazi alliance. The

United States maintained diplomatic relations with Vichy France until the Anglo-American landings in North Africa in November 1942; even then it was Vichy which broke off relations rather than the United States. Nevertheless, President Roosevelt was reluctant to recognize General de Gaulle as spokesman for France; he feared that de Gaulle was a potential dictator, but he also had his suspicions about France, which he saw as a power typical of a decadent Europe with a corrupt political and social system and espousing an exploitative colonialism. Relations between Britain and de Gaulle were prickly, but the British considered a strong, restored France as essential to their own post-war security. They never had relations with the Vichy regime and, in spite of recurrent reservations about, and dislike of, de Gaulle, they continued to press his suit with the Americans. Even so it was not until a month after the D-Day landings that Roosevelt extended recognition to the General and his Free French.

While Roosevelt was suspicious of the French, Churchill was suspicious of Italy. The Italian invasion of Ethiopia in 1935 had posed a threat to British imperial interests, and Churchill and his colleagues wanted to ensure that no such threat would arise again. The United States, with its large Italian minority (many of whom voted for Roosevelt and the Democrats) did not share such concerns. After the fall of Mussolini, Britain and the United States recognized Italy as a 'co-belligerent', even though this meant dealing with a monarch, Vittorio Emanuele, and a Prime Minister, Marshal Pietro Badoglio, who were both tainted by Fascism. In January 1944 representatives of the anti-Fascist *Comitati di Liberazione Nazionale* (Committees of National Resistance) met in Rome and resolved that the King should abdicate and his heir delegate all his powers to a body which would, in turn, appoint a new cabinet made up of all parties in the resistance. Churchill was furious when the Allied authorities in Italy accepted the proposal; he fumed that the anti-Fascists were not representative of the Italian people, and he publicly declared his support for the monarchy. A compromise was reached whereby the King did not abdicate but retired from public life, and his son became Lieutenant General of the Realm. The following June the anti-Fascists engineered Badoglio's resignation and replaced him with a socialist. Again Churchill protested, but the Americans refused to support his demand that Badoglio be reinstated. From Badoglio onwards the Italian governments sought a change in their status from 'co-belligerent', a subordinate position subject to strict controls established under the armistice of September 1943, to full ally. As a part of this aspiration to equality, and to demonstrate their independence as a sovereign nation, the Italians shocked and surprised Britain and the USA in March 1944 by agreeing to a formal exchange of diplomatic representatives with the Soviet Union. The Soviet Union, though a full member of the anti-Nazi alliance, had been excluded from any effective say in the running of liberated Italy.

Exercise   Document II.6 in *Documents 2* is an extract from a speech made by Josef Stalin on the 25th Anniversary of the October Revolution (6 November 1942). Read it now and then answer the following questions:

1   What argument does Stalin contest in this extract?

2   Can you see any way in which the programme of the Allies, as presented by Stalin, differs seriously from that presented in the Atlantic Charter? ■

Specimen answers   1   Stalin challenges the idea that 'an organic defect' within the Anglo-Soviet-

American alliance will undermine it; this supposed defect he identifies as the differing ideologies and social systems of the Allies.

2   In my opinion, there is no essential difference between the programme outlined in the Atlantic Charter and that given in the fourth paragraph of the extract. □

Discussion   Stalin was not present at the Argentina conference, but the Soviet Union subscribed to the Atlantic Charter when, in January 1942, its principles were embodied in the Declaration of the United Nations signed by all governments at war with the Axis powers. In May 1943 Stalin sanctioned a specifically anti-revolutionary move when he authorized the Communist International to dissolve itself. The International (Comintern), founded in 1919 and based in Moscow, had sought to direct the communist parties of different countries during the inter-war years. Admittedly it had not been a great success, yet its dissolution was perceived, by Stalin at least, as a gesture to his allies in the struggle against Hitler. However, at the same time, Stalin was putting a very loose interpretation on the principles of the Atlantic Charter and the Declaration of the United Nations, particularly when he asserted Russia's intention to restore its 1941 frontiers.

Exercise   In what way do you think that the restoration of the 1941 frontiers of the Soviet Union might be said to be against the spirit of the Atlantic Charter? (You might find it useful to refer back to the chronology at the beginning of this unit.) ■

Specimen answer   The Baltic states had been incorporated into the USSR in 1940 and would therefore come into Russia's 'restored' frontiers; so too would much of eastern Poland, occupied by the Soviet Union in 1939 – and, of course, it was Polish independence that had been the reason for Britain going to war in the first place. □

Discussion   The Russians could claim that all of these territories had been lost to them as a result of World War I, the Revolution, and the war against Poland in 1920; at the conclusion of the latter the Poles had pushed their frontier many miles east of the proposed Curzon Line (you can refresh your memory on this by looking at Roberts, p.335). The Polish government in exile, based in London, was incensed by the Russian claim to the 1941 frontiers, and was disappointed and frustrated when, at the Tehran Conference in November 1943, Churchill and Roosevelt agreed to Stalin's demands on the Polish/Russian frontiers. Churchill attempted to build bridges between the Poles in London – who controlled the bulk of the Polish Home Army (the resistance army in Poland) – and Stalin, who was endeavouring to build up the Polish Communist Party into a significant resistance organization. The London-based Poles were reluctant to make any rapprochement with Stalin, especially after the discovery of the graves in Katyn Forest; their suspicions of Stalin appeared confirmed (at least in their eyes) when the Red Army halted on the banks of the Vistula in early August 1944 and failed to assist the insurrection of the Polish resistance in Warsaw. The Red Army insisted that it was compelled to halt for sound military reasons; the non-communist Poles insisted that the Red Army halted so as to see them defeated and discredited.

Exercise   The 'big three' (Churchill, Roosevelt and Stalin) met for the last time at Yalta in the Crimea in February 1945. The concluding declaration of the conference is reproduced as document II.7 in *Documents 2*. Read it now and then answer the following questions:

1   How would you say this declaration differs from the Atlantic Charter?

2   How is the Polish problem to be resolved?

3   Which state is to be invited to share in the occupation of defeated Germany?

4   This invitation was largely at the insistence of the British. Can you think of any reasons why they suggested this? ■

Specimen answers   1   The aims of the two documents are similar, but the Crimea Declaration contains much more precise detail on certain issues. This was possible because the Germans were in retreat on every front and the end of the war was in sight.

2   The Polish problem is to be resolved in Stalin's favour, with the Curzon Line being taken as the frontier; the Poles are to be appeased with territory in the north and west, at the expense of Germany.

3   France.

4   In the aftermath of World War I the United States had withdrawn into isolation. A French presence in occupied Germany following the defeat of the Nazis meant that, if the United States withdrew again, Britain would not have to bear the burden of administrating the west of Germany alone. Moreover, although defeated in 1940, France still had pretensions (especially under de Gaulle) to being a great and an imperial power like Britain; both states were liberal and democratic, in contrast to the power advancing into the east of Germany, the Soviet Union. □

Discussion   There were ideological aspects to the 1939–45 conflicts in Europe. On the Nazi side there was the ideology of racial superiority, the need for *Lebensraum* and security, and the concept of war as a vital element in the development of a successful racial group. The opponents of Hitler did not seek to engage in debate on these grounds, and very little was said during the war about the evil of Nazi racial policy and the systematic attempts at exterminating peoples and social groups. Much of this was due to the fact that the true nature of these policies was probably not understood until Allied troops began overrunning concentration camps and extermination camps towards the end of 1944 and at the beginning of 1945. The extreme propaganda of World War I might also have created a resistance to 'evil Hun' stories. The members of the anti-Axis coalition claimed to be fighting for democracy and a more secure world, but each had very different interpretations of democracy and of what constituted their own security. These interpretations were based partly on their ideological differences, shelved for the duration of the war against Hitler yet re-appearing from time to time, especially as victory came closer. Particularly worrying in the eyes of men like Churchill was the fact that the best organized and most efficient resistance groups were often dominated by communists (Poland was the great exception here). Spheres of influence were drawn up by the anti-Axis coalition as victory seemed certain. As noted in section 4, Stalin acknowledged that Greece lay outside his sphere of influence and, apparently as a result of this, he left the Greek communists to fend for themselves in the civil war. Yugoslavia was supposed to be split 50/50 between East and West influence; the victory of Tito's Partisans seemed to throw Yugoslavia into the Soviet camp, but Tito's independent line, especially when Partisans clashed with British troops over Trieste in the summer of 1945, infuriated Stalin. The 'people's democracies' of Eastern Europe that emerged in the aftermath of the war were expected to follow the lines laid down in Moscow. There is controversy over the extent to which, if indeed at all, Washington exerted, or sought to exert, a more veiled hegemony over Western Europe.

References

Bartov, O. (1985) *The Eastern Front 1941–1945: German Troops and the Barbarisation of Warfare*, London, Macmillan.

Cooper, M. (1981) *The German Air Force: An Anatomy of Failure*, London, Jane's.

Costello, J. and Hughes, T. (1977) *The Battle of the Atlantic*, London, Collins.

Creveld, M. van (1977) *Supplying War: Logistics from Wallenstein to Patton*, Cambridge, Cambridge University Press.

Förster, J. (1986) 'The German army and the ideological war against the Soviet Union', in G. Hirschfeld (ed.) *The Politics of Genocide*, London, Allen and Unwin.

Harris, Sir A. (1947) *Bomber Offensive*, London, Collins.

Hastings, M. (1979) *Bomber Command*, London, Michael Joseph.

Irving, D. (1963) *The Destruction of Dresden*, London, Kimber.

Kaiser, D., Mason, T. and Overy, R. J. (1989) 'Debate: Germany, domestic crisis and war in 1939', *Past and Present*, no.122.

Maclean, F. (1949) *Eastern Approaches*, London, Cape.

Overy, R. J. (1982) 'Hitler's war and the German economy: a re-interpretation', *Economic History Review*, 2nd series, no.xxxv.

Overy, R. J. (1988) 'Mobilization for total war in Germany, 1939–41', *English Historical Review*, vol. ciii, no. 408, July.

Sadkovich, J. J. (1988) 'Re-evaluating who won the Italo-British naval conflict, 1940–2', *European History Quarterly*, vol.18, no.4, October.

Sarafis, M. (1980) *Greece: From Resistance to Civil War*, Nottingham, Spokesman Books.

Shirer, W. L. (1964) *The Rise and Fall of the Third Reich*, London, Pan.

Streit, C. (1978) *Keine Kameraden. Die Wehrmacht und die Sowjetischen Kriegsgefangenen, 1941–1945*, Stuttgart, Deutsche Verlags-Anstalt.

Webster, Sir C. and Frankland, N. (1961) *The Strategic Air Offensive against Germany 1939–1945*, 4 vols, London, HMSO.

UNITS 22–25 THE DEBATE OVER THE IMPACT AND CONSEQUENCES OF WORLD WAR II

Introduction and sections 2.3–2.10 by Arthur Marwick; sections 1–2.2 by Bill Purdue; section 3 by Tony Aldgate

Open University students will need to refer to:

Set book: J. M. Roberts, *Europe 1880–1945*, Longman, 1989

Course Reader: *War, Peace and Social Change in Twentieth-Century Europe*, eds Clive Emsley, Arthur Marwick and Wendy Simpson, Open University Press, 1990

Documents 2: 1925–1959, eds Arthur Marwick and Wendy Simpson, Open University Press, 1990

Offprints Booklet

Maps Booklet

Video-cassette 2

Audio-cassette 1

Audio-cassette 2

Audio-cassette 4

INTRODUCTION

In these units Bill Purdue, Tony Aldgate and I discuss the geopolitical, social and cultural effects of the Second World War, rather as Bill Purdue and I did in Book II for the First World War. We shall again be attempting to estimate the significance of the war experience as against the many other forces which lead to change; we shall try to distinguish between the immediate impact of the war and the more enduring effects. Just as it was important to be clear about the nature and levels of development in the different European countries as they were in 1914, so also we will now have to bear firmly in mind all that you have learned about the different kinds of countries as they developed in the 1920s and 1930s. If, for example, a condition which can be reasonably described as 'mass society' has come into being in these years, then one would not be able to argue that the experiences of World War II 'created' mass society (though they might result in extensions of the facets of that society to new areas – rural ones, for instance – or to new countries; they might result in the further development and exploitation of the artefacts of mass society).

When assessing the effects of World War I, it was very important to make contrasts between autocratic and liberal-democratic societies, and between developed industrial, and less-developed, largely agricultural societies. I want you to spend much of your time in this introduction reflecting on:

1   the main differences between the societies that went to war with each other in the period 1939–1945; and

2   how the likely effects of total war might be influenced or constrained by these differences.

I have already suggested that in explaining the relationship between war and social change (if and where there is one) it is necessary to look for what happens in a society at war that does not happen in a society not at war. Already the notion has arisen once or twice that in total war we get the *participation* of groups which in time of peace had not been very highly regarded. As you may have picked up from Beckett's article in the Course Reader, I have suggested elsewhere (though not in this course so far) that three other processes come into play during war. These are (a) the destruction of resources and the disruption of existing patterns of life (resulting, for instance, in people being projected into new work situations, but also, in face of the destructiveness of war, there is often a great emphasis towards reconstruction); (b) the 'testing' (and therefore frequent modification) of existing social and political institutions and ways of doing things; and (c) the engendering of intensified emotional states (including enhanced loyalties to one's own communities – national, racial, or class – and considerable psychological stresses). The exact way in which these 'processes' (or 'modes' or 'dimensions of war', as I have variously termed them) are expressed is not very important – and indeed no effort is being made in this course to push this particular approach. However, it is possible that, now that you have had time to find your bearings amid all the arguments and counter-arguments involved in a course of this sort, you may find the above four headings useful. (In doing outside reading, making notes, etc., it is always helpful to have headings and issues ready in mind; the latest statement of my own approach is to be found in the introduction and conclusion to the collection edited by me and based on an Open University conference, *Total War and Social Change*, 1988.)

Much more central to the whole course is the question of whether, and how, one can single out war as a cause of change from all the other potential causes. With respect to this conundrum, World War II raises some of the same issues as World War I, but it also embroils us in some rather different debates. To move towards the heart of one of these debates, you will find it extremely useful to read the contribution on Germany which Mark Roseman made to the conference which I have just mentioned.

Exercise   Turn now to the chapter in the Reader by Mark Roseman, 'World War II and social change in Germany'. You will find this article most helpful for several of the aspects of social change which will be discussed later in these units. I therefore suggest that while you are reading the article, apart from making notes on the questions I ask below, you make notes on 'social structure and class', 'social welfare', 'material life and living conditions', 'women and the family', and 'political institutions and values', or at least make annotations in the margin which will later remind you where information on these topics can be found. You may find it useful to apply some of my headings relating to the processes that (I argue) are touched off by war.

The particular issue I want you to address at this stage, and to which I would like you to write down answers, is the following. In contrasting Germany with Britain, Roseman (apart from all the other vitally important ideas and information that he provides) indicates two critical circumstances which severely limit the possibility of identifying the war experience in itself as a separate cause of social change. Write several sentences indicating what (in Roseman's view) the circumstances are, and bringing out the way in which he sums up the issue. Please read Roseman's article now with great care: it is far more important that you should absorb Roseman's expert analysis than my attempt to summarize it. ■

Specimen answer   The first circumstance concerns the nature of the Nazi regime. Germany was *already* experiencing many of the developments which in Britain only came with the actual advent of war. Germany's '"total" peace' entailed the mobilization of society and economy. Labour was already controlled in the way that other countries endeavoured to control it in time of war. There was a 'peacetime war economy', involving a substantial modification (with respect to economic change) of investment activity and raw material allocation and (with respect to social change) occupational structure. The Nazis had already disrupted many aspects of the traditional class structure, had at least made some pretence at giving enhanced status to labour, and had tried to create a kind of national unity through an 'authoritarian corporatism'. The transition from peace to war, Roseman argues, was not a sharp one (as you know, Richard Overy has effectively challenged the notion of Germany merely waging a *Blitzkrieg* war, but this does not, I think, substantially invalidate Roseman's main point).

The second circumstance is that, rather than the experience of war or the responses to the needs of war shaping the development of German society, the decisive influences were those of the occupying powers. The Soviet Union 'totally re-organized society and economy' in East Germany, while West Germany was essentially recreated in the image of the United States.

Roseman sums up these, as he sees them, distinct circumstances (distinct from the British experience, that is) in the phrase 'political discontinuities': that is, the Nazi takeover in 1933, and the Russian and American takeovers in 1945. Because of these, 'total war does not stand out as a revolutionary impulse in the way that it perhaps does in some other countries'. It is evident, says Roseman, 'that "total war" is not an independent cause of social change. Its influence on German society was shaped decisively by the nature of the regime which waged it and that of the regime which followed it'. □

Discussion   In these phrases Roseman shows one of the great historical skills, that of expressing the essence of a problem in a few pithy sentences. In your reading you should be developing the skill of getting into the heart of the arguments being made. The three paragraphs of Roseman's final section make a most effective summing up, and the first of these paragraphs is a splendid summary of the two circumstances I asked you to identify in the exercise. Of course, the final section is of no use to you unless you have mastered the arguments that have led to it.

I hope that (whatever other points you noted down for future use) you did get from Roseman the same two circumstances that I did. Before moving on, do be sure that you really have understood his arguments. Of course, he does also give important instances of the way in which the war experience *did* have effects, but these are to be seen within the general framework of the natures of the regime that waged the war, and the regime (Roseman puts it in the singular because in his conclusion he concentrates purely on West Germany) that followed it.

Roseman's article further pays its way in that it keys us into two general debates of great importance. First, it suggests that in analysing the war we may be able to discriminate between societies that are more or less like Britain (and, incidentally, the United States) and ones that are more or less like Germany. Second, in giving considerable weight to the American and the Russian occupations, he ties in with an important line of thought that has been followed by those belonging to the tradition which likes to generalize about, or build models relating to, historical explanation (the nomothetic tradition, the Marxist tradition, etc.). This is that the major determinant of social change in the aftermath of World War II was the division of Europe into an American sphere of influence and a Russian sphere of influence; thus, for Western Europe 'Americanization' is seen as a fundamental characteristic of social development. Personally, I challenge this view, believing that the roots of social development are much more complex, and that, in particular, the influence of Americanization, as against indigenous Italian, French, British, etc. influences, has being grossly overstated. We hope to help you arrive at informed conclusions of your own on this.

For the purpose of this introduction I want now to concentrate on the first issue.

Exercise   1   What major countries, apart from Germany, could be seen as being affected by 'political discontinuities making it particularly difficult to single out the war as an independent cause of social change' (no one could ever say, of course, that war was ever a *completely* independent cause of social change)? Which country went through one, rather than two, discontinuities?

2   This is a slightly different point, but let's deal with it here. Roseman concludes by stressing the importance of American and Russian occupation policies. But, of course, the war itself was accompanied by occupation policies which had very profound, if not necessarily long-lasting, effects on several countries. What am I referring to here? ■

Specimen answers   1   Italy is the country which went through discontinuities broadly analogous to the German ones. You might wish to maintain, however, that in so far as Italy was less 'revolutionized' than Germany, there was more scope for the war to have a strong impact. Italy was not subject to occupation in quite the same way, but the same arguments about the salience of an American sphere of influence can be advanced. The other country is Russia, which obviously had been 'revolutionized' before the war; clearly it was not subject to any kind of discontinuity and external influence at the end of the war (on the contrary, it extended its own influence).

2   *German* occupation of a number of European countries – touched on by Roseman from the middle paragraph on p.304 to the end of section II. As you know from Unit 21, occupation policies in Denmark, Sweden, the Netherlands, France and Italy were not on the same scale of bestiality as they were in the east. □

Discussion   Those who maintain that the nature of social change after World War II depended upon whether a country fell within the influence of Soviet communism or American capitalism, rather than on the experience of war itself, would seem to have a particularly good example in the case of Poland. Yet Norman Davies, Britain's leading authority on Poland, has maintained almost the exact opposite:

> The changes brought about by the War were deep and permanent. Seven years of slaughter refashioned the state, nation, and society more radically than a century of endeavour beforehand or three decades of communist rule afterwards. (Norman Davies, *God's Playground: A History of Poland*, vol.2, 1981, pp.488–9)

This is perhaps, for rhetorical effect, slightly overstated, but it is certainly not a summary that can be ignored. Perhaps it might be truer to say that some of the more fundamental effects of the war have continued to be concealed by communist rule, but that, if and when that becomes less monolithic, the ways in which Poland is a vastly different country from what it had been in 1939 will become more apparent. (The individual points made by Davies will be discussed in these units under the appropriate headings.)

It may be that from all this we are left with Britain as a unique example, occupied neither by the Germans during the war, nor by the Americans or Russians after the war (though many academics would, not without reason, still apply the Americanization thesis to Britain). Hardach (you may possibly remember the extract I quoted in Book I, Unit 1) is far from the only historian to argue that generalization from the British experience gives a totally wrong impression of there being a connection between total war and desirable social change. Yet, for analytical purposes, it might be worthwhile putting France into the same category as Britain, as a country which on the eve of the war was a Western liberal democracy.

There has been much discussion of the longer-term effects of the destructive aspect of war. F. C. Iklé, in his *The Social Impact of Bomb Destruction* (1958, p.121), has pointed to a distinction between 'passive morale', which shows itself in personal bearing and in private relations and which, as a result of bombing, was generally low, and 'active morale', concerned with public and job activities, which was not adversely affected. In my *War and Social Change in the Twentieth Century* and elsewhere I have suggested that the destruction of war may have some of the same effects on human communities as natural disasters such as earthquakes, and in this connection I have referred to the collection *Man and Society in Disaster* (1962) edited by G. W. Baker and T. E. Chapman. The notion is that bomb (and other destructive) attacks may in fact strengthen morale, creating a determination not just to survive but to rebuild and to reconstruct. One of the most powerful statements of the opposite case is contained in the article 'The impact of World War II on Leningrad' in the Course Reader. The thesis of the article is that the effects of the destruction of World War II were to destroy Leningrad's position as a 'charismatic' city, reducing it to the status of just one of many outside of Moscow. It is not for me to challenge the expertise in Russian history of Edward Bubis and Blair A. Ruble; however, it may be, as is often the case in good historical writing, that some of the evidence they offer suggests qualifications on their conclusions.

Exercise   Read the article by Bubis and Ruble in the Reader now, and then answer the following questions:

1   Can you see any sign of the 'reconstructive' effect of war?

2   Were there any causes, which had nothing to do with the war, that were leading to the reduction in Leningrad's status? ■

Specimen answers and discussion   1   In the second paragraph of the section headed 'The transformation of the city's economic base', the authors say: '*remarkably*, the city's overall industrial output managed to surpass pre-war levels as early as 1950.' I have italicized the remark to show the way in which historians sometimes try to dismiss evidence which goes against their general thesis. Part of one's final conclusion, of course, will depend on how one assesses the significance of the increasing specialization which the authors refer to in the next sentence.

2   Both before and after the war, as the authors make clear, there was a positive policy of hostility to Leningrad emanating from Moscow: in particular Leningrad's scientific and academic institutions were removed or reduced, and national investment in Leningrad was very low   ⬜

The paradigm of the (aerial) blitz in the early stages of the war was that of London. The citizens of Moscow, in late 1941, initially feared that they might suffer a blitz like that on London (though, as we shall see, the destruction and loss of life in Britain was tiny compared with what was later to be suffered in many other countries). Some of the most devastating bombing of all took place on Germany in 1943 and 1944. Albert Speer, in his visits to arms factories and from his 'contacts with the man in the street', derived an impression of 'growing toughness'. Christabel Bielenberg, an Englishwoman domiciled in Nazi Germany, wrote in *The Past is Myself* (1968, p.127): 'I learned when I was in Berlin that those wanton, quite impersonal killings, that barrage from the air that mutilated, suffocated, burned and destroyed, did not so much breed fear and a desire to bow before the storm, but rather a certain fatalistic cussedness, a dogged determination to survive, whatever their policies, whatever their creed.' I would now like you to look at two documents relating to the bomb attacks on Germany.

Exercise   Turn to document II.8, 'Extract from the report by the Police President of Hamburg on the raids on Hamburg in July and August 1943'. When you have read it, write down answers to these questions:

1   What three German air-raid protection services are mentioned?
2   Where does the Police President draw parallels with natural catastrophes? What difference was there in the Hamburg situation?

3   Where is there a suggestion of such destruction having a 'reconstructive effect'?

Before I suggest answers to these questions, I would like you to look at the second extract from document II.9, 'Extracts from *I Lived Under Hitler*', by Sybil Bannister.

4   What indications are there of 'reconstruction' and social change? ■

Specimen answers and discussion   1   The organizations are: Self Protection, Extended Self Protection, and Works Air Protection Services. On the whole, the Nazi air-raid precaution services seemed to have worked reasonably effectively (though, of course, they were completely overwhelmed by something like the Hamburg fire storms); however, it was a feature of Nazi society to have such services divided up into different organizations.

2   There are references to fires in Tokyo, Hamburg (1842), Chicago and the Paris Opera House, and to the 1906 earthquake in San Fransisco. The difference is that these all came unexpectedly, whereas the people of Hamburg were expecting the raids – but they were still overwhelmed.

3   In the last phrase: 'an irresistible will to rebuild'. Of course, this is only an opinion, and an opinion which was in the interests of the Police President to express. I am not trying to identify some universal truth here: I simply want you to consider the possibility that destruction in war can produce reconstructive effects.

4   Despite the appalling destruction, people have 'started afresh', and 'much reconstruction' has been done, etc. With regard to social change, one might detect evidence of 'social levelling' (though that would not necessarily be lasting): prosperous shops are now shacks, one of Hamburg's wealthiest merchants is living in a garage. Again these are hints picked up from only one piece of evidence, but much of historical writing consists of putting together such hints. □

In most of the remainder of these units Bill Purdue, Tony Aldgate and I look at the question of the relationship between war and social change under the series of headings for social change which was introduced at the beginning of the course in Book I. This should be convenient for you, but it runs the risk of misrepresenting the nature of the interaction between war and society. In 'society at war' (as distinct from society not at war), a complex of direct and indirect responses, interaction and cross-action are touched off: changes in one area will often produce consequent changes in other areas. In my own books, as already explained, I have tried to express this complex by speaking of war as simultaneously bringing about destruction and disruption (with, possibly, the reconstructive effects I have just been discussing), operating as a 'test' of and 'challenge' to existing institutions (the French capitulation in 1940 was often seen as a sign that existing French elites had failed the test of war), creating new opportunities for participation, and involving whole populations in an enormous psychological experience. This is only one way, and not necessarily the best one, of expressing complex processes. The point is that you should have a sense of many different effects and counter-effects taking place together in the enormous catastrophe of war.

As in Book II, Bill Purdue starts off with the geopolitical implications of World War II, and then goes on to examine the first two of the areas of change on which we have decided to concentrate in this course. I then take up the topics of social structure, national cohesion, social welfare, living conditions, customs and behaviour, women and the family, high and popular culture, and political institutions and values, concluding with a documents exercise. This is followed by a further study (which runs across several of those topics) of mass society by Tony Aldgate.

For the purposes of your study time Unit 22 comprises sections 1–2.2, Unit 23 sections 2.3–2.5, Unit 24 sections 2.6–2.9 and Unit 25 sections 2.10 and 3.

1 INTERNATIONAL AND GEOPOLITICAL CHANGE

1.1   The war in Europe and the world war

It is conventional, in contrasting the two 'world' wars, to conclude that World War I (I personally prefer its earlier appellation of the Great War) was an essentially European conflict, while World War II, although it began in Europe, became a global struggle which justified the adjective 'world'. To what extent, then, is it justifiable to consider World War II's effects on the international, geopolitical structure without full reference to the progress of the war outside Europe and its effects on the political geography of areas far from Europe?

World War II was in reality two fairly discrete wars – one in Europe (though it spilled over into North Africa and the Middle East) and the other in the Pacific – linked by Britain's and America's involvement in both. Clearly the fortunes of war in the Far East had their effect on Anglo-American strategy in the West and on their military effort in that sphere. But Germany and Japan were at best nominal allies, joined more by the imagination of Joachim von Ribbentrop than anything else, and strategic co-operation between them was minimal; the influence of Mussolini on the Japanese High Command was, to say the least, underwhelming. Things might, of course, have been very different if Japan had chosen to attack the Soviet Union rather than the United States. When the Japanese Foreign minister, Matsuoka Yosuke, was in Berlin in April 1941, Hitler told him nothing about his plan to attack Russia, and Matsuoka accordingly went on to Moscow and signed a neutrality pact with Stalin. The puzzled Matsuoka said to the Japanese cabinet in June: 'I concluded a neutrality pact because I thought that Germany and Russia could not go to war. If I had thought they would go to war . . . I would not have concluded the Neutrality Pact' (Ian Nish, *Japanese Foreign Policy 1869–1942*, 1977, p.242). As it was, the Soviet Union only entered the war against Japan at the last moment in order to safeguard its post-war position in the Far East and was thus enabled to occupy Manchuria and north Korea and to pick up Sakhalin and the Kuriles Islands.

Britain, alone among the major combatants, had a continuous involvement in both spheres and, indeed, it is impossible to understand British foreign policy in the 1930s without an appreciation that 'appeasement' resulted as much from the weakness of the British position in the Far East as from a diagnosis of Europe's problems. Some commentators have seen the United States' involvement in the European war as a natural and inevitable progression from concern at Germany's early successes combined with a protective attitude towards democracy which led, via lend-lease, to Roosevelt being able to bring American public opinion around to the point where entry on Britain's side was possible. However, without Germany's declaration of war on the United States after Pearl Harbor, would the USA have entered the European war?

Exercise   Read Roberts, pp. 549–53, and then answer the following questions:

1   What does Roberts have to say about the pact of 28 September 1940 between Japan and Germany and Italy?

2   What is his assessment of Hitler's action in declaring war on the USA on 11 December 1941? ■

Specimen answers   1   He sees the pact as being designed to discourage the USA from continuing its
and discussion   gestures of support for Britain.

2   He considers it a 'fatal mistake' and an illustration of the irrational origins of Hitler's foreign policy. In the eyes of the Japanese the virtue of the 1940 pact was that it seemed to prevent strong American action in the Pacific. By late 1941, however, American economic embargoes had made Japan decide that war with America was inevitable. But as Roberts says, 'America was not at war with Germany and might well have turned her back on Europe to fight Japan. This possibility was thrown away by Hitler.' □

Once in, America's impact on the war in Europe was colossal and probably decisive, but the impact was akin to that of some mighty *deus ex machina* which threw its power into the European sphere with the sole aim of defeating Germany. The origins of the war in Europe were domestic to the continent while all the European participants had war aims moulded by tradition, geography and self-interest, whereas the United States had no settled convictions as to the geopolitical shape of a post-war Europe. That the military success of American armies had an enormous influence on the *de facto* maps of Europe that emerged in the summer of 1945 is certain, but it was not a politically purposeful influence, for, alone among the Allies, the USA allowed the strategic consideration of the war to be paramount over considerations of post-war advantage.

The view of the closing stages of the war and its immediate aftermath as marking the divided hegemony of two extra-European powers over a diminished Europe is flawed, so far as America is concerned, in that it reads the period from the cold war perspective of 1948. So far as the Soviet Union is concerned, its flaw is the categorization of Russia as somehow not a European power, which would have been news to Metternich. Indeed, far from being a totally novel end to a European war, the situation in 1945 has some similarity with that of 1814–15, with Russian armies penetrating deep into Central Europe, though the main counter-vailing influence is not a semi-detached Britain but its fully extra-continental ex-colony, the United States.

1.2   The role of ideology

The role of ideology in producing the opposing alliances, the war aims of the combatants and the shifting changes to the European political map between 1939 and 1945 is problematic. Were Hitler's and Stalin's war aims determined by the theories of National Socialism and Communism respectively, or did they correspond to the traditional aims of German and Russian leaders, so that they would have made perfectly good sense to many of their predecessors? Was Britain's and France's intervention in 1939 born of concern for the independence of small nations, a vague anti-Fascism, or simply national self-interest and concern for the balance of power in Europe?

Exercise What development at the beginning of the war and during its earlier stages constitutes the biggest single argument against ideology being the dominant consideration? ■

Specimen answer and discussion The Soviet–German Non-Aggression Treaty of 23 August 1939, which was followed by Soviet–German co-operation over the division of Poland between them, together with the attempts of the two powers to reach an agreement over spheres of influence which continued until late 1940. The existence of an understanding or of co-operation between two ideologically opposed powers does not, of course, mean that their respective ideologies were unimportant to them, but it does point to ideology being a less than omnipresent motive for their actions. □

From the early 1920s Germany and the Soviet Union were both revisionist powers with ambitions in East and Central Europe which they were determined to pursue, whether as allies, enemies, or independently. At different times they investigated the possibilities of alliance (as with von Ribbentrop's plan for a Eurasian alliance made up of Germany, Italy, Japan and the Soviet Union), sought to co-exist, and fought. Ideological considerations and the commitment of the Soviet Union to world revolution did put difficulties in the way of the option for France and Britain of an understanding with Russia, similar to that reached before 1914, to balance Germany's strength. However, they did not prevent Anglo-Russia and American-Russian co-operation after 1941, any more than they prevented the Soviet–German Treaty of 1939. Ideology could make alliances difficult and could be used as a justification for territorial ambitions and gains and as propaganda for them, but the alliances entered into, the moves made by the powers, their territorial ambitions, and even the post-war territorial adjustments are all readily comprehensible within the framework of conflicting and traditional national aims pursued as opportunity offered.

1.3 East and Central Europe

It was in East and Central Europe that the origins of the war were to be found, that Russia and Germany had major territorial ambitions, that almost every smaller power had designs on its neighbours' territories, and that the war resulted in major territorial changes.

It is not only with the aid of hindsight that we can see the political geography of East and Central Europe that had emerged by 1922 as ephemeral. The writ of Versailles had not penetrated far into Eastern Europe, but neither the provisions it did make for that region nor its provisions for Central Europe were ever as securely imprinted as those for Western Europe. The Treaty of Locarno had seen the powers guarantee the frontiers of France and Belgium with Germany, but not Germany's eastern frontiers. Further east, as we saw in Book II, Units 8–10, frontiers had been set – not by Versailles, but by the fighting that had continued between 1918 and 1922 and by separate treaties. A month before the Treaty of

Tartu in 1920, by which the Soviet Union recognized 'unconditionally' and 'for ever' the total independence of Estonia, Lenin wrote: 'The borders of these new states are fixed only for the time being'.

The territorial settlements of 1918–22 had left Europe divided between those states committed to their preservation, and revisionist states determined to see them modified.

Exercise
1   Which states were revisionist and which relatively satisfied with existing frontiers?

2   What changes to the territorial arrangements of 1922 had already taken place before the outbreak of World War II? ■

Specimen answers and discussion
1   Revisionist: Germany, USSR, Hungary, Bulgaria and Italy. Upholders of the existing order: Britain, France, Czechoslovakia, Yugoslavia, Estonia, Latvia, Lithuania, Finland, Romania, Belgium and Albania. Poland comes into a category of its own, being a state created by Versailles and by its own military success in the war with Russia. But Poland still had territorial ambitions. A. J. P. Taylor has commented that Poland's problem was that it believed it was a great power but wasn't.

2   Czechoslovakia had, of course, disappeared from the map: the Sudetenland had been incorporated into Germany; Bohemia and Moravia had been declared German protectorates; Poland had taken Teschen; Hungary had taken southern Slovakia and Ruthenia; and the rest of Slovakia had become an independent state. □

Germany's war in the west gave the Soviet Union the opportunity to strengthen its position in Eastern Europe beyond the understanding of the Non-Aggression Treaty. That treaty had provided both for a division of Poland and for Latvia and Estonia to be Russian spheres of influence, while Lithuania was to be under German hegemony. A new German–Soviet treaty of 28 September 1939 gave Germany a somewhat larger share of Poland but assigned Lithuania to the Russian sphere of influence. By the late summer of 1940 the Soviet Union was not only digesting its Polish gains but had fought a winter war with Finland (which, if it brought little glory to the Russian army, did result in territorial concessions by the Finnish government), annexed the Baltic republics and incorporated the Romanian province of Bessarabia. The frontiers of the USSR were almost commensurate with those of Tsarist Russia in 1914.

It remained an open question during late 1939 and 1940 whether or not Soviet and German expansionist aims were compatible. Could accommodations be made and spheres of influence be allocated that would keep the two powers apart or even bring them into alliance? If one sees Germany's decision to invade Russia in 1941 as the inevitable outcome of Hitler's long-standing ambitions or as an atavistic manifestation of an age-old German drive to the east, then the answer must be firmly in the negative. But there are good reasons and considerable evidence for believing that the situation was fluid and that Germany seriously investigated the possibility of accommodation.

Exercise
Why do you think Germany should have wished to accommodate rather than fight Russia in 1940? ■

Specimen answer
and discussion

1   Germany's campaigns to the west had been enormously successful, but Britain, though weak, was not defeated. The familiar problem of a war on two fronts was to be avoided if possible.

2   Germany had made considerable territorial gains and occupied vast areas; it needed time to consolidate.

3   The German economy had not been prepared for a long war. □

None of these reasons ruled out a strike against Russia, but together they provided strong grounds for avoiding it unless absolutely necessary.

I would now like you to read the article by H. W. Koch, 'Hitler's "Programme" and the Genesis of "Barbarossa"', which is reproduced in the *Offprints Booklet*.

Exercise

1   How would you summarize Koch's general thesis?

2   What alternatives to an attack on Russia did Germany consider in 1940?

3   What is Koch's interpretation of Russian policy? ■

Specimen answers
and discussion

1   The German government was considering a number of policy options during 1939–40, and it would have preferred an accommodation with Russia. It was the realization that Russian aims were centred on Eastern Europe and the knowledge of the threat they posed to Germany that persuaded Germany that war with Russia was inevitable.

2   A Euro-Asian alliance including Germany, Italy, Japan and the USSR and the offer to the USSR of a path to expansion in Asia that would give that country control of Iran and then divert it towards the Persian Gulf and India. This would enable Germany to get on with the job of finishing off Britain. Germany wanted peace with Britain, but if Britain was not prepared to come to terms, Operation Sea-lion would have to be undertaken.

3   Essentially Koch sees Russian expansionist aims as being focused on Eastern Europe. Russia had gone beyond the agreement over spheres of interest agreed to in the Russo–German agreements and the further extension of Russian influence, especially if Romania threatened German interests. □

Both Koch and Roberts see November 1940 as the month in whch Hitler made up his mind that Russia had to be dealt with. Roberts writes: 'Now Hitler decided to settle accounts with Russia. But just at that moment he was distracted by the need to send forces to help Italy.'

The failure of the talks between Molotov and the German leaders in Berlin in November 1940 demonstrates that the USSR's main interests and ambitions lay in East and Central Europe. Stalin instructed Molotov to demand as primary requirements that Finland, Romania, Bulgaria and the Black Sea Straits be allocated to the Soviet sphere of influence, but there is evidence of a list of ultimate demands: the allocation of Hungary, Yugoslavia, Sweden and Western Poland to the Russian sphere, with a share for the USSR of the Baltic sea outlets (see Paul Johnson, *A History of the Modern World*, 1983 p.373). As Johnson comments, Stalin's demands, added up, 'are not so very different to what Stalin demanded and in most cases got, as his share of victory at the end of the Second World War. The Molotov 'package' testifies to the continuity of Soviet aims'.

Like Napoleon before him, who had similarly tried to persuade Tsar Alexander to turn his attention to India and the Persian Gulf, Hitler now determined to attack

Russia. An ex-Soviet general staff officer, Victor Suvorov, who defected to the West, has argued that the reason Stalin dismissed rumours of an imminent German attack was that the Russians themselves were in the final phase of deploying 183 divisions on Russia's western frontier, a move which could only have led to a Russian attack. (Suvorov's argument is summarized by H. W. Koch in a further article, 'Operation Barbarossa – the current state of the debate' in *The Historical Journal*, vol.31, no.2, 1988). Were the two powers both seeking the right moment to launch this attack, making their troop movements and reacting to each other's movements? The evidence is complex and confusing and the debate heated.

What seems increasingly clear is that, even after the war between Germany and Russia had begun, diplomatic initiatives were not exhausted. It has been suggested that as the German armies advanced on Moscow in October 1941, Lavrenti Beria, the Soviet Union's chief of secret police, acting on Stalin's orders, approached the Bulgarian ambassador in Moscow to act as a go-between with Hitler. Fearing defeat, Stalin was prepared to conclude a peace treaty on the lines of Brest-Litovsk. This suggestion, made by Dimitar Peyev, now editor of the Bulgarian newspaper *Orbita* and during the war a junior diplomat, and by the Soviet military historian General Nicolai Pavlenko writing in *Moskovskiye Novosti*, could, if true, cast new light on the fluidity of Soviet policy and the fragility of the alliance against Germany. However, as with so much of the information now emerging from Eastern Europe and the Soviet Union, historians have barely had time to evaluate it.

1.4   Eastern Europe moves west

The initial successes of the German armies enabled all the East and Central European losers of 1919, whether states or simply subject nationalities, to make gains under German hegemony. The fortunes of 1919 were almost everywhere reversed. The revisionist states of Hungary and Bulgaria extended their frontiers. Romania, though a victor at Versailles, had been divested of most of its gains but joined the alliance against Russia in the hope of regaining lost territory and even of making further acquisitions. Hungary, like Romania, joined in the war against Russia, although Bulgaria did not. The Slovaks and the Croatians, dissatisfied in 1919, attained a limited sovereignty under German supervision. Those who had gained most at the end of World War I – the Czechs, the Serbs and the Poles – had had their states dismembered. Some other winners in the immediate post-World War I period who had lost all to Russia in 1940 – Latvia, Estonia and Lithuania – retained governments in exile in London, though many of the population supported the German war effort. Finland, having fought a desperate war with Russia, joined combat again on the side of Germany.

Who would have won the war in Eastern Europe had it not been for American intervention is debatable, but the United States' entry into the war ended the deadlock between Germany and Russia in favour of the latter. It is instructive to compare the furthest limits of the German advance in 1942 (see map 8 in the *Maps Booklet* or Map 8 in Roberts) with Germany's position at the time of the Treaty of Brest-Litovsk in 1917. Germany had got a little, but not much, further in the second round, and the new order of 1942 bore some striking similarities to the situation in 1917. This order was to be ephemeral, and that which emerged in 1945 was to be its mirror image, a Russian hegemony.

Should or could the Soviet Union's Western allies have done more to modify the effects of a Soviet victory in the East on the shape and political complexion of East and Central Europe?

From the beginning there were differences between Britain and America on the one hand and the Soviet Union on the other as to both strategy in the war against Germany and a post-war settlement. There were also differences between the two Western allies themselves. Stalin repeatedly pressed the Western powers for an invasion of occupied Europe via the French coast and did not consider the Anglo-American invasion of North Africa and Southern Italy in 1942 and 1943 as sufficient substitutes. For their part both America and Britain still feared in 1942 that the USSR and Germany might make a separate peace.

Relations between Britain and the USA, the latter increasingly the senior partner in the alliance, bore some similarity to those between the USA and its West European allies in World War I. In 1941 Roosevelt had put forward a loose concept of a post-war world based on the rights of all peoples to self-determination and had secured Russian and British association with it. Such a concept recalls the views of Woodrow Wilson, but Roosevelt was conscious of the post-war repudiation of Wilson's policies by the American public, caused in part by the gap between Wilsonian idealism and the more self-interested aims of the European powers. Roosevelt was determined to avoid Wilson's fate, not by cutting back on the idealism, but by disassociating himself and America from any carving up of Europe into spheres of interests which might recall the secret treaties concluded amongst the Allies during World War I.

Roosevelt was both opposed to the British Empire and suspicious of Britain as a practitioner of a worldly approach towards international relations involving spheres of influence and considerations such as the balance of power. He had no illusions that the USSR's twin preoccupations with its security and world communism would make it a satisfactory partner in implementing a world order based on self-determination, but placed high hopes on the establishment of a close relationship between Stalin and himself, a relationship he hoped to make closer by expressing his distrust of British policies. Roosevelt's own policy, so far as Europe was concerned, was to content himself with a lofty moral conception of the future, to concentrate on winning the war against Germany, and largely to ignore the question of the future territorial and political arrangements for East and Central Europe, even as that question became steadily more pressing. He hoped that the Soviet Union would be contained, not by arrangements in East and Central Europe, but by the United Nations, on whose Security Council Russia would be in a minority, and by US military might, together with an Anglo-US monopoly on the atomic bomb.

American lack of concern for the post-war political balance of Europe and distaste for making agreements as to future frontiers and spheres of influence led to both strategic and political disagreements with Britain. Roosevelt was always more sympathetic than Britain to Russian demands for an invasion of France and less interested in alternative strategies which might strengthen the Western position in East and Central Europe. Even after D-Day Churchill supported General Alexander's plan for an operation eastwards from the Allied positions in Italy to cross the Rivers Po and Piave, seize Trieste and the Istrian Peninsular, and march through the Ljubljana Gap, threatening Vienna. The plan, code-named Armpit, was brusquely turned down by Roosevelt and the American Chief of

Staff. Harold Macmillan, Alexander's political adviser, wrote in his memoirs that it

> might have altered the whole political destinies of the Balkans and Eastern Europe . . . But apart from Roosevelt's desire, at that time to please Stalin at almost any cost, nothing could overcome the almost pathological suspicions of British policy, especially in the Balkans. (Quoted in Alistair Horne, *Macmillan*, vol.1, 1988, p.220)

Macmillan was convinced that the war could have ended 250 miles east of where the Iron Curtain eventually divided Europe, with Vienna and Prague firmly in Western hands. Even in the last weeks of his life Roosevelt did nothing to encourage Eisenhower to push on towards Berlin, Vienna and Prague as the British wanted. General Montgomery wrote that, 'The Americans could not understand that it was of little avail to win the war strategically if we lost it politically.'

By the end of 1942 the only firm decision that had been reached among the Allies as to the shape of post-war Eastern and Central Europe was that Austria should be re-established as an independent power. The Tehran Conference of December 1943, however, saw a discussion of the future Polish frontiers. Churchill agreed to the Curzon line of 1920 for Poland's eastern frontier, thus depriving Poland of the territory won from Russia in 1921; he also accepted that Poland should be recompensed with German territory east of the Oder river. Poland was to prove the most contentious issue dividing Britain and the Soviet Union. After all, Britain had gone to war for Poland as constituted in 1939, and the Polish government in exile was based in London. The Soviet Union had not only invaded Poland in 1939 but had behaved with great barbarity there. That there was little to choose when it came to barbarism between the Soviet Union and Nazi Germany – the class determinists and the biological determinists as the historian Ernst Nolte has called them – was largely ignored after 1941 by Britain and the USA, who preferred to represent Stalin as an avuncular figure and the Soviet Union as a courageous ally. But even under the blanket of wartime propaganda, news of the massacre at Katyn of 4,510 Polish officers by the Russians was brought to light by an investigation by the International Red Cross. When asked where these officers and another 9,000 Polish officers and NCOs were, the Russians lied: 'perhaps they fled across the Manchurian border?' (Hugh Thomas, *Armed Truce*, 1986). Nevertheless, Britain, because of wartime expediency and because it could exert little influence on Stalin's determination to impose a compliant regime on Poland, and also nudged by the United States, was steadily to move towards what can only be regarded as a betrayal both of its ostensible reason for going to war and of the Polish forces fighting with Britain.

As Roosevelt rejected Churchill's urgings that there should be Anglo-American negotiations with Stalin to set limits to Russian control of Eastern Europe as Russian armies 'liberated' it – negotiations which would stand a better chance of success while the Soviet Union was still dependent on Western assistance – Churchill attempted to play a lone hand. The so-called 'Percentage Agreement', worked out virtually on the back of an envelope between Churchill and Stalin in Moscow in October 1944, gave the Soviet Union effective control over Romania, Bulgaria and Hungary, Britain and the Soviets joint influence in Yugoslavia, and Britain a free hand in Greece. That Stalin to some extent honoured this agreement in the immediate aftermath of the war suggests that had the United States lent its greater weight towards a wider but equally cynical type of agreement, the eventual Soviet hegemony in Eastern Europe might have been modified.

Churchill, Stalin and Roosevelt met at Yalta in February 1945 to discuss the future of Europe on the eve of Germany's defeat. The very imminence of that defeat had already robbed Britain and America of much of their influence over the Soviet Union. The powers accepted the agreements that their officials had previously arrived at in respect of Germany's division into military zones, although, at Churchill's insistence, France was allocated a smaller zone of its own. It was also decided to set up a four-power military council in Berlin, itself to be divided into four military sectors. An ostensible compromise, which in reality was a Soviet victory, was reached over Poland: the two Western powers agreed that the Soviet-backed Polish Communist Committee based at Lublin in Soviet-occupied Poland should form the nucleus of a Polish provisional government, with a few members of the London-based government in exile given ministerial posts. Stalin promised that there would be free elections in Poland after the war, and the lines of the territorial arrangements sketched out at Tehran were confirmed (though Roosevelt refused to agree publicly to these). The USSR had already ensured by the murder of so many of the Polish officer corps and by allowing the Germans to crush the Warsaw rising in 1944, while Russian armies paused a few miles away, that anti-communist forces in Polish society would be much weakened. The Yalta agreement was thus a blueprint for a Soviet-dominated post-war Poland. In return for these Western concessions on Poland, Stalin was free with words and signed a three-power declaration which included an acknowledgement of 'the right of all peoples to choose the governments under which they lived'.

Stalin's achievement at Yalta was considerable. As Michael Dockrill has written:

> he believed that the West had accepted Soviet control over Poland and Eastern Europe, although he realised that this would have to be achieved behind a facade of self-determination. Roosevelt had said nothing at Yalta which disabused the Soviet leader of this impression. Stalin was willing to pay lip-service to Western principles by encouraging the formation of so-called 'people's' democracies in Eastern Europe whereby communists formed coalition governments with anti-Nazi left and centrist parties. In countries under Red Army control real power of course rested with the Communists (Dockrill, *The Cold War 1945–1963*, 1988, p.22)

The major factor in determining the political arrangements of post-war Europe was not the decisions of plenipotentiaries at peace conferences but the extent of the Red Army's advance at the end of hostilities. By the spring of 1945 Russian troops were in control of all of Poland, the Baltic states, East Prussia, the Karelian peninsular (previously Finnish territory), east Germany, north and east Austria (including Vienna), Hungary, Romania and Bulgaria. The Soviet Union was also a dominant influence, via indigenous communist forces in Yugoslavia and Albania, but it was to prove important that these countries had not been 'liberated' by Soviet forces.

Britain had gone to war in 1939 to prevent the alarming expansion of German power, but if the war had been successful in fulfilling that aim, it resulted in a situation just as threatening to Britain and the other Western European powers.

The defeat of Germany had brought Russian power right into the centre of Europe, and the countervailing power of Germany no longer existed. There was Eastern and there was Western Europe, but the centre had collapsed and the line between East and West was where the Allied armies had met.

Exercise

Let us return to the question we posed previously:

1   What could the Western Allies have done during 1942–5 to curtail the developing Soviet hegemony over East and Central Europe?

2   Why did they do so little? ■

Specimen answers and discussion

1   They could have:

(a)   used their position as the suppliers of aid and war materials to gain more influence over Soviet policy and to extract firm agreements from Stalin on the shape and character of the regime of post-war Europe;

(b)   come to a realistic understanding with the USSR on a *quid pro quo* basis as to spheres of influence;

(c)   aligned their military strategy so as to pre-empt Soviet control in East and Central Europe;

(d)   encouraged forces within Germany, especially within the *Wehrmacht*, to overthrow the Nazi regime and to have concluded an armistice, separately from the Soviet Union if need be, with a new German government.

2   Because the USA under Roosevelt was not prepared to recognize the problem, at least in public. Determined to avoid the fate of Woodrow Wilson, Roosevelt felt that American public opinion would not wear agreements, secret or otherwise, over post-war territorial arrangements or spheres of influence. He also distrusted the British, disliked the British Empire, was preoccupied with the Pacific war, and trusted that the post-war international organization (the outline of the United Nations Organization had already been agreed at Dumbarton Oaks in 1944) would be able to curtail Soviet actions. □

Churchill's 'Percentage Agreement' with Stalin, combined with the British willingness to use British troops in Greece and northern Italy to safeguard Western interests, showed what could be achieved by a combination of options (b) and (c). It was British initiatives that largely preserved the Mediterranean from Soviet influence, but British power was severely limited and Churchill's actions were disapproved of by the US State Department, though Roosevelt himself seems privately to have been more sympathetic.

Option (d) may be considered a purely theoretical course of action. America and Britain had bound themselves to unconditional surrender at Casablanca in 1943, though whether that had been wise is doubtful. There is some evidence, however, that the British Cabinet had contemplated a negotiated peace with Hitler in 1940, so, logically, an armistice with a putative anti-Nazi regime which had overthrown him should not have been impossible in late 1944.

The Potsdam Conference of the three powers produced little in the way of constructive agreements but succeeded in temporarily papering over the cracks between East and West – cracks which were widening as Truman, who had succeeded to the presidency on Roosevelt's death on 12 April 1945, became aware of Russian intentions in Eastern Europe. The main decisions of Potsdam concerned the future of Germany: it was agreed that eastern Germany be considerably reduced from its pre-war frontiers; that Poland be expanded eastwards at Germany's expense; that the Soviet Union receive half of East Prussia; that authority in Germany be exercised by the Commanders-in-Chief, controlling their own forces and acting together in a control council; and that Germany should be treated as a single unit. This latter decision marked the formal abandonment of the plans for the dismemberment of Germany that had been mooted in 1942 and 1943, but the differences between the Western Allies and the USSR were soon to result in the effective separation into two Germanys.

As in 1919, the major changes to frontiers occurred in East and Central rather than in Western Europe (see map 13 in the *Maps Booklet*). The frontier between France and Germany remained much as in 1919, while there were only minor rectifications to the Italian-French frontier, and that between Austria and Italy was also unchanged. The Italian-Yugoslavian frontier was a matter of considerable contention, and Italy lost most of its post-First World War gains; indeed Italy, without the presence of British troops in northern Italy, would almost certainly have lost more. The status of Trieste continued to be disputed until 1954. Hungary and Bulgaria were reduced to their pre-1938 frontiers, save that Bulgaria retained southern Dobruja. Romania recovered Transylvania from Hungary, but its loss of Bessarabia and northern Bukovina to Russia was confirmed. Finland had to yield to Russia the territory it had lost in the 'Winter War', plus some additional territory that gave Russia a common frontier with Norway. Austria was restored to its pre-*Anschluss* frontiers, and even Czechoslovakia had to give up some territory to Russia, losing Subcarpatho Ruthenia. Although peace was not made with Germany, 'temporary' arrangements were treated by its eastern neighbours as final and, in accordance with Potsdam, East Prussia was partitioned between Poland and the USSR: the USSR received the northern half and Königsberg, while Poland gained territory up to the Oder-Neisse line. Poland, as has been noted, lost land to the east of the Curzon line to Russia. The Baltic states were incorporated in the Soviet Union.

A feature of the post-1945 settlement, if settlement is not an inapposite term, was the brutal displacement of population. Whereas in 1919 the attempt had been made to make frontiers coincide with ethnic divisions, the less civilized world of 1945 saw the device of making ethnic divisions fit frontiers. In particular, millions of Germans were expelled from East Prussia, from the German territory ceded to Poland and from the Sudetenland, while there were parallel movements of Poles from the territory ceded to Russia into that gained from Germany.

Such movements, which we will return to in sections 2.1 and 2.4 below, were both part of and symbolize the general westward momentum of Eastern Europe. The eastward momentum of Germans over many centuries was instantly reversed, and the westward social, political and cultural inclination of the old Habsburg Empire was abruptly ended. *Mitteleuropa*, or Central Europe, was, for several decades at least, to be Eastern Europe.

2 SOCIAL CHANGE

2.1 Social geography

The effect of World War II on the size of the population within different countries and on the distribution of population in Europe was enormous, and the consequences are still being felt. The war resulted not only in a colossal loss of life but in the intra-European migration of vast numbers of people, both during the war because of the victories and defeats of armies, and at its end because of the realignment of frontiers and the desire of many to escape new uncongenial regimes.

Exercise Do you suppose that the loss of life in World War II was greater or smaller than in World War I? ■

Specimen answer and discussion The loss of life in World War II was far greater, and this was largely due to the very high war losses in East, Central and Southern Europe. As with World War I, one must consider the impact on fertility and morality as well as losses directly due to the fighting. It would be understandable if you got the above answer wrong, for the losses of World War II are not seared on the British memory in the way that those of World War I are. British and, indeed, French losses were far fewer. Consult the war memorial in your town or village and the servicemen commemorated on it for having died in World War II will be much fewer in number than those who fell in the Great War. Of course, British civilian casualties were far greater than in the previous conflict (30,000 were killed during the Blitz and the total for civilian casualties during the war was approximately 60,000, while until September 1941 the enemy had killed more civilians than combatants), but by the end of the war Britain with some 260,000 victims of war and France with 620,000 had both suffered far less than in World War I.

The loss of life in Central and Eastern Europe, however, was enormous: Poland lost more than 20 per cent of its total population and Yugoslavia 10 per cent, while more than five million Germans died. Russian losses are the subject of some debate. Probably some seven million military casualties were suffered, but the loss of civilian life was considerable, so that altogether there were over 20 million premature deaths, some due to food shortages, some to enemy action, and some to forced labour. It is impossible, however, to distinguish between losses of civilians due to the Germans and those due to the Soviet Union's reign of terror over its own subjects. The disproportionate loss of males caused a severe drop in the birth rate. □

As with World War I, estimates of the effect of the war on the populations of individual countries are made difficult by changes in frontiers. For instance, the Soviet Union grew enormously in size, incorporating 360,000km^2 of new territory which had been inhabited before the war by 17.4 million people, then the citizens of other countries; the three Baltic states with a combined population of 5.7 million were also incorporated into the Soviet Union.

Leszek Kosinski, in his *The Population of Europe* (1970), refers to the estimate of League of Nations demographic expert G. Frumkin that, excluding Albania and the European parts of the Soviet Union and Turkey, the population of Europe fell by 7.9 million between 1939 and 1945, a decline caused by 15.1 million direct war losses; these losses contributed to an excess of deaths over births of 3,160,000 and the removal of 4,770,000 prisoners of war outside Europe.

The map below (Figure 22–25.1) indicates percentage changes of population between 1940 and 1950 based on the present territories of countries; it is taken from Kosinski's book. The figures, Kosinski admits, do not provide a fully satisfactory solution to the problem of getting accurate figures after the population transfers and boundary changes. Because he excludes all of the Soviet

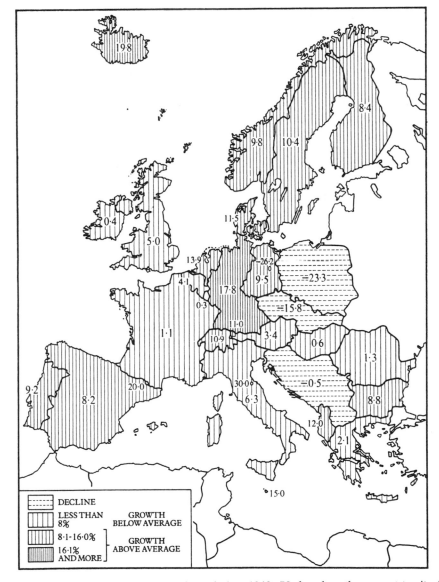

Figure 22–25.1 *Percentage changes of population, 1940–50, based on the present territories of countries*
Source: Kosinski, *The Population of Europe.*

Union, the eastern boundaries of his Europe have all been changed by the war. However, it does demonstrate certain broad trends.

Exercise What significant variations in population change do you detect? ■

Specimen answer 1   The decline or low rate of growth of Central and East European countries with certain exceptions such as Albania and Bulgaria.

2   The relatively high rates of growth of neutral countries or those which were fought over for only short periods.

3   The highest rate of growth is achieved by West Germany. This last factor should alert us to the great migrations of population that accompanied and followed the war. □

The movement of population

The Nazi 'New Order' in East and Central Europe saw an ambitious attempt to change the ethnic maps of East and Central Europe between 1939 and 1944. Basically this *Generalplan Ost* consisted of the expulsion of Czechs, Poles and Slovenes from lands incorporated into the expanded Germany and their replacement by some 1.5 million Germans either from areas of Eastern Europe or from the interior of Germany. At the same time there was a movement into Germany of foreign workers recruited or forcibly mobilized to take the place of German workers drafted for military service. By the end of the war this foreign workforce was estimated to be about seven million, including five million civilians and two million prisoners of war.

With Germany's defeat in the east came a general westward movement of German civilians, but this left large numbers of Germans in Poland, Czechoslovakia and Hungary and, of course, in the eastern provinces of Germany which at the end of the war were incorporated into Poland.

The number of Germans transferred to within the new frontiers of occupied Germany between 1945 and 1949 was about six million. The German minority in Poland was thus much reduced, and only tiny numbers of Germans were left in Hungary and Czechoslovakia.

During 1939–40 there were large movements of population to and from the lands and countries incorporated in the USSR: some 485,000 Finns, for instance, were evacuated from the territory ceded by Finland and about 2.5 million Russians were settled in ex-Polish territory. By the time of Stalin's death 10 per cent of the population of the Baltic republics of Estonia, Latvia and Lithuania had been removed by several waves of deportations, with the population of Estonia being a quarter smaller than it had been at the time of the Russian occupation. The place of the indigenous population was to be taken by Russians brought in to work in new factories and to help secure Soviet control of the territories.

If the Versailles Settlement had sought to make frontiers fit people, the more ruthless and less civilized expedient at the end of World War II was to make peoples fit frontiers. Germans were pushed westwards and their place was taken by Poles and Czechs; Poles and Czechs were in their turn pushed westwards and their place was taken by Russians. There were exchanges of population between Czechoslovakia and Hungary and between Hungary and Yugoslavia. Well over 200,000 Italians left territory gained by Yugoslavia, while 103,000 Hungarians were repatriated from Romania.

Macro-demographic trends

Prior to the war the rate of growth of the European population had been falling, with the West European rate slowing spectacularly and even the East European growth rate beginning to slow down. The West European growth rate had been 9 per cent in the period 1920–30 and 7 per cent over the ten years 1930–40. Between 1940 and 1950, however, the West European growth rate was to be the highest in Europe (8.1 per cent) and this trend continued for another two decades. Part of the West European increase can be attributed to a higher marriage rate followed by higher fertility in the post-war period. Even France overcame its long-term problem of low fertility. This trend should not automatically be seen as a result of the war, since the populations of neutral countries such as Ireland and Sweden saw similar increases. But the major factor in the high growth rate for Western Europe was immigration into the region, particularly into West Germany but also into France and Switzerland. An important cause of the lower rates of population growth in Eastern Europe in the years after the war was the constant decline of the population of East Germany until the building of the Berlin Wall in 1961, as migration to West Germany proceeded apace.

World War II thus had a very considerable impact, at least in the medium term, on the social geography of Europe. Though the loss of life was colossal, the shift of populations as a result of frontier changes and ideological pressures was probably the more significant factor. Movements of more than 25 million people took place. The importance of the German migration can be demonstrated by the fact that, excluding the Soviet Union, Germany with its pre-war frontiers had in 1939 the largest population in Europe with 69.6 million people; the United Kingdom was second with 48.0 million. By 1950 the United Kingdom had the largest population with 50.3 million and West Germany was second with 47.8 million. But by 1966 West Germany was to head the list with 59.5 million and the UK was second with 54.7 million. Even today a stream of migrants from isolated German (*Volk deutsche*) communities in the Soviet Union are making their way to their homeland of West Germany.

Over the longer term it is doubtful whether the war's impact can be compared to the well documented tendency towards a lower birth rate in technologically sophisticated societies, where children are not considered as an economic advantage. Thus Europe's population increase in the post-war decades was modest in comparison to that of Africa and Asia. The increase in Eastern and Southern Europe slowed from its already decreasing pre-war levels, but by the 1950s it was higher once more in Southern than in Northern Europe. Save for the haemorrhage of immigration to the West, it would also have been higher in Eastern than in Western Europe during that decade.

Urbanization

The term 'urbanization', like 'industrialization', becomes increasingly imprecise when we consider recent history. One sense in which urbanization is now often used is to describe the spread of an urban way of life into the countryside; in that sense rural areas of Western Europe can be considered urbanized. Even if we take a yardstick such as population density, there may be no firm divide between town and country such as we could discern in much of nineteenth-century Europe, but a spectrum moving from densely populated towns or cities, through suburbia, to a more thinly populated countryside, with that spectrum disrupted by new towns. In considering cities and their respective sizes we are confronted with problems of definition. Do we go by legal and administrative definitions of cities, or do we consider conurbations?

The increased percentage of the urban population of Europe, despite a variety of definitions of urban (some legal, some based on population density, and some based on economic activity) was a major phenomenon of the post-war decades. The lead taken by Western Europe in the process of urbanization continued to be reflected in post-war statistics. Only one of the ten most urbanized countries in Europe in 1960 was in East or Southern Europe, namely East Germany, while of the ten countries with the highest percentage of population employed outside agriculture, only two – East Germany and Czechoslovakia – were outside Western Europe (Kosinski, p.102). But if Western Europe was more heavily urbanized, parts of Eastern Europe were rapidly moving in the same direction. Poland, for instance, despite the destruction brought by the war, had eleven cities with populations over 100,000 in 1931 and twenty-three (with 25 per cent of the population) in 1966. The article on Leningrad in your Reader ('The impact of World War II on Leningrad') demonstrates how even a city reduced to a garrison at one stage in the war and unfavoured by central government in the post-war years, nevertheless managed by the late 1950s to surpass its pre-war population level, while the proportion of the Russian population living in an urban environment passed the 56 per cent mark in the 1960s.

It was in Western Europe that the polycentric urban systems that geographers have identified as the most modern phase of high-density urban development became apparent in the immediate post-war decades. The four largest European conurbations by the early 1980s were London, the Rhine-Ruhr region, Paris, and Randstad Holland. The Ruhr area was well established by the early twentieth century as a major zone of industrial/urban development, but its expansion into the major European conurbations – consisting of the areas of the Inner Ruhr (Essen-Dortmund-Duisberg), Hamm, Krefeld-Mönchen-Gladbach-Rheydt-Viersen, Düsseldorf, Wuppertal-Solingen-Remscheid, Cologne and Bonn – was the combined result of the German 'economic miracle' of the 1950s and the resettlement of German immigrants from East Germany and the *Volk deutsche*.

2.2   Economic performance and theory

The haunting image of a Europe in ruins, a wasteland, pervades most accounts of the state of the European economy in 1945 and 1946. Walter Laqueur comments that, 'All visitors to Central Europe reported a feeling of unreality: lunar landscapes dotted with enormous heaps of rubble and bomb craters, deserted and stinking ruins that had once been business centres and residential areas' (*Europe since Hitler, The Rebirth of Europe*, 1982, p.16). Richard Mayne refers to Europe, and above all Central and Eastern Europe which had seen so much of the fiercest fighting, as

> a land laid waste. In the cities, the skyline was jagged with destruction: amid the ruins and craters, rubble and wreckage blocked the streets . . . Much of the countryside was charred and blackened. Mutilated trees, burned bushes, and fields ploughed by tank tracks marked the site of battles. (Mayne, *The Recovery of Europe. From Devastation to Unity*, 1970, p.24)

You will notice that the titles of both the books from which I have quoted point towards the successful expansion of the European recovery from the nadir of 1945–6. Silver linings must have been pretty hard to find in the summer and autumn of 1945, but within a few pages of the quotation above Laqueur is writing: 'The preconditions for a spectacular recovery existed in 1945 but were hidden beneath the surface; not even the most sanguine expected rapid economic expansion.' Well, yes, sanguinity must also have been in short supply along with food, housing and clothing. Again, though, Laqueur is clearly correct in that a sustained recovery of the European economy, to say nothing of the social structure, was to take place in a very short period. By 1950 European output of almost everything was to be substantially above pre-war levels.

World War II and the years immediately after the war highlighted two economic developments: the European economy relative to the world economy had declined in its strength and importance from the position it had held earlier in the century, but in absolute terms it not only remained dynamic and sophisticated but had considerable potential for expansion. The performance of the wartime economies of the European powers is instructive on both counts.

The wartime economies

Prior to the war, the more optimistic British politicians and commentators were inclined to point to weaknesses in German military preparedness and to cast doubts on Germany's ability to fight a war lasting any length of time. The success of German arms between 1939 and 1942 and Germany's ability to sustain its war effort for over five years would appear to have proved them entirely wrong. Yet there were weaknesses in the German military position in 1939: although the army was spearheaded by well-armed mobile divisions, much of the reserve was underequipped and in the process of being trained, while munitions stocks were low; the surface navy was greatly inferior to the Royal Navy, even if U-boats were being produced in large numbers; and the *Luftwaffe*, although it outclassed the British and French air forces, also suffered from a lack of reserves. More importantly, given that it is the strength and the production power of the economy that are held to determine the potential military strength of a modern state, Germany's rapid re-armament had strained and overheated the economy and had exposed the shortcomings of the administration and management of the economy within the National Socialist state. Germany was also highly dependent upon imported raw materials, so there was some sense in the view that Germany was not in a good position to fight a long war.

Germany's success in the first stages of the war and its ability to withstand greatly superior odds for so long between 1942 and 1945 can be attributed in large part to a non-economic factor, the calibre and the operational doctrine of the German army. The use of tank formations and motorized infantry by Guderian in the French campaign of 1940 is an outstanding example of German operational doctrine, but throughout the war German training emphasized decentralized commands and maximum flexibility on the battlefield. To a considerable extent, therefore, German military ability was able to compensate not only for the fact that they were usually fighting an enemy numerically superior in men and tanks, but also for the shortcomings of the German economy and armaments production.

Another factor in Germany's early successes was that many of the problems facing the German economy were able to be solved, at least in the short term, by Germany's expansion. It has been suggested (see, for example, Tim Mason's 'Some origins of the Second World War' in E. M. Robertson (ed.) *The Origins of the Second World War*, 1971) that the whole logic of German economic development under National Socialism pointed towards the plundering of power and materials by wars of conquest. Certainly the answer to a heated economy and shortage of raw materials was found first in Czechoslovakia and then in the 'New Order' in East-Central Europe. Germany was able to gain labour, raw materials and new productive capacity from its advance to the east. At the same time failings in the German economy and disadvantages in Germany's position against enemies actual and political were disguised by the nature of the 'phoney war' and by the pact with the Soviet Union which permitted Germany to take imports from Eastern Europe without interference. Thus it was that until 1942 Germany was able to do without the imposition of a total war economy – unlike Britain and, indeed, unlike the Soviet Union, whose economy was geared to war well in advance of the war.

Exercise   You are already familiar with the article in the Reader, 'World War II and social change in Germany' by Mark Roseman. Say how and why Roseman thinks Germany avoided a total war economy. (Pages 302–4 give you the outline of his arguments.) ■

Specimen answer and discussion   For the first two years of the war Germany was able to fight a type of war suited to 'its state of half preparedness'. The Nazis were unwilling to impose too many sacrifices on the population. Competing authorities and interest groups made mobilization of the economy difficult. There was a reluctance to involve women in war work (here Roseman rather sneeringly refers to the 'traditional cosy bourgeois view on women's place at the hearth', though I personally can't see why either 'traditional' or 'cosy' should be considered pejorative words; the working classes have always been as attached to this idea as the middle classes). The exploitation of the occupied territories also served to protect the German population from the hardships resulting from a total war economy.

Here, it is suggested, is one of the great paradoxes of the war. The state which had been taken as virtually the model totalitarian state and the rhetoric of whose leaders was full of words like 'planning', 'corporation' and 'autarky' in fact allowed its business interests, its workers and consumers to enjoy more 'business as usual', to take a phrase current in Britain at the beginning of World War I, than any other European participant. □

But is Roseman correct in his analysis? Another article in the Reader which you are again familiar with, 'Hitler's war and the German economy: a re-interpretation' by Richard Overy, attacks the '*Blitzkrieg* economy' concept put forward by Roseman.

Exercise   Where does Overy disagree with Roseman? ■

Specimen answer and discussion   Overy accepts the shortcomings of the German armaments programme in the early years of the war and agrees that before 1942 the German government did not restrict the civilian sector in favour of military production. He does not, however, think this was because the regime planned only to fight a short war or a number of short *Blitzkrieg* type wars, nor that it was reluctant to impose sacrifices upon the civilian population. (In another article, 'Mobilization for total war in Germany' in the *English Historical Review* (1988), Overy has challenged the notion that the *Reich* made little use of female labour in the early stages of the war, asserting that a greater percentage of the female population was employed in Germany than in Britain.) According to Overy, Hitler planned a major war of conquest which he believed could last for a decade. However, he did not expect war to break out in 1939 with any of the great powers, and thus foreign policy and the economic preparations for war got out of step, 'a dislocation that was exacerbated after 1939 by a combination of poor planning, structural constraints within German industry, and weaknesses in the process of constructing and communicating policy.' As with so many issues relating to World War II, we come back to the central question of Hitler's plans and motives.

   A successful mobilization of the German economy for total war only came with the appointment of Albert Speer, who became minister of munitions and armament in February 1942, and with the realization of the desperate situation Germany was in, once the *Wehrmacht* had failed to knock out the Russians and the Americans had entered the war. Speer established a centralized machinery of control, the Central Planning Board, and by 1943 he had complete control of the economy. The production of armaments and munitions soared. This German economic miracle was based on a combination of centralized planning and a belated embargo on the production of luxury commodities, together with the intensified exploitation of occupied territories, the plundering of their raw materials, and the conscription of foreign labour, though Overy insists that the main factor was simply that under Speer existing resources were used better. Despite British and American concentration on destroying Germany's production capacity by bombing, Germany attained its highest levels of munitions production in August 1944, of aircraft in September 1944, and of weapons production in December 1944 (William Carr, *A History of Germany 1815–1945*, 1969, p.388). □

The approach of the Soviet Union was very different. Indeed, one might say that for most of its history the Soviet Union has had, whether in war or peace, a war economy. During the 1920s the Soviet Union devoted some 12–16 per cent of the state budget to armaments (estimates from within the Soviet Union put the 1989 share at between 25 and 34 per cent), and although the percentage fell during the early 1930s, the years after Hitler's succession to power saw an accelerated armaments programme. But a concentration on armaments *per se* only gives us a partial picture, for the Soviet Union's potential strength as a military power lay in the fact that private consumption's share of Gross National Product (GNP) had already been driven down to an abysmally low level, and the resources of the state directed to heavy industrial production; such industrial production both supported an armaments industry and could quickly be re-directed to concentrate upon it. Thus despite weaknesses in the Russian army due to the purging of nearly all its generals and colonels and the obsolescence of so many of its tanks and aircraft, the Soviet economy could move to a ruthless concentration on the production of armaments with greater ease than other European powers, and by 1940 the share of the state budget directed to armaments had increased to 32.6 per cent.

   Table 22–25.1 shows the armaments production of the powers between 1940 and 1943, and illustrates a number of facets of the balance in military might between the powers.

Exercise   What conclusions do you draw from Table 22–25.1? ■

Table 22–25.1   *Armaments production 1940–43 (in billions of 1944 dollars)*

	1940	1941	1943
Britain	3.5	6.5	11.1
USSR	(5.0)	8.5	13.9
United States	(1.5)	4.5	37.5
Total of Allied combatants	3.5	19.5	62.5
Germany	6.0	6.0	13.8
Japan	(1.0)	2.0	4.5
Italy	0.75	1.0	—
Total of Axis combatants	6.75	9.0	18.3

Note: brackets indicate that these countries had not yet entered the war.
Source: Paul Kennedy, *The Rise and Fall of the Great Powers*, 1988, p.355.

Specimen answer and discussion

The table clearly illustrates the large discrepancy between the opposing sides in terms of armaments production. It also reveals the massive part played by the United States in that discrepancy. We can see a shortfall between German and Russian production in 1941, bearing out the view expressed previously that on its entry into the war Russia was already running a war economy. By 1943, although the USSR has greatly increased its production, Germany under Speer's direction has virtually equalled Soviet levels of production. The tremendous stride made by Britain between 1941 and 1943 is also revealed.

Clearly, had it not been for United States involvement in this war, the sides would have been much more clearly matched, although even if we take Japanese and half of the American armaments production out of the picture in order to see the European sphere more clearly, Germany and Italy in 1941 and Germany alone in 1943 were failing to match Britain and the USSR, and were falling well short of Britain, the USSR and the USA. □

J. M. Roberts (set book, p.555) comments that 'England and Russia achieved the greatest subordination of economy and society to the war effort.' As we have seen, this was scarcely surprising in the Russian instance, where both Russian history and communist doctrine supported the subordination of civil society to the state, and where everything had been subordinated to industrial production and armaments under a system of state planning before the war. But why and how did Britain, with its liberal and individual traditions, impose such a subordination of economy and society to the war effort and achieve such a startling leap in armaments production?

As Roberts suggests (p.556), 'the experience of the Great War was there to be drawn on'. Britain had gone a long way in the direction of 'war socialism' in the previous war, and the Lloyd George coalition had, in particular, identified itself with the idea that civil liberties, private property and consumers' needs and desires should be subordinated to the war effort. The legislation and planning machinery that had been prepared for the event of war was based on the assumption that a similar approach would be required for the next war. Britain thus went to war with the assumptions of 1918 rather than those of 1914, and these had been strengthened by the widespread popularity of 'planning' during the 1930s among centre and left political circles. The rearmament programme of the Baldwin and Chamberlain governments must, however, be given some credit for Britain's ability to expand its production lines so rapidly, especially as regards aircraft production. New factories rather than the immediate production of aircraft were the aim, and by 1941 the efficiency of this approach was making itself felt.

The renewed emphasis on central planning in Britain during the war was endorsed by the economic section of the Cabinet and given maximum scope by the fact that Churchill left so much of the 'Home Front' to Labour ministers like Ernest Bevin at the Ministry of Labour, Herbert Morrison at the Home Office and, later on, Hugh Dalton at the Board of Trade. The government moved in a corporatist direction as Bevin attempted to enlist the support of trades union leaders for the direction and allocation of labour. An equality of hardship was imposed as rationing was imposed on clothes as well as food, and income tax rose to ten shillings (50p) in the pound; by 1941 personal consumption was 14 per cent less than in 1941. The coal mines, shipping and the railways came under government control. More and more of the population were working for the state in one way or another – 49 per cent by 1941 – and more of them were women as the government implemented conscription of the female population. This siege economy was in part supported by high taxation and a high level of personal savings, but above all it was based on the sale of Britain's dollar assets and financial aid from the United States.

Britain's wartime controlled and planned economy was perceived by contemporaries as a great success, and it has been argued that this perception of the success of a state-controlled economy did much to ensure the Labour Party's victory at the 1945 general election. Britain, it was thought, had won through by harnessing the skills of its people and its resources by intelligent planning and with a beneficent egalitarian ethic which had melted class and industrial antagonisms. It was not just that the production figures were so impressive; there were the major technological and scientific innovations that the war effort had produced – penicillin, jet-propelled aircraft, radar, major innovations in photographic equipment, and, of course, Britain's contribution to the atomic bomb. Britain's success in the war was to be hailed as demonstrating the advanced state of its science and technology, the resilience of its manufacturing capability, and the miracles wrought by planning, collectivism and the generous participation of all classes in the war effort.

A rosy picture. Or was it a mirage? Was the true picture much bleaker, as Correlli Barnett has argued in *The Audit of War. The Illusions and Reality of Britain as a Great Nation* (1986)? It is true, argues Barnett, that the war produced some specialized products such as high-speed cameras and Rolls-Royce engines and a major advance for one industry, chemicals, but otherwise the war found Britain wanting in every branch of second-industrial-revolution technology. The much-vaunted effects of wartime controls and planning resulted in low productivity per person. The image of the enthusiasm and dedication of shipyard workers returning to yards unused since the 1920s presented by the wartime propaganda film, *Tyneside Story* (item 17 on video-cassette 2), can be contrasted with the rigid adherence to craft demarcations and the overmanning insisted upon by unions. Far from a 'people's war' with everyone working for a common cause, the figures for strikes and absenteeism during the war reveal a home front in which the trades unions and workforce simply took advantage of wartime full employment. The impressive figures for war production can be seen as only being possible because of lend-lease and sterling area credit, which relieved Britain of any need to export.

Certainly, Britain's life-support system came in the shape of American dollars. The great economic phenomenon of the war, and the one that had the decisive impact in the European sphere as in the Pacific, was the astonishing growth of the US economy. The war revealed the degree to which during the Depression the US economy had been ticking over below its capacity. Stimulated by war expenditure, the American GNP measured in 1939 dollars grew from 38.6 billion in 1939 to 135 billion in 1945, by which time the value of the dollar stood much higher. Industrial expansion in the period 1940–44 grew by over 15 per cent a year, and the physical output of goods rose by over 50 per cent. Alone among the combatants, the USA was able to expand the production of goods that were not part of the war effort, so that civilian standards of living were able to rise. By the end of the war the United States not only possessed two-thirds of the world's gold reserves, but its economy produced a third of the world's goods of all types (figures taken from Paul Kennedy, *The Rise and Fall of the Great Powers*, pp.357–8), while at the same time its aid buttressed its European allies.

As the war moved towards its close, the dictum that economic strength combined with manpower would prevail in modern war was being fulfilled. The efforts and ingenuity of Speer and Germany's industrial managers and workforce enabled Germany to produce 17,800 tanks and 39,807 aircraft in 1944, but these totals must be compared with those of the Allies. In the same year the USA produced 17,500 tanks (29,500 in 1943), Russia 29,000, and Britain 5,000; the USA produced 96,318 aircraft, Russia 40,300, and Britain 26,461 (figures again from Kennedy; as Kennedy points out, the fact that the Anglo-American figures include a large number of heavy bombers disguises the even greater strength of Allied air power). It became clear also that the end of the war would witness (a) a German economy which, although it had reached its production peak in the war's penultimate year, would be razed and devastated by the final months of the conflict; (b) a Soviet Union capable of sustaining great levels of war production but with the rest of the economy in an abysmal state: (c) a Britain overstrained and overstretched by its military and economic effort; and (d) an American economy in a position to dominate the post-war world.

We need now to consider what plans the Allied powers had made for the European economic crisis that was bound to follow the end of hostilities and whether the individual economic ambitions of the powers and their hopes for the economic shape of a post-war Europe were compatible.

The economic ambitions of the big three

The views of the three Allied powers, the USA, the USSR and Britain, as to how to refashion the economic structure of the post-war world were, inevitably, conditioned by a mixture of their self-interest, their political and economic philosophies, and their relative strengths and weaknesses, together with their analysis of the failings of the world economy as it had existed in the 1930s. Just as inevitably, economic and political ambitions faded into each other.

Exercise   What sort of differences were likely to divide the Allies? ■

Specimen answer   The USSR was a communist state and the ruble had never been a convertible
and discussion   currency, so one might well have expected that the Soviet Union would not be as eager as the Western powers for the re-establishment of the international capitalist economy. In particular it would much prefer to keep capitalism well away from its own frontiers and wish to impose socialist economies on its East and Central

European neighbours. The sheer strength of the US economy, the economic powerhouse of the alliance against Hitler, was an invaluable asset to the Soviet Union during the war but could inspire Soviet fears that it would be overwhelmingly influential after the war, especially as the USSR, with the devastation heaped on it by the war, would be in poor condition to compete.

However, the situation was more complex than this, for there was no clear community of interests between the United States and Britain any more than between the two Western powers and the Soviet Union.

Since 1900 it had become increasingly obvious that the USA was the dominant economic power in the world. If after World War I the USA had withdrawn into political isolation, it had not withdrawn into economic isolation, and the implications of its actions and its fortunes had been profound, whether as the underwriter of agreements over German war reparations via the Dawes and Young plans or as the catalyst for the Depression as the effects of the Wall Street Crash reverberated around the European economies. American economic policy towards the outside world since the late nineteenth century had combined a demand for 'open doors' for American goods with a readiness to impose protective tariffs wherever American industries were threatened.

The 1930s had been a period of protectionism during which most states had sought to protect their native industries against foreign goods, with adverse consequences for the international economy; the United States had been no exception. Yet the New Deal had not been very successful in taking the American economy out of depression – far less successful than Hitler's economic policies for Germany – and it was essentially the effects of World War II and the need for armaments that gave the USA full employment and got its industries humming. Even the vast US home market was arguably insufficient to absorb America's productive capacity on a peacetime basis. By the early 1940s not only was American political policy moving away from isolationalism, but American economic policy was becoming posited on a belief in international free trade, which would open up the world to American goods. Like Victorian Britain before it, the United States, coming into its prime, believed that a free trade dominated by the most successful economy, itself, was not only in its own best interests but a positive moral good which would both lead to prosperity and bring liberal values in its wake.

The post-war world was almost certain to see an American economy, untouched by bombing or by fighting on its own territory, suffering from problems of over-capacity and in search of markets; and a Soviet economy, devastated by war and disabled by inefficiencies endemic to its system, suffering from problems of under-capacity. The Soviet leadership, not surprisingly, did not welcome the prospect of seeing the Soviet Union drawn into a world economy dominated by the USA and the dollar, although it might have made Soviet society more prosperous. Though prepared to accept American aid in the short term, the Soviet Union was determined to keep its own economy, those of its neighbours in Eastern and Central Europe, and as much of Germany as possible out of a future world economy dominated by the USA.

Britain, the free trading power *par excellence* in the late nineteenth and early twentieth centuries, was also threatened by US economic ambition. With many world markets closed because of protectionist policies, Britain in the 1930s had increasingly relied on the Empire and the sterling area for its exports and imports. From the time of the lend-lease agreement onwards, the USA was bent on exacting as the price for its aid the end of the sterling area and imperial protection. As Wilfred Loth has written,

> Negotiations with the British Allied partner which were conducted from Washington at a very early date on account of the economic importance of Great Britain in the pre-war world, turned out to be an endless series of American demands for liberalisation, British refusals, American threats of the most brutal nature and eventual British capitulation out of their concern for the indispensable support of the Americans. (Loth, *The Division of the World*, 1988, p.24)

Neville Chamberlain's fear that another war would mean the end of the British Empire and the further decline of Britain's economic position was being fulfilled.

On strictly economic grounds Soviet and British fears of a world economy dominated by the USA and the dollar were probably unjustified. It can be argued that the world economy works best when dominated by a single power and a single economy – Britain and sterling before World War I and, as events were to show, the USA and the dollar between 1945 and 1970. It also seems true, as Paul Kennedy's *The Rise and Fall of the Great Powers* argues, that, just as political dominance contains within it the seeds of decline as the dominant power taxes its strength and its worldwide military commitments, so the corollary of economic supremacy, the possession of the strongest currency, has effects which are by no means entirely to the benefit of the possessor. The stimulation of the West European economy by the USA after 1947 was, for instance, to be as economically necessary to the USA as it was politically desirable. But neither Britain nor the USSR was thinking purely of the long-term economic effects of the emerging US-controlled world economy; they were more concerned at the effects of such a development on their political and strategic positions. □

The problems of Germany

Although the Allied powers had their economic ambitions and fears for the shape of the world and European economies after the war, they were muddled and even individually inconsistent as to policies for the immediate economic problems that Europe would face at the end of hostilities. The defeat of Germany and its East and Central European allies was bound to leave an economic hole in the centre of Europe. From the late 1930s the *Reichsmark* regime of East-Central Europe had increasingly become an economic unit dependent upon Germany. This *Reichsmark* area had indeed prospered up until 1942, and Austria and much of Eastern Europe had rapidly industrialized. In many ways the economic effects of the Nazi New Order were beneficial, with rises in real wages in Bohemia-Moravia and mini-booms in Slovakia, Hungary and Romania. Soviet policy at the end of the war was clearly to reverse the direction of these economies towards the Soviet Union, while the Anglo-American aim was to co-opt these states into a multilateral free trade system. But what of Germany itself, the strongest economic power in Europe since the early twentieth century?

Exercise   Bearing in mind what had happened after World War I, what do you think was the Allies' view as to what should be done about the German economy? ■

Specimen answer and discussion   They could have adopted one of two contradictory views:

(a)   They could have gone along with the Keynesian analysis of Versailles and seen reparations and the desire to punish Germany as having led to a German economic weakness in the early 1920s which had had deleterious repercussions on the whole European economy, as well as fuelling German desires for revenge.

(b)   They could have taken the view that Versailles was in fact 'too lenient for its own severity', as Tony Lentin has described it, and argued that the German economy should be permanently weakened. ☐

Their initial view was close to that of (b), but from 1946 on, the Allies increasingly favoured the reconstruction of the German economy.

Such views could not, of course, be disassociated from plans for Germany's political future. The decision to demand unconditional surrender from Germany ensured that Germany (and most of Central Europe) would have its economy temporarily destroyed, while the eventual agreement to divide the state into four zones of occupation resulted in four very different policies towards the economies of those zones. The most important difference was to be between policy in the Soviet zone and that in the rest.

The most explicit plan for the permanent destruction of Germany's capacity for industrial production was that put forward by the US Secretary of the Treasury, Henry Morganthau, who demanded that all but the lightest of German industries be dismantled and that the country be made 'primarily agricultural and pastoral in character'. For a time such ideas interested Roosevelt: 'If I had my way, I would keep Germany on the breadline for the next twenty-five years'. Furthermore, he stated, 'We have either to castrate the German people or . . . treat them in such a manner . . . that they just can't go on reproducing people who want to continue in the way they have in the past.' Churchill's response was that the result of such a plan would be that 'England would be chained to a dead body'. 'I'm all for disarming Germany', he said, 'but we ought not to prevent her living decently.' Even Churchill departed from this magnanimity for a while, arguing for the destruction of the principal industries of the Ruhr and the Saar, although by 1945 he had returned to his previous moderation. Roosevelt and his successor, Truman, distanced themselves from the Morgenthau plan. Yet its influence can be discerned in the directive JCS/1067 drawn up by the US Joint Chiefs of Staff to guide their occupation authorities. By this, 'no steps looking forward to the rehabilitation of Germany, or designed to maintain or strengthen the German economy should be taken'. Between a Soviet Union which at Yalta had demanded that Germany pay 20,000 million dollars' worth of reparations in the form of plants, goods and labour, and a USA which seemed destined to leave the German economy in whatever parlous state it was in at the end of the war, the future of the economic heartland of Europe did not seem good.

The economic wasteland

The economic crisis that awaited Europe at the end of the war was by no means to be confined to Germany and its allies, and there can be little doubt that the victorious powers had made inadequate plans for dealing with it. The Soviet Union was essentially concerned to salvage its own ailing and war-stricken economy by exacting resources from Germany and East-Central Europe, while what plans the Western Allies made were based on colossal underestimates of how great the economic crisis would be.

Early in the war, Churchill had pledged British relief to continental Europe, and the decision to set up UNRRA, the United Nations Relief and Rehabilitation Administration, in 1943 followed this spirit. UNRRA was to do a good deal in countries such as Italy, Poland, Austria and Greece by dispensing food, clothing, raw materials and even machinery, but, largely because the US government feared that Congress would frown upon long-term assistance to future industrial competitors, none of its aid was supposed to go to the long-term rehabilitation of economies. Nor was aid supposed to go to ex-enemy countries, though in practice Austria and Italy came to be admitted, and to a lesser degree Finland and Hungary. A means test was imposed on potential recipients, so that those who had means of foreign exchange were disbarred. This excluded the greater part of Western Europe, and Britain, France, Belgium, the Netherlands, Luxemburg, Norway and Denmark did not apply for aid.

What was available to such countries up until the end of the war was lend-lease. Originally designed to provide defence equipment to the recipients, the principle of lend-lease became widely interpreted by Roosevelt: 'Success in restoring the countries we free will be a powerful factor in shortening the war and giving the liberated peoples their chance to share in the victory' (quoted in Mayne, *The Recovery of Europe*, p.68). But lend-lease ceased immediately on Germany's surrender; even ships carrying lend-lease goods turned around and began to unload in American ports. Although Truman quickly rescinded the order for the discontinuance of lend-lease made in May 1945, the programme was finally cancelled five days after the end of the war in the Far East. It ensured that a devastated Europe and a near bankrupt Britain were without any effective form of US aid.

The extent of that devastation must now be briefly investigated. Its extent was such that many experts thought that economic recovery could take many decades. Not only was the loss of human life due to World War II much greater than that caused by World War I, but material losses were also much greater than in the previous war.

Exercise Which areas of Europe and which countries do you suppose suffered the most extensive devastation? ■

Specimen answer and discussion Central Europe was particularly badly affected, because there the German army had battled for every mile against the advancing Russians, but every part of Europe where there had been fierce fighting exhibited its wounds: Poland and Russia, Yugoslavia and Greece, Italy and Northern France, Belgium, Holland, Germany, Austria, Hungary and Czechoslovakia. Britain might have seen no land battles, but air raids had done damage enough. Warsaw and Berlin were almost completely destroyed, and virtually every major city in the countries involved in the war had suffered extensive damage, with only Paris, Prague, Brussels and Rome among capitals escaping large-scale destruction. The scorched earth policies adopted by the Russians and the Germans in their respective retreats had left millions homeless and had destroyed not only industry but also farms and crops; to the West, the invasion of France by the Allied forces had resulted in enormous destruction to the coastal and northern region, while in Holland large areas had been flooded.

The devastation was much more general than that which had been caused by World War I. That many wondered whether reconstruction in some areas was even possible is illustrated by the case of Berlin:

> Ninety-five per cent of its urban area lay in ruins. There were three thousand broken water mains, and only twenty-five stations out of eight

were in operation. 149 of the city's schools had been demolished, and not one of its 187 Evangelical Churches was untouched. In the streets were over 400 million cubic metres of rubble: one estimate reckoned that if ten trains a day with fifty wagons each were used to remove it, the process would take sixteen years. (Mayne, *The Recovery of Europe*, p.30) □

The pressing economic problems that were either pan-European or affected much of Europe were formidable:

(a)   Most basic of all there was a widespread shortage of food. Immense tracts of arable land had been laid waste and nearly 40 per cent of Europe's livestock was gone. There were shortages of seed, fertilizers, pesticides, draught animals and agricultural machinery. Hunger was therefore a common problem and malnutrition a threat. The countryside was not always eager to supply the towns and be paid in inflated currency, so peasants ate better than urban dwellers and black markets flourished. A United Nations report suggested that in 1946 140 million Europeans were receiving fewer than 2,000 calories a day and 100 million of them less than 1,500 (quoted in Mayne, p.74).

(b)   Industry, where it had not been damaged by enemy action, was beset by shortages of machinery, raw materials and power. Coal production outside the Soviet Union was down to two-fifths of its pre-war level and electricity supplies accordingly found it difficult to cope with demand. Production capacity was therefore almost everywhere greatly below pre-war levels.

(c)   Communications problems were caused by paralysed transport systems: roads and bridges were closed or impassable, vast numbers of vehicles had been destroyed, canals and rivers were unnavigable, and long stretches of railway tracks were out of commission.

(d)   War is an expensive business: bombing and shelling destroys fixed assets, military expenditure diverts money from investment in civilian industrial production, and most governments find it necessary to sell assets and get into debt. As in World War I, Britain, faced with greatly increased expenditure and with many export markets closed, was forced to liquidate overseas investments (£1,118 millions' worth) and borrow heavily from the United States. All European participants on the Allied side were recipients of lend-lease, but when that ended Britain, France, Belgium and the Netherlands found it necessary to raise US loans.

(e)   Inflation affected most European countries and was worst in Belgium, Bulgaria, Czechoslovakia, Finland, France, the Netherlands, Norway, Spain and Turkey. In Greece and Hungary the currencies collapsed completely, while Germany became a barter economy with cigarettes the main means of exchange.

Certain features were common to most of the European economies in the immediate post-war years. Almost everywhere the standard of living fell *after* the war. Victorious powers like Britain and France were dismayed to find that there were few fruits of victory. Rationing intensified in Britain: bread, which had never been rationed during the war, was rationed in 1946. In France all goods were scarce, inflation soared, and an enormous black market defied attempts at regulation. It was no great comfort to the British and French to know that things were incomparably worse in defeated Germany and in East and Central Europe, where the individualist looting by Red Army units paled in comparison to the looting by the Soviet government of the raw materials and the factory machinery from the countries it controlled.

Reflecting a general political shift towards the left, the tendency in the immediate post-war years was for a move towards statism and collectivism in the European economies. The process of war elevates the state and results in a diminution of the individual's economic and political rights. Societies emerged from war accustomed to look to the state for decision-making. Shortages resulted in demands for government intervention in the interests of 'fairness'. The great nostrum of the centre-left during the inter-war period had been central planning. Now, with the immensity of the task of post-war reconstruction before them and accustomed to government direction during the war, many European societies turned towards major extensions of public welfare and public ownership.

British historians are not unnaturally divided about the effects of the post-war Labour government's shift towards central planning and increased social welfare. For Kenneth Morgan, the record shows that 'deliberate government policy' was able to 'significantly influence the geographical spread of new industry and employment', and the welfare state 'offered an essential base for future social advance (*Labour in Power 1945–51*, 1984). For Correlli Barnett, the Labour Party in power were the architects of future decline. Grossly overestimating the success of collectivism and planning during the war, which had largely been paid for by American loans, Labour made a decrepit economy pay the price for a romantic social vision: 'By the time they took the bunting down from the streets after VE-Day and turned from the war to the future, the British . . . had already written the broad scenario for Britain's post-war descent' (*The Audit of War*, p.304).

State directives and controls were the order of the day, whether in Britain, France, the Netherlands, Italy or Germany, via the controls established by the Allies, to say nothing of Eastern Europe as it was pushed increasingly towards the Soviet model. For a while such controls seemed to succeed well in reconstructing European economies.

We began this section with Walter Laqueur, who pointed to the fact that the preconditions of a European recovery existed but were 'hidden beneath the surface in 1945'. The infrastructure of the European economy had been damaged but not destroyed by the war and, if the last years of the war had destroyed industrial capacity, the early years of the war had actually seen it increase. The potential, especially strong in the western zones of Germany, remained awaiting enlightened economic policies to release it. The possibility of agricultural inno-vation and the intensified use of agricultural machinery, which would release vast numbers for industrial production, was only beginning to be realized in continental Europe.

It may also be the case that the experience of war and the scientific and technological changes that came with it were to have some beneficial effect on the post-war economy. Besides the obvious benefits of medical advances associated with the war (sulphonamides, penicillin and anti-infection agents) and the discoveries and innovations which clearly demonstrated a potential for peacetime uses (more sophisticated photographic equipment, radar, the jet engine and the atom bomb) the challenge of war production had resulted in important changes in methods of production. Productive technology improved, more machine tools were used, and the organization and management of factories changed radically. The European combatants moved towards a more American model of industrial production which would allow the post-war German economy in particular to build on the experience of war.

Most of the preconditions for industrial recovery did indeed exist bar one –

perhaps the most important, dollars. Many of the European countries' currencies were grossly inflated and their overseas assets had disappeared or were shrinking fast. Even trade between European countries was difficult, for a fistful of francs or lira was of dubious worth to the recipient, and a quasi barter system was resorted to. Exports were well below pre-war levels, and by 1947 Europe's current account deficit with the dollar area was 7,000 million dollars. In 1947 Europe's industrial production and its farm yields were still considerably below peacetime norms, and Western Europe could no longer rely on food and raw materials from Eastern Europe or the Far East. European governments urgently needed to import capital goods and farm machinery as well as food and raw materials, but lacked the money to pay.

The loans made by the US government since the war (650 million dollars to France, 3,750 million to Britain) had been inadequate and quickly used up by 1947. Europe was living on capital and imports it could no longer afford. The American Congress showed little enthusiasm to make further loans.

The bad harvest of 1946 and the harsh winter of 1946–7 brought the crisis to a head, a crisis which appeared to imperil not only Europe's economic but also its social and political stability. It also affected Britain's ability to continue with its world political role.

Yet the crisis of 1947 was largely a financial or, more narrowly, a shortage of dollars crisis than the more general social and economic crisis it is made out to have been. The reconstruction of the European economy was bound to involve massive imports of capital goods from the United States, and it was as much in America's as in Europe's interests that arrangements should be made to facilitate such imports and that this sensitive phase in European recovery be put in the past.

The US reaction to the European crisis was, however, not primarily determined by the needs and ambitions of the US economy. It was in large part determined by the fear of Russian and communist expansion. The US response and its economic and political repercussions will be considered in Unit 26.

You should note that sections 2.3–2.10 are written by Arthur Marwick.

2.3 Social structure

The central debate in considering social structure or class is over whether the experiences of World War II did or did not involve what is usually referred to as 'social levelling'. The phrase is in many ways an unsatisfactory one. The notion of class, whether Marxist or non-Marxist, involves a sense of social aggregates existing in some kind of hierarchy, of being inferior, or superior, to each other. If classes were 'levelled' (that is to say, brought to the same level), that would in effect mean the end of classes – that a 'classless society' had actually been achieved. (Indeed, many of those who use the phrase 'levelling' have in mind the idea of some kind of progress towards a classless society.) Since the article which I am going to ask you to read in a moment, 'The "levelling of class"' by Penny Summerfield in the Course Reader, explicitly reacts to some writing of my own, I would like to make it clear that I do not myself anywhere speak of the war as 'levelling' social classes. My book *Class: Image and Reality in Britain, France and the USA since 1930* (1980), to which Summerfield specifically refers, firmly concludes that Britain and France were still manifestly class societies in the 1970s. Mark Roseman, you may remember (now is the time to bring to hand the notes you took, or the annotations you made on his article), did perceive some changes in the nature of class in West Germany as between the Weimar Republic and the German Federal Republic, though he put as much weight on Hitler and the Americans as on the war itself. The debate, then, should be about how far there were changes in the nature of class, in the social structure itself, in relationships between the classes, and in attitudes about class in general, and about individual classes: whether there were such changes, and what part, if any, the war experience played in them. Class, as we are all by now aware, is one of those topics in which the general approach one follows, the way in which one defines one's terms, can be significant in the answers one comes up with. Penny Summerfield's article is a splendid example of careful, meticulous research, which deliberately avoids all easy generalizations and places great emphasis on detailed quantitative analysis. You will find that you have to concentrate very carefully, but I think that if you do so you will feel the pleasure of joining with Summerfield in trying to tease out precise answers to precise questions. Regretfully, I do have to comment that since Summerfield concentrates on only one chapter of quite a large book, she misses the fact that I do, at the beginning of the book, make very clear what my own definition of class is. However, for present purposes it is much more important to be clear about the way in which Summerfield is defining class. Her article is extremely useful to us here for two main reasons. First, it gives a vivid insight into some of the detailed methodological problems inherent in trying to discuss class, and brings us into contact with the concrete realities of actual earning and expenditure which are so often obscured in wider generalizations. Second, it gives us an intriguing start to our comparative study of changes in class across Europe: if (allegedly) 'exceptional' Britain went through so little change, won't there be even less change in all of the other countries? Or, on the contrary, can we expect the more catastrophic events on the continent to have brought about much more significant change? It might be added that the article is a model of forensic skill, of how to develop an argument: in essence it takes in turn the arguments that have been made, or could be made, in favour of the argument that there was 'levelling' because of the war, and rebuts each one in turn. As you read the article I want you to follow the careful, stage-by-stage way in which the overall argument is built up; that in fact forms the purpose of the main exercise I am about to set. However, there are some other issues as well: for instance, the article is not, as Summerfield readily makes clear, a complete treatment of its subject.

Exercise   I suggest that you read once carefully through the entire article by Penny Summerfield in order to get a complete sense of its scope and structure, then go back through it noting down answers to the following questions.

1   How does Summerfield define class? What two aspects does it have? One of these aspects is deliberately omitted from this article: in what ways might one tackle that aspect? Entailed within this definition, what is taken to be a significant indicator of belonging to, or joining, the middle class?

2   What alternative way is there of defining class, and what criticisms of Summerfield's approach would it involve?

3   Now the main question. I want you to prepare a table in which you set out on the left-hand side each argument in favour of the 'levelling' hypothesis that is being discussed, and then on the right-hand side each answer made by Summerfield. ∎

Specimen answers and discussion

1   Class is an economic relationship, 'whether in terms of income, occupation or ownership of capital'. The two aspects are (a) stratification with respect to these economic categories, and (b) class consciousness and activity, or 'political identity of separate social classes'. To analyse the latter, one would presumably have to look at voting figures (to establish correlations between belonging to a particular class and voting for a particular political party), and membership of specific political or industrial organizations (political clubs, professional associations, trades unions). The indicator of middle classness is saving, or the 'accumulation of capital' (see, for example, the last sentence of the first paragraph on p.264).

2   An alternative definition would see class as involving more than an economic relationship (for example, lifestyle – where you live, what you eat, recreational activities, etc., what class you think you belong to, what class others think you belong to, whether your occupation, whatever the level of pay, is manual or not, etc.). It would query the automatic association between saving and middle classness (what class is a butcher, a bookmaker, a publican, in a working-class area?) Above all, it would query the notion of class consciousness as an indicator of class (arguing, for instance, that a man can be manifestly working class while having absolutely no political opinions, or, indeed, being a Conservative voter). It is possible to envisage a manual worker moving into a middle-class occupation, for instance bank clerk, without ever accumulating any capital.

3   My table looks like this:

Argument	*Rebuttal*
D. C. Marsh's argument, based on tax returns, that the gap between rich and poor had narrowed.	Tax returns are inaccurate, ignore those below taxable levels, and also the hidden income of the rich. They refer to individual, not family, income, and do not take account of inflation. In short, they do not deal with *real* incomes, and thus greatly exaggerate 'levelling up'.
Seers, Cole, and Westergaard and Resler all showed that there had been a 'levelling' of real incomes, partly because of the overall rise in the Gross National Product during the war, and partly because of taxation and food subsidies. Change in taxation and subsidies policies after the war meant that the 'levelling' trend was short-lived.	Even so, the amount of levelling during the war may still have been overstated. The figures dealt with overall growth in working-class incomes, rather than with growth in individual incomes. Also, the distinctions made between middle class and working class may not have been accurate (some of the growth may actually have been among middle-class incomes). Even if there was levelling up of incomes, a possibly more important question is that of the distribution of property. In fact, the investigations of Charles Madge showed that only a tiny minority of workers were saving towards the accumulation of capital.

Argument	*Rebuttal*
Numbers in paid employment rose during the war, and average earnings rose by 80 per cent. Averages suggest that full employment made manual workers better off than they had been before the war.	But these are just averages. There were great differences between different groups within the working class, and there was no levelling between these groups: indeed (last paragraph on p.262) 'differentials widened'.
A small minority of men did have exceptionally high wartime earnings.	However, they did not use these earnings to save, and thus be assimilated into the middle class. Furthermore, their conditions of work, and their job security, was totally different from that of middle-class earners.
There was some improvement in conditions for working-class earners, and some deterioration for some middle-class earners. For some manual workers there were greater opportunities for promotion.	But all that this adds up to is greater variety within the working class, without any automatic levelling up for the higher paid manual workers.
Government departments would have liked to have seen a levelling of income among manual workers.	In fact, those in 'essential' industries did very well, but not those in 'non-essential' industries. Thus 'the war had the opposite effect on manual workers' earnings to "levelling"'. (One might possibly argue here that in moving from levelling between classes to levelling within the working class, Summerfield obscures an important point: she does seem to be admitting that *some* workers were levelled up; however, I suppose she could respond that she has already explained the limits upon that.) Arguments about general levelling are controverted not just by the variations in available income per head between families (large families being worst off), but also by the different practices of husbands in giving money to their wives.
Undoubtedly women's earnings made a significant contribution to family incomes in wartime.	But this did not amount to a general redistribution: it simply meant that there was more paid employment among wives of lower-income than higher-income husbands.

Argument	*Rebuttal*
There was social mixing among women workers.	In fact, only a very tiny minority of women who took paid jobs in wartime came from the higher social classes (such women tended to prefer to go into voluntary work).
Women's wartime employment contributed more to the working-class share of the national income than to the middle-class share.	But the effects of this depended very much on the number of mouths to feed, other items needed, etc.
There was levelling in the services.	Servicemen's wives were the 'new poor' of the war. In fact the service hierarchy was very energetically maintained, outside as well as inside the services.
The rise in the working-class share of the national income meant for that class (or a substantial part of it) a process of permanent 'levelling up', either as between the working class and the middle class or within the ranks of the working class.	Probably the permanent levelling up affected only a tiny group of self-denying savers, while the war probably increased differentials rather than diminished them.
The relative fall in the middle-class share of the national income meant a permanent 'levelling down' for them. As Seers put it, 'the real net incomes of the working class had risen over nine per cent, and those of the middle class had fallen over seven per cent'.	In fact, Guy Routh's analysis of average earnings over a longer period than that of the war itself revealed that while lower-middle-class groups had done quite badly, some higher groups had actually improved their position. The picture 'was not one of overall levelling, but of differing fortunes for different groups'.
The shortage of manual labour in the munition industries and the enhanced power of the trades unions narrowed differentials between middle-class and working-class occupations.	But, as Routh stated, the changes were only partly caused by changes in the pay of individual occupations, and were also caused by fluctuations in the numbers in different occupations. Some of the reduction in middle-class incomes could be explained by the substitution of female for male labour. Summerfield cites figures to indicate that there was indeed a great influx of women into white-collar work. Relative to the jobs done, women were even worse

Argument	*Rebuttal*
	paid here than in the working-class jobs they took on.
There was a growth of a 'cross-class' group of low salaried workers and better-paid manual workers, leading to a breakdown of all the class distinctions.	On the contrary, there is a good deal of evidence that mixing of social classes and other groups creates social friction.
Levelling of consumption (because of rationing, etc.) suggests a 'levelling of class'.	In fact, many middle-class families were making up for this, and in fact maintaining their positions, by saving. □

Discussion I hope you were able to identify the main stages in argument and counter-argument, though you may not always have linked up the points on the right-hand side as I have done. Also, I have made the points on the left-hand side more extensively and repeatedly than Summerfield (who after all is writing a polished article, not producing a schematic table).

The general conclusion is that there was little in the way of social levelling, and possibly some trends in the other direction. I hope you noted the other major points made by Summerfield:

1   She describes her conclusions as 'tentative', and presents her article as 'an antidote to a focus entirely upon images and attitudes'. (The approach of my book on class does explore images and attitudes very fully, though it seeks to integrate these with statistical information.) It is not altogether clear whether Summerfield (given her very firm Marxist, or perhaps Weberian, definition at the beginning) feels that further light could be thrown by paying attention to images and attitudes. Anyway, that is what I shortly propose to do .

2   Summerfield usefully identifies the 'three camps' in the debate over war and class (this is in the middle of p.256): 'those who believed that levelling took place in World War II and was permanent; those who argued that by some criteria levelling can be seen to have taken place but that it was not necessarily permanent; and those who concluded that no levelling took place at all.' Keep these categories in mind for our discussion of the other European countries.

3   The argument contained in the last sentence of the first paragraph on p.270. You may well not have thought this sentence worthy of any special attention. I want you now to consider its significance.

Exercise Here is the sentence:

> It is almost irresistible to conclude (with Madge) that most male members of the working class were drinking and smoking their wartime 'excess incomes' rather than using them as a means by which to 'level up' socially, because for the majority such a shift in class position had very little meaning.

If this is true, what significance does it have in the debate on the 'levelling of class'? ■

Specimen answer and discussion   Well, I do sympathize if you don't quite see what I am getting at. What is being said is that most of the working class weren't interested in moving up the social scale, in 'levelling of class' in that sense. Thus there is perhaps little point in worrying over whether the working class, or substantial numbers of them, did move up the social scale. What was presumably of importance to members of the working class was whether, within a basically unchanged class structure, their conditions, their job security, etc., improved. That is what I have argued took place; note, however, that the Summerfield article is most effectively questioning even that.

If Summerfield is correct, that would certainly throw serious doubt on the validity of the whole participation argument. It is my contention, Summerfield's excellent article notwithstanding, that the indispensable contribution of the working class to the war effort – whether in the forces or on the home front – the absolute necessity for keeping working-class morale high, and its strong market position, did produce clear gains over the condition of the working class in the 1930s, though these were within a broad class structure which (I have never maintained otherwise) did not significantly alter. I would make four points:

1   While I agree that Penny Summerfield is absolutely right in bringing out the variegated detail behind the broad averages, that some families were much better off than others, and that there were pockets of relative deprivation, she cannot escape the overall fact that working-class real earnings did steadily rise throughout the war and that (this is the really significant point which her article does not explore) these formed a platform for long-term change when immediately after the war new agreements on wages and hours ratified and perpetuated the broad 50 per cent gain in real earnings that had been made. If we are looking at the working class as a class, then we have to look at the aggregate figures relating to the class as a whole. The point Summerfield makes about the experience of individual families – particularly about women's earnings – is very important. But she leaves out of her account the fact that a significant section of the working class, as it was to be in the post-war years, was serving in the army and was not therefore included in the figures she quotes: what was important from the longer-term point of view was that when these men came back they took up employment at the new enhanced wage rates. Certainly there were many difficulties and contrary cross-currents during the war, but there was a general upward movement in earnings levels once the war had ended. Without doubt, an important factor was the control on the cost of living exercised through food subsidies. Though these were removed in the post-war years, this did not necessarily have a serious adverse effect, since, in a time of high demand for labour, wage rates continued on the steady upward movement that (in contrast to the inter-war years) had been established. Average weekly earnings, standing at 53s 3d in October 1938, rose 30 per cent (while the cost of living rose 26 per cent) to 69s 2d in July 1940, and 80 per cent to 96s 1d in July 1945 (when the cost of living was only 31 per cent above 1938). Wartime changes were ratified in 1946 when there were general reductions in the working week from 47–48 hours to 44 or 45.

2   That the workers were in a strong market position as against the employers, and a strong moral position as against the government, is shown in the way in which, despite the national emergency, and despite the overwhelming commitment of everyone to the defeat of Hitler, strike action was successfully resorted to. At the height of the war crisis in 1940 and 1941 there was a slight drop from the

1939 figures in the number of days lost due to strikes, but thereafter there was no shyness on the part of local labour leaders over using their power to press their claims, and the number of days lost due to strikes steadily mounted throughout 1942, 1943 and 1944, dropping slightly in 1945, when it was still double what it had been in 1939. Summerfield is absolutely right that workers in 'essential' industries did best; but my main point remains valid.

3   Attitudes towards the working class on the part of other sectors of society changed. I have to be careful here, having already talked about the prestige and status which the working class gained due to its participation in World War I. What essentially happened was that the working class became more homogeneous, the marginal elements of Edwardian times becoming established within the working class. The place of the working class in society was clearly recognized, but members of the working class were expected to stick very firmly in that place. A 'statutory working class' was clearly singled out in social welfare legislation as being the class to which such legislation applied alone. While not utterly alone in suffering from the slump, it was the class which could expect nothing in the way of job security in the face of economic vicissitudes. Expressions of opinion, if unrelated to any actual action, do not count for much; yet if attitudes generally do change among a significant number of people, that is a change. Vested interests and entrenched attitudes do not change overnight; indeed, they often do not change at all. The balance between stirrings of change and a determination to retain the existing structure of relationships is well brought out in the history of a Ministry of Labour memorandum on industrial morale of September 1942. The first draft was drawn up within the Ministry, and depended upon reports sent in from all over the country by regional controllers, industrial relations officers, labour supply inspectors, employment exchange managers, welfare officers and factory inspectors, all of whom were well qualified to present an authentic view of what was happening in the realm of industrial relations. Their draft provided a neat and true encapsulation of how the participation dimension of war was modifying the class relationship between employers and workers:

> Many employers still cherish the right to discipline their workers and to manage labour in their own way and resent the alleged curtailment of managerial rights. Management are slow to realise that times are changing and that their relationship with their work people must change also.

Yet a small committee of senior civil servants insisted on redrafting the passage in a manner which brings out well the resistance to, and total unwillingness to accept, any change in relationships between employers and workers:

> Many employers still consider it important that they should have the right to discipline and manage their workers in their own way, and dislike curtailment of managerial rights. (Drafts from the Bevin papers, Churchill College, Cambridge)

But the Federation of British Industry had declared in respect of the London Blitz, 'So great a people deserve the best', and was arguing two years later: 'we are on the threshold of a new world, and the theories and practices of the past cannot be taken for granted in the future'. 'It is hard', wrote Constantine Fitzgibbon, 'to persist in looking down upon, or resenting, a man who night after night is sharing the same dangers and doing exactly the same work as yourself' (*The Blitz*, p.118). The practical implications show themselves most obviously in government social policy at the end of the war, which would take me to the topic of social welfare. But if one simply concentrates on the literature associated with the establishment of the welfare state which poured out from the government presses after the war, one can see a complete change in tone from that of the official attitude towards the working class in the 1930s. Photographs, drawings and histograms proliferate: there is a clear intention to communicate in a civilized and friendly fashion with a wide audience, to be accessible to all.

4   The obverse of this point is that one can detect within the working class a greater self-confidence, a greater assertiveness. When, in his chairman's address to the 1941 conference of the Transport and General Workers' Union, Harry Edwards, a docker, expressed his conviction that this war was a 'people's war', he was echoing a sentiment which was remarkably widespread, as can be seen from the secret reports the government itself compiled on civilian attitudes, from letters sent abroad, which naturally passed through the hands of censors, and from private letters and diaries. Henry Penny, a London busdriver who wrote a diary on scraps of paper during the long nights in his air-raid shelter, noted in the early stages of the Blitz: 'we are all in the "Front Line" and we realise it'. Throughout, his diary is marked by a tone of reasoned self-confidence, of pride in himself and his fellow working men, and by an acceptance of the established order of society and Churchill's leadership. A Methodist minister reported on his encounters with soldiers on leave: 'Most of them are thinking of a world where there will be better opportunities for everyone, and more economic security than there has been since the early ages of mankind.' (Reports on morale are filed with the Cabinet in the Public Records Office; the private papers are in the Imperial War Museum.) The mood continued in the post-war years. Here is a Transport and General Workers' conference chairman, Edgar E. Fryer, in 1949: 'Let there be no mistake about it, we have made substantial progress in working-class conditions during the lifetime of this government.' Here is an ordinary plumber interviewed in 1951: 'There is now so much work to be done and so little unemployment, so if the boss rattles at you or threatens you with the sack you can just up and leave. There is no poverty anymore so that makes a lot of difference. The working people are better off and the bosses have lost a lot of their grip.' (Documents in Modern Records Centre, University of Warwick, and in Josephine Klein, *Samples from English Cultures*, 1965). Labour politicians with manifestly proletarian attributes, such as Ernest Bevin and Herbert Morrison, were, and were seen to be, important members of the wartime government.

Whether or not the figures are used to support the idea of growing class consciousness (in Summerfield's sense, though this would cut across her main argument), they certainly do demonstrate an increased confidence and assertiveness. More workers than ever before voted Labour in 1945, which is one of the reasons for Labour's election victory; and trades union membership rose over the war period from 6 million in 1938 to 8 million in 1944.

Summerfield is right to be scornful of notions of 'social mixing' during the war. In the chapter from *Class: Image and Reality* to which Summerfield refers, I quote from the diary of a spinster who on the second day of war (somewhat prematurely one might think) remarked: 'there is one thing, and one only, about this war – it is an instant and complete leveller of "classes"'. I continue:

Throughout the war, and after, there was much talk in this vein: of the war 'breaking down' the social structure, 'levelling' or 'mixing' social classes, and creating class unity. To talk of levelling or breaking down the class structure might be to imply the differences between classes, in power, wealth, life-styles, and so on, were so reduced as to lose almost all significance, so that everyone was left on the same social plain. More often what was probably meant (the war did tend to provoke the exaggerations of genuine self-delusion as well as those of interested intent) was that significant reductions in class differences did indeed take place, but within a class structure which basically remained unchanged. Likewise with social mixing: this could imply that there was so much mobility, such a startling elevation of the material conditions of those lowest in the old hierarchy (the working class) and such an accretion of power to them, so many instances of miners hobnobbing with top civil servants, bank clerks issuing orders to barristers, and duchesses bunking down with dustmen, that the old class reference points had become meaningless. Or again mixing could simply mean that, within the recognisable continuance of the old structure, there was more mobility, and that, in greater numbers than ever before, members of different classes were associating with each other – 'mixing', indeed. Most of those who spoke of class unity were in fact recognising the continued existence of classes: they did not usually mean that the nation was being united into one homogeneous class, but rather that the middle and upper classes were showing greater sympathy for, and understanding of, the working class, and a greater willingness to support improvements in working-class conditions.

That is indeed what they meant, and that it did indeed coincide with what was really happening is what I endeavoured to show in that particular book. □

During the war itself, much was made of the experience of the evacuation of the country's children from urban areas likely to be bombed, to safer rural areas. This was said at the time to have amounted to a 'social revolution' and to have aroused the consciences of the better-off in sympathy with the terrible plight of the products of the country's urban slums. Probably the ultimate wisdom has been pronounced in Travis L. Crosby's *The Impact of Civilian Evacuation in The Second World War* (1986): evacuation aroused as much bitterness between the classes as it did sympathetic responses on the part of middle-class individuals; it intensified working-class aspirations, and contributed to working-class determination to vote Labour in 1945. Cross-class encounters through air raids, and through evacuation, have been given too much attention. Where they did occur consist-ently throughout the war was in the voluntary activities almost exclusively undertaken by upper- and middle-class women. Summerfield is right to remove the majority of such women from alleged mixing in the factories, but she fails to allow for the 'social mixing' of voluntary air-raid, ambulance and canteen work.

There is certainly no need to weep over the fate of the various groups that make up the middle classes. But the fact is that taxation levels in the post-war years did remain far higher than would have been acceptable in the inter-war years. That persistent upper class of which I have spoken several times continued to maintain its position (indeed, several leading members of the post-war Labour govern-ment, and almost all leading civil servants, belonged to it). In the upheavals of war this class recruited even more actively from below than previously (D. N. Chester – Sir Norman Chester – made his way up through being a wartime civil servant;

Edward Heath through active service in the Guards). Broadly speaking, for the older-established middle-ranking professional middle class, real disposable income was reduced. The research organization Mass-Observation, which in pre-war days had concentrated its attention on the working class, felt it worth while in 1949 to carry out two investigations into 'The London middle-class housewife and her food problems' and 'The London middle-class housewife and her expenditure'. In the previous year it also collected interview material which makes a fascinating source for 'images and attitudes'. A woman civil servant aged fifty-sixty declared:

> I definitely think of myself as middle-class. It is difficult to say why. I had a typical middle-class education (small private school and secondary school). I have a middle-class job and I live in a middle-class district. But none of these things would make me middle-class in themselves. If I had been clever enough to get a higher post or profession, or rebellious enough to choose a more attractive manual job, I should not thereby have changed my class. Nor should I change it by living in a different district. Besides, my education and job and residence (to a certain extent) were determined by the fact that my parents were middle-class, so it is like the old riddle of the hen and the egg. Income has something to do with it but is not in itself a deciding factor nowadays, as many working-class people get higher pay than the lower-middle class, and many upper-class 'new poor' get less.
>
> I suppose it is rather a question of being born into a family and social group with particular customs, outlook and way of life – a group, that is (in my case), in which it is normal for the children to go to a secondary school, which usually chooses black 'coat' or professional careers, but which cannot afford university education or the higher professions – which has a certain amount of leisure and culture and expects to have time for such things as books, music and social activities, but does not go in for extravagant entertainment, expensive dinners and hotels, and so on; which chooses theatres in the balcony or pit rather than the stalls or gallery – which lives, generally, in dining room or lounge rather than in the kitchen or in various rooms for different times of the day, which speaks and writes generally correct English, and is, generally speaking, thrifty. And so on! (Mass-Observation archives, University of Sussex, file 3073)

My case is that while the contemporary phrases 'levelling' and 'social mixing' are over-dramatic, they do refer to something which, in a rather limited way, did actually happen. The working class in general gained in living conditions and in self-confidence; it was treated less contemptuously by members of other social classes. While the class structure itself did not appreciably alter, much of the middle class relatively lost. The upper class remained mainly unchanged, but recruitment from below into the various elites expanded. Summerfield's case is that nothing changed.

France

Let us see how these thoughts and counter-thoughts apply to the experience of France. Let me start once more with the notion of participation. Using this line of argument, one would expect social gains to be made by those who participated in the Resistance, in the Free French, and in the Liberation – particularly since a Liberation government was in power in the closing stages of the war. It is here that we should look for evidence of 'levelling' and 'mixing'. Associated with this approach is the idea that since the groups and classes that dominated in the inter-war years had failed, their position in the social hierarchy would be adversely affected. This whole approach, then, contrasts the Vichy and collaborationist regime with that of the Liberation: participants in the former lose out, participants in the latter make gains. However, that view was challenged thirty years ago by the American historian Stanley Hoffmann in an article to which the much over-used adjective 'seminal' may properly be applied. For the moment, I just want to get at the essence of the Hoffmann thesis.

Exercise   Turn to Hoffmann's article, 'The effects of World War II on French society and politics' in the Course Reader. Just concentrate for the moment on reading the second paragraph. In discussing social change in France, how does Hoffmann relate the war to the 1930s, and how does he relate Vichy to the Liberation? ▪

Specimen answer   Hoffmann believes that the social system that had flourished since 1878 began to
and discussion   change in 1934 (and thus not with the war – here we have a curious parallel with what Roseman was saying about Germany), though the changes which amount to 'death blows' for the old system come with war itself. In this summary Hoffmann is not making any distinction between the Vichy regime and the Liberation: the changes begin with Vichy in 1940, not with the Liberation in 1944.

Before attempting to sum up where all this takes us with regard to the effects of the war on class in France, let us see what the Resistance experience suggests in the way of levelling or mixing. □

Exercise   Turn to documents II.11, II.12 and II.13 in *Documents 2*, the interviews with former Resistance workers carried out by historian Dr Rod Kedward in the early 1970s and printed in his *Resistance in Vichy France*.

1   As sources, what are the strengths and weaknesses, collectively and individually, of these documents?

2   What in them would tend to suggest that there was little or no levelling or mixing of classes?

3   What in them suggests that there was mixing or levelling of classes?

4   Which do you find more impressive, the evidence for question 2 or the evidence for question 3? ▪

Specimen answers   1   Collectively, these documents have the strength that they are accounts by
and discussion   individuals who participated directly in the circumstances they are describing (also, the interviews were conducted by a highly qualified historian). Even these three documents give us a range of social backgrounds and attitudes (Kedward printed eighteen 'profiles' altogether; I shall mention some of the others shortly). It is a strength of oral history that it can provide us with details that simply would not be available in any other sources (Resistance workers did not have time, nor would it have been prudent, to keep diaries, and they certainly could not speak of their activities in letters, given the nature of the German censorship). The collective weakness of this oral history is that it was recorded thirty years after the events took place and thus depends on possibly fallible memories. There might always be a temptation for individuals to exaggerate their own roles. Clearly each individual had his own class and political viewpoint, which may have affected his perception. Malafosse calls himself a patriot. He was rich (but this perhaps enhances the value of his testimony about the role of working-class figures). Pestourie is a Communist Party member, Chauliac a pacifist socialist.

2   Wittingly, Pestourie would seem to be indicating an absence of 'mixing' when he says 'our Resistance was a class struggle' (on the other hand, in so far as this was successful, it could be held to be achieving 'levelling'). Chauliac brings out the point that the Resistance was not a movement of the people till August 1944: if it only involves a tiny minority, it can perhaps have little effect in mixing and levelling. Malafosse notes that 'we recruited mainly among workers', which would seem to suggest there was not a lot of social mixing, though on the other hand it could have the effect of raising the status of those workers.

3   You have noted how, in giving answers to question 2, I felt bound to indicate points which more properly answer question 3. This is all part of the complexity of historical source material, which frequently does not point unambiguously in any one direction. For all his insistence on class struggle, Pestourie reveals that he did work with those whose concern was purely the liberation of the country and with 'good republicans'; he also admits that Gaullism (which was based on a notion of class unity) 'spread much faster than we did'. Chauliac states quite straight-forwardly: 'there were all types of people in the Resistance. There was a great fraternity of different jobs and different political backgrounds.' Malafosse clearly is mixing 'downwards': as a barrister he defended Communist Party members – 'I was also a patriot, and more and more of a democrat'.

4   You can see the way in which the evidence can be read in different ways. For myself, I do think there is clear evidence of social mixing, of unity in a common purpose. But we do have to bear firmly in mind that until 1944 resistance was very much a minority activity (involving perhaps 4 per cent of the population). ☐

Note that Chauliac says that he never thought Pétain was playing 'a double game': this phrase is often used by supporters of the Resistance, and refers to the argument that, while pretending to collaborate with the Germans, the Vichy regime was really looking after the best interests of the French people. This is not a part of the Hoffmann thesis, except in so far as Hoffmann says that Vichy felt it better to set up its own institutions of social and economic reorganization rather than have the Germans impose them. Kedward also interviewed an aristocratic landowner who traced his inheritance back six hundred years, declared himself 'a man of the Right, a man of order', an opponent of the Popular Front 'because it was revolutionary', and an upholder of the 'cardinal virtues' of '*patrie* and *famille*'. Considerable force therefore attaches to his statement:

> There were all types of people in the network by the end, though at the beginning it was the humble people who were most easily recruited. As Jaurès said, and Socialists do say something true occasionally, 'The fatherland is the only wealth of the poor'. No cottage door was ever closed to me in the Resistance.

Another Kedward interviewee was a university-educated engineer in a small factory, who was a member of the main trades union confederation CGT. He noted signs of the Resistance as a social leveller:

> Within the Resistance, prejudices tended to disappear, since people were united by something essential – the defence of liberty, justice, dignity, and the fatherland. For myself Resistance was the direct continuation of my pre-war ideas. I had always dreamed of revolution, the remaking of the economic and political structure, and the movement towards a peaceful

world of people united in a common cause. Resistance was a sense of Utopia, and it is always necessary to envisage Utopia, even though serious-minded people at the time saw this Resistance as mad and ridiculous.

The needs of the Nazi war machine did, in a crude, ambivalent and strictly circumscribed way, confer a certain power on labour: there could be no concealing the essentiality of labour to the war effort, nor of the possibilities which labour had of sabotaging that effort. During the Liberation period a famous film, *La Bataille du Rail* (*The Battle of the Railways*) was made which symbolized the unique power that railway workers had to sabotage the Nazi war effort, and which celebrated their heroic participation in the national resistance. (I wanted to include this on video-cassette 2, but unfortunately we ran out of tape; perhaps you'll see it at summer school.)

With regard to the working class as a whole, I would say that the effects of World War II in the longer term were very similar in France to what they were in Britain. The working class did not change its position in the hierarchy, but it benefited from the social legislation introduced after the war, in accordance with the Liberation programme (see document II.14, 'Programme of the CNR'). The experience of the Popular Front had shown how much resentment of, and contempt for, the relatively small and isolated working class existed throughout middle-class France. The way in which the working class was now integrated into French life is symbolized by the treatment of Léon Blum in the French newsreels: mocked in the 1930s, he is treated as a returning hero in 1945.

There is no need to embark on a controversy over wartime wages, such as is featured in the article by Summerfield. Workers in vital industries did have preferential rations, but in general during the war people suffered lower standards and much deprivation. Harsh conditions continued in the immediate post-war years, but in the long run wage standards after the war were relatively much better than they had been in the 1930s. However, this was due more to a world-wide upsurge in demand than to any participation in the war effort.

The one social group who were able to do quite well during the war were the peasants, as they could eat their own produce or make it available through the black market. Gérard Walter, in his *Histoire des paysans de France* (1963), argued convincingly that the war did substantially change and improve the lifestyle of the peasants (as industry continued to expand, the proportions of those working on the land declined sharply in the post-war years, but that does not negate the argument that those who remained enjoyed high living standards). Nevertheless, François Bédarida, in his contribution to the Open University conference on total war and social change, not only argued that the effects on the peasantry were temporary, but saw little other change in class relationships:

> From the point of view of relations between the classes, the war endorsed and accentuated the existing state of affairs, save with respect to one area, the relationship between town and country. As a result of the widespread shortages the peasants, the producers and purveyors of foodstuffs, acquired the dominant and privileged position, and they benefited greatly from inflation and the black market. Here we do have a reversal of a pre-war trend, but a temporary reversal, directly related to immediate circumstances, and one which disappeared towards the end of the 1940s when the food supply situation returned to normal. Apart from this

temporary phenomenon, social mobility changed little, while class divisions tended to sharpen.

Bédarida does recognize that, 'Incontrovertibly there was a shift within the political elites'.

> New men, fresh from the clandestine struggle, now occupied the corridors of power. They were the ones who directed the government and held the ministerial portfolios in place of the figures of the Third Republic (Daladier never recovered from Munich; Reynaud was destroyed by the events of May to June 1940; Herriot was all but a shadow after the war . . .). In the parliamentary assemblies, the phenomenon was no less marked: deputies and senators from the Third Republic had for the most part been cleared out and largely replaced by men (and some women) from the Resistance. The numerical importance of *Résistants* among those elected to the assemblies was to be one of the characteristics of the Fourth Republic throughout its entire existence, even if many notables in the localities survived all changes of regime. (Bédarida, 'World War II and social change in France', in A. Marwick (ed.) *Total War and Social Change*, 1988)

Bédarida also speaks of a 'profound regeneration both in business enterprises and in administration' and of 'the formation of a modernizing elite which took control of the commanding heights of the economy, here through new men taking positions of power, there through amalgamation with directors from former times.' Does this amount to a change in class composition? As with Britain, it amounts to changes *within* the upper class, much greater recruitment from below, and perhaps quite far below compared with Britain, taking into consideration the strongly working-class composition of the Resistance.

Italy

As in World War I, many Italian workers were subject to quasi-military discipline, and the Fascist regime was in any case very restrictive of workers' rights. However, after October 1939 representatives of the Fascist syndicates were sent into the main engineering factories to settle individual grievances and smooth over potential unrest. As always, workers' participation in vital national production had some pay-offs. Wages held up reasonably well until 1943, and workers secured extra unrationed food in factory canteens. But from the point of view of social change, the most important factor was the failure of the government to rise to the challenge of war: opportunities were thus created for workers, and political groups, to show their hostility to the Fascist regime. In October 1941 a Committee of Action was founded, bringing together liberals, republicans and liberal socialists, as well as communists and socialists; on 1 July 1942 *L'Unità*, the communist paper, reappeared as a clandestine monthly. In April 1943 came the United Freedom Front, which provided the essential basis of the collusion between Catholics, communists and socialists that carried through the reform policies of the post-war Italian republic. Allied bombing raids, against which defences were particularly ineffective, also helped to stir up discontent.

Document II.15 in *Documents 2*, the Committee of Action poster, shows how the disruption of bombing could be exploited by the Committee of Action both to denounce Mussolini, and to offer assistance itself during air raids. As we have seen, there are debates about the effectiveness and consequences of bombing.

Partly because of the inherent weaknesses of the regime, the bombing of Italian cities did produce definite direct results with respect to disruptions in production, the shattering of morale, and causing people to flee from the cities. Workers in industrial plants were particularly vulnerable. By the end of 1942, 25,000 buildings had been wrecked in Turin and 500,000 people had left Milan. The government was forced to grant what was called the 192 hours evacuation allowance (that is to say, an extra month's wages). The government's subsequent decision that only heads of families who could prove that they had in fact moved house were to receive this allowance was one of the grievances which provoked the celebrated 'internal strikes' that began in Turin on 5 March 1943 and spread to other industrial centres in Piedmont, Milan, Bologna and Florence. The strikes took the form of downing tools for relatively short periods. But in a desperate war situation they were extremely effective, and on 2 April the government secured a return to work on the basis of a pay increase. Martin Clark, in his *Modern Italy* (1985, p.289), has commented that: 'The strikes were the first mass protest demonstrations in Axis Europe; they revealed how weak the Fascist regime had become by March 1943.'

I now want you to read document II.16 in *Documents 2*, *L'Unità*'s report on the strike of 100,000 Turin workers, relating it to the information I have just given you. Later in these units I will set an exercise on this document.

It is a moot point whether (mainly non-violent) resistance to Mussolini, or the military resistance to the German occupation which took over in the north of Italy in September 1943 (see document II.17, the statement issued by Field Marshal Rommel) were more important in stimulating social change at the end of the war. Given that armed resistance was largely confined to the north of Italy – the Committee of National Liberation of Northern Italy was formed on 17 October 1943 – while the Allies were advancing up through the southern half of Italy, it is probably true to say that the critical factor was the inadequacy of the Italian regime in face of war, rather than participation in resistance activities, though these contributed to the general reformist atmosphere at the end of the war. The popular rising of the ordinary people of Naples against the Germans in the 'Four Days' at the end of September 1943 did bring some prestige to the working class in the south, while the great strike of March 1944 in the north again drew attention to the special role of the working class.

As elsewhere, then, the story is of general working-class gains (though intense privation after 1943) within a basically unaltered class structure. Wartime conditions were again favourable for the peasants who, as in France, could keep their food to themselves or put it on the black market. In the words of Martin Clark, 'As in 1915–18, many peasant families became relatively prosperous. They began buying land, and inflation soon reduced their mortgages. Sensing their chances, they simply ignored the regime: it was in the countryside, not the towns, that the Fascist system first collapsed.' Peasant resistance activity also, as Tannenbaum has stressed (*The Fascist Experience*, 1972, p.323), contributed to bringing them into the mainstream of Italian life.

Germany

I hope that you took the opportunity earlier to take notes from, or make annotations on, Mark Roseman's article on Germany in the Reader.

Exercise   What are the main points made by Roseman with respect to changes in class and the relationship of the war to these changes? ∎

Specimen answer and discussion   Roseman's first point is that the pre-war Nazi regime had already brought changes in class relationships, particularly with respect to mobility from manual to white-collar positions, upward mobility through Nazi organizations, and the abandonment of traditional working-class dress. The war maintained and, as Roseman says, increased the already high level of geographical and social mobility. This had long-term significance for rural communities and also substantial sections of the working class. With reference to the extension of working-class cultural horizons, note Roseman's phrase about 'war as the continuation of tourism by other means'. Both economic mobilization and the army itself offered opportunities for upward social mobility: 'in practice a good war career proved advantageous at most levels of the post-war job market.' Furthermore, the influx of foreign forced labour created 'a form of collective upward mobility for German workers.' Many German employees found themselves elevated to positions of overseers and foremen; from interviews, Roseman tells us, we know that many workers did perceive their new responsibilities as a sort of promotion. Roseman also sees war conditions as fostering harmonious relations between employers and workers. Again and again, though, Roseman returns to the importance of the pre-war period, throwing out more neat formulations:

> In general we can say that the war undermined the Nazis' own appeal while reinforcing many of the social changes which they had initiated in the 1930s . . . Yet through isolation and terror, through collective and individual mobility and through the forging of new loyalties and solidarities, the war confirmed the Nazis' assault on class traditions . . . Of greater long-term significance for the German working class were the subtler changes to perceptions, behaviour and relationships, above all the weakening of traditional class identities and antipathies which had been wrought by fascism and war.

Roseman also refers to the effect of the Allies in preventing 'the bitter conflicts between labour and capital that had resulted after 1918 and would otherwise probably have resulted after 1945.' Personally I am dubious about this reference to the influence of the Allies: Roseman seems to me to have already adequately explained the development in working-class attitudes. But that is yet another issue for you to think about and do more reading on. What is certainly beyond dispute is the emergence of a 'hard-working, consumer-orientated, sceptical and unpolitical working class'. As Roseman neatly adds, a strong suspicion of the bosses co-existed with the feeling that labour's status had collectively improved: 'The boom economy of the 1930s with its possibilities for individual advancement and the toughening experiences of soldiering and surviving the hardships of the Occupation years had encouraged in many workers a confidence in their ability to stand up to those in authority and to profit from the capitalist system.' □

It would be naive, I think, to take the view that the class structure that emerged in post-war West Germany was simply imposed on it by the Americans. Clearly some of the features of East Germany were determined by the Russian occupation, but Professor Ralf Dahrendorf, in his study of *Society and Democracy in Germany* (1969), brought out that in East Germany 'a society with its own peculiar structure has emerged'. In general, it was a society in which political elites replaced the upper and middle classes as they had developed in the early twentieth century. Specifically, there were major land reforms which brought a final ending to the pre-eminence of the Junker landowners, many of whom fled to the west. There was a working-class rise in status in that they were guaranteed social and economic rights in the form of full employment and welfare benefits. Dahrendorf has offered this comparison between the German Democratic Republic in the east and the Weimar republic:

> In the Weimar republic the role of the citizen was formally guaranteed to all, but this offer was undermined by the absence of the social preconditions of its realisation. In the DDR [German Democratic Republic] the preconditions are present, but the realisation is made impossible by numerous formal restrictions on the citizenship rights that are part and parcel of the constitution of liberty. De facto, there is no universal, equal, free and secret suffrage, no liberty of the person and of political activity, no equality before the law; but there is a society that would enable its members to make effective use of these liberties, if only they had them.

Russia

Russia suffered greater destruction and devastation, and greater loss of human life, relative to its population than any other country involved in World War II, save for Poland (see section 2.6 below). Yet such was the firm grip of the Soviet regime as it had established itself by the late 1930s, that it has been argued that far less in the way of change in the social structure took place there than in the other countries we have been discussing. The American analyst, Edward L. Keenan, put the matter this way in an article published in 1986:

> The very fact that this devastating war, more costly for Russia in human and economic terms even than the first, produced so few significant changes in the structure or political culture of Soviet society is, in my view, the most eloquent evidence that the society had become restabilized, and its political culture 're-knit', before the outbreak of the war. Evidence of long-term economic and social processes bears this out: the fundamental and dramatic processes of social change – industrialization, urbanization, the creation of the new elites – although they had not entirely run their course, were slowing by the beginning of the 'forties, and had already established the basic patterns and relationships that were to be reconstituted and redefined in the post-war period. (Keenan, 'Muscovite political folkways', *The Russian Review*, 45, 1986, pp.167–8)

Paul Dukes, who quotes the above passage from Keenan in his contribution to *Total War and Social Change*, links up with a debate which I identified in my Introduction in discussing Germany: he has suggested that Russia's relationships with the outside world in the 1940s imposed profound constraints on social change. In particular, the Cold War put a stop to any modifications in Soviet society which might have developed out of the war.

What evidence is there of change in social structure? You will recall Bernard Waites's discussion of internal war in the Soviet Union in Book III, Unit 16. It can be argued, and it has been argued by Susan J. Linz in her introduction to *The Impact of World War II on the Soviet Union* (1985), that in the Great Patriotic War internal war gave way to a new social cohesion. The effect of war service in broad-ening horizons was encapsulated in Roseman's phrase about war as tourism by other means. Dukes has an even finer phrase to express the same idea: 'It was diffi-cult to keep them down on the collective farm now that they had taken Berlin.'

The evacuation of industry eastwards (see document II.21 in *Documents 2*) created an expansion in industrial employment. However, the extensive applica-tion of compulsion, the appallingly cramped accommodation, the generally low wages, meant that there were no gains for the working class. There was some talk during the war of improvements for the peasants (who suffered desperately at the hands of the Germans) but in fact in the post-war years very harsh quotas were imposed on the collective farms. It was, as Alec Nove has put it, 'as if Stalin was determined to make the peasants pay for the necessary post-war reconstruction' (*An Economic History of the USSR*, 1972, p.298). The currency reform of December 1947 was in part meant to hit at black marketeers and those who had managed to hoard savings, but it failed to curb inflation, while the turnover tax payable by everyone was scarcely kind to the least well-off. There were no structural changes in the political elites, 'the new class', but Dukes has indicated that there were qualitative changes here (perhaps comparable with the kind of changes that took place in the upper class in Western countries):

> Allowing for those dismissed from the Party, a guarded estimate indicates that about 75 per cent of the membership in 1952 had joined since the outbreak of war in June 1941, and that roughly the same percentage was under 45 years of age. While the bulk of the new recruits were of peasant and worker origin, they appear to have risen for the most part to managerial level. The educational level had gone up, too, the percentage of those having completed secondary education having climbed from less than 15 per cent in 1941 to about 20 per cent in 1947. In 1952, nearly 12 per cent had experienced some degree of higher education. (Dukes, 'The social consequences of World War II for the USSR', 1988, pp.54–5)

Other East European countries

With regard to the social structures of the other East European countries, the question that arises is this: is the critical factor their position within the Soviet sphere of influence, or are there any significant internal developments springing out of the experience of war? A number of issues need to be clarified:

1 We are now moving from the detailed study of relatively limited (though, I would maintain, still significant) changes within the major countries, to a broad comparison taking Europe as a whole; rather than taking the separate aspects of social structure, we are essentially taking social structure together with political systems and values. Just as one could pose the question with respect to the First World War as to whether it contributed materially to the division in the inter-war years between one-party dictatorships and liberal democracies, so now we are considering whether the Second World War contributed to the broad division of Europe between one-party communist states and liberal democracies.

2 We have to be clear about what exactly the distinction is: is it really true to say that, with regard to the particular question of class and social structure, the two groups of societies are very different in the position and status of the working class, the nature of the 'upper class', etc.; is one group more 'classless' than the other – has levelling proceeded further in one than in the other?

Actually there were some structural changes which outweigh the ideological and political division of Europe, the most noteworthy being the acquisition of coal-fields and industrial areas by the new westward-shunted Poland (although it lost agricultural areas): thus, for the first time Poland had the basis for a large, skilled industrial working class.

3   We have to be clear about when exactly the division of Europe came about. As hostilities ended, there was certainly an occupation of the two halves of Europe by, respectively, Soviet and Western forces. But for a few years after 1945 there were coalition governments of various sorts, and forms of democratic government, in several of the countries later to fall within the Eastern bloc.

4   How far is the division essentially a function of Russia's emergence as a world power (very definitely, of course, a consequence of the war) and how far, if at all, is it related to internal developments within the various countries, in particular with reference to occupation and resistance during the war?

5   It may be that, compared with the brute facts of the physical presence of Russian military power, all other issues are drained of significance. However, it would be worth looking at the nature of the various East European regimes and social systems as they were on the eve of war, with a view to asking whether, under the impact of war, they might have undergone some transformation even if Russia, after the war, had exercised a restraint not usual in great powers. Few East European regimes in the 1930s were full liberal democracies on the Western model (Czechoslovakia is the noteworthy exception, but after 1938 it was in effect absorbed into the Nazi system). Where there was manifestly Nazi or Fascist influence in a pre-war regime, did that mean that oppositional impulses (which, as in Italy, might gain new opportunities in war) would be towards the Soviet system or the Western one?

'Divided Europe' is a topic that is discussed in Unit 26.

In discussing what the differences were in social structure and class relations between Eastern and Western countries as they finally emerged, it is difficult to steer clear of overtly political judgements. Perhaps the extract I quoted from Dahrendorf with respect to East Germany is as good a basic proposition as any. There is, as in Russia, the problem of the particular nature of Stalin, and of the insecurities bred by the Cold War: might the East European societies otherwise have come closer to realizing the nobler aspects of Marxist philosophy? We know that these societies, while clearly not offering political liberties to their citizens, failed (even after allowance is made for the desperately destructive effects and after-effects of war, including the reparations exacted by Soviet Russia) to provide them with decent living standards. With regard to the other issues I have raised, let me conclude with a few questions which you should be able to answer on the basis of your reading in the course so far.

Exercise   1   Which East European country achieved a one-party socialist form of government and social system almost exclusively through the efforts of its own liberation fighters? Which foreign country provided most assistance?

2   Which East European country, left to its own devices, would have been most thoroughly opposed to any form of Soviet socialist system? Explain your answer.

3   In which country was there the greatest welcome for the Russians as genuine liberators from a detested previous regime? Explain your answer. ■

Specimen answers and discussion

1   Yugoslavia. Britain provided most assistance. (See Roberts, p.572; see also document II.18 in *Documents 2*, the letter from Tito to the Italian command – I will discuss the context of this document later).

2   Poland. Poland had been divided up between Russia and Germany at the beginning of the war (there is a catalogue of further Polish grievances against the Russians which I don't need to go into here). (See Roberts, p.571.)

3   Czechoslovakia. The Western powers had failed to support Czechoslovakia's liberal democracy in 1938, the country in fact (in two stages) being handed over to the Nazis. (See Roberts, p.571.) ☐

2.4   National cohesion

In our discussions of the origins, causes and consequences of World War I nationality was a prominent issue. In the eyes of idealists, World War I was in part fought over, and in part succeeded in, securing the rights of the different nationalities to their own independent nation states. The question of nationality had featured most prominently with respect to the Austro-Hungarian empire, but it was an issue which affected Central and Eastern Europe in general. Before the war, Russia figured largely in Western eyes as the champion of all Slav populations; that Russia was itself a multinational empire only became more obvious in the later stages of the war. By the time of World War II, questions of nationality and race were being stridently emphasized in a rather different way.

Exercise

1   Which country was most outspoken on matters of nationality and race? Write a few sentences on this issue.

2   Which major power had very genuine nationality problems? Where else was nationality a significant issue immediately before or, more important, during the war?

3   What overall effect did the war have on nationalities? ∎

Specimen answers and discussion

1   Germany. There are two, or perhaps three, aspects to the issue. A particularly obnoxious feature of Nazi philosophy was the emphasis on 'racial purity', involving anti-semitism in particular. This led before the war to policies designed to expel Jews from Germany and, during the war, to their extermination. Associated with this was the notion of the *Herrenvolk* (the superior race), which entailed the deplorable treatment of *Untermenschen* (sub-humans) such as the Slavs. At the same time there was the drive to unite all Germans, scattered as they were throughout Central and Eastern Europe, in one great German empire.

2   Russia (the problems had not gone away). As noted earlier by Bill Purdue, there were pockets of Germans throughout Europe: some had been dispersed for centuries, some found themselves included in a foreign country (for example, Poland or Belgium) because of the way in which the Versailles frontiers had been drawn. In Czechoslovakia, apart from the German minority in the Sudetenland, there was the problem of national rivalries between Czechs and Slovaks. There were Hungarian minorities in Romania and Poland. But the country I particularly hope you thought of is Yugoslavia, where the Germans and Italians were able to exploit the national rivalries between the Croats and the Serbs (remember from Unit 21 the setting up of the puppet kingdom in Croatia).

3   The two main points, which I hope you got, were that the war both induced

great movements of population, and also resulted in the redrawing of frontiers. The ultimate expression, as in so many other spheres, was Poland. After 1945, Poland was, for the first time in history, a homogeneous nation state. Though its boundaries had been shunted westwards, the people within them, following the mass transfers of Germans, were exclusively Polish. There are rather more subtle, and perhaps more problematic, possible consequences. It is probably true that in some cases unity was forged in the face of the common German enemy (see Roberts, p.565). At the same time, given that the upheavals of war bring into question the legitimacy of certain states, and given that (as I have suggested) wars tend to stimulate communal feelings, there could be encouragement of national self-expression within established states. Both forces, I think, are true with respect to the growth of Flemish sentiment within Belgium, and the latter is important with respect to the growth of Scottish nationalism within the United Kingdom (where there were also particular grievances, such as the conscripting of Scottish girls to work in English factories). One point that you almost certainly will not have thought of is that with the dreadful destruction of male lives in the war, women, if they were to have a husband at all, often took one from outside their own national group. It has been argued that this was a factor in producing greater cohesion between the nationalities in Russia. □

One of the most tragic consequences of World War II was the destruction of European Jewry. In Germany, where Jews in the past had contributed so much to national culture, there was in effect no longer any Jewish population. The post-war settlement left a number of areas of friction. Russia moved its boundaries westwards, and Poland was then, as it were, 'shunted' westwards. The boundary between Italy and Yugoslavia continued to be a matter of contention in the post-war years. A result of the settlement was the considerable transfer of populations. In many cases what people feared was not an alien national regime, but an alien form of government. On the whole it could be said that the general movement which had accelerated earlier in the century towards each nationality having its own nation state was consolidated in the aftermath of World War II. If you turn to document II.10 in *Documents 2*, 'extracts from the *Protocol of the Proceedings of the Berlin Conference*', you will see that great transfers of German populations were envisaged, with only a rather cursory reference to these being carried out in an 'orderly and humane' way.

2.5   Social reform and welfare policies

Two documents have long been taken as symbolizing the aspiration that World War II should result in a world in which there would be better social conditions and better social provision for the ordinary people: the Atlantic Charter (the statement of common aims subscribed to by Churchill and President Roosevelt in August 1941, four months before the USA's entry into the war) and the Beveridge Report (formally the report of a committee appointed to 'undertake . . . a survey of the existing national schemes of social insurance and allied services . . . and to make recommendations', the report being published in December 1942).

Exercise   Turn to document II.5 in *Documents 2*, the Atlantic Charter. As you will quickly see, it is not basically concerned with issues of social policy. However, it is a good illustration of the notion of participation, in so far as it was the Labour members participating in the Churchill coalition who insisted that a clause be inserted referring to the better world to be created after the war. Which clause is this? ■

I can't believe that you need an answer to that one, though I will mention the clause number later just to make sure that no one has gone off on the wrong track. Because of this single clause the Atlantic Charter did come to represent that psychological reaction to war which produces the argument that all the destruction and sacrifice must be for something better. We find it being mentioned in Resistance literature, and Beveridge himself, in a radio broadcast of 2 December 1942, said of his plan: 'It's the first step, though it is one step only, to turning the Atlantic Charter from words into deeds.' The Beveridge Report also emphasizes the idea of participation, since the committee was, in the first instance, set up at the behest of British trades union leaders whose co-operation was, of course, essential to the war effort.

Exercise   In this exercise, for once, I shall be doing most of the work. I want you to have beside you the extracts from the Beveridge Report which are printed in *Documents 2* as document II.19. I propose to talk you through this very famous and very important document, clause by clause, with just a few preliminary general questions for you to answer.

1   Where does the document, in the very strongest terms, express the view that the war is in itself a time of change, and that it is a time when there must be plans for further change?

2   What specific aspect of social policy is this report basically about?

3   Where is it stated that this aspect is not in itself enough? What other aspects of social policy are advocated in the report? ■

I shall now comment paragraph by paragraph, with the answers to these questions emerging clearly in my commentary.

It is evident from the first paragraph that we have come in about half-way through the report, and that up to this point the report has consisted of a survey of the existing system, prior to the making of recommendations. It is the second paragraph which, in its last two sentences, contains what I was referring to in my first question above. The general sentiment is an important one and was much quoted, thus helping to add to this sense that there must be a better world after the war, particularly since, thanks to the efforts of the British Ministry of Information, the contents of the Beveridge Report were widely known across the world. However, we must be cautious. One trap which earlier, and unthinking, commentators on the relationship between war and social change often used to fall into was to take phrases of this sort at face value, to assume that because someone like Beveridge said that the time was right for revolutionary change, revolutionary change therefore took place. In discussing programmes put forward in wartime, it is essential always to continue into the post-war years and see whether they were actually put into practice.

The specific reference to 'sectional interests' is to the various bodies who gave evidence, particularly the insurance companies and to a lesser extent employers' organizations and trades unions. In the existing social insurance system, as originally set up by Lloyd George (remember document I.23 in *Documents 1*), the private insurance companies (known as the 'approved societies') had a part in running the system. Beveridge is giving a warning here that whatever the companies may think, they will be cut out of his system which will be administered directly by the state.

The next paragraph is the one which helps to answer my second question, and provides the main part of the answer to the third question. Although this document is specifically concerned with the narrow aspect of social insurance, Beveridge also wants there to be 'a comprehensive policy of social progress'. Then comes the Dickensian language of the five giants (actually taken from the opening pages of *A Tale of Two Cities*). The meaning may not be very clear to you: Want is loss of income, to be dealt with by social insurance; Disease stands for all kinds of ill-health and physical incapacity, and is to be dealt with by a National Health Service; Ignorance means inadequate education, and is to be dealt with by a new Education Act; Squalor basically means poor housing, and it is to be dealt with by a Housing Act; Idleness signifies unemployment, and it is to be dealt with by policies directed towards the avoidance of high unemployment. Thus we see what Beveridge means by a comprehensive policy, though in fact education and housing are not again dealt with in the report. Nevertheless, in that the Beveridge Report was widely taken as the blue-print for what was already in some circles being spoken of as a welfare state (to contrast with Hitler's warfare state), that welfare state was taken to embrace positive policies on all of these matters.

Beveridge was a Liberal. Like Margaret Thatcher four decades later, he believed that individuals should be encouraged to take action to provide for themselves – this idea is embodied in his 'third principle' of co-operation between the state and the individual. The post-war Labour government which was responsible for implementing the Beveridge proposals aimed actually to provide benefits above the mere subsistence level which Beveridge recommended, though in practice these benefits quickly fell behind inflation. Certainly Labour policies did not aim to encourage private insurance coverage as Beveridge had hoped: that is the basis of the Thatcherite accusation that a 'dependency culture' was created.

The next paragraph gives the full and explicit answer to my second question. The report is essentially concerned with the 'limited contribution' of an immediately achievable plan of insurance. The next paragraph sets out what social insurance is seen as covering: interruption (for example through unemployment or sickness) and destruction (through permanent disability or retirement) of earning power, and also special expenditures arising from birth, marriage or death. The six fundamental principles are very important: they contain the essence of the Beveridge view – many were not followed in continental European plans, and many have been abandoned in Britain in more recent times. The term 'flat rate' is a key one: everybody was to pay the same level of contribution, and everyone, whatever their ordinary earnings, was to receive the same level of benefit (this contrasts with earnings-related schemes, where the better-off pay more, but then get higher benefits). The various British social insurance schemes (we took an overview of them in Book II, Units 8–10) had continued to grow in piecemeal fashion; Beveridge's idea (spelled out later) was that there should be one Ministry of Social Security to bring everything together in one united scheme. Benefits were to be genuinely of subsistence level, but, as already noted, it was expected that through private provision individuals would build on these. 'Comprehensiveness' is another key word, sometimes rendered as 'universality'. In my discussion of class, I mentioned that social security and other services prior to World War II were essentially and explicitly aimed at the separate working class. The new idea, which it was hoped would genuinely create a more united society, was that this social security scheme would bring in everyone, rich as well as poor. The exact meaning of 'classification' is spelled out in (ii) below – it is a functional classification and one which cuts right across the conventional notion of social classes. 'National assistance' figures again later in the document. Because the Beveridge scheme depended, like that of Lloyd George, on insurance stamps being bought, there were inevitably people not covered by this scheme; hence the need for national assistance, for which contributions were not required, but which for many working-class people had overtones of the old Poor Law and the dole of the 1930s. If we look ahead to what actually happened after the war, we find that while national assistance featured quite prominently in the post-war years, voluntary insurance (or private provision) did not play a great part for ordinary people. Several socialists argued, unsuccessfully, that the insurance principle should be abolished, and that all benefits should be made available to anyone in need, without the distinction between contributors and non-contributors. Nevertheless, the aim of the plan 'to make want under any circumstances unnecessary' is a noble one, and expresses well the noble side of the aspirations engendered by war.

I now come on to the individual points (i) to (xii):

(i)   This spells out the 'comprehensiveness' or 'universality' principle. The idea of 'different ways of life' is not related to social class, but to the classification spelled out in (ii).

(ii)   The basic classification is between I, employees, and II, employers and the self-employed. That this is scarcely a class distinction is clarified when one realizes that I included top professional people 'under contract of service', while II could, for example, include a self-employed window-cleaner. III obviously covers all social classes, while IV includes both the idle rich and those unable to secure employment. V simply means children, and VI, of course, is those who have qualified, or now will qualify, for some kind of old-age pension.

(iii)   Retirement pensions of a sort had existed since before the First World War, but the idea of children's allowances, or family allowances as they were actually called when introduced by the Churchill coalition in 1944, was something new (though long agitated for). Paid on the universalist principle, this has so far (1989) survived, as child benefit, all Thatcherite reforms. The 'appropriate' conditions relating to the other four classes are spelled out in the next two sub-sections, (iv) and (v).

(iv)   The critical points here are that employed persons will have a contribution from their employer, thus creating for themselves a higher entitlement to benefits. The self-employed and non-employed will simply have their own contribution. Housewives do not make any contribution, it being part of the assumptions about the nature of the family of the time that the benefits they can receive will be covered by the contributions that men have to make for that very purpose (bear in mind Summerfield's figures for the earnings for men and women).

(v)   This sub-section spells out the wider range of benefits available to employees (with their higher total contributions) than the other classes. Again we see what housewives are to get, by virtue of their husbands' contributions.

(vii)   The means test was a hated symbol of the 1930s, and it was the intention of the Beveridge plan, and its Labour and trades union supporters, that this was now to be abolished. However, a form of means test would remain for national assistance (see below).

(x)   In the post-war years the 'limited number of cases' proved not to be quite so limited, though many were deterred from claiming national assistance because of the overtones of means test. It should be said that the whole spirit in which needs were assessed in the post-war years differed totally from the viciously inquisitorial means test of the 1930s.

(xi)   This was not, strictly speaking, part of Beveridge's brief, but is one of the items he felt to be essential to 'a comprehensive policy of social progress'. Already, to meet the expected needs of war, there was in existence an Emergency Hospital Scheme which could form the basis for a future National Health Service. The Churchill coalition government was responsible for a separate white paper, *National Service for Health*, which recommended the establishment of a National Health Service after the war. Again the principle is that of universality ('all citizens').

(xii)   In fact a Ministry of Social Security was not set up (until the 1960s and the advent of supplementary benefits), so the system created by the post-war Labour government was less unified than Beveridge had envisaged. The phrase 'social security' did not come into general usage: instead there was a Ministry of National Insurance, and an autonomous National Assistance Board.

The next paragraph, in perfectly clear language, sums up the essentials of the Beveridge insurance scheme. It picks up the point about social insurance in itself not being enough, and returns to the notion of 'a concerted social policy', which, in so many ways, was what made the Beveridge Report famous. Three particular assumptions relating to 'a concerted social policy', the paragraph is saying, are essential for the implementation of the social insurance scheme. The first assumption is the institution of family allowances (as they were actually called in the 1944 Act). The Beveridge Report does not state who these are to be paid to, but in fact by 1944 feminist sentiment was strong enough (or at least the fear that husbands would waste the money was) for it to be enacted that the family allowances were to be paid direct to mothers. Family allowances expressed the universalist principle in its fullest form: as the next paragraph makes clear, they are not to depend on insurance contributions, but are payable to everyone and are financed out of taxation. The second assumption (or assumption B) is that there will be a National Health Service. This too involves a very full statement of universalist principles. It was in fact decided that a portion of the cost of the National Health Service (which began in 1948 under the terms of the Labour government's National Health Service Act of 1946) would be met from insurance contributions made by those who paid them, but this is a minor detail since the service was to be completely open to everyone. Its administration was also to be totally detached from social insurance, and it was in fact the responsibility of the Ministry of Health in England and Wales, and of the Department of Health of the Scottish Office in Scotland. If one looks at the rather tentative and fragmented proposals that were being made for health provision before World War II, then I think a good argument can be made that the war experience (particularly the nationalization of hospitals in the Emergency Hospital Scheme) did make a significant contribution towards the comprehensive National Health Service that finally emerged (this at least is the argument of my article 'The Labour Party and the welfare state in

Britain', in the *American Historical Review* vol. 73, no. 2, 1967). The phrase 'prior to any other consideration' is worth noting: this means that treatment should be provided whether or not a patient has money or insurance cover, considerations which loom large in societies which do not have a comprehensive National Health Service.

Britain after the war became, for a considerable period, a full-employment society: that, indeed, is one of the crucial differences between conditions before the war and conditions after the war. The Beveridge Report, in assumption C, expresses a commitment to the maintenance of employment. In intention, the Labour government went even further, though the most important influence was the high level of world demand after all the destruction of resources during the war. It is important to note that Beveridge did not expect, and did not call for, full employment. As you will see as you work through the paragraph, he expected an average unemployment rate of 8.5 per cent, though he does immediately express the hope that unemployment might be reduced to below that level. The report does not explain how maintenance of employment is to be achieved; Beveridge, on his own initiative, wrote a separate report on this, while the government published its famous *Employment White Paper*, which announced the aim of avoidance of mass unemployment. What all had in mind were Keynesian policies of managing total national expenditure so as to keep up demand in times of potential recession. Beveridge does not expect it to be possible to control 'completely the major alternations in good trade and bad trade'; in fact Keynesian policies were fairly successful in this respect throughout the 1940s, '50s and '60s. Beveridge expects some short-term unemployment: the evil he is concerned to eradicate is long-term unemployment for the same individual. His implication is that a fair amount of labour mobility will enable an unemployed man to find another job within about 26 weeks.

The penultimate paragraph again brings out the essence of Beveridge's liberal principles. Unlike traditional socialists, he does not believe that the main kind of redistribution of wealth and income required is that between land, capital, management and labour (in the direction of the last, of course). He believes that the main problem is within classes, between those earning and those not earning, between those with large families and those with no families. He then rests much of his case on better administration, which he believes will eliminate waste. Clearly he would be worried by the creation of a 'dependency culture' – he intends that his plan will not have a depressing effect on incentives. In the final paragraph he is saying that want could have been abolished before the war. The phrase 'abolition of want' is very much a phrase of the 1940s, and very much a concept which, like the Beveridge Report itself, achieved international circulation. His key-note now is that it should be regarded as a post-war aim capable of early attainment. In saying this he was anticipating the criticisms of people like Churchill, who did not want any discussion of such post-war aims to distract from the prime task of getting on with the war. Churchill was also to warn at the end of the war that the country was too impoverished for radical social schemes.

That ends my detailed textual commentary, which you will find very useful should you yourself, in a TMA or exam, have to write a commentary on an extract from the report. There remains the question of what it all adds up to: what is the ultimate historical significance of these extracts from the Beveridge Report? Well, as I have indicated from time to time, the basic provisions were adopted in the post-war Labour government legislation which is usually seen as establishing the

British welfare state. The Beveridge Report, to put in summary form what really should be spelled out in a little more detail, forms a vital link in any chain joining the war experience to the enactment of social legislation. It also had symbolic significance when resistance fighters and progressive elements in other countries discussed the kind of society there should be after the war.

In this course we have tried to avoid placing too much emphasis on Britain, but with the Beveridge Report it really is a case of the British document being a seminal one. I want to keep it in mind as we turn to the relationship, if any, between war and social welfare in some of the other main countries. Let me see whether, on the basis of what you already know, you can make any connections.

Exercise   Let us consider France, Italy, Germany and Russia. Remembering their differing experiences of war, occupation, resistance, and so on, say which of these countries you think would have been most susceptible to the influence of Beveridge's ideas on welfare, and which would have been least. Briefly explain your lines of reasoning. Don't struggle too long with this one if it seems beyond the bounds of your present knowledge, but try at least to set down a few odd thoughts. You may find it easiest to start with the country where the influence of Beveridge would be least. ■

Specimen answers
and discussion   With respect to that last helpful sentence, I hope you immediately thought of Soviet Russia, where the liberal-capitalist ideas of Beveridge would be unlikely to have much appeal. In any case, we have already seen that there were severe limits on the extent to which change was permitted to take place in Russia at the end of the war. You may then have found it very difficult to say which of the other three countries was most 'susceptible'. During the war, France, because of the contacts between the British government and the French Resistance, was most open to ideas from Britain, and certainly it is in French Resistance documents that we see the clearest signs of the influence of Beveridge. I'll come back to this again in a moment. Next (this may surprise you) I would actually put Germany. Britain, remember, was an important occupying power at the end of the war and (we'll also look at this in a moment) it was under the Allied occupation that various reformist ideas from the West could be put forward. In Italy there were no immediate comprehensive social welfare reforms as there were in France and Britain. Although some older British traditions had some influence in post-war Italy (for instance, with respect to the nature of independent, non-political newspapers), there was no effective mechanism for such 'new' ideas as those of the Beveridge Report to make a great impact. In fact, while there was a definite commitment to social welfare on a better scale then ever before, post-war Italian social welfare, very much in the spirit of Christian Democracy, depended heavily on voluntary and local organizations. □

I'm going to end this section by encouraging you to take a detailed look at France, followed by a briefer one at Germany.

I want you now to return to Hoffmann's article on 'The effects of World War II on French society and politics' in the Course Reader. Forgetting Beveridge and the Resistance for a moment, note down the extent to which, according to Hoffmann, the development of welfare policies was initiated by the Vichy regime.

Exercise   Note down the main relevant points made by Hoffmann. ■

Specimen answer   Here is my own summing up (some of the points I make are less directly relevant to social welfare than others):

Hoffmann lists four types of new organization set up by the Vichy regime: 'organization committees' within the world of business, on which the post-war *Conseil National du Patronat Français* was modelled; the Vichy government's Peasant Corporation, which provided the structure for the Liberation's *Confédération Générale Agricole* (established in reaction against the Peasant Corporation) and the leadership of the *Fédération Nationale des Syndicats d'Exploitants Agricoles* of post-war years; the workers' groups established within the Vichy Labour Charter, which continued to flourish in the post-war years; and finally the various professional organizations of lawyers, doctors, and so on, which were also preserved and consolidated in the post-war period. In theory at least, the Vichy Labour Charter recognized the just needs of the working classes, and the regime made much of its main contribution to social insurance policy, the institution of old-age pensions for retired workers. The new Vichy organizations, Hoffmann claims, were put in the hands of a dynamic new generation of businessmen (partly, indeed, as a result of pressure from the Germans, who were anxious to squeeze as much out of France as possible). One of the top figures he especially singles out for mention, Jeanne Bichelonne, is important in respect of economic planning, rather than social welfare; but Pierre La Rocque, one of the main drafters of the Law of August 1940 which set up Vichy's business committees, later, according to Hoffman, 'built . . . the social security system of the Liberation'.

Hoffmann, I think, overstates his case. However, his thesis does bring out the 'neutral' pressures of war which had significance, rather than the ideological commitments of groups, parties or governments. Several Resistance organizations put forward programmes which went far beyond social welfare of the Beveridge type, but rather envisaged a complete social and economic re-organization of society. □

I want now to look at some of the French Resistance organizations and the sorts of programmes for economic and social reform that they proposed. France's greatest authority on World War II from the older generation is Henri Michel. In an invaluable collection of documents which he compiled with Boris Mirkine-Guetzovitch, he sought to draw attention away from 'sabotage and para-military activities' to 'social and political policies'. Questions that we would have to ask are: were these policies put into practice, and, if so, was this due to the Resistance? (Or would they have been put into practice anyway?) In April 1942 Jean Moulin parachuted into France to group together the various Resistance organizations, and set up a General Committee to draw up political and social policies for the Liberation. In a main report of 1943 the committee declared that 'the working masses expect from the Liberation the birth of a new world where everyone can develop to the full without constraint'. At the same time a Catholic Resistance journal insisted: 'the working class is the most important. It has the right to speak and the right to responsibility.' Of course, the various statements I am quoting here are of relevance also to our earlier discussion of class; however, I put them here because they are really dealing with future policy rather than with changes in class structure actually taking place. Many of them, indeed, seem to be spoken *for* the working class, rather than *by* the working class. The non-socialist Resistance group *Défense de France* published an important statement in March 1944:

> The governing class has abdicated. The bourgeois class is shown to be incapable of directing by itself the destiny of the country. It senses obscurely the arrival of a new social structure and, while its best elements devote themselves already to trying to establish and to promote its main features, the rest weep for a dead past and whine uselessly over the uncertainties of the time.
>
> The moment is propitious to ratify anew the social unity of the nation, destroyed by the birth of large-scale industry and by the accompanying birth of a capitalist bourgeoisie and of a proletariat of mechanical beings, whose work, tears, clothes and even the quarters to which they are relegated, separate them from the rest of the nation. The revolution must consist of re-integrating all classes of society into the nation, thus giving to the workers [*travailleurs*, meaning all workers, whether by hand or brain] the place which must be returned to them. (Quoted in H. Michel and B. Mirkine-Guetzovitch, *Les idées politiques et sociales de la Résistance*, 1954, pp. 376–7; trans. Arthur Marwick)

Trades unions, the statement said, have improved the material conditions of the workers, but there is still a chasm between 'proletarians' and 'non-proletarians'. The very condition of being proletarian must be suppressed (and this will not be done through the empty rhetoric of the Pétain regime). There must be an end to the 'absolute dependence in regard to terms of employment, to the perpetually re-born fear of tomorrow, of the deprivation involved in an immense mechanistic organization in which the worker [*ouvrier*, industrial worker], an anonymous peon, is buffeted around at the whim of sovereign and mysterious forces'. Having long since achieved its political, administrative and territorial unity, France is now, in the Resistance, 'forging its moral unity'. Next it must establish its 'social unity'. To achieve this social unity, liberal capitalism would have to be abolished:

> It will be necessary to institute an economic structure in which all Frenchmen can participate both in prosperity and in common set-backs. It will be necessary to re-make 1936, with different methods and a different spirit, suppressing not only the hostility of the Right towards the leaders of the popular masses, but also the efforts of the 'revolutionary' to avoid real revolution, and the 'socialists' to save capitalism. It would be necessary to put the economy at the service of the nation. Then, having eliminated the material cause of the chasm between our children, France can hope to re-find her internal coherence and to march in harmony towards a better future.

Certainly we seem here to be a long way from the ideology of Beveridge. The programme of the Lyon region of the *Mouvement de Libération Nationale* (into which *Défense de France* was merged) stressed the need for the whole war experience to yield benefits for the working class and the peasants (*cultivateurs*). *Organisation Civil et Militaire* (OCM) suggested that the companies of private capitalism might be replaced by 'groups of workers' brought together to carry out a common labour and using the help of capitalists; collective agreements would unite together the enterprises and those working in them. Many Resistance organizations supported 'the politics of the family' very much along Vichy lines (here is a point in favour of the Hoffmann thesis). OCM wanted a Ministry of Social Life to deal with abandoned mothers and children, and to rehabilitate criminals, prostitutes and beggers. The *Défense de France* statement announced that every man and every woman should feel 'the obligation to transmit life'. Calling for the equal distribution of the charges involved in bringing up children, it declared that 'an important part of the increase in salaries should be granted in the form of an increase in family allowances accompanied by marriage loans, tax relief, and a battle against abortion'. So one can see that many traditional considerations were mixed in with what seem like revolutionary utterances. Bearing these various quotations in mind, and also a further observation by Henri Michel that 'in politics, economics and in democracy, the members of the Resistance were constructing a new France', I want you to turn to document II.14 in *Documents 2*, the programme of the CNR (National Resistance Council) (you worked on a brief passage from this in Book I, Unit 1.

Exercise First, I want you to work your way carefully through the document, indicating:

1 which paragraphs merely deal with the immediate circumstances created by the war;

2 which paragraphs indicate, in very broad terms, the idea of a complete break with France as it was in the 1930s;

3 which paragraphs deal (a) with proposed political reforms and (b) with proposed economic reforms;

4 which paragraphs deal (a) with matters that were also central to the Beveridge Report, and (b) with other matters touched on by the Beveridge Report. What proposal mentioned by Beveridge does not feature at all in this programme?

5 There is a long list of proposed social reforms of other types: what particular aspects of French life do they reflect?

When you have completed this preliminary exercise, which is useful in helping you to grasp the content of the document, try these two more wide-ranging questions:

6 In two or three sentences say what this document suggests about the relationship between the war experience and social welfare legislation.

7 What indication is there in the document that the proposed legislation will be implemented once the war is over? ■

Specimen answers and discussion 1 Paragraphs 1–3. In paragraph 1 it is stated that the Provisional Government will re-establish the independence taken from France by Germany; the other two paragraphs concern traitors, profiteers, the actions of enemy citizens, etc. Paragraph 5(b) talks of compensation for war victims. In other places, as for instance where 5(b) talks of the 're-establishment' of trades union freedoms, there is the suggestion that what is being dealt with is the evil wartime situation.

2 I think it can be seen that with each point there is the suggestion of going further and introducing better conditions, more rights, etc., than existed in the 1930s. This is made most explicit in the final section where, in addition to references to the 'vile' Vichy regime, there is also reference to 'the organs of corruption and treachery' that existed *prior* to the surrender to the Germans.

3 (a) Paragraph 4, though note that this deals with political *rights* rather than any precise proposals for institutional reform; (b) paragraph 5, which we discussed in Book I, Unit 1.

4 (a) 'A complete social security plan', etc. (b) 'Security of employment', though the devices mentioned differ from the regulation of the trade cycle envisaged by

Beveridge; also the paragraphs on education and 'retirement pensions'. There is no mention of a national health service.

5   The other proposals reflect the relative weakness of French trades unions and the comparative lack of legislation on hours of work, etc. (and probably also the long hours of work enforced during the war); the instability of the franc over the period of the First World War and again in the Second World War, and its general decline in value in the 1930s; and the great importance in French life of the agricultural community. You should be able to pick out for yourselves the different proposals which relate to these issues.

6   First, this is the programme of the body which brings together the various Resistance organizations, and is also linked to General de Gaulle, leader of the Free French: it is the document of a body brought into existence only by the need to carry on the war against the Germans. We have already seen how individual Resistance organizations related their policies to the idea that surrender to the Germans demonstrated the inadequacies of the old system, which now must be reformed. This document, as we have just seen, links together proposals dealing with immediate problems caused by the war and longer-term proposals that will create a better society. Both at the beginning and the end of the document the sense of unity in national resistance is stressed, a unity to be perpetuated in a fairer and more equal society.

7   The fact that this document unites not just the Resistance organizations, but also major political parties and General de Gaulle and his supporters. □

Provided, then, that the Germans were indeed defeated (as, of course, we know they were), one could expect this document to have practical consequences. To see what exactly did happen, I turn to the leading authority, Jean-Pierre Rioux, whose two volumes on *The Fourth Republic* have now been translated into English. In the original French, the appropriate section was entitled *Le 'New Deal' social*, which might suggest an American influence, though I don't think there was on this French legislation. Rioux in fact begins with the ordinance of 22 February 1945, dealing with the issue of workshop delegates and workers' rights – issues featured in the CNR programme. Rioux says that this ordinance also built on the Popular Front legislation of 1936, and the Vichy Labour Charter. The demands in the CNR programme relating to the agricultural community were met in the statute of 13 April 1946.

The 'New Deal', Rioux continues, was finally cemented by a new concept which should transform the condition of the worker – social security: 'The "revolution" so often promised passed, this time, into the daily life of a large proportion of the French people.' Two ordinances of 30 December 1944 established social security contributions. Further ordinances of 4 and 19 October 1945 brought together all the old piecemeal insurance schemes under one single organization and brought all wage and salary earners within the social security system. Benefits referred to the same areas as identified in the Beveridge Report, with a special emphasis on family benefits. There was no separate national health service; instead the French social security scheme included provision for reimbursement of 80 per cent of all medical expenses. A law of 22 May 1946 extended social insurance to some of the self-employed. Maurice Larkin (in his *France Since the Popular Front*, 1988, p.128) has declared that 'it is arguable that the reforms of the brief liberation era were a more significant advance on the past than Labour's creditable six-year record in post-war Britain'. The pre-war baseline is the crucial element in such a judgement. In absolute terms the British welfare state was indisputably more effective and more comprehensive.

Germany

Finally, I turn to Germany, guided by the article by H. G. Hockerts, 'German post-war social policies against the background of the Beveridge plan', in W. Mommsen (ed.) *The Emergence of the Welfare State in Britain and Germany* (1981). That the Beveridge plan should be under consideration in post-war West Germany was partly because of the British presence as an occupying power. Hockerts shows that the Americans also had an interest in it, but that the main pressure for its application came from the German trades unions. In fact, particularly from the German Christian Democrats, there was considerable resistance to such a unified state-sponsored plan. Hockerts has a neat formulation, reminiscent of points made by Roseman:

> In Britain the war experience had engendered a sense of national solidarity and confidence in state intervention and had thus prepared the ground for the Beveridge reform; in Germany, by contrast, the experience of Nazi misuse of power had provoked opposition to any form of any government-imposed centralisation or collectivism.

Furthermore, the Germans were proud of their own indigenous tradition of social insurance, which went back well before the Lloyd George reforms in Britain. Addressing a mass rally of the Christian Democrats in August 1946, their leader Konrad Adenauer, the dominant figure in the first years of the West German Federal Republic, declared:

> We must hold on to this social insurance. We are proud of it. And as for the proposals Beveridge has recently made in Hamburg [the occupying authorities sent Beveridge on a tour of West Germany] I can only say we Germans have already had such things these past thirty years. (Quoted in Hockerts, 'German post-war social policies')

Between 1949 and 1953 there was in fact a reconstruction of what was very largely the traditional structure, embodying different, and much more favourable, conditions for white-collar workers compared with manual workers (this, incidentally, is a significant piece of evidence that West Germany was very far from being a classless society in the years after 1945). The Child Allowances Law of 1954, however, was very much in the Beveridge tradition. Germany's big pensions reform came in 1957 when, in effect, it set the pattern for breaking from the Beveridge flat-rate principle by introducing earnings-related pensions. Hockert's general summing up is as follows:

> For the instances cited here, the Beveridge plan had provided some important initial ground work. Even if some of the proposals no longer seem to provide entirely convincing solutions, hindsight nevertheless shows how momentous the new ideas generated by his plan have proved to be.

Our concern, of course, is not specifically with the Beveridge Report. I simply started with it, because it is, without doubt, a key document in the study of war and social change. But what my discussions have brought out is the complicated series of interrelationships involved in any study of war and social change: the direct effects; the indirect effects; the cross-currents; the 'feedback'; the inter-action between unguided forces, direct responses to war necessities, and the guided actions of major political powers; the forces of tradition; and the desire for innovation, often part of the psychological response to war.

Finally, what about the countries which fell under Soviet influence? These, in theory, abolished unemployment by providing a job for everyone, and offered a free and universal welfare state. In practice there was usually a system of supplementary fees payable for medical and social services. On the whole, however, the result of the war and associated events was the spread of welfare systems on a more thoroughgoing basis than ever before.

2.6   Material conditions

The Summerfield article we have already studied gives a general idea of the relative scale of material conditions in Britain: whether or not wages overall improved for the working class (as I would maintain), we are certainly not talking about conditions of starvation, the terrorization of civilian populations, and so on. The Blitz of 1940–1, sporadic later raids, and the V1 and V2 attacks of 1944 were frightening enough. In all, 60,000 civilians were killed in bomb attacks: this is a significant figure in that it amounts to about a fifth of the total number of combatants killed in action, but it is of course small compared with the immense civilian losses in other parts of Europe; the French, it may be noted, lost almost exactly the same number of civilians through British and American bombing raids. Life in Britain was strictly regimented during the war, some goods disappeared altogether, and there was rationing of all basic commodities, save bread and vegetables. But the result was a fairer distribution than ever before, involving, for many families, higher nutrition standards than had obtained before the war. In a country which was not occupied, did not have a regime imposed on it by an external power, had a government which, whatever the exigencies of war, was mindful of the principles of liberal democracy, material conditions were sometimes unpleasant and even worse, but one cannot unreasonably speak, over the longer term, of a desirable redistribution.

At the opposite extreme were Poland and Russia, which experienced war as destruction in its most unmitigated form. Poland, as Norman Davies has put it (*God's Playground: A History of Poland*), 'became the killing-ground of Europe, the new Golgatha'. Altogether 18 per cent of the Polish population was killed; the figure for Russia is 11.2 per cent, for Yugoslavia 11.1 per cent. This can be compared with 7.4 per cent for Germany, and 0.9 per cent for Great Britain. In Poland the Russians exterminated those whom they regarded as class enemies, the Germans those they regarded as race enemies. From 1941 Poland was in the grip of Nazi terrorism, the selective executions of 1939–40 giving way to indiscriminate shootings and hangings. Poland, again in the words of Norman Davies, 'became the home of humanity's holocaust, an 'archipelago' of death-factories and camps, the scene of executions, pacifications and exterminations which surpassed anything so far documented in the history of mankind'. In the countryside hundreds of Polish villages were razed to the ground, their populations massacred. In the towns, prisoners and suspects were shot out of hand. 'In Warsaw, hardly a street corner did not witness the death of groups of citizens by the score and the hundred'. As German power began to collapse in 1944–5, 'hundreds of thousands of underfed slave-labourers of both sexes and every conceivable nationality were marched back and forth, from project to abandoned project, amidst the endless retreating convoys and demolition squads of the defeated *Wehrmacht*'. The Germans had segregated the Jewish population in the winter of 1939–40. Even had they wished to do so, there was little that the Polish population at large could do, circumstances in Poland, as Davies puts it, bearing 'little relation to the relatively genteel condition of occupied Denmark, France or Holland'. Anyone caught sheltering, feeding or helping Jews was liable to bring instant execution upon his or her entire family.

From June 1941 the horrors of the German 'barbarisation of warfare' (to quote part of the title of the analysis of Omar Bartov) were visited upon Russia. Bartov quotes documents (see document II.20 in *Documents 2*, orders issued by General Lemelsen) to show that barbarity was practised from the very beginning.

Exercise   Turn now to document II.20 and answer the following questions:

1   Bartov points out that the German commanders were not opposed to Hitler's orders, nor to shootings as such, but that they were worried by disorderly activities among their troops, and about their soldiers' actions encouraging frenzied desperation in the opposing Russian forces. What in this document would tend to support these points?

2   What role is Lemelsen envisaging for non-Bolshevik, non-Jewish, non-partisan Russians? ◼

Specimen answers   1   The last sentence of (a), and the references in (b) to 'Bolshevism', 'a Jewish and
and discussion   criminal group', and 'instruction of the Führer' indicate Lemelsen's support for his orders. The phrases in (b) about 'an irresponsible, senseless and criminal manner' and 'only by order of an officer' suggest the worry about disorderly conduct. The last phrase of (b) indicates the worry about stimulating further Russian resistance.

2   To serve as labour for the German army. In fact such labour was exacted under the most inhumane conditions, with masses of deaths from exhaustion and starvation – even populations which might well have welcomed the Germans as liberators from Russian rule were, as Roberts points out, treated in this way. □

Bartov suggests that even the apparently slightly more restrained attitudes of commanders like Lemelsen were effectively blank cheques for the mass killings of civilians that took place on the faintest of pretexts.

Within the appalling general situation of horror and barbarity, there were individual episodes that have become particularly well known, most notably the siege of Leningrad. I have already discussed the Bubis and Ruble article in the Course Reader from the point of view of the long-term impact on the city. Here my concern is with actual conditions at the time. The winter of 1940–1 was appalling beyond description, with deaths from starvation running as high as 50,000 per month. Loss of one's ration card meant certain death. Any offence against the food regulations was punished by summary execution. Desperate, hunger-crazed citizens resorted to murder to gain food and ration cards, and to cannibalism. Frozen corpses were to be seen everywhere. Conditions lightened only slightly in the spring, when it was possible to evacuate about a million of the survivors. The remaining population, about one million out of a pre-war total of three million, settled down to face the second winter of blockade. Now, though conditions were still desperately hard, better order was maintained. The streets had been cleaned up, and some of the trams were running again. Yet in July and August 1943, with the population down to a select, proud and still near-starving 600,000, there came the worst shelling of the whole war: new street signs went up: 'Citizens: in case of shelling this side of the street is the most dangerous'. The military success which finally broke the siege did not come till January 1944. At least a million Leningrad citizens had died of starvation, another 200,000 or so from bombing and shelling.

Leaving Leningrad to starve, in October 1941 the Germans were rapidly advancing on Moscow. On 16 October many top Moscow citizens took to flight. However, Stalin remained; and Moscow, in fact, did not fall. Moscow's winter was not as desperate as that of Leningrad, but, to quote the Russian-born British correspondent there, Alexander Werth, 'many individual stories were grim – stories of under-nourishment, of unheated houses, with temperatures just above or even below freezing point, with water-pipes burst, and lavatories out of action; and in these houses one slept smothered – if one had them – under two overcoats and three or more blankets' (*Russia at War*, 1964, p.370). As in all major cities, there was food rationing: 800 grams of bread a day for workers, 600 for office staff, and 400 for dependants and children; 2,200 grams of meat a month for workers, 600 for dependants and children. In June 1941 bread was selling on the open market in Moscow at 150 rubles a kilo (£1.50 a pound). Milk, sugar, fats and tobacco were all very hard to come by. Cabbage and other vegetables had disappeared, having been commandeered either by the German or the Russian armies. Werth noted 'a peculiar form of profiteering which had developed in Moscow during the spring, when the owner of a cigarette would charge any willing passers-by 2 rubles [nominally equivalent to the then British shilling] for a puff – and there were plenty of buyers'. Werth reported further:

> People in the Moscow streets looked haggard and pale, and scurvy was fairly common. Consumer goods were almost unobtainable, except at fantastic prices, or for coupons, if and when these were honoured. In the big Moscow department stores strange odds and ends were being sold, such as barometers and curling tongs, but nothing useful. In the shopping streets like the Kuznetsky Most, or Gorki Street, the shop windows were mostly sand-bagged and, where they were not, they often displayed cruel cardboard hams, cheeses and sausages, all covered with dust.
>
> There were other deplorable shortages. In dental clinics – with the exception of a few privileged ones – teeth were pulled without an anaesthetic. The chemists' shops were about as empty as the rest . . .
>
> Moscow itself was very empty, with nearly half its population still away. Only half a dozen theatres were open in June, among them the Filialé of the Bolshoi, and tickets were easy to obtain. In the buffet, all they sold, for a few coppers, was – glasses of plain water. The Bolshoi itself had been hit by a ton bomb, and was out of action. There was a good deal of other bomb damage here and there, and the sky was dotted with barrage balloons.
> (*Russia at War*, pp.218–19)

I referred earlier to document II.21 in *Documents 2* (*Pravda* report on factory moved from the Ukraine to the Urals) and the relocation of Russian industry. We may count this as a positive long-term consequence of the war, but conditions for workers at the time were dreadful:

In most places, living conditions were fearful, in many places food was very short, too. People worked because they knew that it was absolutely necessary – they worked twelve, thirteen, and sometimes fourteen or fifteen hours a day; they 'lived on their nerves'; they knew that never was their work more urgently needed than now. Many died in the process. All these people knew what losses were being suffered by the soldiers, and they – in the 'distant rear' – did not grumble much; while the soldiers were risking so much, it was not for the civilians to shirk even the most crippling, most heart-breaking work. At the height of the Siberian winter, some people had to walk to work – sometimes three, four, six miles; and then work for twelve hours or more, and then walk back again, day after day, month after month.

It is impossible to work out a balance-sheet between material conditions, physical suffering, risk to life, and the moral aspects of life. In the German puppet regimes, as in Hungary, Romania and Bulgaria, the material basis of life was perhaps a little more secure than in the countries we have been discussing (I shall come to Czechoslovakia in a moment). Yugoslavia was divided between the puppet regime in Croatia, areas effectively controlled by the Germans or the Italians, and the area centred on Montenegro where most of the Partisan activity took place. Elements of the nature of life in this region are apparent in document II.18, the letter from Tito to the Italian commander. The context of this document is that the Italian occupying forces had learned that Tito had moved his Partisan head-quarters to Varanjak, but by the time they got there, Tito had already moved on. The Italians then took out their frustration on the inhabitants of Varanjak and the neighbouring village of Drenova. The officer and the other soldiers had been captured in an ambush on 3 December, and interrogation, the Partisans claimed, had revealed him as being a Fascist party member. Tito's letter of protest was forwarded from the garrison in Prijepolje to General Giovanni Esposito, com-mander of the 'Pusteria' Alpine Division at Pljeulja. Esposito addressed a reply to 'Signor Commander of the Partisans' requesting release of the officer. The request was refused, provoking Esposito into sending a second letter full of threats, this time addressed to 'Bandit Commander'.

Exercise   Turn now to document II.18 in *Documents 2* and answer these questions:

1   What are the most significant points that emerge from it (I think there are two)?

2   What other points need explanation or elaboration? ∎

Specimen answers and discussion   1   The significant points, I think, are (a) the evidence of brutality of the Italian occupation forces, and (b) the evidence of the power possessed by Tito and the Partisans. With regard to (a), one might also comment on how the document indicates the escalation in the circle of violence – something, of course, which would bear heavily on the ordinary population (previously, according to the letter, captives had been exchanged or set free).

2   The reference in the final paragraph is to the Battle of Moscow and the Russian counter-offensive which began on 6 December and which started the German retreat, with the Germans sustaining heavy losses. However, 'turning point' or not, victory for Tito was still some way off. □

In Czechoslovakia conditions were basically determined by Hitler's intention to exploit the material and human resources of the country to the greatest possible extent, but without driving the Czechs to such desperation that he risked guerilla warfare to his rear. At the same time Hitler's policy was one of ruthless Germanization, and he believed that 'by firmly leading the Protectorate, it ought to be possible to push the Czech language in about twenty years back to the importance of a dialect' (see Gotthold Rhode, 'The Protectorate of Bohemia and Moravia 1939–45', in *A History of the Czechoslovak Republic 1918–1948*, edited by V. S. Mamatey and R. Luza, 1973). Against intellectuals a policy of terrorization and liquidation was followed, while some concessions were offered to the working class in order to maximize productivity. Bouts of terror were particularly associated with Reinhardt Heydrich, who effectively was in control from September 1941. The men who succeeded in assassinating Heydrich on 27 May 1942 were parachuted in by the Czechs in exile, and protected by the Czech underground. Nazi retaliation took the form of the destruction of the villages of Lezhaky, where 33 male inhabitants were shot, and Lidice, all of whose male citizens were shot, whose women were sent to concentration camps, and whose children were dispersed. One measure of the differences between the treatment of Czechoslovakia and the treatment of Poland and Russia was that the Germans officially publicized these measures, whereas the atrocities in Poland and Russia simply proceeded as a matter of course. Altogether the Czechs lost to German reprisals and punitive actions between 360,000 and 500,000 citizens; 250,000 were killed in bomb attacks and military operations.

What, then, of Germany itself?

You should have notes from, or annotations on, the article by Roseman to refer to here. I have particularly referred you to the sixth and seventh paragraphs in section IV, and also the fifteenth and sixteenth paragraphs in that section. Note also the paragraph in section II which refers to the way in which state terror became an increasing part of everyday life. You should refer to document II.9 in *Documents 2* (extracts from *I Lived Under Hitler* by Sybil Bannister) for the food situation in May 1943, and for the reduced housing circumstances of one of Hamburg's wealthiest merchants in January 1945. For the truly horrendous effects of the Hamburg fire raids in July and August 1943, which created the housing situation described by Sybil Bannister in 1945, turn to document II.8, the extract from the report by the Police President of Hamburg. Probably the most instructive comparisons are with Italy, where conditions began to deteriorate very badly in 1943 (a year earlier than in Germany) and were desperate by the last stages of the war. The general trend is well indicated in figures given by David Ellwood in his *Italy 1943–45* (1985, p.130) (see Table 22–25.2). Martin Clark (*Modern Italy*, p.290) gives a horrendous summary. In 1945 prices were at twenty-four times the 1938 level, even after a freeze on gas, electricity and rents. Over three million houses had been destroyed or badly damaged, as well as most of the railway stock, lorries, bridges and ports. Industrial output in 1945 was about one-quarter of the 1941 figure, and about the same as 1884; the gross national product was about the same as that of 1911, and income per head lower than 1861. In July 1946 the average Italian was taking in only 1,650 calories per day, compared with 2,650 before the war.

As I keep emphasizing, we have to distinguish between the immediate effects of war, and long-term effects. Almost everywhere recovery was remarkably quick, largely because of the new levels of demand engendered by the war, and by the destruction of war. Roseman refers to malnutrition disappearing in Germany after 1948, and to the high standards achieved by 1955. After referring to the harsh

Table 22–25.2   *Percentage of food available and price index, Italy, September 1943 and July 1944*

	Sept. 1943	July 1944
Percentage of food available in:		
Rationed market	10.9	3.4
Free market	23.5	22.6
Black market	65.6	74.0
Price index in:		
Rationed market	100	127.6
Free market	100	397.8
Black market	100	465.0

Source: D. Ellwood, *Italy 1943–45*, 1985.

conditions of wartime, Alan Milward, the distinguished economic historian, continues:

> Nevertheless the basic economic circumstances of a high and increasing demand for labour did change the conditions which had long prevailed for most employees in most industrial countries. These changes were effected more through the altered aspirations of labour than through substantial increases in real earnings . . .
>
> The history of labour during the war was not simply a history of a factor of production, it was the history of most human beings involved in the war. The big changes in their economic circumstances which took place inevitably expressed themselves in important shifts in social aspirations and political opinions. And these went far towards making the post-war economic world a very different one from that of the 1930s. (Alan Milward, *War, Economy and Society*, 1977, p.244)

2.7   Customs and behaviour

This aspect of social change relates to the topic of 'mass society' which was introduced in Book III and to which Tony Aldgate will be returning later in this book. Here I will confine myself to a few general points. In discussing the effects of the First World War, I suggested that it was in the more 'backward' countries that one could expect to find the greatest upheavals in customs and behaviour induced by war. With the further developments in mass society of the interwar years there was less scope for change as a result of World War II. Yugoslavia was probably the country brought most forcibly into further contact with Western ideas. In general, one might expect the war to have influenced customs and behaviour in two main ways: through the upheavals of population and the alterations in class relationships already discussed; and through the damage to civic morality caused by violence, terror tactics, and all the dodges and subterfuges people had to resort to in order to survive. On the former point, it would be broadly true to say that there was less formality, less sense of hierarchy in most countries (possibly Britain remained the stuffiest in this sphere). On the second point, civic norms were in fact established remarkably quickly: there was no substantial general increase in criminality, though the behaviour of dissident youth in the post-war years was often related back to the dislocations of war. Once again the extreme circumstances of Poland draw attention to themselves. I have already mentioned the geographical shift and the need for rebuilding on a massive scale. Polish cities were meticulously rebuilt, but with subtle modifications which reflected Russian influence. At the same time Poland continued to be more open to Western popular culture than Russia. Poland was both terribly new, and not new at all. The French philosopher/writer Jean-Paul Sartre, writing in 1960, found Poland 'the world of perfect absurdity'.

One question often raised, and one that I've already mentioned, concerns the extent of Americanization in the aftermath of the US encroachment on the European continent. As we shall see later, there was something of a flowering in the war years of, for example, both Italian and British film-making, which acted as a counterpoise to the Hollywood influence already there in pre-war days. For all European countries the major spectator sport was association football, a pastime totally resistant to all American forces. Among certain sections in Paris there was a fad for certain things American, including jazz, but this scarcely adds up to widespread Americanization. What a number of commentators have singled out, perhaps rather surprisingly, is the question of developments in religion. I shall say something about them, and then conclude with what I take to be one of the most important developments of the war, the passing of a further critical stage in the bringing of mass communications directly into the home.

A significant feature of the immediate post-war world in southern and western countries was the political role of Christian Democracy, which was particularly important in West Germany and Italy, but also apparent through the MRP (Popular Republican Movement) in France. The various crises of war had forced Catholic organizations into involvement in, and taking up positions favourable to, moderate social reform. In his paper to the Open University conference on total war and social change, François Bédarida argued that during the war there was a considerable transformation in the connection between religion and society:

> Not only was a new brand of secularism introduced, allowing Catholics to be reintegrated into public life, but Catholicism suddenly pervaded the whole civil society. It is true that French Catholicism was then undergoing a process of renewal, theological, pastoral and liturgical. At the same time it was the war which gave birth to the experience of the worker-priests. It was in the middle of the war that the famous book, *France, pays de mission?*, which sounded the alarm over the depth and extent of the decline in Christianity, was published. It was in face of the great crisis of conscience provoked by the war and the immediate post-war period – and in spite of the support given to Vichy by most bishops – that the most advanced wing of Catholicism affirmed its position (*Témoignage Chrétien, Temps Présent, Esprit, Jeunesse de l'Eglise*, etc.). Whether in the political realm, with the creation and rise of the Mouvement Républicain Populaire [Popular Republican Movement], the trade union sphere with the CFTC [Confederation of Catholic Unions], the domain of youth and culture with the JOC, the JEC, the JAC [Catholic Youth Organizations], in the media (in particular the press), in economic modernisation, in intellectual life, everywhere could be seen the vitality of a Catholicism which was to pervade everyday life, and the entire social fabric. (Bédarida, 'World War II and social change in France', p.91)

That there should be comparable developments in the Soviet Union may seem still more surprising, yet this is the case convincingly argued in an article by William Fletcher in the Linz collection which I referred to earlier (*The Impact of World War II on the Soviet Union*). This development (as in France) comes largely under what I would term the psychological dimension of war. For Russia, the Second World War was the 'Great Patriotic War', in which older traditions of Russian society were appealed to, as well as more recent ones. In particular, as Fletcher brings out, a bargain was struck between church and state: the church gave the state political support, and in return the church was granted the right to exist as an institution in Soviet society. The Russian Orthodox Church, in short, at the expense of limiting itself to a purely spiritual mission, won for itself during the war a legal, as distinct from an underground, existence in society. Furthermore, in the areas that were under German occupation during the war, the populations were both freed from Soviet restrictions and greatly in need of the traditional comforts of religion: thus, argues Fletcher, a 'bible belt' of firm religious belief and practice grew up in western sectors of the Soviet Union. Although no bargains were struck, it could also be argued that the horrific experiences and upheavals in Poland served to consolidate sentiment behind a Polish Catholic Church which came to stand for the independent spirit of the people. These are all, in East and West, important developments; but, of course, the wider trend of a general decline in religious observance continued.

During the war peoples everywhere, and often peoples who had hitherto shown little interest in national or world news, became heavily dependent on radio communication. When Tito boasted to the Italian commander of Russian victories, that news would have come to him by radio. In occupied Europe, resistance groups everywhere depended on news broadcasts from London, as a counter to the propaganda and misinformation broadcast by the Germans. The crucial point about radio is that it brings news (and entertainment) directly into a person's own home; there is no need to go out, as with the purchase of a newspaper, or a visit to a cinema (where, of course, newsreels also had a special importance). Today we speak of the information technology revolution which is making the home the basis for everything – work as well as entertainment. This process is associated with television and visual display. Yet I believe there is a strong case for seeing World War II as a turning point in so far as it brought a new salience to radio, and a notion of news and entertainment in the home at the touch of a button – what television, of course, also brings in a more elaborate way.

2.8 Women and the family

In *Documents 2* (document II.9) I have included extracts from the wartime reminiscences of Sybil Bannister; I have also referred to the reminiscences of Christabel Bielenberg. Now both of these women were in slightly unusual circumstances, in that they were English women domiciled in Germany. What we learn from them, and from other sources, is the manner in which women had to cope with appalling upheavals, great reversals in fortune, while continuing always to *manage* their own lives and those of their families. One of the best sources I know is the diary of an Englishwoman, published as *Nella Last's War*, which brings out most effectively the way in which, through both organizing a family and doing a great deal of invaluable national work through the Women's Volunteer Service, Nella comes to realize that she is a much stronger and much more capable person than her husband. Women's work in the auxiliary military services and, even more, in the European resistance movements, is legendary.

The battle lines in the historiographical debate over whether or not the experiences of World War II broadened the roles and improved the status of women in society are familiar ones. Those for whom the overriding issue is the continuing inferior status of women today argue that, accordingly, the war cannot have had much effect, that even when women seemed to be doing new jobs they were always kept in an inferior position to men, and that if there were any changes these were due, not to the war, but to long-term structural forces. Certainly the image of woman as potato-peeler or as pin-up was not suddenly obliterated; in some ways it was strengthened. But overall I would stand by the position I took in *War and Social Change in the Twentieth Century* (p.175, where I was referring to the USA, though I consider the statement of general applicability): 'The conclusion is inescapable that the Second World War offered women opportunities normally unavailable in peace time to improve their economic and social status, and to develop their own confidence and self-consciousness. In many cases these opportunities were firmly grasped; whether they would be extended depended very much on women themselves, for, without doubt, old attitudes, overpoweringly strong in 1941 [or 1939], were still influential in 1946.' I lay particular stress on changed opportunities for married women, and the weakening of the prejudices against married women taking jobs (often only part-time jobs, but still, by the account of many women themselves, liberating). My arguments, with particular reference to Britain, have been challenged by Harold L. Smith in his own chapter in the collection edited by him, *War and Social Change* (1986). In her paper to the Open University conference, Penny Summerfield, by examining in great detail the statistics of married women's employment, has on the whole confirmed my view against that of Smith.

Exercise   I want you to read what François Bédarida said to the Open University conference on the subject of the effects of the war on French women. Then answer the questions that follow.

> The changes brought to the condition of women by the second world conflict have been greatly exaggerated, both at the time and during the immediate post-war period. People have been too quick to interpret the Resistance as a demonstration of progress towards equality of the sexes. On the other side we perhaps have a tendency today to under-estimate the changes. Within the workplace changes in employment were qualitatively real, though quantitatively slight. If the female working population increased both absolutely and relatively from 1936 to 1946 (an increase of 560,000 individuals), the figures have to be corrected, because they include agriculture where they were over-estimated. If agriculture is left out, the proportion of women in employment only rises from 20.6 per cent to 22 per cent.
>
> On the other hand, to the extent that the Resistance served as a channel for social promotion, one well might think that women, who played an irreplaceable role, would also benefit from this. But all studies on this theme have illuminated how far in reality they became the 'forgotten people' of history. Besides, even in their clandestine activities, women were for most of the time confined within their traditional roles, above all carrying out subordinate secretarial or social service work. Here for example are the terms in which a leading figure described the work of one of his female collaborators: 'Like all her female comrades, she had the worst job, typing letters, fetching and carrying mail, putting people in touch with each other, taking part in secret rendezvous, emptying our

letter boxes, clandestine and under surveillance, seeking out meeting places, and, whenever that became necessary, doing the shopping with genuine or forged ration books.' And he concludes that if 'the women of the Resistance had their place, their important place in all the networks,' in the end 'they were the Marthas of the clandestine movements.'

One must not minimise to the same extent the progress made, in particular with regard to the acquisition of the vote, a right which suffragist women, in spite of all their efforts, had not been able to gain between 1919 and 1938 in particular because of the opposition of the Senate dominated by the Radicals. Again in 1944, when the Conseil National de la Résistance wanted to include votes for women in its programme, the Radical party tried to obstruct this, but without success, for the text adopted on 15 March 1944 recognised the feminist claim: to become citizens. At the same time, and on the same subject, de Gaulle in a speech on 18 March 1944 declared: 'to establish democracy renewed in its institutions and above all in its practices, the new regime must be based on representatives elected by all men and all women of our country.' Consequently, the ordinance drawn up in Algiers in April 1944 by the Comité Français de Libération Nationale on the constitutional organisation to be set up at the Liberation specified: 'Women are voters and candidates under the same condition as men.' The new right was exercised for the first time in the municipal elections (29 April), then at the time of the referendum and the legislative elections for the constituent assembly (21 October).

This revolution in basic principles was fully achieved in the Declaration of Rights placed at the head of the Constitution of 1946. While the first article declared, 'All men, and all women are born and live free and equal before the law', the second clause added, as the result of a campaign orchestrated by the Union des Femmes Françaises, a para-Communist organisation, 'The law guarantees to women equal rights to those of men in every domain.' But the familial vocation of women was explicitly recalled by article 24 which tried to reconcile equality of the sexes with specifically feminine characteristics: 'The nation protects all mothers and all children through appropriate legislation and institutions. It guarantees to woman the exercise of her functions as citizen and worker in conditions which permit her to fulfil her role as mother and her social function.' One can see here how potent the traditional mould remained and how slowly the relations between men and women evolved. (Bédarida, World War II and social change in France', pp.89–90)

Questions   1   Is Bédarida saying that women did or did not make gains? How would you characterize the tone of the passage with respect to this issue?

2   Turn to document II.14, the programme of the CNR, and identify the place where the 'old feminist claim: to become citizens' is recognized.

3   Can you think of any other reasons for article 24 than mere traditionalism? ■

Specimen answers and discussion   1   Bédarida clearly wants to caution us against exaggerating the amount of change, but on the other hand he does recognize that important changes did take place. I would say that the tone is very much in the fashion of today ('shilly-shallying' would be too unkind a word), not wanting to offend the feminists by overstating the changes brought by the war, but, on the other hand, forced to admit that some changes did take place. (It may be noted here that, with respect to Italy, Tannenbaum, *The Fascist Experience*, p.323, declares roundly that 'the active role played by many women in the Resistance helped to change the status of women as a whole in the postwar period'.)

2   There is actually no explicit mention of women, but the point is implied in the first clause ('universal suffrage') and the last ('equality of all citizens') of paragraph 4. (Maurice Larkin, in *France since the Popular Front*, 1988, argues that the absence of explicit mention of women was deliberate, because of the fears of both the Radical Party and trades unionists of the supposed Catholic sympathies of women; I prefer Bédarida's version.)

3   Worries about the low birth-rate and the destruction of life in the war. □

Formally, equal rights for women were more of a reality in Russia than anywhere in the West. Paul Dukes (in his paper in *Total War and Social Change*) has noted an increase in the percentage of women in the Communist Party, from 15 per cent in 1941 to over 19 per cent in 1942. However, he also points out that in that latter year only two out of 125 full members of the Central Committee were women. Wartime employment changes for women were least in evidence in Germany, in keeping with Nazi ideology. If you turn to document II.22 (Germans in the industrial labour force 1939–44) you will see that the numbers of women in employment went through minor fluctuations, but did not show any large or steady increase, even though, because of military requirements, the total labour force was declining. The table as a whole says a lot about the inefficiencies of the German war effort. One might well conclude overall that the new responsibilities women had to assume as home-makers were as important as the taking on of new jobs. The absence of men, the dislocation of war, the strident intrusions of government (particularly of the Nazi government) may well have made family life seem more precious.

The previous paragraph, which represents a widely held view among experts, was written before I had seen the article by R. J. Overy, 'Mobilization for total war in Germany, 1939–1941', in *English Historical Review*, July 1988 (referred to earlier by both Clive Emsley and Bill Purdue). Overy does not dispute the accuracy of the statistics in document II.22. He writes (pp. 627–8):

> While it is certainly true that the number of German women employed between 1939 and 1945 hardly increased at all, it would be quite wrong to conclude from this that women were not mobilized for war work. The fact is that by 1939 women already constituted a very much larger part of the workforce than in other industrialised countries. If we compare Britain and Germany, we find that the proportion of women in the German workforce *in 1939* was already higher than the proportion of women in the British workforce at the very height of the British war effort in 1943. In 1939 women made up 25.7 per cent of the labour force in Britain, but 37.4 per cent in Germany. The corresponding figures for 1943 were 36.4 per cent in Britain and 48.4 per cent in Germany. More women were brought into the workforce in Britain because there was a much larger pool of non-employed or unemployed women before 1939, as might be expected given the great difference in British and German unemployment levels. The high 1939 figure reflects the large part played by female labour in the German countryside, which continued during the war as women were forced to cope with family tasks usually carried out by conscripted men . . .
>
> Not only were women already a large proportion of the workforce by

1939, but there was substantial *redistribution* of the female workforce, as might be expected, away from consumer sectors into war and war-related industries.

Overy [I have omitted his footnotes] concludes with the uncompromising statements that: 'It is clear that the "failure" to mobilize women for war work is a statistical illusion' (p.628); and, 'A higher proportion of German women were at work at every stage of the war than was the case in Britain.' I am not an expert myself, but certainly Overy's use of the figures is convincing. Be sure, anyway, that you have understood his version of the traditional view. Perhaps the last conclusion would be that despite their ideological commitment to women's place being in the home, the Nazis recognized that the necessities of total war entailed their moving into the factories.

Finally in this section, I want you to consider the attitudes about the role of women being transmitted in British wartime films, and also other issues discussed throughout these units.

Exercise   Item 6 on video-cassette 2 consists of the last quarter-of-an-hour or so of *The Gentle Sex*, a British World War II film which, through the device of a narration by its director Leslie Howard, explicitly sets out to follow the experiences of seven young women (fictional, of course) who enlist into the ATS. Item 5 comes from quite early in another British wartime film, *Millions Like Us*, and runs continuously for about twenty minutes (we have made a few minor cuts in the sequence showing people coming to work).

One feature film might be dismissed as unrepresentative; with two similar films we can be on more solid ground in identifying certain images and representations as being characteristic of popular films of the time. Little in a fictional film can be taken as fact; however, our attention may be drawn to issues which we would then wish to follow up in other more reliable sources. I have deliberately selected fairly long extracts so that, among other things, you can relax and enjoy them.

I also want you to set down some of your reactions. As these are bound to be very varied, I shan't be able to anticipate all of them. At the same time there are particular points that I do want to be sure you have noted. Therefore I am going to put some questions in the usual way, hoping that they will help you to relate what you see in the films to what you have learned elsewhere in the course. I suggest you read through my questions first, then sit back and enjoy the two film clips. Then write down answers where you can. After that, if necessary and if you have time, go back through the films trying to find answers to any remaining questions.

1   What is the main subject matter of the two films?

2   What do you feel about the tone of the two films?

3   What responses, relative to the war effort, are the films intended to arouse in audiences? *Millions Like Us* seems to try to allay worries some viewers might have – did you notice this?

4   Both main plots take the form of girl meets RAF boy (a sergeant in one case, a commissioned officer in the other), they fall in love, boy is killed in action. Why do you think the plots took this particular form?

5   Try to pin a class label on each of Celia, Gwen, Jennifer and Annie in *Millions Like Us*. Try also to pick out precise examples, or symbols, of class or (alleged) class

behaviour. Would you agree that the general message in both films is of the mixing of classes (cite precise examples)? What, in *Millions Like Us*, seems to conflict with the views of Penny Summerfield? What had Jennifer done before coming to the factory? Any comments?

6   Would you agree that both films suggest that social reform and social change will, or should, come after the war? Give examples. These films form a very different type of evidence from, say, the Beveridge Report: what significance do they have in the discussion of war and social change?

7   Finally, one very precise question on *Millions Like Us*: where were the machine tools you see made? Is there any wider significance to this? ■

Specimen answers and discussion

1   Women's part in the war effort: military in *The Gentle Sex*, civilian in *Millions Like Us*.

2   *The Gentle Sex*, particularly at the end, is perhaps rather patronizing; yet the intentions, and the goodwill, are (I think) genuine. Perhaps *Millions Like Us* seems a little patronizing too. I am not sure, but you must decide for yourself.

3   To encourage women to participate enthusiastically in the war effort, and to encourage acceptance of this among men. The harsh conditions feared by Celia and Gwen (in different ways) do not materialize.

4   In 1940–3 (the films were both released in 1943) the air war was the most immediate one for civilians – hence both young men being in the RAF. Many in the audience would have lost loved ones: both films have the function of trying to reconcile such people to their losses. More mundanely, there had to be a story line to maintain interest (*The Gentle Sex* becomes dangerously documentary-like at times).

5   Celia: lower middle-class ('middle-class' would be fine; the 'lower' is clearer when you have seen the whole film). Gwen: upwardly mobile working-class (her father is a miner, but she has been to college). Jennifer: upper-class or upper middle-class (clearly, in all sorts of ways, she is intended to be a cut above all the other girls; note her accent and compare it with those of the others). Annie: working-class (sleeping in her underclothes is intended as the clear symbol here).

I certainly detected signs of mixing (common, but by no means universal in British films of the time): Jennifer does clearly becomes less snobbish and tries to integrate herself with the others; in *The Gentle Sex* Maggie (subject to the snide comment about Glasgow docks) makes an accommodation with the snooty corporal (however, differences here may be more personal and psychological than social). Penny Summerfield argued that upper-class figures were not gener- ally to be found in factories (however, that does not mean that Jennifer's situation was a completely unlikely one). Jennifer had been canteening in the West End – among rich officers, the film implies. Actually canteen work could often involve the very mixing of classes which Summerfield tends to deny.

6   Again, I think 'yes'. The most obvious example in our clip from *Millions Like Us* is in the speech by Gwen when she first meets up with Celia (play it again if you are in doubt). I wonder what you made of the exchange between Annie and Mrs Sheridan in *The Gentle Sex*? Women had served in France in the previous war, yet that was apparently forgotten: perhaps service in war does *not* lead to gains for women. However, the film is saying, both here and in later words by the narrator, that this time things will be different, women are now clearer about what they

want, and, indeed, the influence of women will be felt not only in the new position of women, but in social reform generally.

The Beveridge Report is an actual plan for reform; attitudes expressed in the films are not actuality. However,

(a)　film-makers are themselves influential people and come from a privileged group in society: these attitudes *may* be seen as representative of an important section of middle- and upper-class opinions;

(b)　films were watched by large audiences who may well have been encouraged to believe that the war must result in social change (perhaps they were even influenced to vote Labour in 1945).

7　America, as the label Cincinatti indicates. Some commentators, in particular Correlli Barnett in his *The Audit of War*, have argued that the much vaunted British war effort was a sham, because it was so dependent on the USA (I don't agree with him, but it's worth thinking about). □

2.9　High and popular culture

Although the characteristic features of modernism in the arts were already clearly apparent well before 1914, it would be widely accepted that the catastrophe of the First World War did have profound effects on the subject matter, beliefs and modes of expression of artists and thinkers. The Second World War came to a much less naïve world, and therefore did not have the same effect in transforming modes of thought and expression. It was, nonetheless, an experience of enormous intensity, and resulted in the production of a considerable body of work related directly to that experience. It can indeed be argued that while the trauma of World War I turned intellectuals in on themselves and towards the esoteric modes of modernism, World War II, as a war of peoples and partisans, induced a turning back towards realism. The least significant work, I think it can be safely said, emanated from Germany, the guilty country, ultimately humiliated, ruthlessly controlled, and from whom most of the truly distinguished figures in all spheres of culture had emigrated in the 1930s. Many years had to pass before works of true distinction, having digested the experiences of war, as distinct from works of immediate emotional intensity or graphic experience, were produced. One of the greatest, Günter Grass's *The Tin Drum* (1959) was a ferocious and rumbustious allegory on the more recent German experience, pre-war, wartime, and post-war (an extract from the *The Tin Drum* is reproduced as document II.23 in *Documents 2*). The other profound novel of the war experience was in fact American, Joseph Heller's *Catch 22* (1962), while another American, Norman Mailer, had consciously written 'the great war novel', *The Naked and the Dead*. One upshot of the pre-war flight from Nazi power, of the war itself, and of the triumphant entry into Europe of the Americans, was the new ascendancy of New York in the art world.

Exercise　1　Play Part 2 of your music cassette (audio-cassette 1).

2　Play Part 2 of your art cassette (audio-cassette 2), entering fully into the spirit of my discussions with you. ■

In the rest of this section I am going to look in turn at Germany, France, Italy, Britain and Russia, taking high culture and popular culture together. Tony Aldgate's separate section on mass society will go into greater detail on popular culture.

Germany

It is significant that two of the writers who were among the first in the post-war years to try to come to grips in literary form with the Nazi and war experience were both exiles from Germany during the war period itself. One is our old friend Erich Maria Remarque, whose *A Time to Love and a Time to Die* (1951) is generally considered to be a much more contrived and less satisfactory work than his truly heart-felt *All Quiet on the Western Front*. The first serious engagement was that of Carl Zuckmayer, who in the 1930s had fled to Austria, then to Switzerland, then to France, then finally to the USA, but who returned to Germany at the end of the war, and whose play *The Devil's General* was produced in 1946. In essence the play is about Hitler and his entourage. A central character is a flying ace named Harras, who has enjoyed professional and personal success all his life without any help from the Nazi Party. Party members, as his girlfriend points out, envy him his successes, particularly his successes with women. In that area they are 'way below zero'. For them, joining the Party was a way to setting things right (Frederick Harris, *Encounters with Darkness: French and German Writers on World War II*, 1983, p. 104).

In the 1920s German film-making had been one of the most imaginative and innovative in the world. With the advent of Hitler, advances came almost to a total stop. But, as almost everywhere, during the war visits to the cinema became more widespread and popular than ever; in bombed areas open-air cinemas were set up, and film vans turned out to remote villages (there was partly a desire to meet the needs of hard-pressed civilians, partly a desire to continue to pump out forms of Nazi propaganda). By the closing stages of the war, long queues were forming in the early afternoons outside the Berlin cinemas. Many cinemas, of course, had been put out of action by bombing raids, and a considerable black market in tickets developed. Throughout the war soldiers (of whom there were not many around) had been granted the right to go straight to the head of queues, but as the front line came closer and closer to the capital, this privilege was revoked. The enormous wartime audiences provided the basis for the two greatest box office successes of the entire Third Reich, *The Great Love* and *Request Concert*. The first of these 'focused on the solidarity of suffering of women separated from the men folk at the front. Characteristically omitting any reference to the events or the background of the war, it made wartime separation seem to be a form of alchemy whereby the gold of marital love could be purged of all dross'. In the same vein 'of sympathetic magic, the film gave married soldiers a more favourable statistical rating than single ones by implying a wife's loving concern for her husband at the front could – like some incorporeal bullet-proof vest – shield him from harm' (Richard Grunberger, *A Social History of the Third Reich*, 1971, p. 87). *Request Concert* took its name from a weekly radio programme linking soldiers and their families through musical requests. Artistically these films were of no merit, but they do bring out both the importance of family in wartime Germany, and that critical significance of radio to which I have already referred.

With respect to radio, there was a two-and-a-half-hour Sunday afternoon programme of 'request concerts', incorporating a medley of requests by soldiers for their families, and by families for their serving men. The new and unique power of radio is highlighted in Hitler's crucial broadcast after the attempt on his life in July 1944: the broadcast reassured the public as no other medium then could have done.

Most, but not all, of the great musicians, composers, performers and conductors had fled from Nazi Germany. The most popular excerpts from the great German classics were exploited for Nazi puposes. Wagner's great opera house at Bayreuth became a kind of culture centre for the deserving, convalescent soldiers, hyper-industrious munitions workers, nurses, and so on. Hitler had always been hostile to Western dance music, and the war meant that Germany was practically cut off from this influence. The playing of such music, and dancing to it, was an activity indulged in, at great personal risk, by youthful rebels.

France

The intellectual and literary scene in post-war France was dominated by Jean-Paul Sartre and Albert Camus. In no way, however, can one talk of the war as 'creating' existentialism. Camus rejected the label, and Sartre's purely existentialist works date back to before the war. Both men had played their part in the Resistance, and what their wartime and post-war writings implied was, within a broader perception of the irrationality and absurdity of the world, the affirmation of social and political commitment. Later, Paris was the home of the 'new novel' (Alain Robbe-Grillet is mentioned in the Reader article by Josipovici), which went far beyond the stream-of-consciousness techniques of James Joyce and completely destroyed the narrative structure of the traditional Western novel. It is not easy to detect any direct links between this development and the disruptions of war. The best generalization one can make about the most significant developments after 1945 is that writers and artists were responding to an entire twentieth-century crisis, of which World War II was one major symptom, rather than to the war as such. In any case, I propose here to concentrate on two examples of more immediate, and therefore more limited, responses to the war (and ones which tend to support the contention that, in contrast to World War I, World War II provoked a reaction towards realism).

Exercise   Turn to document II.24 in *Documents 2*, the extract from the short novel *Le silence de la mer* (*The Silence of the Sea*). This was the first in the clandestine series *Editions de Minuit* ('Midnight Editions') published in France by supporters of the Resistance, and smuggled out to Britain. The novel was completed in October 1941, and published in February 1942. In a moment I want you to consider this novel in relationship to the poetry of Louis Aragon, who in 1939 was editor of *Le Soir*, a left-wing evening paper with a circulation of nearly half a million. Aragon served with great distinction in the French army, winning several medals and being evacuated from Dunkirk, prior to the capitulation. He published one volume of heavily coded poetry (poetry lends itself naturally to coding) under the Vichy regime, before it was banned by the Germans; subsequently, as an active Resistance organizer, he published four more volumes through the clandestine Resistance press, and then one volume at the time of the Liberation. In reading (now) the extract from 'Vercors' (document II.24) and (in a minute) the poems by Aragon (document II.25) you might wish to bear in mind the words of Paulhan, the distinguished French critic of the time: 'art benefits by being clandestine and subversive'. 'Vercors' was the pseudonym of Jean Bruller, an artist and writer of hitherto modest distinction. In his novel a German officer is billeted with an old Parisian (the narrator) and his niece. The old man warms a little to the officer, but the niece treats him with unrelenting silence. Only at the end, when the officer is called to the eastern front, does the old man hear her mutter to him 'Adieu'.

Now write a commentary on the extract, commenting on any significant or difficult points in it, and saying what you think its significance is. ∎

Specimen answer and discussion

The first part of the extract informs us that the German officer is a man of high culture, and indeed of tolerance. He recognizes the great French authors, and also the English one, Shakespeare. When he turns to music, his obvious implication is that German and French civilization complement each other; France has the literature, but Germany has the music. His ideas, apparently genuine, are those which the Nazis put forward, of France and Germany coming together in a greater civilization in the 'New Order'. The officer suggests that it is a tragedy that there should have been a war at all, and expresses a view that this must be the last one: 'we will marry each other!'

The phrasing here indicates that the novel is operating on several levels: the relationship between Germany and France, the relationship between the officer and the niece (who, it later becomes apparent, is in the room), and the later discussion of the story of Beauty and the Beast.

The novel becomes more politically pointed when the officer refers to his initial entry into France at the border at Saintes. First he had thought the population genuinely welcomed the Germans, then, when he realized that they were simply acting out of cowardice, he felt contempt for France. Thus he actually rejoices in the stern silence of the niece, who is seen as upholding the honour of France. The niece, accordingly, is seen as a metaphor for the Resistance, however cultured and seductive some German claims might be. The next part concerns the conflict between national necessities and personal sentiments (we must bear in mind that this is a novel, fiction, and that although much of this extract is in the form of comments by the German officer, the whole thing has been created by a French writer). It is apparent that the niece is in fact attracted to the officer. The officer then recalls the Beauty and the Beast story which, of course, symbolizes both Germany's relationship with France and the officer's relationship with the niece.

The novel is saying three things:

1 Whatever the temptations, we in the Resistance must be, and are, unflinching.

2 Doing one's duty, in time of war especially, brings personal pain.

3 We in the Resistance are not brutal and ignorant propagandists – we can recognize that there are civilized Germans, even if it is our duty totally to resist them.

The historical significance lies in the very circumstances of the production of this work, the way in which it was both distributed in France and smuggled over to Britain (without being translated). It is a symbol of cultural life, in its most noble-spirited and least partisan sense, being continued in occupied France. □

Now I want you turn to the two poems by Louis Aragon (document II.25). The stanzas of the second poem, about a quarter of the total length of the poem, are very clear, and may even, in English translation, seem slightly banal. The first poem, 'Tears are alike', is more in the spirit of *Le silence de la mer*, and indeed of the famous film *La Grande Illusion*. It may not be immediately clear to you, but what the speaker is referring to in stanzas 1–3 is his experience as a soldier occupying the German Rhineland in 1922. Stanza 4 is the key stanza: he did not know then about how he would feel when his own country was occupied, as it now is: the reference to 'false prophets' is to the Vichy regime and the French collaboration-ists, in whom most Frenchmen (though not Aragon) found 'hope'. The next stanza takes us back to the narrator's experience in the Rhineland and the signs he could not decipher. Stanza 6 is also a critical one, linking the tears of the Rhinelanders with the tears of France in 1942. Stanza 7 is again memory, of the 'blank looks' of the 'vanquished' Rhinelanders. Aragon has been termed *the* poet of Western resistance in the Second World War. He was a Communist, but an independent-minded one; despite the Nazi-Soviet pact, he was an enthusiastic soldier for France. Aragon can be seen as representing the bringing together of the spirit of resistance and the spirit of reform, the impulse towards a genuinely better post-war world. If we go back to the imagery of Beauty and the Beast in the novel, we may see that as a kind of anticipation of the movement for European union which in fact developed after the war.

The German occupation of France saw the creation of the German company La Continentale, which was intended to be the Hollywood of Nazi Europe. Many leading French film-makers remained in France, there being some argument among historians and film critics as to how far they expressed 'coded' resistance through their films. *Symphonie Fantastique* (1942) attempted some kind of national-ist statement through the life of the great French composer Hector Berlioz. Goebbels was not amused: 'the French must content themselves with light films, empty, even a little stupid, and it is our business to give them such films . . . Our policy must be identical to that of the Americans with regard to the American continent. We must become the dominant power on the European continent. We must prevent the creation of any national cinema industry' (quoted by Georges Sadoul, *Le cinéma français*, 1962, p.91). What French film-makers did do, in the view of Sadoul, the greatest authority, was to take refuge in what he calls 'stylism' – beautifully made films without any obvious message. The three greatest box office successes of wartime French cinema were *La Nuit Fantasque, Les Visiteurs de Soir*, and *L'Eternel Retour*. The second of these, made by Marcel Carné with a screenplay by Pierre Laroche and Jacques Prévert, was originally set in the contemporary era, then was prudently switched to the Middle Ages. It is possible that the chained and tortured lovers are meant to represent France, while the devil may represent Hitler. The third of these films, made by Jean Cocteau, was based on the famous theme of Tristan and Isolde. Since this theme had its most celebrated incarnation in Wagner's *Tristan und Isolde*, the film was denounced by the British as being collaborationist: Sadoul points out that the original legend originated from Brittany, so that the film could be seen as expressing a form of French nationalism. Sadoul, incidentally, doesn't think much of it, speaking contemptuously of 'gratuitous baroque episodes'. The 'stylistic' tendency of the occupation reached its culmination in *Les Enfants du Paradis*, made by Carné and Prévert under the most difficult conditions in the later stages of the occupation, with the Germans not being at all clear exactly what the film was all about. This is (in my opinion) one of the greatest films of all time, an allegory of good and evil, of reality and representation, of different kinds of love, of the existentialist agent Lecaneur, who in the perfect gratuitous act, assassinates the arrogant, all-powerful nobleman (symbol of the occupation?), all set in the Paris of Balzac. I simply recall the words of Paulhan: 'art benefits by being clandestine and subversive'.

Italy, Britain and Russia

Of *Les Enfants du Paradis* one thing can be said with absolute certainty: it betrays not the slightest whiff of Americanization. The same I believe could be said of the one great creative outburst of wartime and liberated Italy, that of neo-realist cinema. This is a topic fully explored in the Open University course *Liberation and Reconstruction*, and one which cannot be taken further here, though I would like you to reflect on the proposition that the realism of such films as *The Bicycle Thieves* is the realism of the war of peoples (as is maintained, for example, by Tannenbaum in his *The Fascist Experience*, p.337, where he also contrasts the neo-realism of the painter Guttoso with the surrealism of de' Chirico developed at the end of World War I). Similar points – national, non-American, self-expression and 'democratic' realism – could be made about the great efflorescence of British film-making which accompanied the war (though such films were often very conscious of continuing class distinctions). With the great concentration of effort and resources on national survival, British film-makers who, in the 1930s, had too often been confused through aiming at US standards and attempting to reach US audiences, developed a genuinely British tradition, examples of which you have already seen in *Millions Like Us* and *The Gentle Sex*. However, the issue of the extent of Americanization (as of Sovietization) brought by World War II is a contentious one, on which, as with other such issues in this course, you should seek to develop your own views.

Finally, I come to Russia, drawing on the article by Deming Brown in the collection edited by Linz (*The Impact of World War II on the Soviet Union*). Because of the way in which literature had been politicized in Soviet Russia, the impact of the war was enormous, with the efforts of Soviet writers between 1941 and 1945 being almost completely devoted to the war. Brown comments on a process which we have already seen at work in other spheres. In the middle stages of the war, writers had more freedom than usual, and were able to draw on the reserves of Russian historical traditions. But as the war came to an end, official control returned. Literature then became as debased as ever it was in Nazi Germany, being almost confined to celebrating the glories of Stalin. In assessing the consequences of war we have always, as noted several times, to be aware of other constraints (dictatorship, occupation by a foreign power, etc.) which may contain or terminate forces released by war itself. While creative artists in France had to beware of the alien regime imposed by Germany, artists in Russia had to beware of their own regime. Sergei Eisenstein was able to exploit Stalin's admiration for the historic Russian figure Ivan the Terrible in making his film of that name; at the same time he was able to hint at a parallel between the 'gang of degenerates' (as a critical Communist Party Central Committee later put it) surrounding Ivan and the Communist Party bureaucrats.

The horrific, powerful and sometimes uplifting experiences of World War II were deeply etched into cultural artefacts at all levels, but there was no significant general shift in direction, such as it is possible to associate with World War I. However, as noted before, one contrast that can be made, though it should not be pushed too far, is that intellectuals, 'scorched' or 'traumatized' by the cataclysmic collapse of civilized values after 1914, sought isolation and the new modes of modernism, whereas some intellectuals in the Second World War, seeking an identification with struggling peoples, turned back towards naturalism and realism.

2.10 Political institutions and values

Exercise on four French newsreels

These newsreels, items 7–10 on video-cassette 2, are dated respectively May 1940, April 1944, May 1944 and June 1944. We discovered the first one by accident, having actually asked the Imperial War Museum for another issue from 1944. It occurred to me immediately that looking at the four items together gives a very good sense of the beginning and ending of the war for France, and of some of the particular ways in which the war impacted on French society. I shall talk you through each item separately (because of shortage of space we have made cuts in all of these; item 9, which is in the condition in which we found it, starts rather abruptly), but you should try to find time (perhaps when revising for the exam) to play the four items together to get a general overview of certain important developments in France. The aims of this exercise, then, extend beyond the single topic of political institutions and values:

1   Film material can make vivid to you (as it made vivid to audiences at the time) events and developments (which you already know about from your *written* course material; you, of course, are in a position to make a detached historical analysis, knowing how events unfolded – a position not open to film audiences at the time).

2   You can see the *uses* that were made of this particular form of mass communication, a subject to which Tony Aldgate will return shortly.

3   You can see (and hear) some of the political, social and ideological responses to invasion (two rather different ones) and occupation.

4   You can see directly and physically something of the impact of the war on civilian life.

Exercise   Play item 7 on video-cassette 2, noting down answers to the following questions:

1   What military stage of the war is being reported here?

2   Against whom is the commentary directed, and for what in particular?

3   The film shows two of the most characteristic tragedies inflicted on civilians by twentieth-century war: what are they?

4   What device is used by the film-makers to heighten the sense of tragedy?

5   Do any scenes strike you as obvious clichés, possibly deliberately set up, presumably to impress French audiences? (I have in mind a scene near the beginning of the extract.)

6   Had you been a French person of the time would you, overall, have found this film reassuring? Give reasons. ∎

Specimen answers
and discussion   1   The German 'blitz' on Holland, Belgium and Luxemburg, which, of course, preceded the invasion of France itself. There are references to Allied troops having been thrown in, but a month later there came the evacuation from Dunkirk.

2   The Germans, particularly for the barbarity of bombing civilian targets.

3   The flight of refugees (note the reference to the horrific memories of the Belgians of the previous war), and bombing.

4   Music.

5   Maybe you noticed other things as well, but I was struck by the civilians

welcoming the 'rescuing' Allied troops (here French) – particularly the girl giving the soldier a bottle of beer and the little boy offering cigarettes.

6   I would think not, despite the scenes of 'rescue' first mentioned. The film does reveal that French civilian targets had been bombed. It is often held that newsreel film was always exploited to maintain morale, but here, I suspect, the naked actuality may well have contributed to the mood of defeatism in France. □

Exercise   Now play item 8, and then answer the following questions:

1   Note the date of this newsreel: what is the general military situation at this time; what indications come through in the film? Which major document that you have already studied dates from exactly this time?

2   Look back to question 2 of the previous exercise: what comments occur to you this time (reflect a little on the horrible ironies of war)?

3   The bombing of civilians and the question of evacuation (particularly of children) are much in evidence. Are there any signs (however limited) of a stimulus to social welfare? What, according to Feldman, is the significance of Bichelonne in this context?

4   Pay very careful attention to the world of politics sequence referring to the Milice (you may have to play it two or three times). What has happened? What is the attitude of the commentator? What do you learn about the internal situation in France? ■

Specimen answers   1   The Germans are in slow retreat on the Russian front. British and American
and discussion   bombing raids on France are intensifying in preparation for the invasion of France, which the Germans know to expect, but don't know where to expect it. The only direct manifestations in our example are the Allied bombing raids. The document is the programme of the National Resistance Council.

2   Again, the barbarity of aerial bombardment is being denounced, but the evil perpetrators this time are not the Germans, but the British and the Americans!

3   The Workers' Committee for Immediate Assistance (COSI) is a direct response to bombing; however, since it obviously depends on voluntary contributions, it is rather limited as a social welfare organization. Bichelonne was credited by Feldman as being one of the Vichy ministers who pioneered social welfare policies later adopted by the Liberation.

4   A policeman has been killed (obviously by the Resistance). The commentator, inevitably, takes the government line in speaking of the bravery of the police in the face of what he calls 'crime and banditry'. It is clear that by this stage the Resistance is having an impact which even an official newsreel cannot conceal. □

Exercise   Now play both items 9 and 10.

1   At what stage do we realize that a new turning-point in the military war has been reached? In what sense does it echo the first item you looked at?

2   What characteristic feature of this war, evident in both of the previous items, is again central to these two issues? Did any particular details stand out this time?

3   The opening titles for item 9 are missing. The opening shot is a hoary old, and very phoney, film cliché. Explain.

4   What three symbols of French patriotism are exploited in the film? Did you learn anything about popular French support for the occupation regime?

5   What impression was the sequence on the Russian front at the end of item 9 intended to give French audiences?

6   What does item 10 do to try to keep up the morale of audiences: for example, what does it concentrate on in portraying the Allied invasion? What about other sequences?

7   I have spoken from time to time of workers' *participation*. Did you see any hints of this? ■

Specimen answers and discussion   1   Where item 10 begins to discuss 'the war in France'. We began with the German invasion of the Low Countries; now we have the Allied invasion of German-occupied France.

2   The bombing of civilians (note the similarities of music and moral indignation expressed by the commentaries). I noted the indignation on the destruction of the library at Chartres (the Nazis, of course, were the great burners of books), and the chalked messages on bombed houses (all of these were optimistic – were the cameraman, editor, etc. secretly pro-Allies; do we again see the 'constructive' response to bombing?)

3   Bombs issuing from planes is one of the oldest tricks in the business. They can never, of course, be the same bombs as do the damage, and anyway a French cameraman could not have got such shots of *enemy* planes.

4   Joan of Arc (sword blown off by the wicked Allies); Marshal Pétain, hero of World War I, here represented as France's only true leader; the 'Marseillaise'. There does seem to be popular support for Pétain – it's not faked; on the other hand, the persuasive powers of the Milice, the Gestapo, etc., were considerable. The evidence in general is that Pétain *was* popular.

5   One of cheerful German soldiers prepared to fight to the death against Bolshevism, contrasted with (this at least was the intention, though we are perhaps less susceptible to such racism) very Slavic-looking Russian prisoners, made to appear as '*Untermenschen*'.

6   Apart from the emphasis on destruction and the deaths of Frenchmen, the invasion sequences feature burnt-out American tanks and anti-aircraft defences against Allied planes. The penultimate sequence (the Milice again – referred to as the 'forces of order' – and Laval) is on the theme of Life Goes On; the last item tries to wring 'Hope' out of the launching of a civilian ship.

7   I don't want to press this, but, while grossly exploited, workers were essential to all aspects of the war effort: we *see* them at work in this final launching scene. □

Comparative study of political institutions and values

Clearly, the ten areas of social change that I have identified for study throughout this course overlap each other. There is, in any case, considerable dispute over what exactly constitutes the 'political'. Some people argue that everything is in essence political; others that, compared with broader economic and social forces, politics are relatively unimportant. Even if I limit myself here to changes in forms of government, electoral laws, prevailing political ideas (liberal, collectivist, democratic, etc.) and political parties, it will quickly become clear that much of this has already been covered in our discussions of other areas of change. So also has a major question for debate: were political institutions and values in 1945 and after shaped more by war experiences (the participation of labour, Resistance ideas, etc.) or by whether or not countries fell under Russian influence or that of, say, the Western occupying powers in Germany? Certainly the establishment of one-party dictatorships (similar to that of Russia, different from those of Hitler and Mussolini) was a major political consequence of the war.

You will probably remember the chart I asked you to construct when you were working on Book I, Unit 5 (simply a country-by-country list of headings under which you could note down changes in political institutions and values).

I want you now (a) to read Roberts from p.573 ('This prolongation . . .') to p.577 ('. . . entered the war') and then (b) to reflect on what you have learned about political change so far in this book. Take the United Kingdom, France, Italy and Germany (I am taking it that the *broad* developments in Eastern Europe are essentially similar to each other – the detail will be examined in a later unit) and note down the main changes of 1945 and after (of course, *during* the war countries often had to make temporary changes in their political organization). Note how, if at all, the changes relate to the war experience.

Instead of providing an extensive answer, I am simply going to highlight certain points that may not have come out clearly from Roberts or from your earlier reading in this book.

United Kingdom

In its essentials the political system did not change ('victory' in war was taken as a vote of confidence in the system). This time, for instance, there was no striking reform of the franchise (the Labour government did, however, improve democracy by abolishing the second vote which businessmen could cast). Most historians (see, for example, Paul Addison, *The Road to 1945*, 1975) would agree that, as a result of the war experience, there was a general shift towards a political consensus in favour of collectivism and the welfare state. Some middle-class voters moved left, and more workers than ever before felt a clear commitment to voting Labour. Thus the election of a Labour government had much to do with changes touched off by the war.

France

It is a commonplace that the spirit of Resistance evaporated quickly and that although some of the forms of the Fourth Republic were different from those of the Third, France continued to be governed by shifting middle-of-the-road governments, as in pre-war years. Crucially, however, the whole French civil service was renewed (the 'regeneration of elites' of Bédarida, product of the 'test' of war, as I would put it) and provided France with the kind of leadership and planning initiatives, and reconstruction of the economic infrastructure, which turned out to be so lacking in Britain.

Italy

Much the same is often said of Italy (save that no one has accused the Italian civil service of being infected with anything much akin to efficiency). After the brief and not very competent government of Ferrucio Parri, who, in the words of Martin Clark (*Modern Italy*, p.317), 'symbolised the values of the Resistance', Italian politics was dominated by the Christian Democrats. However (remember the golden rule: look at what a country was like *before* the war you are assessing),

Italy before 1914, unlike France, had not had a secure democratic system imbued with democratic values; hence, in part, the ease with which Mussolini came to power. The moderately progressive democratic system of the years after 1945 *was* something different, and its spirit was essentially that of the anti-Fascism and community welfare politics stirred up in the war years (see Tannenbaum, *The Fascist Experience*, pp.325–39). Attention must also be given to the special position obtained by the Italian Communist Party, largely through the leadership it provided during the Resistance. Though kept out of central government, it had great prestige throughout the nation, most notably in agricultural areas (in part at least because it was able to assert its independence of Moscow); it was a great social influence in many communities, and a power in local politics in such important cities as Bologna. There was a new balance of political forces, committed to democracy and tending towards community welfare. Many writers see only a lost revolution (consider that argument carefully); I, however, believe that, with Germany, Italy underwent the greatest political change of all Western countries.

Germany

Post-war forms of government emerged more quickly in Italy than in Germany, where the occupying power spent more time nurturing a new German democracy, eventually also dominated by Christian Democracy. You will recall the arguments so well expressed by Roseman. I shall add only one thought. It is hard ever to assert that the appalling carnage and suffering of war is worthwhile. At least World War II did obliterate Nazism and the peculiar 'liberal' and nationalist political values which, in part, lay behind it.

A final reflection on Eastern Europe

'Europe divided' was not an instant consequence of war. The situation of Czechoslovakia, in particular, is worth reflecting on. Although many Czech political leaders at the end of the war looked warmly towards Russia, there was a widespread belief in the West that Czechoslovakia could become a new showcase of progressive democratic government. The *coup d'état* which clamped Soviet rule on a country till then governed by a coalition government and operating democratic elections (one was due in May 1948) did not come till February 1948. Even then some historians have blamed the Democratic ministers who walked out, rather than being pushed out, of government, as much as Soviet machinations. In the post-war political history of Czechoslovakia we see different sorts of forces released by war taking effect at different times.

Final documents exercise

To give you practice in the kind of document exercise you will have to do in the examination, and, of course, to give you some guidance on how to do it, I am now setting the exercise I mentioned earlier.

Exercise   Turn to document II.16, the report of *L'Unità* on the Turin strikes of 1943. Imagine that in front of you in an examination is printed the third, fourth and fifth paragraphs, that is to say from 'What are they striking for' to 'the profiteers and the party leaders'.

Write a commentary on this extract, saying what the document is, setting it in its historical context, commenting on specific points in the text, and summing up the extract's historical significance for the study of war, peace and social change.

In order to make a really serious attempt at this you may find it desirable to refer back to my discussions of Italy, particularly in the section on class. Please do make a serious effort to write out an answer to this question, then compare your answer with mine. ■

Specimen answer This extract is from the Communist paper *L'Unità*; that is to say, it is a newspaper report from a very politically committed newspaper. While we might expect left-wing bias, we would also expect this source to be closely in touch with events affecting the working class. Mussolini's Fascist regime was being severely tested by the war, and found to be seriously wanting. By early 1943 discontent with the regime was openly breaking out. *L'Unità*, banned along with the Communist Party by the Fascists, had been revived the previous year and was now coming out as a clandestine monthly. RAF bomb attacks on northern Italy had been especially disruptive, and particularly affected the workers in the industrial areas. Although the incomes of workers, essential to the war effort, had held up reasonably well, they were now deteriorating rapidly. The extracts are from *L'Unità*'s report on the strikes which broke out in Turin on 5 March 1943, known as 'internal strikes', since the workers simply downed tools at 10.00 a.m. for short periods, rather than going continuously on strike. The *L'Unità* article has begun by giving a very colourful account of the strikes, and of the way in which Fascist officials have been unable to do anything about them. The report now turns (in the extract in front of us) to the reasons for the strikes.

The extract explains that the first demand is that the evacuation allowance (equivalent to 192 hours, or one month's wages) should be paid to all workers. Although the bombing raids had caused widespread distress, the government was trying to limit these allowances to those who could prove incontrovertibly that they had to take up a new residence. In part, of course, the claims were simply a means towards increasing earnings. But they do also show the real effects that the bombing raids were having. The second claim is for a straight rise in wages to meet the considerable rise in the cost of living. The third claim is for an increase in basic rations (Italy, of course, had had to impose basic food rationing, the workers generally doing better than other ordinary people, but by this time rations had severely deteriorated). The remainder of this second paragraph expresses most accurately the general feelings of frustration, war-weariness, and the determination to protest which lay behind the strike. It may be noted that in time of war the Italian Communist Party developed a policy of very precise, realistic demands (as distinct from the call for revolution); it continued this position in the post-war years.

The next paragraph begins with the more fundamental Communist Party principle, that of the power of the working class, provided it is united. There is a triumphant tone about the first sentence, which was justified since the government did give way to the workers' demands. The remainder of the paragraph is about the need to extend the Turin strike to other areas of Italy. Again, what is spoken of did come to pass: there was a series of strikes in other industrial areas.

The significance of the document is that it demonstrates the power workers can have in time of war because of the desperate need for their participation in the war effort. It has the particular significance of describing, as Martin Clark has put it, the first open workers' protest against Fascism. The fact that the strikes spread, and that the government had to make concessions, demonstrate both the potential of the working class and the weaknesses of the Fascist regime exposed by war. There was much suffering and repression still to come, particularly when the Germans took over all of northern Italy, but events presented in the document (with very little ideological or propagandist exaggeration) can be seen as marking a stage towards the defeat of Fascism and the emergence in Italy of a more equal and democratic society. The document also indirectly reflects the fact that British bombing raids on northern Italy, unlike many other bombing raids, did achieve some of their objectives. □

Discussion There is no absolutely right answer, of course, but I hope you were able to make some of these points and, more important, can now see the sorts of points you should be making. Let me just summarize a few guidelines:

1   In stating what the document is, any indicators of its reliability, likely biases, etc., will be welcomed.

2   In setting the context you have to refer to wider knowledge derived from secondary sources (particularly the course units) and you also have to show how the extract fits into the document as a whole, or even, in some cases, into a group of similar documents. The date of the document will almost certainly be of great significance.

3   Note the way of working through line by line, making any appropriate comments (for example, explaining the '192 hours'), commenting on wider significance (there *were* other strikes), on reliability (especially, as compared with your general comment at the beginning). This is a reliable document, though the opening paragraphs of the report, not used in my exercise, are rather rhetorical and highly coloured.

4   The historical significance can be at several levels. The point about bombing, though important, is obviously less important than the point about the place of these events in the development of the Italian war experience.

You should note that the following section is written by Tony Aldgate.

3 *MASS SOCIETY 1939–45*

Only those people can compass what is needed who are in sympathetic understanding with the masses of the people they address, who know or can learn about their common condition of life, their common interests and their common hopes. (F. C. Bartlett, *Political Propaganda*, 1942, p.143)

The Germans are fighting a revolutionary war for very definite objectives. We are fighting a conservative war and our objectives are purely negative. We must put forward a positive and revolutionary aim admitting that the old order has collapsed and asking people to fight for the new order. (Clement Attlee, July 1940, reported in Harold Nicolson, *Diaries and Letters 1939–45*, 1967)

The cynically-minded observer might be disposed to comment that it took a total war for the British governing classes to show real and practical concern for the condition of the people. (Ian McLaine, *Ministry of Morale*, 1979, p.260)

I would like you to begin this section on mass society during World War II by looking, once again, at the clip you looked at earlier from the 1943 British feature film, *The Gentle Sex* (item 6 on video-cassette 2), Leslie Howard's sincere if occasionally patronizing tribute to the ATS. Watch, in particular, the initial sequence where the women are enjoying afternoon tea, and note the exchange between the characters of Anne Lawrence and Mrs Sheridan. Arthur Marwick has already raised some questions about this scene, so you have doubtless formed an opinion regarding its depiction of the role of women in Britain during the course of that war.

I want you also to read document II.26 in *Documents 2*. This is an extract from the novel, *Not So Quiet . . . Stepdaughters of War*, which was published in 1930 and written by 'Helen Zenna Smith' (a pseudonym adopted by the journalist Evadne Price). Though initially conceived by a British publishing house as an opportunistic spoof on Erich Maria Remarque's successful *All Quiet on the Western Front* (1929) – the publisher fancied the idea of a riposte entitled 'All's Quaint on the Western Front' by 'Erica Remarks' – Price chose instead to produce a serious account of a young woman's experiences during the First World War. She based her novel on the diary kept by an ambulance driver at the front in France and soon found that she too had a bestseller on her hands. It was serialized in *The People* and *Collier's Weekly* (in the USA) and went through three British editions in two years. The film rights were sold, it was turned into a play and staged, was published in French translation by Gallimard and awarded the Prix Severigne as the 'novel most calculated to promote international peace', and, finally, it resulted in four sequels between 1931 and 1934. While Price's account has not been afforded the lasting and 'classic' status usually granted to that of Remarque – though a recent reprint by Virago Press suggests it might yet enjoy some revision of reputation – it was clearly a 'popular' novel in its day.

Exercise   Watch item 6 on video-cassette 2 and read document II.26. Then answer the following questions:

1   What obvious points of difference do you detect between the 1930 novel and the 1943 film in their depiction of women's experience during the two world wars?

2   What do you think would account for the differences? ■

Specimen answers   1   While the novel, like Remarque's, fits generally into that genre which was intended to heighten people's awareness of the horrors of war, it was also meant to convey the harsh realities of life for those women serving at the front in the ambulance corps. In this regard, however, it was plainly dealing with what can only be termed 'exceptional women'. One could hardly call their experiences, as rendered in the extract, the everyday experience of ordinary women during the course of World War I. The women at the front in that war were in a minority, and as a consequence their lives were little understood. In fact, Price pointedly refers to the gap between her protagonist's experience of the war and that of her parents back home – notice especially the vehemence of the reaction to her mother's social climbing on the back of a daughter doing her patriotic bit. There is both a generation gap, you might say, and a gap caused by first-hand experience of the war. Here, incidentally, I am reminded of a comment by Roberts (on p.499) about the 'physical and psychological blows of the Great War . . . The gap of generations was suddenly widened by millions of deaths and a difference of experience between those who had been in the trenches and those who had not.'

By contrast, Leslie Howard's 1943 film paints a very different picture of women's role during World War II. One must not make too much of its intentions, of course. Unlike Price's account, it was produced during the war itself, when plainly there was still an inspirational, morale-boosting job to be done in recruiting women for the forces. There again, it is little wonder his fictional character of Mrs Sheridan proves so responsive and sympathetic to Anne's speech and cause. She was clearly one of the exceptional women in that she, too, had driven a front-line ambulance during the Great War (and was precisely the sort of person, one might imagine, whom Price had been prompted to write about). She can therefore easily identify with Anne and share her feelings.

Whereas Mrs Sheridan was an exception in her time, however, Anne and the other ATS women are not. Howard obviously intends that this group should be seen as more representative of women's experience generally during World War II. Hence their diversity of background, class, character and even nationality – notice that in addition to the token Scots girl, there is the refugee Czech (played by Lili Palmer). Anne, of course, apologizes to Mrs Sheridan for blithely thinking that 'probably for the first time in English history, women are fighting side by side with the men'. But Mrs Sheridan excuses her lack of historical knowledge and insight. So, too, does the Scots girl, who chastises Anne mildly yet, surprisingly, fails to correct her all-too-casual equation of English = British. However, as Arthur Marwick has already noted, Anne's comment that 'this is going to make a tremendous difference to the status of women after the war's over', is clearly meant to apply to women in a wider social context and not just to those who experienced life in the forces (and the like). Significantly, it is Mrs Sheridan who reassures her for thinking that way:

> Oh my dear, you must believe in all those things with all your heart and soul. And you must fight for them as you are fighting for them. We didn't really know what we wanted. But I believe you do. And I believe you'll get it.

2   The advent of another war and the nature of that war undoubtedly account for the differences and the new-found emphasis given to women generally. In Price's novel, she was looking back on a comparatively isolated experience. By the time of Howard's film, he was dealing with a more common phenomenon. I am sure it must be obvious that the sheer need and presence of women in the forces in greater numbers than ever before was the major reason why they came to figure so prominently in World War II propaganda.

It is not surprising, therefore, that official bodies like the Ministry of Information were increasingly aware of the value of 'propaganda devoted exclusively to women'. Indeed, on 3 April 1941, the MoI's Policy Committee had agreed that, 'Since the women are being mobilized it would be good publicity to show what they are doing in the services and the factories.' Furthermore, at a meeting with the British Film Producers' Association on 7 May 1942, Jack Beddington, head of the MoI's Films Division, had suggested that 'The change in the status of women during recent years' would make an 'excellent subject' for a film; hence the making, by 1942 and especially 1943, of such films as *The Gentle Sex* (Leslie Howard was a member of the Films Division's Ideas Committee) and *Millions Like Us* (which started life as a proposal for a MoI documentary before it was handed over to a feature film company for commercial exploitation).

One further aspect is worth noting, which is perhaps most evident in the scenes of the anti-aircraft battery at work in *The Gentle Sex*. In World War II, unlike World War I, women simply did not have to go off to France to be in 'the front line', any more than did the rest of the population. □

Discussion The extent of this total involvement of society in warfare between 1939 and 1945 has been well summarized by Michael Howard:

> The Second World War awoke a new interest in the relationship between war and social change. Not only did it accelerate within all the societies involved, the processes of change catalysed by the Great War, but it brought social involvement in belligerent activity to a new level of intensity by eliminating the distinction between 'front line' and 'base'. This distinction had characterised not only the 1914–18 war but the great majority of wars in Europe since the seventeenth century. During the First World War heavy and prolonged pressures had been brought on civilian populations to find vast and continuous resources of men and material for the Front – a word which itself became heavy with sombre meaning – and these pressures were in themselves highly catalytic of social change. But the pressures arising from a situation in which the Front was *everywhere*, whether because of air bombardment as in Britain, Germany and Japan, or because of invasion and occupation as in continental Europe and the Soviet Union, were of a different order of magnitude altogether. ('Total war in the twentieth century: participation and consensus in the Second World War', in Brian Bond and Ian Roy (eds) *War and Society. A Yearbook of Military History*, 1976, pp.216–17)

As the civilian populations of the belligerent nations were compelled to withstand certain 'pressures' arising solely from war – conscription, evacuation, the increased likelihood of destruction and devastation, the enhanced threat of death – their leaders, too, were confronted with problems of 'a different order of magnitude' – the need to achieve widespread consensus for the waging of war, to maximize the people's participation in the war effort, to continue the mobilization, and to maintain morale among civilian and military populations alike. The war, in short, as Arthur Marwick has repeatedly stressed, posed a 'test' for society, not least of the relationship between the leaders and the led.

During the inter-war period, I suggested in Book III, Unit 19, this relationship was based upon sometimes naive psychological and sociological assumptions which presumed that people's attitudes and behaviour were especially susceptible to manipulation in the conditions of modern mass society. The people were malleable. Hadn't World War I established the value and need of mass propaganda, for instance? Certainly this was the lesson that Adolf Hitler drew from that war, as we have seen from the passages in *Mein Kampf* where he developed his theory that the key to both military and political achievement lay in the successful manipulation of the masses. Hadn't the very success of the 'totalitarian' dictators merely confirmed this view and demonstrated that the masses acted in response to crowd psychology, and not according to rational political calculations? Didn't the mass media of radio and cinema prove conclusively that the people were eminently persuadable? Why else would critics worry so much about commercialization, levelling, the lowering of standards, and the supposedly pervasive and pernicious influence of the USA on the realms of popular culture? Why else would governments in the liberal democracies as well as the totalitarian states strive so hard to control and direct the media to their best advantage?

Clearly, the war was to test many of these elitist notions about mass society and, in particular, the fear that the new technology of destruction, such as mass bombing, would lead to the collapse of society and the breakdown of civilization. Additionally, of course, it was a test of the effectiveness of propaganda generally. In the remainder of this unit we shall be looking at several examples of wartime propaganda. I intend to concentrate upon German and British sources, which you might feel is somewhat limited in scope. However, there are distinct advantages to be gained from this approach. First, it allows you to familiarize yourself thoroughly with a manageable amount of propaganda material and to explore the nuances in the methods and techniques applied. Second, the propaganda organizations in Germany and Britain set up bodies to record and assess public responses to their output, so one is able to judge its effectiveness with a good deal more confidence than is sometimes the case. Third, it is still possible for you to compare the propaganda emanating from a 'closed' and tightly controlled form of government, of the sort traditionally associated with the totalitarian states, with that in a more 'open' society of the liberal democratic variety. (Nevertheless, you should bear in mind that in wartime even the democracies sought to exert a greater measure of control over the media and to centralize their direction in official bodies such as, in Britain, a Ministry of Information which was established at the outset of hostilities.) Fourth, it permits comparison between two systems imbued with distinctly different and opposing ideologies: one, as in Germany, which was committed to the 'revolutionary' task of re-educating the people for a new society based on a drastically restructured value system; the other, as in Britain, with the relatively simpler and more 'conservative' role of building on the general acceptance of a just and necessary war in defence of existing values. Those, at least, are the terms in which the function of wartime propaganda in Germany and Britain has often been construed, in both contemporary and historical accounts. (A brief example of the former can be found in the quote from Clement Attlee reproduced at the beginning of the section. There are many historians who continue to categorize the difference between German and British war aims and propaganda in terms of a divide between 'revolutionary' and 'conservative' objectives.) It remains to be seen whether the terms hold good at the end of our survey.

Now listen to items 2 and 3 on audio-cassette 4, and watch the three extracts from the 1941 film *Ohm Kruger*, to be found on video-cassette 2 as items 11, 12 and 13. Read both document II.27 (the SD report on the audience response to *Ohm Kruger*) and the synopsis for the complete film, which you will find below.

> Gold is discovered in the land of the Boers, the Transvaal, and Orange Free State. The English decide they must acquire this land: Cecil Rhodes and Joe Chamberlain try to provoke them into war; Paul Kruger, the leader of the Boers, goes to England and signs a treaty which provides the English with many advantages but retains the Boers' independence. Returning home, however, Kruger starts to prepare for what he knows is an inevitable conflict. The English start the war but the Boers repel them, London changes its tactics and appoints Kitchener Supreme Commander. He decides not to engage the Boer Army but the helpless civilian population. Their homes are burnt, their herds are destroyed, their wells are poisoned,

the Negroes are armed, and women and children are forced into concentration camps where they are brutally treated, starved, and infected with diseases in an attempt to break down the morale of the Boer men still fighting. Thousands of men and women are killed in this way whilst Kruger travels around the capitals of Europe imploring help. English diplomacy assures his failure, and while the Boers are finally forced to sacrifice their independence and become part of the British Empire, a broken Kruger finds asylum in Switzerland. (Extract from *Aktuelle Filmbücher*, Berlin, 1941, reprinted in David Welch, *Propaganda and the German Cinema 1933–1945*, 1983, pp.271–2)

Exercise   1   Who were these examples of German propaganda directed at?

2   What was their purpose?

3   How were they meant to achieve their desired effect? ■

Specimen answer   1   The radio items were clearly intended for overseas broadcast and foreign consumption, i.e. by British listeners, whereas the feature film was straight anti-British propaganda and obviously aimed at the domestic market and the population in Germany.

2   Put bluntly, the former was meant to sap the enemy's morale, and to undermine the confidence of the British people in their leaders; the latter was meant to denigrate the British further in the eyes of the German people, to paint a 'historically valid' picture of the enemy they were confronting, and thereby boost their resolve and determination to continue the conflict.

3   By simple propagandist techniques. Thus 'Lord Haw-Haw' (William Joyce) mentions the damage done to the British cruiser *Exeter* in an engagement with the *Admiral Graf Spee*, though he noticeably fails to add that the final result of the battle of the River Plate was the scuttling of the German battleship in December 1939 – one of the few British successes in the early months of the war. This decidedly partial and highly selective broadcast harps upon the British losses while, from the German point of view, it goes out of its way to accentuate the positive aspects of the episode and to eliminate those negative aspects which were considerable, though short-lived. To substantiate his point, William Joyce resorts to information gleaned from a neutral source, the *New York Times*, which purportedly lends greater credence to his overall account. The story on tin hats is more trivial, even eccentric, and serves merely to emphasize the everyday inconveniences of war while allowing for a sly gibe at the expense of the 'Ministry of (Mis)Information'.

The New British Broadcasting Station item was a piece of 'black' propaganda purporting to come from within Britain itself. It supposedly represents the voice of alternative opinion which is increasingly disenchanted with the official version of wartime events, as reported by such organizations as the BBC, and, indeed, which is altogether unhappy with the British system of government. (NBBS professed, Asa Briggs records, to be 'entirely run by British people who put their country above their own interest and are resolved to speak the truth for their country's sake'.) There is much stress on 'the grievances of ordinary people' which are obscured by the mainstream media, at government instigation, and the fact that 'the masses of the people have never had any real heart in the war since it began'. 'Social injustices' such as 'the shocking state of poverty' are highlighted, and leading church and civil campaigners are applauded for their efforts to rid the country of slum conditions and the like. The broadcast is meant to provoke discontent with the existing system by playing upon social divisions and by giving vent to oppositional arguments on what should obtain in a fair and just society. It seeks, in short, to undermine British morale by posing the question whether the war is worth fighting for the values represented by the country's governing elites.

Ohm Kruger (Uncle Kruger) uses the full array of cinematic techniques to depict Britain as the brutal enemy of any kind of order or civilization. That much is evident from the first extract you see, with its heavily ironic juxtaposition of imagery and soundtrack, as bibles and guns are given out to the natives in equal measure against a backdrop of missionaries singing the national anthem. The *Illustrierter Film-Kurier*, incidentally, commented on this scene as follows: 'When England realizes that even with cannon and rifles she cannot crush the little nation whose heroic struggle is jubilantly acclaimed by the whole world, she decides to commit one of the most obscene acts in the history of the world.'

The full obscenity of Britain's role during this war is revealed when the spotlight is turned on the harsh treatment meted out to defenceless Boer women and children, culminating in the dramatic and emotional massacre in the concentration camp (which was closely modelled on the Odessa steps sequence at the climax of Eisenstein's *Battleship Potemkin*, a film that Goebbels privately admired). The message, plainly, is that Germany has a mission to rid the world of such an enemy and to restore peace and stability under the Nazi new order. It is reinforced with Kruger's words at the end of the film, when he declares: 'One day, great and powerful nations will resist the British tyranny, and then the way will be clear for a better world . . . There can be no coming to terms with the British.'

To lend an air of impartiality and objectivity, however, the film is set in a historical context, some forty years earlier, and omits any direct reference to Germany. Talk of this film being objective is perhaps difficult to imagine now. The British characters seem grossly caricatured, even comical (in addition to the obvious caricature of Churchill as the camp commander, there is an earlier caricature of a whisky-drinking Queen Victoria, which you do not see). Furthermore, the Nazi propaganda emphasis on the British invention of concentration camps (with the possible implication that the camps in Germany were somehow different and less brutal) becomes, with the benefit of hindsight, loaded with tragic irony.

The Security Service (SD) summary of audience reactions to the film gives you a better idea of how it was received in its day. Such reports have to be treated with some degree of caution, since people were always capable, as the Nazi authorities well recognized, of saying one thing in public and quite the opposite in private. But historians still consider that they provide a reliable indicator of public opinion and that they were characterized by an honesty which was uncommon in the Nazi state. Note, in the SD report on *Ohm Kruger*, the repeated emphasis on the film's 'plausibility' and 'historical authenticity'. Apart from the inevitable reservations about occasional scenes being 'too heavily loaded' with propagandist intent, the film does appear to have been a considerable success. It seems also to have genuinely fulfilled its function in helping to stiffen anti-British sentiment and resolve. □

Discussion   The Nazi leadership certainly held *Ohm Kruger* in great esteem. Emil Jannings, who came up with the original idea for the film and played the leading role of Kruger, was presented by Goebbels with the 'Ring of Honour of the German Cinema' for his achievement. The film was also the first to be awarded the accolade 'Film of the Nation', and it went on to win the Mussolini Prize for the best foreign film at the Venice film festival. In terms of its success at the German box office, the film did very well, with receipts amounting to RM 5.5 million, as against box office figures of RM 8 million and 7.5 million for *Die Grosse Liebe* (*Great Love*, 1942) and *Wunschkonzert* (*Request Concert*, 1940), the two top hits at the German box office during these years. Despite *Ohm Kruger's* popular success, however, it did not make a profit for the state, since Goebbels had invested more than RM 5.5 million in its production.

Judging the success of Nazi radio propaganda on British public opinion is difficult, since it was, by definition, intended to be a covert operation. The best estimate from informed sources (see Asa Briggs's *The History of Broadcasting in the United Kingdom* for the war years, vol.3, *The War of Words*, 1970, pp.140–59) is that 'black' German radio stations like NBBS could only be picked up by 38 per cent of British listeners with powerful enough receivers. Nor, it seems, did other stations such as Radio Caledonia, which sought to play on nationalist sentiment in Scotland and Wales and even reported the news in Gaelic, fare much better. Anti-British nationalist fervour, incidentally, found its echoes in many German films, with titles like *Der Fuchs von Glenarvon* (*The Fox of Glenarvon*, 1940), *Mein Leben für Irland* (*My Life for Ireland*, 1941) and *Das Herz der Königin* (*The Heart of a Queen*, 1940), about the life of Mary Queen of Scots and starring the immensely popular Zarah Leander.

Lord Haw-Haw, by contrast, built up a regular audience for a short while in the late autumn of 1939 and the early months of 1940. The opening announcement to his programmes, 'Germany calling, Germany calling', quickly became a catch-phrase and a ready stand-by for comedians up and down the country. He was variously dubbed 'the Humbug of Hamburg' and 'the Comic of Eau-de-Cologne' (and worse) in popular songs and jokes of the period. But his broadcasts caused genuine fear and alarm in the Ministry of Information and the War Office because of the likely effects and potential of his 'socially subversive message'. The BBC was prompted to conduct an enquiry into the extent and impact of 'Hamburg Broadcast Propaganda'. An interim report, in January 1940, found that of the 16 million people (over 50 per cent of the listening public) listening to a typical 9 p.m. BBC news bulletin, some 9 million would stay tuned to the BBC if the news was followed by a talk. Six million, however, would switch over to the Hamburg station and listen to Joyce. Among this 'Hamburg audience', as the final report confirmed in March 1940, there was a distinctly strong interest in current affairs. The report concluded:

> The blackout, the novelty of hearing the enemy, the desire to hear both sides, the insatiable appetite for news and the desire to be in the swim have all played their part both in building up Hamburg's audience and in holding it together. The entertainment value of the broadcasts, their concentration on undeniable evils in this country, their news sense, their presentation, and the publicity they have received in this country, together with the momentum of the habit of listening to them, have all contributed towards their establishment as a familiar feature in the social landscape.

Haw-Haw's appeal soon diminished, however, when popular programmes such as *Band Waggon* were switched to compete directly with his slot and when, shortly after, the *Postscripts* series was evolved with the express aim of projecting 'reasonable explanation' rather than 'exaggerated propaganda'; the series was to be presented by speakers who 'should not hesitate to admit our own short-comings'. When speakers like J. B. Priestley were invited to the microphone, the BBC found it had commentators who could do all that was required of them, and more besides.

Now watch the extract from *Der Ewige Jude* (1940), to be found on video-cassette 2 as item 14; read the translation of the extract's commentary (document II.28 in *Documents 2*), and the SD report on audience reaction to the film (document II.27); and read the synopsis of the complete film which follows. It is the synopsis that accompanied the film on its initial release.

> The film begins with an impressive expedition through the Jewish ghettoes in Poland. We are shown Jewish living quarters, which in our view cannot be called houses. In these dirty rooms lives and prays a race, which earns its living not by work but by haggling and swindling. From the little urchin to the old man, they stand in the streets, trading and bargaining. Using trick photography, we are shown how the Jewish racial mixture in Asia Minor developed and flooded the entire world. We see a parallel to this in the itinerant routes of rats which are the parasites and bacillus-carriers among animals, just as the Jews occupy the same position among mankind. The Jew has always known how to assimilate his external appearance to that of his host. Contrasted are the same Jewish types: first the Eastern Jew with his kaftan, beard and sideburns, and then the clean-shaven, Western European Jew. This strikingly demonstrates how he has deceived the Aryan people. Under this mask he increased his influence more and more in Aryan nations. But he could not change his inner being.
>
> After the banishment of the Jews from Europe was lifted, following the age of Enlightenment, the Jew succeeded within the course of several decades in dominating the world economy, before the various host nations realised, and this despite the fact that they made up only 1% of the world population. An excerpt from an American film about the Rothschilds, made by Jews, reveals to us the cunning foundations of their banking empire. Then we see how Jews, working for their international finance, drive the German people into the November Revolution. They then shed their anonymity and step out openly on to the stage of political and cultural life. Thus the men who were responsible for the disgraceful debasement of the German people are paraded before us. Incontestable examples are shown of how they robbed the country and the people of immense sums. As well as gaining financial supremacy they were able to dominate cultural life. The repulsive pictures of so-called Jewish 'art' reveal the complete decline of cultural life at that time. Using original sequences from contemporary films, the degrading and destructive tendency of Jewish power is exposed. For hundreds of years German artists have glorified figures from the Old Testament, knowing full well the real face of Jewry. How the Jew actually looks is shown in scenes shot by Jews themselves in a 'culture film' of a Purim festival, which is still celebrated today to commemorate the slaughter of 75,000 anti-Semitic Persians, and the doctrine with which future Rabbis in Jewish schools are educated to be political pedagogues. We look into a Jewish 'Talmud' class and experience the oriental tone of the ceremony in a Jewish synagogue, where Jews conduct business deals among themselves during the holy services.
>
> However, the cruel face of Judaism is most brutally displayed in the final scenes, in which original shots of a kosher butchering are revealed. These film documents of the inhuman slaughter of cattle and sheep without anaesthesia provide conclusive evidence of a brutality which is simply

inconceivable to all Aryan people. In shining contrast, the film closes with pictures of German people and German order which fill the viewer with a feeling of deep gratification for belonging to a race whose Führer is fundamentally solving the Jewish problem. (Extract from *Illustrierter Film-Kurier*, no.3152, reprinted in David Welch, *Propaganda and the German Cinema 1933–1945*, pp.292–3)

Exercise   An opening title to *Der Ewige Jude* (*The Eternal/Wandering Jew*) states it was intended as 'a film contribution to the problem of world Jewry'. As you will be aware by now, it is a particularly virulent and repulsive example of Nazi propaganda. Indeed, after the war, the Allied Commission's *Catalogue of Forbidden German Film* concluded that it was, 'One of the most striking examples of direct Nazi anti-Semitic propaganda, probably the vilest and subtlest of its kind ever made for popular consumption by the masses'.

What methods were being employed in this instance to convey the film's meaning and to what effect? ■

Specimen answer   The film-makers adopted the documentary format, utilizing actuality film for the most part, but also feature film extracts (ironically using Alfred Werker's 1934 American film *The House of Rothschild*, a thinly veiled statement against Nazi anti-Semitism, yet turned cleverly here into an indictment of Jewish financial practices), along with maps, animated inserts, statistics and the like, to build up an apparently factual piece of reportage on the so-called 'Jewish problem'. The commentary reinforces the visual impact of the images by equating Jewish migrations into Europe with the spread of disease brought by rats; by marshalling an array of 'facts and figures' designed to prove that these 'parasites' were involved in every aspect of international crime; and by highlighting the process whereby Jews had been assimilated into various national cultures and had insinuated themselves into positions of financial power, thereby having a supposedly deleterious effect upon the course of social, political and economic events everywhere. The message throughout was that the Jews remain an essentially alien race, a pernicious influence, and a threat to Western civilization and culture: an odious message for an odious film.

In assessing the film's impact, as no doubt you have spotted, the SD report noted that an extensive advance publicity campaign provoked 'great interest' in it and 'remarkably high audience figures' after its first release. Subsequently, audiences seem to have fallen off somewhat except among the 'politically active sections of the population'. Two reasons are given for this reaction. First, the feature film *Jud Süss*, which had been released just two months earlier and had already enjoyed huge success, clearly captured a lot of its potential audience – that film, too, displayed a vitriolic anti-Semitic slant, though more attractively couched in the trappings of costume drama. Second, word-of-mouth reports about the ritual slaughter scenes at the climax of *Der Ewige Jude* simply put a good many people off – a point anticipated by the Nazi authorities, who approved two versions for release. One, without the slaughter scenes, was exhibited at afternoon showings. The other, complete with slaughter scenes, was shown in the early evening. Advertisements announced that 'those of a sensitive disposition are recommended to see the 4 o'clock performance'.

The slaughter scenes are, indeed, gruesome. But it is perhaps revealing of both the Nazi regime and Nazi society that it was these scenes which compelled attention and required careful thought to be given to avoid placing undue 'strain on the nerves' of 'those of a sensitive disposition' in the cinema audience, while the rest of the film openly espoused racial hatred of the most virulent kind. 'The repulsive nature of the material' is a judgement that could be made on the whole film and not just the scenes of ritual slaughter, which really depend for their effectiveness upon public antipathy towards cruelty done to animals – a factor acknowledged in the official synopsis of the film. Interestingly, by contrast, no comments are to be found in the SD report which even begin to question 'its starkly realistic portrait of the Jews'. The most frequent reaction there, you will note, is one of complacency and indifference – 'a Jew is always a Jew', 'We've seen *Jud Süss* and we've had enough of Jewish filth'. □

Discussion   Apparently, then, the German cinema-going public was growing increasingly tired of anti-Semitic propaganda of the sort found in *Der Ewige Jude*. That, though, did not invalidate its purpose as far as the film's director was concerned. Two days after his film was released on 28 November 1940, Fritz Hippler wrote:

> I can envisage that film audiences may feel they have had enough of this subject. I can hear the comments: 'Not another film about the Jewish problem'. But I must reply to this and it is the intention of the film to stress the fact that the Jewish problem only ceases to be topical when the last Jew has left the *Volkisch* fabric of all nations.

Consequently, and unsurprisingly, *Der Ewige Jude* was dubbed and distributed to all Nazi-occupied countries. It attracted very large audiences, not least in France, where free exhibitions ensured its success despite the proven popularity, once again, of *Jud Süss*. Furthermore, a specially edited and adapted French version was released ten days before the round-up of some 13,000 Jews in preparation for their mass deportation to the East. The film was clearly intended to prepare public opinion for such an event, and it is in this regard that the importance of such films to the Nazi regime can be seen. As David Welch has concluded:

> By the late 1930s the increasingly fanatical tone of propaganda reflected the growing radicalisation of the regime's anti-Semitic policies. Not only had racial propaganda convinced the population that a 'Jewish Question' existed (a point acknowledged by Sopade [the Social Democrats' exile organization] as early as 1935), but Jews were now being openly driven from public posts and their property confiscated. The Jewish stereotype depicted in Nazi propaganda served to reinforce anxieties about modern developments in political and economical life, without the need to question the reality of the Jewish role in German society. The massive increase in the circulation of the obnoxious and virulently anti-Semitic *Der Sturmer* was an indication of this trend. It may well be true that the 'Final Solution' did not follow a more or less 'programmed' development and that Hitler was not its prime mover, but what remains unchallenged is that the culmination of such a policy resulted in a network of concentration camps where thousands were confined without trial, and eventually [led] to the slaughter of six million Jews during the Second World War. At precisely the time that Jewish persecution was being intensified and final details of the 'solution' arrived at, the SD reports were noting either boredom with or massive indifference to the 'Jewish Question'. Such indifference proved fatal. From the Nazis' point of view, the Jew provided an important escape valve from serious political and economic problems. The 'image' of the Jew portrayed in the mass media as 'self-seeking' and 'parasitic' was outside

Stills from the Nazi feature film Jud Süss *(1940, dir. Veit Harlan), showing* (top left) *the Nazi image of the 'enemy within' and* (bottom right) *the typical Aryan hero (photos British Film Institute, copyright © Rank Film Distributors).*

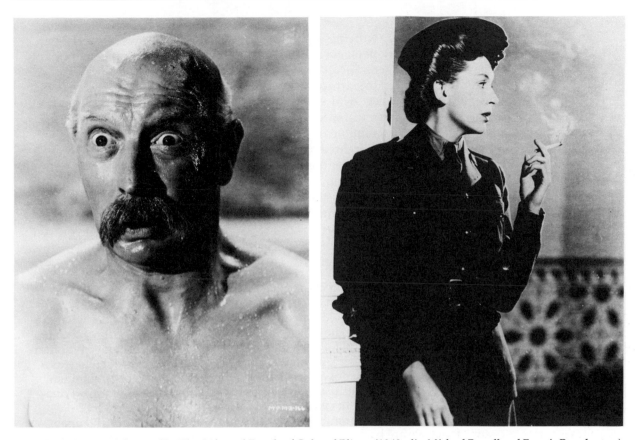

Stills from the British feature film The Life and Death of Colonel Blimp *(1943, dir. Michael Powell and Emeric Pressburger), showing the benign Blimp (Roger Livesey) – the most Britain could conjure by way of an enemy within – and 'the new woman' (Deborah Kerr) (photos British Film Institute, copyright © Rank Film Distributors).*

the range of serious intellectual analysis, and that was its strength. In this way, racial propaganda was able to rationalise any doubts that may have existed, minimise possible dissent, and at the same time provide the emotional basis for a totalitarian solution to the 'Jewish problem'. ('Propaganda and indoctrination in the Third Reich: success or failure?', *European History Quarterly*, vol.17, no.4, October 1987, p.415)

Listen now to items 4–6 on audio-cassette 4, watch item 15 (*Miss Grant Goes to the Door*) on video-cassette 2, and read document II.29 in *Documents 2* (transcript of commentary to *London (Britain) Can Take It*).

I do not want to set a full-scale exercise on this particular selection of material, but you might care to note down what you think were its various aims and what differences you can spot in emphasis and approach between the individual items.

Clearly, the two initial broadcasts are examples of straightforward exhortatory ministerial announcements. In the first talk, Ernest Brown, the Minister of Labour, was seeking to recruit the additional workers required to meet the engineering industry's needs for the war effort. Despite his emphasis on the non-compulsory nature of the appeal ('You are free men' compared with those in 'the totalitarian states') and the complacent assumption by the Ministry that the million and a quarter unemployed at the war's outset would provide a ready reservoir of labour, Brown found he had his work cut out during the early months of 1940 to meet the targets fixed for the expansion of employment in the wartime industries. It was only with the appointment by Churchill in May of Ernest Bevin, who concocted a very personal mixture of conscription and voluntarism born of his experience as General Secretary at the TGWU, that the Ministry of Labour was sufficiently revitalized to start seriously on the urgent task that was required of it. It was Bevin, of course, who enthusiastically supported the idea for *Workers' Playtime*, despite some reluctance on the part of the BBC, calling it 'a great work for great people'. The first edition, on 31 May 1941, came from a factory in Wrexham, and by the end of that year three programmes were being broadcast each week. It continued for many years after the war.

The appeal by Lord Woolton, newly arrived as Minister of Food by the time of this broadcast, was directed at 'the housewives of Britain' – 'the army that guards the kitchen front'. Woolton, a former social worker in the slums as well as head of a large chain of department stores, was a philanthropic businessman who proved more than keen to learn the art of broadcasting. Angus Calder comments on this speech in the following passage:

> The philanthropist radiated goodwill towards all. At his very first public appearance as minister, in the phoney war period, Woolton's homely phrasemaking had marked him out as a man on the people's side, when he had urged housewives, not, in so many words, to make weaker tea, but to give only 'one spoonful for each person . . . and none for the pot'. Woolton had been to Manchester University, not to Oxford or Cambridge; he was a man of the provinces, not a slick metropolitan personality; his somewhat potato-like face was suffused with earnest sympathy. In the words of one citizen (whose comments were passed on to Woolton by the postal censors), 'When he harangues us on the radio, as he does now and again, we fancy we are back at dame school. He speaks with the firm precision of a talented school marm and we all sit quiet and say, "Yes, teacher".'
> (Calder, *The People's War*, 1971, p.441)

Woolton was certainly 'media-conscious', and after his appointment there was an immediate speeding up and strengthening of Ministry of Food propaganda. By May 1941, his ministry was the second largest spender on advertising, investing well over half a million pounds on press and poster publicity alone. The major theme of leaflets issued to every household and thousands of 'Kitchen Front' exhibitions was the difference between the three main kinds of food groups – energy, protective and body-building – and by September 1941 roughly two-thirds of London housewives claimed to have a pretty good idea of what foods they should take to represent those groups. MoF literature advised on everything from how to make Christmas puddings without eggs, to preserving fruit without sugar, and improvising such 'delights' as pilchard layer loaf and corned beef rissoles. The results, if a jingle from *Housewife* for June 1941 are to be believed, were significant:

> Pat-a-loaf, pat-a-loaf
> Baker's man,
> Bake me some wheatmeal
> As fast as you can:
> It builds up my health
> And its taste is so good,
> I find that I *like*
> Eating just what I should.

Furthermore, from April 1940, an experimental series of nightly five-minute broadcasts after the 6 o'clock news, given by the popular comediennes 'Gert and Daisy' (Elsie and Doris Waters), convinced both the MoF and the BBC that there was an audience for regular radio talks dealing with domestic cooking problems and dispensing useful recipes. They were an undoubted success, though the time of broadcast proved unsuitable, not surprisingly, for many housewives. From June, it was placed in the more convenient slot of 8.15 every weekday morning. *The Kitchen Front* series 'on what to eat and how to cook it' was to command close on six million listeners by October 1940, and more when it included such contributors as 'the Radio Doctor', Dr Charles Hill. His 'vulgarity' while talking of Christmas Day over-indulgence or referring to 'the belly' and the like, did not exactly recommend him to everybody. But then, as Wilfred Pickles was to find when he started reading the news, the new 'stars' of wartime radio could not hope to please all listeners all the time, even in the changed circumstances of war. Besides, as we shall shortly hear in the case of Pickles, some listeners were plainly inclined to write in and complain on the merest pretext. In that regard, nothing had changed.

Wynford Vaughan Thomas's documentary interview with 'women at the benches' is, I am sure you will agree, similar in spirit to the scene you saw in Launder and Gilliat's 1943 feature film, *Millions Like Us*, where Eric Portman is introducing the latest band of 'mobile' women to the Castle Bromwich factory front. Portman, though, never patronizes the new recruits quite so much as Vaughan Thomas, with statements like 'the lady who is regaling that technical information so confidently was only a few months ago only interested in house-wives' work'. You might also have noticed that Vaughan Thomas's piece of reportage was being broadcast around the time when the MoI's Home Policy Committee was deliberating on the need to give more publicity to women's work in the factories and the services as the nation was fully mobilized. The BBC could act faster than the film-makers, of course, at putting into effect official policy on where the latest propaganda push should be directed. Janet Quigley, a talks producer who had pioneered *The Kitchen Front*, was moved over to work on programmes mainly for women in the forces by the autumn of 1941. She came up with *Women at War*, with a format that included 'brainteaser's trust' as well as the predictable spot for advice on 'beauty hints'. We shall hear more of the role allotted to women in BBC output when we come to the end of audio-cassette 4 and listen to extracts from a very popular woman on British wartime radio, Vera Lynn.

Nazi radio of the period seems to have given much less thought to the role of women in society and consigned them largely to the realms of traditional stereotyping. There were certainly many talks addressed directly to them which were broadcast on both the national network and regional stations. But the regional programmes appear to have confined themselves to the ubiquitous topics of 'purely feminine interest', including household advice, care of children, health, social conditions, and the perennial fashion tips, though these were mainly concerned with the remaking of worn clothes. *Here Starts Another Week*, presented by Charlotte Koehn-Behrens, was one national programme given over entirely to making the idea of factory work increasingly palatable to women, and it clearly proved popular, since it was moved to a peak listening slot. But it is perhaps indicative of the pervasive feeling in Nazi radio towards women that when an American radio reporter, Harry W. Flannery, approached Goebbels' office in August 1941 with the intention of interviewing 'a heroine of the home front', he could not convince them that such 'a human interest story would make good propaganda'. Flannery reports: 'Calls on the women's organisation, *Frauenschaft*, were met', furthermore, 'with the statement that it was the duty of the German people to be heroic and that they deserved no publicity for being so.' Similarly, in the Nazi cinema, women were required to accommodate a predominantly male ethos. 'As far as I am aware', David Welch states, 'no film made during the Third Reich features a heroine as the main protagonist.' 'Women were certainly prominent in a number of films', he continues, 'but they invariably took on submissive roles, generally acting as loyal comrades to their menfolk, rather than assuming heroic stature in their own right.' The result, he concludes, was that 'Actresses were encouraged to represent the Germanic ideal of genuine *Volkisch* womanhood as opposed to the painted and perfumed "degeneracy" of Hollywood.' The hugely popular and undeniably talented Zarah Leander (who in fact was Swedish) was star of the most successful German box office hit of wartime years, *Die Grosse Liebe*, but was not really required to demonstrate more than the song and dance skills that this melodrama demanded.

Women were very much to the fore, of course, in the British Ministry of Information short film of *Miss Grant Goes to the Door*, which you have just seen. Made by the feature film director, Brian Desmond Hurst, with screenplay and dialogue provided by Rodney Ackland and based upon a story by Thorold Dickinson and Donald Bull, the film was given a cinema release in August 1940 and put on the non-theatrical circuit (that is, it was shown by 16 mm mobile film units) in October 1940. It was meant to boost British morale by assuaging some of the home front's fears about invasion which were keenly and justifiably felt early in the summer of 1940. There was considerable emphasis, as you must have spotted, on the simple precautions people might take in order to thwart enemy infiltration, and the film was clearly intended to be instructional as well as reassuring and entertaining. Along with other films of a similar nature, though on a different theme – *Now You're Talking, Dangerous Comment, Albert's Savings, The Call for Arms, Food for Thought, Salvage With a Smile*, and *Miss Know-All* – it formed part of a series initiated by the MoI. As Sir Kenneth Clark put it during a radio broadcast in October 1940, the series was intended to 'help people to remember government messages by putting them in a dramatic form'. They were small-scale feature films which were often enjoyed, perhaps not surprisingly, more for their dramatic than their instructional content.

In the case of *Miss Grant Goes to the Door*, which proved especially popular among the first wave of MoI films, the organization monitoring the public reception of the films on behalf of the MoI, Mass-Observation, found that audiences liked the 'strong story'. By contrast, the instructional elements were unfavourably received, not least because of some improbable features. For example, success in dealing with live spies, so it was implied, lay in having a dead German parachutist conveniently to hand, with a revolver on him. The class base of the characters was also picked up – you may have noticed it in the distinctly middle-class flavour of the Grant household – with comments noting that Miss Grant lived in 'a big house' (a point also noted about *Miss Know-All* and other films, particularly the early 'Careless Talk' ones, where unfortunately the spy or gossiper causing untold if inadvertent damage was usually working class).

In the main, however, *Miss Grant Goes to the Door* was adjudged a success and was well liked. It was felt that the film registered with audiences in significant ways and that, for example, 'The sight of this untrained hand wielding the weapon, however ineffectively . . . was incidental propaganda for a "people's war"'. The film did show the people dealing resourcefully with the problems that confronted them. It at least advocated action, which was a good deal more than was advocated in some of the other MoI material related to the prospect of invasion. 'Stay put and do nothing' seemed to be the basic message emanating from the official leaflet of instructions, *If the Invader Comes*, which was issued to all households throughout the country in mid-June 1940. Alfred Duff Cooper, Minister of Information at the time, reported that the leaflet had 'a good reception' but acknowledged that it left people 'expecting further instructions' and guidance, not least about such essential matters as '(a) whether they, the civilians, are to fight, or (b) whether they might even take steps to protect themselves'. *Miss Grant Goes to the Door* suffered no such shortcomings. Far from it. The two sisters living alone in the country deal resourcefully in the main with the danger that threatens them.

This film did suffer, however, from the problem that beset much propaganda, especially film propaganda, namely that it was tied to and used in conjunction with particular campaigns. In these instances, of course, timing was of the essence. It was vital to get material out in time to be relevant; and doubtless the credibility of a film like *Miss Grant* was undermined slightly because of the time it took in production and before release. In fact, the film-makers worked quite speedily on this production. It was completed on 2 July 1940 and released on 5 August 1940. But in between, at the end of July, the Local Defence Volunteers referred to in the film had been renamed the Home Guard. Also, as Ian McLaine recounts, 'from mid-July onwards reports showed people passing from acceptance of the possibility of invasion through to a tendency to doubt its imminence and then, with the exception of people living near the eastern coast, to a stage late in August when expectation of invasion seemed to have almost receded' (*Ministry of Morale*, p.77). There was a sense of widespread relief with the passing of those dates that were popularly held to be of particular significance – 19 July, when it was thought the invasion would start, and 15 August, the date it was believed Hitler had chosen for his arrival in Britain. (Mass-Observation confirmed these peaks of expectation, as its various 'morale' reports indicate throughout July and August.)

Though also made for the MoI, *Britain Can Take It* was quite a different proposition to *Miss Grant Goes to the Door*, as I am sure you could tell from a reading of the script alone. (You may be familiar with the film, since it is shown often enough on television. In case you are not, it is my intention to include it in our programme of summer school films.) Directed by Harry Watt and Humphrey Jennings, with a commentary written and narrated by Quentin Reynolds, the London war correspondent for the US magazine *Collier's Weekly*, it was released to cinemas in October 1940 and put on the non-theatrical circuit in December 1940. It was made in two versions: a five-minute film for domestic consumption (the script for that runs to the asterisks in your documents reprint), and a longer version (with the complete commentary) for exhibition in the United States under the title of *London Can Take It* and with a running time of ten minutes. Its theme is expressed in the latter title, suggested by Reynolds, and its story is of London in the Blitz. The story is related in a deadpan and underplayed style, with the emphasis on a seemingly straightforward and factual narration of events. It is not dramatized at all, nor does it use actors; it was plainly intended as a piece of descriptive reportage and was meant to convey the impression, 'this is how it is in wartime London'.

'These are not Hollywood sound effects', Reynolds points out as he proceeds to show the devastation caused by 'the nightly siege of London'. Actuality is everything ('I am speaking from London'), and there is an insistence upon objectivity ('I am a neutral reporter'). It is a highly personalized account, but the message is one of quiet confidence and continued hope among the people ('London raises her head', 'London looks upward'), and there is repeated reference to the moulding of a new 'people's army' and to the high morale of the population despite its tribulations. The film was greeted with much critical acclaim in Britain – even the generally jaundiced *Documentary News Letter*, voice of the documentary film movement, reviewed it kindly in its issue for November 1940 – and it went on to enjoy considerable success with cinemagoers. As Mass-Observation assiduously reported to the MoI, this film 'received nothing but praise', and it topped their popularity poll of official films. Audiences felt it was 'factual, honest, and to many of them it was part of an actual experience they had gone through . . . People were delighted to see themselves recognised as fully involved in the war and not in any way being spoken down to.'

Britain Can Take It, then, was a popular success because it recognized and acknowledged the role of the population at large in the war effort. It should be said, though, that one or two of the other major cities across the country took it mildly amiss that London should have been chosen to represent Britain as a whole. The Co-operative Wholesale Film Company in Manchester, for instance, produced its own variation on the same theme, entitled proudly *Manchester Took It Too* (1941), which included an impressive array of footage showing the effects of the Blitz on that city during Christmas of 1940.

It was *Britain Can Take It*, of course, that Quentin Reynolds took with him to America to show on a lecture tour he was engaged to deliver there. The film was shown without any British credits, and only Reynolds' name appeared on the titles, as war correspondent for the American *Collier's*. Thereafter, it was booked by the prestigious Warner Brothers corporation for nationwide release in their cinemas. Once more, it proved to be immensely popular. The MoI was delighted and commissioned both Reynolds and Watt to do a follow-up, *Christmas Under Fire*, this time about London during the Christmas of 1940, and again for American as well as British distribution. In all, Quentin Reynolds wrote and narrated the commentary on three documentaries for the MoI, and appeared as himself in the 1942 Ealing feature film *The Big Blockade*. In addition, he penned a series of personal messages in the radio *Postscripts* series entitled 'Dear Dr . . .' (Goebbels) and 'Dear Mr Schickelgruber' (addressed to Hitler). Churchill was not very pleased when Reynolds persisted in trying to reinstate a censored reference to Rudolf Hess in one of his broadcasts, after Hess had landed in Britain on 11 May 1941. Churchill, like Hitler, had placed an embargo on mention of him. But for every one person against Reynolds' talks, Mass-Observation found, there were thirty in favour. Furthermore, along with Edward R. Murrow, Eric Sevareid, Vincent Sheean, Alastair Cooke, and a band of like-minded commentators, Quentin Reynolds proved an invaluable ally to Britain's cause in the USA. (I have included items 10–12 on audio-cassette 4 as examples of British radio propaganda directed specifically at audiences in the United States and broadcast over the North American Service. They are intended as a resource, but are well worth listening to since they bear out many of the points made already with regard to

Britain Can Take It. There is an Ed Murrow broadcast on London in the Blitz and broadcasts by Lord Lothian and Leslie Howard, which show how the BBC sought to promote Anglo-American relations.)

Listen to items 7–9 on audio-cassette 4; watch items 16 (*The Dawn Guard*) and 17 (extract from *Tyneside Story*) on video-cassette 2; and read document II.30 (the J. B. Priestley broadcasts of 5 June and 21 July 1940). Please note that document II.30(a) transcribes the first part of radio item 8, which was missing from the sound archive recording.

Exercise   There is a distinct difference in purpose, I would suggest, between, on the one hand, the Priestley talk on the 'Epic of Dunkirk' and the extract from Churchill's 'finest hour' speech, and, on the other, the remaining pieces of film and broadcast propaganda. What differences do you detect, and what would you say they were trying to achieve? ■

Specimen answer   The simple division I would make in the first instance is between plain inspirational propaganda, which tries to turn moments of undoubted national disaster into something approaching success, and propaganda with a larger ideological and idealistic purpose, which relates to wider sea changes in society brought about by the country's wartime experience generally.

Priestley's talk of 5 June 1940, his first in the *Postscripts* series, and Churchill's broadcast to the nation on 18 June 1940, both seek 'to snatch victory from the jaws of defeat' and turn the setbacks they refer to into reflections on the strength of the national character (very much along the lines of what the film *Britain Can Take It* was to do during the Blitz). They extol the virtues of the British people as a prelude to exhorting them to expend greater effort in continuance of the war, if the nation is to survive. The extract from Priestley's 'A New "English Journey"' (a radio follow-up to his 1934 book of the same title) and his *Postscript* of 21 July 1940, are more ruminative in character and require the people to deliberate on the reasons why the war is being fought, and to consider what sort of world they would like to see emerging at the end of it. For his part, Priestley believes there can be no going back to 'the old days'. The war has brought about social and economic changes in British society and the only thing to do is to capitalize on them with the aim of producing a new and better order. There is a good deal of homespun philosophizing – much more so, as you would expect, than is evident in Churchill's impressive and eloquent report on the state of affairs for this nation, given the imminent fall of France. But it is not so difficult to spot why Priestley also proved popular. His talks are powerfully persuasive, simply and succinctly expressed. They are evocative but have no recourse to party political rancour, though clearly they are arguing for change and 'no going back', which implicitly suggests no return to the Conservative rule of before the war (a point not lost on some people at the time who complained that his talks were decidedly 'leftish'). BBC listener research soon reported that Priestley was second to Churchill in size of audience: two out of every three adults on average listened to Churchill's broadcasts, one out of three to Priestley's. □

The two films you have just watched echo the same themes evident in Priestley's 'new world order' broadcasts. Roy Boulting's *The Dawn Guard* (released to cinemas in January 1941 and the non-theatrical circuit in March 1941) and Gilbert Gunn's *Tyneside Story* (given a non-theatrical release in January 1944 but not released to cinemas), harp upon the idea of war as 'the midwife of social progress'. Both vividly contrast 'the bad days' of the 1930s, with the potentially beneficial changes wrought by war, and argue that these should point the way to a better planned, more rational, fair-minded and equitable society in the future. In the former case, the overall effect is rather benign and beneficent, perhaps because of the idyllic rural imagery and the resort to the use of Bernard Miles and Percy Walsh as typical country yokels. In the latter, the effect is definitely hard-edged and sharper, doubtless because the film is brought to an abrupt and peremptory halt with the interjection of an actor, from the People's Theatre Company of Newcastle-upon-Tyne, who consciously disturbs any hint of complacency that might possibly have crept in, with his remarks: 'Aye, but wait a minute. Tyneside is busy enough today . . . but just remember what the yards looked like five years ago . . . Will it be the same again five years from now?'

Discussion   As you will be well aware by now, historians disagree about the question of whether World War II was a catalyst for change and about the extent to which it altered British society. As you saw earlier in this book, they continue to engage in a debate over how profound the changes were and how far the war was responsible for them. Some, like Henry Pelling (in *Britain and the Second World War*, 1970) and Angus Calder, contend that 'The effect of the war was not to sweep society on to a new course, but to hasten its progress along the old grooves' (Calder, *The People's War*, p.20). Arthur Marwick, of course, is one of the proponents, indeed an architect, of the view that war causes change, and has repeatedly outlined what he sees as the social consequences of the war for Britain.

Similarly, Paul Addison has charted the significance of the war in effecting political change. After the fall of France, and especially after the setback at Dunkirk, there was a distinct swing to what might loosely be called 'the left' in Britain. This tide of popular feeling was not necessarily of a political character, nor indeed was it always channelled along Labour Party or socialist lines, though clearly Labour was to be an immediate beneficiary in 1945. But it was 'directed against the Conservative Party' in so far as this represented, despite Chamberlain's departure and his replacement by Churchill, 'the so-called "Men of Munich", "the old gang", "Colonel Blimp" and similar diehard types' (Addison, *The Road to 1945*, 1975). It manifested itself, furthermore, in a feeling of revulsion against 'vested interests' and 'privilege', and in a general agreement that 'things are going to be different after the war'.

In addition to the movement in popular opinion, there was a change in thinking at the top. 'A massive new middle ground had arisen in politics', Addison continues, and a new political consensus evolved which was quite unlike the species of consensus that existed before the war, when Baldwin and MacDonald adopted 'safety first' policies and resolved 'to prevent anything unusual from happening'. 'The new consensus of the war years was positive and purposeful', and there was a convergence of opinion in favour of 'pragmatic' economic reform and social amelioration. Beveridge and Keynes inspired those 'socially concerned professional people' who lent their weight to the reform programme, and though little was actually achieved during the war in the way of new laws, except on family allowances and education, nevertheless much of the ground was prepared by the time the Labour Party came to power in 1945. (*The Road to 1945*, pp.14–15, 162–5, and 276–7.)

As you would expect, the evidence provided by the British media and sources such as the films and broadcasts you have just been examining, does not provide an easy or obvious answer to the overarching question of war and change, any more than does the evidence put forward by other historians in the debate. But it does bear eloquent witness, I am sure you will agree, to the fact that many people felt profound changes were afoot in society, born largely of the country's wartime experiences, and that these changes could prove beneficial. It also provides abundant evidence of the desire and commitment to build 'a better world' once the war had been won. It is clear that cinema and radio played a positive and purposeful role in their own right in generating adherence to the new-found consensus of the war years.

This did not happen overnight, of course. Films such as *Ships with Wings* and *The Demi-Paradise*, in 1941 and 1943 respectively, continued throughout the war to purvey the conventional image of gallant officers doing heroic deeds or to project the traditional image of the nation as a class-bound, hierarchically structured society (and proved very popular). But there was increasing emphasis on the idea of 'the people's war', in such films as *Britain Can Take It*, and the contribution made by 'ordinary' people in films like *The Foreman Went to France* (1942). Working-class figures were given a fuller and more rounded characterization, not least in *Millions Like Us*.

Furthermore, subjects were broached in the cinema, as on radio, that had been barely touched upon before. For instance, the director John Baxter could now contemplate making a film of Walter Greenwood's 1933 novel, *Love on the Dole*. This had not been possible in the 1930s, you will recall from my reference to the matter in Book III, Unit 19, because the British Board of Film Censors had informed would-be producers that they felt it could only show 'too much of the tragic and sordid side of poverty'. Significantly, no such objections were made in 1941, and John Baxter turned the novel into a serious and moving film. Its message for a Britain at war was enhanced by a postscript caption at the film's end, which was signed by A. V. Alexander, the Labour MP and First Lord of the Admiralty. It read: 'Our working men and women have responded magnificently to any and every call made upon them. Their reward must be a new Britain. Never again must the unemployed become forgotten men of peace.'

John Baxter's next film, *The Common Touch* (1941), also evoked the new consensus. This time, he began his film with a caption that proclaimed: 'This picture is dedicated to the humble people of our great cities whose courage and endurance have gained for us all the admiration and support of the free countries of the world.' Thereafter, Baxter treated audiences to a whimsical social fantasy in which a young toff experiences life in a doss-house as well as at the top of the firm he has just inherited. His adventures teach him a lot about human nature and the values of life. He leaves the doss-house 'better fitted to start on the work of rebuilding', and the film ends with an exchange of dialogue between two of the doss-house characters:

> TICH: All this talk about better things, homes and all that. Do you suppose they really mean it or will they forget?
> BEN: No, I think they really mean it this time, Tich.
> TICH: Blimey, it'll be like heaven on earth.
> BEN: And why not?

Such sentiments were neither uncommon nor incidental. For his part, Baxter reiterated them endlessly in his later films like *Let the People Sing* (1942, based upon

J. B. Priestley's novel of the same name which had actually started life as a BBC radio serial) and *The Shipbuilders* (1943, from George Blake's 1935 novel of the Clydeside during the depression). The sentiments were as much in evidence in the work of other film-makers – everything from Roy Boulting's short film *The Dawn Guard*, made for the MoI and which you have seen, to the Ealing Studios feature film of J. B. Priestley's allegorical play, *They Came to a City* (1944), which ends with the following exchange between Googie Withers and John Clements as they leave their 'ideal' city:

> ALICE: Goodbye, my lovely city. I don't know when I'll ever see you again.
>
> JOE: Now, Alice, take it easy kid.
>
> ALICE: I don't want to go. And it'll seem worse than ever when we get back.
>
> JOE: No, it won't. Because, to begin with, we'll remember. That's why we've got to go back – because we're the ones who've been, and seen it all . . . And then we'll hope. And keep on hoping. And every time we find a spark of hope and vision in anybody, we'll blow it into a blaze . . . They will tell us we can't change human nature. That's one of the oldest excuses in the world for doing nothing. And it isn't true. We've been changing human nature for thousands of years. But what you can't *change* in it, Alice – no, not with guns or whips or red-hot bars – is man's eternal desire and vision and hope of making this world a better place to live in. And wherever you go now – up and down and across the Seven Seas – from Poplar to Chunkink – you can see this desire and vision and hope, bigger and stronger than ever beginning to light up men's faces, giving a lift to their voices. Not every man, not every woman, wants to cry out for it, to work for it, to live for it and if necessary to die for it – but there's one here, one there, a few down this street, some more down that street – until you begin to see there are millions of us – yes, armies and armies of us – enough to build ten thousand new cities.
>
> ALICE: Like our city?
>
> JOE: Yes, like our city. Where men and women don't work for machines and money, but machines and money work for men and women – where greed and envy and hate have no place – where want and disease and fear have vanished for ever – where nobody carries a whip and nobody rattles a chain. Where men have at last stopped mumbling and gnawing and scratching in dark caves and have come out into the sunlight. And nobody can ever darken it for them again. They're out and free at last.
>
> *(They look back to the city)*
>
> I dreamt in a dream I saw a city invincible to the attacks of the whole earth, I dreamt that was the new city of Friends.
>
> ALICE: Come on, Joe, let's get going.
>
> (Priestley, *They Came to a City*, 1944, pp.64–5).

All these films were imbued with the same vision of a 'brave new world' arising from the ruins of the old, and of the war as a harbinger of social progress. It was a message that was especially suited to Britain's wartime circumstances. C. G. H. Ayres, who wrote the original story on which the screenplay of the film *The Common Touch* was based, expressed it simply but effectively in 1942 when discussing with the director, John Baxter, some ideas for their next project together: 'The political outlook for our type of stuff was never more promising'.

There was among these film-makers something of a 'mild revolution', to borrow producer Michael Balcon's phrase. Balcon described its nature in the following terms: 'We were middle-class people brought up with middle-class backgrounds and rather conventional educations. Though we were radical in our points of view, we did not want to tear down institutions . . . We were people of an immediate postwar generation, and we voted Labour for the first time after the war; this was our mild revolution.'

With hindsight, then, Balcon qualified the nature of the 'revolutionary' impulse which reportedly inspired him and others like him, and concluded that its 'radical' import was really quite 'mild'. It did not necessarily appear so during the war. Though many shared the feeling that change and reform ought to be an inevitable outcome of the harsh experiences of war, and though questions of post-war expectations and reconstruction were definitely on the agenda for public discussion as far as official bodies such as the MoI were concerned, these matters, in fact, were not always easily aired. Churchill, in particular, was of the opinion in January 1943 that 'Ministers should, in my view, be careful not to raise false hopes as was done last time by speeches about "Homes for Heroes", etc.'. 'The broad masses of people face the hardships of life undaunted but they are liable to get very angry if they feel they have been gulled or cheated', he continued, and 'It is for this reason of not wishing to deceive the people by false hopes and airy visions of Utopia and Eldorado that I have refrained so far from making promises about the future.' Churchill was adamant that winning the war was the priority, and he was opposed to anything which he felt might detract from that purpose. Thus, in one well-known instance, he badgered Brendan Bracken, the Minister of Information, to stop production of Michael Powell and Emeric Pressburger's mild critique, *The Life and Death of Colonel Blimp* (1943). Without ever having seen the film, he felt it could only serve to 'undermine the discipline of the army'. In the event, Bracken knew better and Churchill's efforts simply delayed the film's release at home and abroad.

Nor did talk of reconstruction pass unchallenged. When Priestley returned with a second series of *Postscripts* in January 1941, his tone was decidedly more aggressive and political over war aims. The listening figures for that second series were the highest ever. But the Conservative 1922 Committee protested about the 'socialist' tendencies in the talks and Priestley was forced off the airwaves for a while as far as Britain was concerned (though he continued broadcasting successfully on the North American Service and returned to domestic radio in 1943). Despite, furthermore, the unprecedented public acclaim which greeted publication of the Beveridge Report on 1 December 1942, that too was the cause of much dissatisfaction in cabinet circles. It was also included in Churchill's January 1943 ban on the ventilation of post-war topics by government speakers (except for overseas, where 'It was proudly broadcast through the world as an advertisement of our Democratic accomplishments and aims'). Arthur Marwick has already discussed the implications of the report with you in considerable detail. I want to deal with it along with the final items which make up my compilation of wartime broadcasts. They have been chosen to spotlight the changes in style and content of radio programming and the BBC's reaction to the conditions of wartime broadcasting generally, to highlight its strengths and its limitations. I have appended commentaries to help contextualize the individual broadcasts.

Listen to the remaining items of audio-cassette 4, extracts 13–18, and read document II.31 in *Documents 2* (transcript of the Dimbleby broadcast of 19 April

1945). Refer to the notes below before you listen to or read the appropriate item.

Item 13: 'War with Japan', Wilfred Pickles (1 p.m. News, 8 December 1941)

> The [news] readers up to September 1939 had performed in evening dress. This consorted with the fact that their voices, while pleasant, were all southern English and impeccably upper middle class. In mid-war, this convention was broken when a Yorkshire character actor named Wilfred Pickles was called south from the BBC's northern headquarters in Manchester to become a regular 'front line' newsreader. There was a press furore over the prospect of a reader who pronounced his 'A's' short in the northern manner. Excitement increased when he ended the midnight news by saying a special 'Good Neet' to all northerners. Though his voice was very popular (especially in the south), Pickles himself asked to return to Manchester. (Calder, *The People's War*, p.415)

Item 14: 'Operations against Pantelleria', Lt Cmdr Anthony Kimmins (22 June 1943)

> . . . it is all too easy to forget the astonishing wartime growth in the function of broadcasting. Such was the novelty of eyewitness descriptions of scenes of combat that there was angry criticism of a recording made at Dover in 1940, during the battle of Britain. Many people felt that an eyewitness's account of a dogfight overhead between RAF fighters and the Luftwaffe was not a proper thing to broadcast. The contention was that an incident in which men were losing their lives was being treated as if it were a cricket match or a horse-race.
>
> Public opinion had changed radically by 1943 . . . It would be ludicrous to suggest that there is any equivalent to direct experience of the hardships and hazards of battle. But at least broadcasting does help to diminish the gap between the combatant and the civilian – and not merely in the details of battle but also in their lesser items of song, of slang, of tone of speech, which are a not inconsiderable part of the measure of an army's exile from the homeland. If Caen and Arnhem seemed less remote psychologically than were Mons or the Somme thirty years earlier, it was largely because of the power of broadcasting to act as an immediate link between the battlefront and home. Every fireside could entertain the voices, the personalities, of men in action, of men stepping out momentarily from the smoke and confusion of battle to talk in those intimate terms of informality – as between two or three people – which are peculiarly the gift of radio. (Desmond Hawkins (ed.) *War Report*, 1985, p.21)

Items 15 and 16: 'Report on Social Insurance and Allied Services', Sir William Beveridge (2 December 1942) and 'The Story of a Thirty Years' Fight', Sir William Beveridge (28 December 1942)

> This short feature programme [item 16] was a potted biography made to celebrate the great man after his Report. Within two weeks of its publication (1 December 1942) a Gallup Poll found that 19 out of 20 people had heard of it, and 9 out of 10 believed its proposals should be adopted . . . At first the Ministry of Information intended to give the Report the widest possible publicity, but shortly afterwards that decision was reversed. From dawn on 1 December the BBC broadcast the details in 22 languages; it was yet another proof for the rest of the world, enemies

and allies alike, that democracy was still alive and flourishing in England if nowhere else in Europe. Beveridge gave a short talk about his proposals to the home audience on the next day [item 15]. But after that there was virtually nothing. The feature programme you hear is about the only thing, in the wake of the Report, to refer to it direct – and most of the programme is about Beveridge himself. There is very little reference to the social and political implications of the Report in the programme.

The government was taken aback by the enormous popular interest in, and support for, the Beveridge Report. Churchill did not want to arouse 'false hopes and airy visions of Utopia'. The cabinet sat on the Report, which was not discussed in the Commons until late February 1943. The official line was to welcome the proposals in principle, while declaring that no firm commitments could be made. (David Cardiff and Paddy Scannell, 'Radio in World War II', U203 *Popular Culture*, 'Broadcast Notes', The Open University, 1983)

Document II.31: transcript of Richard Dimbleby war report (19 April 1945)

Richard Dimbleby was the first British correspondent to reach a camp. He broadcast a report, 'The Cesspit Beneath', from Belsen, on 19 April 1945. Belsen, he wrote, was 'the first of these places to be opened up'. He had only gone to Belsen with the advance team of medical services to follow up a story of an outbreak of typhoid. But they expected nothing different from the many POW camps they had already been through. He described the horrific conditions that he saw and, like [Richard] Crossman, the surreal otherworldly nature of life in the camps, where apparently all order and all rules had broken down. Dimbleby emphasised the appalling shock: 'No one could have imagined a scene like this, no one even hinted at what I was to see.' He broke down five times while he was recording the broadcast. But when the recording was received at the BBC, he wrote, it was queried. The broadcast was delayed by over a day, 'and the BBC kept coming back to him to check the authenticity of the account'. Apparently the Corporation was anxious. 'When they heard it some people wondered if Dimbleby had gone off his head or something. I think it was only the fact that I'd been fairly reliable up to then that made them believe the story.' Dimbleby, who was to return to Belsen several times later, emphasised that he had no idea of the role of the camps and that he had been totally unprepared for what he saw. No briefing had dealt with it. . . .

Thus the dominant theme in eyewitness accounts of the opening of the camps was one of shock and unpreparedness. This was obviously an attempt to deal with the appalling things they saw. Almost unanimously the eyewitnesses claimed that they had not known what they were going to see. In the spring of 1945, when the full horror of the camps was revealed, the problem crystallised into one of why more was not known. . . .

Some people had knowledge, other people did not. Knowledge was not uniformly available. Some people believed what they knew. Others did not. Many perhaps could not. The disbelief was subtly structured. It was as if the most accurate and vivid accounts were often undercut by a refusal to focus on the consequences if the accounts were real. That information about what was happening to Jews was widely available and widely broadcast is clear. But its focus did not encourage campaigning or action. More was not done because, rightly or wrongly, it was felt that nothing could be done except win the war. The BBC might have taken independent action – but it saw the world with government eyes in the war. When the camps were opened, it seemed like the unveiling of an obscene evil, of which nothing had been known, yet one which proved a final, irrefutable justification for the anti-German war. Yet our conclusion must be, in some way, grimmer than the secret that was disclosed. It was a secret known by some, understood at least by some, but over which there was no political will to act. (Jean Seaton, 'Reporting atrocities: the BBC and the holocaust', in Jean Seaton and Ben Pimlott (eds) *The Media in British Politics*, 1987, pp.157 and 179)

Items 17 and 18: ITMA *(13 April 1944) and* Sincerely Yours *(8 March 1942)*

(a)   By 1945 the Corporation had apparently become less aloof. Programmes like *ITMA*, *Hi Gang* and *Workers' Playtime* introduced a more vigorous tradition of speech and humour to broadcasting, one that was closer to the music hall tradition than the well mannered 'variety' of pre-war programmes. They were part of a feeling that the British war, unlike that of the prudish Germans, was taken seriously, but never solemnly . . . Humour was part of the protective self-image with which the British faced air attacks and the possibility of invasion. It was an image that the BBC helped to create, and was determined to encourage. Harold Nicolson even broadcast talks on the subtle superiority of English humour to that of the status-conscious Germans.

There was, of course, another war which did not get much broadcasting time. This was one of apathy, and dingy making do rather than cheerful resilience. Life in shelters was not always a protracted East End party; it was squalid, with inadequate sanitary arrangements, little food and chaotic overcrowding. Novels of the period document the dreariness and austerity of life in England after several years of war, and newspapers campaigned against the pettymindedness of official regulations and bureaucracy. The BBC did not campaign for the public on any of these issues.

However, the Corporation succeeded in producing a dignified but humorous image of what kind of people the British were. It was not that the BBC 'came closer to the people'. Rather it represented them as a liberal, compassionate, reforming administrator might have seen them. Subsequently, it has been argued that there was a significant change in public mood during the war. The people became determined that there would be greater social justice after it. Certainly the war changed the BBC, and it changed public taste. (James Curran and Jean Seaton, *Power without Responsibility*, 1981, pp.189–90)

(b)   *Sincerely Yours* deplored, but popularity noted. (BBC Board of Governors, minutes, 4 December 1941, quoted in Asa Briggs, *The War of Words*, 1970, p.578)

Conclusion

What, then, at the end of our survey, can be said of the relationship between the people and their leaders in Germany and Britain respectively? And what do we learn about mass society during World War II?

First, to repeat a point made at the outset of this section, both sets of leaders were confronted with much the same problems – to mobilize their populations for the continual effort required in waging total war, and to maintain civilian and military morale at a level sufficient to help achieve a successful outcome. The elites in both countries, furthermore, set about that task with similar ideas on the power of propaganda as a significant force and basically the same views on the malleability of the masses in the face of sustained propaganda. Both, however, shared an essentially pessimistic vision of the likely effects on society of such new-found methods of destruction as mass bombing. How many of these assumptions remained intact by the end of the war?

Mass bombing did not result in a complete collapse in civilian morale in Germany or Britain, but it did not necessarily result in a wholesale stiffening of civilian morale, either. Clearly, the scale of personal loss and hardship suffered was the initial factor in determining how people reacted to bombing raids. Thereafter, however, the success of official propaganda in mitigating these effects depended on the extent to which individual sacrifice was recognized and merged into a sense of group unity with the feeling that all parts of the community were sharing the burden. This required of the propagandists, of course, a willingness to change their approach and to extend their horizons to accommodate somewhat different reactions than expected.

When the time came, Goebbels proved slow off the mark in acknowledging frankly that German cities endured any bombing at all, and he was unable to prevent Germans so afflicted from feeling resentment towards 'the good fortune of their countrymen who had not been bombed'. To compound his errors, Goebbels proceeded to indulge in exaggerated and early promises of a retaliatory response which only materialized in June 1944, when the first V1 long-distance missiles landed on London. If the German population's will to fight was strengthened during late 1942 and 1943, as there is reason to believe it was, it owed little to Goebbels' propaganda on the matter of Allied bombing and more to such factors as the increasing threat from Russia and the fear of bolshevization. (For a detailed study of these issues see Gerald Kirwin's articles, 'Allied bombing and Nazi domestic propaganda', in *European History Quarterly*, vol.15, no.3, July 1985, and 'Waiting for retaliation – a study in Nazi propaganda behaviour and German civilian morale', in *Journal of Contemporary History*, vol.16, 1981.)

Britain, of course, had to deal with the problem of bombing before Germany. As we have seen, its propagandists proved capable of revising their pre-war opinions about the people when actually suffering from the onslaught of aerial bombardment. They recognized their role, not least during the Blitz, as being 'fully involved in the war'. 'The British public as a whole shows a very high degree of common sense', observed Dr Stephen Taylor of the MoI's Home Intelligence Division. 'Given the relevant facts,' he concluded, 'they will listen to and accept explanations when they will not accept exhortations.' His comments seem sensible and straightforward enough, but they were a long way away from the disdainful and elitist view of the British people that obtained in the 'official' mind during the 1930s. The war had changed that.

Nazi propaganda definitely scored some notable successes. It was effective during the first phase of the war in painting Britain as the major obstacle to peace and order. 'Building on a store of traditional anti-British feeling,' Ian Kershaw has argued, 'enormous hostility to Britain was whipped up in the summer of 1940, though Goebbels realized that this was engendering a dangerous impatience and optimism about Germany's ability to steamroller Britain as it had done the rest of Europe, and the protracted build-up to the German offensive against Britain and the inability to force a victory again put strains on the confidence in German propaganda.' ('How effective was Nazi propaganda?', in D. Welch (ed.) *Nazi*

Propaganda, 1983, p.195) Clearly, a film like *Ohm Kruger* sought to capitalize on this store of anti-British feeling and consolidate it.

Yet again, as Kershaw has stated, German propaganda was effective 'in spreading the conviction that there was such a thing as a "Jewish Question"' (p.191). However, he does not believe the film we have seen, *Der Ewige Jude*, to be a key factor. The 'successes' on this front, he maintains, were mainly achieved before the onset of war; furthermore, 'despite an increasing rather than diminishing volume of anti-Jewish propaganda during the war, anti-Semitism was for most Germans now so abstract and so routine that there was apparently difficulty in keeping alive a real interest in the "Jewish Question"' (p.192). (You should remember, though, that David Welch feels differently about this matter. For him, the continual reinforcement that such films offered was significant.)

Kershaw is also less sure about the revised propaganda policy that Goebbels was compelled to adopt after the momentous German setback at Stalingrad. He states: 'Though the new "realism" as portrayed in Goebbels' "total war" speech in February 1943 and in related propaganda was in the short term effective, and though in the remaining period of the war there were still propaganda successes . . . the final two years were in general a period of decreasing propaganda effectiveness and culminating sense of failure' (p.198). Certainly, as all commentators agree, propaganda success was exceedingly difficult in those final two years of the war when the circumstances had turned so decidedly in favour of the Allies.

It may be, indeed, that Nazi propaganda had reached its peak by 1939. Fear of war was as pervasive in Germany by 1939 as elsewhere in Europe. Ironically, as Kershaw continues, 'an important feature of [Nazi] propaganda success lay not so much in its militarism as in its bolstering of the Hitler image in such a way that, perversely, the Führer appeared to act as a guarantor of peace, not a bringer of war' (p.187). Thus the onset of war was a test of the Hitler myth which the propaganda machine had helped to create, of the German people's genuine trust in their leader, and of the credibility of Nazi propaganda.

From the start of the war Hitler delivered immediate results, but that allowed Goebbels no respite – quite the contrary in fact. 'It could also be argued', suggests Richard Overy, 'that the easy victories of the early years of war created an unfortunate psychological climate.' He elaborates further: 'In the summer of 1940 and again in October 1941 the popular feeling was that the war was over, and all the propaganda effort before 1939 directed at preparing the population for sacrifices and privation seemed curiously inappropriate' ('Mobilization for total war in Germany 1939–1941', *English Historical Review*, vol.ciii, no.408, July 1988, p.635.) What price the propagandist's job when it is popularly thought that victory has been won?

Perhaps it is no surprise that Ian Kershaw is prompted to the following conclusion:

> The anxieties of war made Germany keener than ever for reliable information. Yet the 'closed' and tightly-controlled information provided by the propaganda agencies gave rise in such circumstances – to a far greater extent than in wartime Britain – to the construction of a frequently powerful counter opinion which contributed significantly to the growing general scepticism about the reliability of 'official' information. The part played by rumour – often started by foreign broadcasts which, despite draconian penalties, found ready listeners – in forming resilient counter

opinion and prompting scepticism about the 'official' version, was extraordinary. And stories told by eyewitnesses – soldiers home on leave or bombed out evacuees – often conflicted directly with optimistic press reports and were listened to eagerly. The veracity of German propaganda was in these and other ways increasingly called into question, and general confidence in official information gradually undermined. Of course, there were certainly phases of propaganda success and themes which were undoubtedly highly effective, but the general picture of wartime propaganda which can be gleaned from sources such as press directives and especially SD reports is one of growing and eventually almost total propaganda failure long before the end of the war. The more propaganda seemed to conflict with reality, the more discredited it became. The process began even in the 'triumphant' phase of the war, before the invasion of the USSR. (Kershaw, 'How effective was Nazi propaganda?', pp.194–5)

Kershaw, you will note, uses the word 'closed' to describe the German context. It is a word I used myself at the outset of this unit to contrast totalitarian Germany with 'open' liberal democratic Britain. Do the terms really have any meaning in trying to distinguish between one variant of mass society and another when engaged in total war? What also of the suggested divide between 'revolutionary' Germany and 'conservative' Britain? If the descriptions are relevant for the onset of the war, how might they be applied by its end?

I think by now you must have enough sources and arguments at your disposal to answer questions like those for yourself. Just in case you feel otherwise, I shall direct you to the one remaining document for these units and the last two pieces of film. Document II.32 in *Documents 2* is the transcript of a newsreel extract covering Goebbels' 'total war' speech of 18 February 1943. Ian Kershaw referred to it earlier as marking a point of departure in Goebbels' propaganda approach with the adoption of a new found 'realism'. You should really be watching the film of this speech, and my apologies for the fact that you are not. Ironically, though, the printed extract fulfils my purpose. Notice the well orchestrated nature of the proceedings. The audience of party members had been rehearsed beforehand and knew exactly what was expected. It shows in the exhortatory question-and-answer sequence which elicits the appropriate amount of 'spontaneous' consent for Goebbels' message. Little had changed, in fact, from the propaganda techniques used years earlier in *Triumph of the Will*, and, as far as we can judge, the relationship between the leadership and the led had changed little. One was still exhorting the other and urging greater sacrifice.

Contrast that approach with the one adopted in the second story of item 18 on video-cassette 2. Here we see Field Marshal Montgomery talking to factory workers. Again, you will doubtless note, there is the same sense of the proceedings being well orchestrated, with the appropriate amount of careful editing to convey a feeling of 'spontaneous' rapport between 'Monty' and everyday folk. Despite the editing, however, some things cannot be hidden. Notice the distinctly autocratic air and the patriarchal tone. Monty and the workers ('and women too') were one 'big happy family', yet they remained classes apart. But it is surely not insignificant that Monty was appearing on the factory front. Furthermore, there is little exhortation, just explanation (however limited in scope). I wonder if, like myself, you feel that despite the obvious manipulation this newsreel does still convey a sense of genuine agreement and unity? Is this a sign of change between the leaders and the led in Britain, do you think, resulting from the conditions of war? The purpose of item 19, I think, should be obvious.

Now read document II.32 and watch items 18 and 19 on video-cassette 2.

Selected bibliography (note: works cited in the text are listed in the references)

Balfour, M. (1979) *Propaganda in War 1939–1945. Organisations, Policies and Publics in Britain and Germany*, London, Routledge and Kegan Paul.

Calder, A. and Sheridan, D. (1984) *Speak for Yourself: A Mass-Observation Anthology 1937–1949*, London, Oxford University Press.

Cardiff, D. and Scannell, P. (1981) 'Radio in World War II', Unit 8 of U203 *Popular Culture*, Milton Keynes, The Open University.

Ehrlich, E. (1985) *Cinema of Paradox: French Filmmaking under the German Occupation*, New York, Columbia University Press, 1987.

Kershaw, I. (1987) *The 'Hitler Myth'. Image and Reality in the Third Reich*, Oxford, Clarendon Press.

Kris, E. and Speir, H. (1944) *German Radio Propaganda*, London, Oxford University Press.

Landy, M. (1986) *Fascism in Film: The Italian Commercial Cinema, 1931–1943*, Princeton, NJ, Princeton University Press.

Leiser, E. (1968) *Nazi Cinema*, London, Secker and Warburg.

Priestley, J. B. (1967) *All England Listened. The Wartime Broadcasts*, intro. by Eric Sevareid, New York, Chilmark Press.

Pronay, N. and Thorpe, F. with Coultass, C. (1980) *British Official Films in the Second World War: A Descriptive Catalogue*, Oxford, Clio Press.

Richards, J. and Sheridan, D. (eds) (1987) *Mass-Observation at the Movies*, London, Routledge and Kegan Paul.

Short, K. R. M. (ed.) (1983) *Film and Radio Propaganda in World War II*, London, Croom Helm.

Short, K. R. M. and Dolezel, S. (eds) (1988) *Hitler's Fall: The Newsreel Witness*, London, Croom Helm.

Taylor, P. M. (ed.) (1988) *Britain and the Cinema in the Second World War*, London, Macmillan.

Welch, D. (ed.) (1983) *Nazi Propaganda. The Power and the Limitations*, London, Croom Helm.

Zeman, Z. A. B. (1973) *Nazi Propaganda*, 2nd edn, London, Oxford University Press.

Selected filmography

Feature films:

'The Alexander Korda Classic Film Library' (Central Video)

The Lion Has Wings (1939, Michael Powell, Brian Desmond Hurst and Adrian Brunel)

Newsreel:

'Music, Memories and Milestones' (Visnews Video): *Volume 2: The 1940s*

References

Addison, P. (1975) *The Road to 1945: British Politics and the Second World War*, London, Cape.

Aldgate, A. and Richards, J. (1986) *Britain Can Take It. The British Cinema in the Second World War*, Oxford, Blackwell.

Baker, G. W. and Chapman, T. E. (1962) *Man and Society in Disaster*, London, Basic Books.

Barnett, C. (1986) *The Audit of War. The Illusions and Reality of Britain as a Great Nation*, London, Macmillan.

Bartlett, F. C. (1942) *Political Propaganda*, Cambridge University Press.

Bédarida, F. (1988) 'World War II and social change in France', in A. Marwick (ed.) *Total War and Social Change*, London, Macmillan.

Bielenberg, C. (1968) *The Past is Myself*, London, Chatto and Windus.

Briggs, A. (1970) *The History of Broadcasting in the United Kingdom*, vol.3, *The War of Words*, London, Oxford University Press.

Calder, A. (1971) *The People's War: Britain 1939–1945*, London, Granada.

Cardiff, D. and Scannell, P. (1983) 'Radio in World War II', U203 *Popular Culture*, Broadcast Notes, Milton Keynes, The Open University.

Carr, W. (1969) *A History of Germany 1815–1945*, 3rd edn 1987, London, E. J. Arnold.

Clark, M. (1985) *Modern Italy 1871–1982*, London, Longman.

Crosby, T. L. (1986) *The Impact of Civilian Evacuation in the Second World War*, London, Croom Helm.

Curran, J. and Seaton, J. (1981) *Power without Responsibility: The Press Broadcasting in Britain*, London, Fontana.

Dahrendorf, R. (1969) *Society and Democracy in Germany*, New York and London, Doubleday.

Davies, N. (1981) *God's Playground: A History of Poland*, vol.2, *1795 to the Present Day*, London, Oxford University Press.

Dockrill, M. (1988) *The Cold War 1945–63*, London, Macmillan.

Dukes, P. (1988) 'The social consequences of World War II for the USSR', in A. Marwick (ed.) *Total War and Social Change*, London, Macmillan.

Ellwood, D. (1985) *Italy 1943–45*, Leicester University Press.

Fitzgibbon, C. (1957) *The Blitz*, London, Wingate.

Grunberger, R. (1971) *A Social History of the Third Reich*, London, Weidenfeld and Nicolson.

Harris, F. (1983) *Encounters with Darkness: French and German Writers on World War II*, New York, Oxford University Press.

Hawkins, D. (ed.) (1985) *War Report. D-Day to VE-Day*, London, Ariel Books.

Hockerts, H. G. (1981) 'German post-war social policies against the background of the Beveridge plan', in W. Mommsen (ed.) *The Emergence of the Welfare State in Britain and Germany 1850–1950*, London, Croom Helm on behalf of the German Historical Institute.

Horne, A. (1988) *Macmillan*, 2 vols, London, Macmillan.

Howard, M. (1976) 'Total war in the twentieth century: participation and consensus in the Second World War', in B. Bond and I. Roy (eds) *War and Society. A Yearbook of Military History*, London.

Iklé, F. C. (1958) *The Social Impact of Bomb Destruction*, Nottingham, W. S. Hall.

Johnson, P. (1983) *A History of the Modern World*, London, Weidenfeld and Nicolson.

Keenan, E. L. (1986) 'Muscovite political folkways', *The Russian Review*, no.45.

Kennedy, P. (1988) *The Rise and Fall of the Great Powers*, London, Unwin Hyman.

Kershaw, I. (1983) 'How effective was Nazi propaganda?', in D. Welch (ed.) *Nazi Propaganda. The Power and the Limitations*, London, Croom Helm.

Kirwin, G. (1981) 'Waiting for retaliation – a study in Nazi propaganda behaviour and German civilian morale', *Journal of Contemporary History*, vol.16.

Kirwin, G. (1985) 'Allied bombing and Nazi domestic propaganda', *European History Quarterly*, vol.15, no.3, July.

Klein, J. (1965) *Samples from English Cultures*, London, Routledge and Kegan Paul.

Kosinski, L. (1970) *The Population of Europe: A Geographical Perspective*, London, Longman.

Laqueur, W. (1972) *Europe since Hitler. The Rebirth of Europe*, revised edn, Harmondsworth, Penguin.

Larkin, M. (1988) *France since the Popular Front: Government and the People 1936–86*, London, Oxford University Press.

Linz, S. J. (1985) *The Impact of World War II on the Soviet Union*, Totowa, NJ, Rowman and Allanheld.

Loth, W. (1988) *The Division of the World 1941–55*, trans. C. Krojzlova, London, Routledge and Kegan Paul.

McLaine, I. (1979) *Ministry of Morale. Home Front Morale and the Ministry of Information in World War II*, London, Allen and Unwin.

Marwick, A. (1967) 'The Labour Party and the welfare state in Britain, 1900–1948', *American Historical Review*, vol.73, no.2, December.

Marwick, A. (1974) *War and Social Change in the Twentieth Century*, London, Macmillan.

Marwick, A. (1980) *Class: Image and Reality in Britain, France and the USA since 1930*, London, Collins.

Marwick, A. (1988) *Total War and Social Change*, London, Macmillan.

Mason, T. (1971) 'Some origins of the Second World War', in E. M. Robertson (ed.) *The Origins of the Second World War*, London, Macmillan.

Mayne, R. (1970) *The Recovery of Europe. From Devastation to Unity*, London, Harper and Row.

Michel, H. and Mirkine-Guetzovitch, B. (1954) *Les idées politiques et sociales de la Résistance*, Paris.

Milward, A. (1977) *War, Economy and Society, 1939–45*, London, Allen Lane.

Morgan, K. (1984) *Labour in Power 1945–51*, London, Oxford University Press.

Nicolson, H. (1967) *Diaries and Letters 1939–45*, ed. Nigel Nicolson, London, Collins.

Nish, I. (1977) *Japanese Foreign Policy 1869–1942*, London, Routledge and Kegan Paul.

Nove, A. (1972) *An Economic History of the USSR*, Harmondsworth, Penguin.

Overy, R. (1988) 'Mobilization for total war in Germany, 1939–41', *English Historical Review*, vol. ciii, no. 408, July.

Pelling, H. (1970) *Britain and the Second World War*, London, Collins.

Priestley, J. B. (1944) *They Came to a City*, London, Samuel French.

Rhode, G. (1973) 'The Protectorate of Bohemia and Moravia 1939–45', in V. S. Mamatey and R. Luza (eds) *A History of the Czechoslovak Republic 1918–1948*, Princeton NJ, Princeton University Press.

Rioux, J-P. (1987) *The Fourth Republic 1944–58*, trans. G. Rogers, Cambridge University Press.

Sadoul, G. (1962) *Le cinéma français*, Paris, Flammarion.

Seaton, J. (1987) 'Reporting atrocities: the BBC and the holocaust', in J. Seaton and B. Pimlott (eds) *The Media in British Politics*, Aldershot, Gower.

Smith, H. L. (ed.) (1986) *War and Social Change: British Society in the Second World War*, Manchester University Press.

Tannenbaum, E. R. (1972) *The Fascist Experience: Italian Society and Culture 1922–1945*, New York, Basic Books.

Thomas, H. (1986) *Armed Truce: Beginnings of the Cold War 1945–46*, London, Hamish Hamilton.

Walter, G. (1963) *Histoire des paysans de France*, Paris, Flammarion.

Welch, D. (1983) *Propaganda and the German Cinema 1933–1945*, Oxford, Clarendon Press.

Welch, D. (1987) 'Propaganda and indoctrination in the Third Reich: success or failure?', *European History Quarterly*, vol.17, no.4, October.

Werth, A. (1964) *Russia at War, 1941–45*, London, Barrie and Rockliff.

UNIT 26 EUROPE DIVIDED

Sections 1, 2, 6 and 7 by Bill Purdue; sections 3, 4 and 5 by Clive Emsley

Open University students will need to refer to:

Documents 2: 1925–1959, eds Arthur Marwick and Wendy Simpson, Open University Press, 1990

Maps Booklet

INTRODUCTION

This unit looks at the division of Europe in the aftermath of World War II. Its aims are to help you to develop an understanding of:

1   the way in which political divisions were made and evolved in post-war Europe; and

2   the relative importance of ideology, contingency and pragmatism in this division.

The unit has seven sections. Sections 1, 2, 6 and 7 are written by Bill Purdue, and sections 3, 4 and 5 are by Clive Emsley.

1 YALTA AND THE SHAPE OF THINGS TO COME

General Jaruzelski, in the aftermath of his temporarily successful crushing of the Solidarity movement in Poland in 1981, argued that:

> Poland is being regarded as a tool, as a lever for putting pressure on the Soviet Union, on the socialist community . . . It has been allotted the role of a detonator under the edifice of the peace founded on agreements signed in Yalta and Potsdam which cannot be separated from each other. (Quoted in Jacques Rupnik, *The Other Europe*, 1988, p.64)

General Jaruzelski's purpose in linking Yalta, an agreement widely detested in Poland, with Potsdam, the Protocol of which contains Poland's best documentary claim to its present western frontiers, was plain. His comments also draw our attention to the view of Yalta and Potsdam as the basis for the post-war division of Europe (almost the equivalent of Versailles in relation to inter-war Europe) and to the importance of the dispensations for Poland, especially those made at Yalta: Poland was the most intractable problem between the Western Allies and the Soviet Union, and Poland's fate, sealed at Yalta, set the pattern for the subsequent fate of East Central Europe as a whole.

For a brief period in 1939 Neville Chamberlain had succumbed to the illusion that East Central Europe was a British sphere of influence. In so doing and in handing out guarantees to Poland and Romania, he had abandoned his policy of appeasement and had paved the way for the Hitler-Stalin pact and the Second World War. By 1945 the long-term consequences of that illusion were evident: East Central Europe was a Soviet sphere of influence and Poland was to be abandoned to one of the two powers that had partitioned the country in 1939. The Poles, as Adam Zamoyski (*The Polish War*, 1987, p.371) has written, were 'the nation who really lost the Second World War'.

When the leaders of the three principal Allied powers met at Yalta in the Crimea in February 1945, the war in Europe was as good as won. Britain, the Soviet Union and the United States had embarked on war with Germany at different times and under very different circumstances and, as we saw in Units 22–25, their views on a post-war settlement and on the structure of post-war

Europe were by no means harmonious. However, Yalta maintained the façade of harmony, largely because it combined real concessions by Britain and the USA *on behalf of* Poland (and an agreement on Germany which provided for four allied zones of occupation, but little else) with more lofty innovations and sentiments – the inauguration of the United Nations, foreshadowed at the 1944 Dumbarton Oaks conference, and the Declaration on Liberated Europe which bore witness to a verbal adherence to democracy and self-determination. It can be argued that the real problem with Yalta was that the high-flown sentiments of the Declaration on Liberated Europe obfuscated, while they contradicted, the 'realism' of the provisions for Poland. Yalta was thus an agreement which not only General Jaruzelski but also the Soviet Union and even the United States can claim was a sound agreement – if only its provisions, properly interpreted, had been upheld.

Exercise   Read again article 5 of document II.7 in *Documents 2*, the Declaration on Liberated Europe.

1   Can you find any contradictions or loopholes in this article which might enable the power actually in control of a liberated country to evade its apparent intentions?

2   What were its essential weaknesses? ∎

Specimen answer   1   I suppose a purist might wonder whether destroying the last vestiges of Nazism and Fascism and the holding of totally free elections might not have been incompatible. What if electors wanted to vote fascist? But in the circumstances of 1945 few would have thought it permissible to allow fascist parties the right to exist. Yet parties that were not fascist could be so defined in order to justify their banning: thus the National Democracy, Poland's largest pre-war party, was banned under a very broadly defined anti-fascist policy, as were the largest pre-war Czechoslovakian parties, the Agrarian Party (Czech) and the People's Party (Slovak). The formation of interim governments 'broadly representative of all democratic elements' left plenty of room for subjective or self-interested interpretations: what was 'democratic' and who were 'broadly representative'?

2   The essential weakness was that this was simply one of those 'solemn and binding declarations' (the work of that wise old fool 'Solomon Binding') that bind no one because they can't be enforced and on whose meaning everyone disagrees. The 'Allies' were not in control of the liberated countries: America and Britain were in control of some, and the Soviet Union was in control of others. □

At Yalta the two Western powers not only agreed to changes in Poland's frontiers that ran directly counter to the Atlantic Charter and, in Britain's case, to a Foreign Office Note of July 1941 on the non-recognition of any territorial changes in Poland since August 1939; by accepting Stalin's proposal that the communist-controlled Lublin Committee should become the basis of Poland's future government, they also repudiated the government in exile for which Britain had gone to war. Yalta was indeed Churchill's Munich. Yet Norman Davies is almost certainly correct in saying that, 'At Yalta and Potsdam, there was no way that Churchill or Roosevelt, *by diplomatic means*, could have deflected Stalin from his chosen solution' (*God's Playground. A History of Poland*, 1981, p.15). British and American public opinion, nurtured on a wartime propaganda diet of amity with the Soviet Union, would have taken much persuading that any other than 'diplomatic means' should be employed. Yet that same public opinion would have been aghast at a frank exposition of the reality that Poland and East Central Europe were to be placed under Soviet hegemony whatever their own wishes. So, as Davies goes on to argue, 'matters were not decided at the conference table, but by the situation on the ground and by the men who held the reins of political power'.

To put Yalta into context we need to return to and to continue our discussion from section 1 of Units 22–25 of the war aims of the Allied powers, their hopes and fears for the post-war world, and the interaction between military and diplomatic strategy.

Exercise   What do you consider were the main aims of each of the principal Allied powers? How did they align their diplomatic and military strategies to further their ambitions for the post-war world? ■

Specimen answer   *The Soviet Union*
Debate over the Soviet Union's aims tends to be dominated by the question of whether Soviet policy was based on an overarching desire to further world communism or a traditional Russian perception of national self-interest. The interests of both, however, could be interpreted as pointing towards security for the Soviet Union to be achieved by a domination of East Central Europe, with the bounds of that domination set as far west as circumstances and opportunity made available. As the war drew to its close, the success of the Soviet forces made circumstances more favourable and opportunities greater. Whatever long-term and far-reaching plans Stalin had for the spread of communism outside the immediate western front zone, there can be no doubt that that zone was his first priority and that he was prepared to be pragmatic over spheres of influence, as the 'Percentage Agreement' with Churchill shows. The Soviets closely integrated diplomatic and military strategy, being well aware that whose army occupied which territory would be of crucial importance at the end of the war. Thus they were prepared to subordinate military advantage to long-term political aims, as with the decision to allow the Germans to crush the Warsaw uprising.

The United States
America had no territorial ambitions in Europe, disapproved of plans for the allocation of territory after the war, and disliked the idea of spheres of influence. The military strategy of the United States was just that – a military strategy unaffected by diplomatic considerations or worries about where its armies might be positioned when Germany surrendered. Like Woodrow Wilson before him, Roosevelt placed great faith in the idea of a post-war international organization (the United Nations) and in the appeal and influence of ideas of democracy and self-determination, while he looked askance at what he saw as the old-fashioned and corrupt power politics of his allies.

Great Britain
Britain was attempting to play realistic politics with a weak hand. Its aims were to safeguard the Empire and to achieve as favourable a balance of power in Europe as possible. To this latter end Churchill had supported plans for an advance from Italy into Central Europe and urged that the British and American armies attempt to reach Berlin before the Russians. The 'Percentage Agreement' was Churchill's attempt at damage limitation. □

All the above is basically true, but is it the whole truth? Did the United States' lack of concern for spheres of influence, and its apparent refusal to adopt Clausewitz's dictum of war as the continuance of diplomacy by other means, in fact disguise ambitions so far-reaching that they made the territorial boundaries and the political complexities of European states seem unimportant? Was the USA seeking to use its military and economic might, not to make short-term gains in East Central Europe but to impose a *'Pax Americana'* upon the world? The thesis can be put in either the Machiavellian or missionary modes. The Machiavellian version, put forward not surprisingly by Soviet historians and by a revisionist school of Americans, sees a United States reaching towards the peak of its economic and military strength and determined to extend its power throughout the world. As the end of the war would inevitably bring with it a crisis of overproduction, the USA sought to turn the whole world into a free market that it could dominate and in which it could find new markets and investment opportunities. The missionary version sees a conjunction between traditional American values – liberty, democracy, constitutionalism – on the one hand and the United States' new-found military and economic power on the other. Thus, as Michael Dockrill has argued, 'Before 1941 the United States did not have the power to project her ideology beyond the shores of the continent (except in Latin America which the United States had long claimed as her special sphere of interest)' (*The Cold War 1945–1963*, 1988, p.4). By 1945 the USA felt it had that power.

It could well be argued that, even had American politicians possessed no strong views on the shape of the post-war world, on its political or economic structure, the enormously favourable economic and strategic position would have ineluctably led it to become the actively dominant world power. Paul Kennedy, in his study of *The Rise and Fall of the Great Powers*, has seen the USA as to some extent in thrall to its power and the position in which the world-wide success in war had placed it: 'Like the British after 1815, the Americans in their turn found their informal influence in various lands hardening into something more formal – and more entangling; like the British too, they found 'new frontiers of insecurity' wherever they wanted to draw the line' (p.359).

At the time of the Yalta Agreement, the USA was unaware of the consequences of its new-found power and the degree to which the implementation of its vaguely formulated plans for a world economic and political order would involve it in a continuous and active, political and military involvement overseas. Nor did the Americans realize that they would have to adopt many of the traditional stratagems of the other great powers they saw as morally inferior. United States foreign policy sought a post-war world much like that envisaged by Woodrow Wilson in 1918 – a community of self-governing nations existing on the basis of self-determination within an international constitutional framework. At the same time its political liberation was to be accompanied by an economic liberation, at once self-serving and idealistic, in which free convertibility of currencies and open competition would open up overseas markets to American goods and capital. Yet the illusion persisted that these goals might be achieved without great opposition, armies overseas, alliance commitments or the embracing of the 'corrupt' methods and the 'old' diplomacy used by the great powers of the past.

Thus, in pursuit of great goals the USA felt it could remain aloof from the undignified jostling for position in the post-war world that marked Soviet and British policy. Where armies met, questions of frontiers and the political complexion of regimes in East Central Europe were of minor importance because the post-war world would exist within an international, democratic and liberal economic structure. Such an inclination was reinforced by the determination both to bring about Woodrow Wilson's aims and avoid his fate: the aims must be achieved without embarrassing commitments.

The result of this policy was that the United States denied itself or failed to use the weapons and strategies that might have furthered its aims and improved its post-war position. A fundamental misreading of the nature of Stalin and the Soviet Union led Roosevelt to believe that the Soviet Union would not stand clear of an essentially liberal capitalist post-war system. American policy therefore failed to subordinate military to diplomatic considerations. It also failed to use economic loans to gain influence with the USSR, and US-Soviet discussions on new loans to replace lend-lease came to nothing. Nor were US policy-makers prepared to countenance the notion of spheres of influence.

The uncertainty and ambivalence of the Yalta Agreement, uplifting in its Declaration on Liberated Europe, cynical in its treatment of Poland, and vague as to the future of Germany, thus reflected the uncertainties and ambivalences of US foreign policy. 1947 saw the USA utilize some of the weaponry it could have employed at Yalta but in a far less favourable context.

One can downgrade the importance of the Yalta Agreement on two counts. First, what really mattered was the absence of either clear or united strategic thinking on the part of the Western Allies during 1941 and 1943 when things were still in a state of flux (Tehran had first revealed the likelihood of the Soviet Union becoming the dominant power in East Central Europe). Second, the significant point was what Yalta did *not* do, namely come to detailed agreements for tripartite control of all occupied territories. Yet much can be traced to Yalta. The decisions on Poland convinced Stalin that he had a free hand in East Central Europe, and he was not slow to act on this: immediately afterwards he sent Vishinsky to Romania with an ultimatum to King Michael to instal a communist-controlled government, and when a Polish delegation representing the Home Army resistance went to Moscow it was arrested on arrival. The lack of a detailed agreement for Allied government of Germany did much to ensure that all zones were treated differently and that distinctions between Western and Soviet zones of occupation foreshadowed the division of Germany.

Yalta, which attempted a temporary resolution of inter-Allied differences, can thus in many ways be seen as the position from which the 'Cold War' and the division of Europe developed. The period 1945–47 saw a progressive hardening of the divide between East and West as the Soviet Union tightened its grip on East Central Europe, the delineations of the future West and East Germany appeared, Western and Southern Europe were securely bound to the liberal capitalist world, and the propaganda war between the Soviet Union and its erstwhile allies increased in volume and bitterness.

Historians, as is both customary and inevitable, have disagreed about their interpretations of this period and the reasons for the Cold War in accordance with their nationalities and, where and when it was possible for them to express them, their political or ideological positions.

The main theories may be summarized as follows:

1   The Soviet Union, with its Marxist ideology which insisted on world-wide revolution and the victory of international communism, was entirely to blame for the division of Europe and the Cold War.

2   The fundamental hostility of capitalism and particularly American capitalism to socialism and the Soviet Union was to blame. The Soviet Union's policies were primarily defensive.

3   Ideology played little part, save as justification for policies that were intended to further the interests of the great powers and especially of the two super-powers.

Such theories do not, of course, cover the entire range of possibilities, nor are they or parts of them incapable of permutation. Thus it is possible to argue that the Soviet Union's policies were the main cause of the division of Europe, but that their motivation was more national than ideological. Or it could be argued that the failure of the United States to understand and allow for Soviet insecurity was a major factor in the hardening of attitudes, but that lack of realism rather than liberal capitalist ideology was the main reason for this.

A more empirical approach has tended to see the Cold War as a product of miscalculation. However, as Dockrill has written: 'in the last analysis Western writers see the Soviet Union as the prime motivator: her suspicions and mistrust of the West condemned the world to a bipolar struggle for power while the United States was criticised for over-reacting to Soviet activities' (*The Cold War*, p.4).

2   *THE ROLE OF IDEOLOGY*

Do the causes of the division of Europe and the Cold War lie primarily and inescapably in ideology, in the clash between liberal capitalism and Marxist socialism? Or are they more accurately to be located in a conflict between great powers with opposed geopolitical ambitions who happened also to have conflict-ing political ideologies? It is often difficult to see whether ideology was the servant or master of the policies of states.

This is particularly so in respect of the Soviet Union, in whose foreign policy aims so many historians have detected a continuity with Tsarist policy: the desire to regain for the state territory lost at the end of World War I; the drive for hegemony in East Central Europe with its overtones of Pan-Slavism; the push into Manchuria in 1945 recalling the eastward expansion of the Russian Empire; the attempt to detach the province of Azerbaijan from Iran, which similarly seemed a continuance of the long Russian advance down the shores of the Caspian Sea; and Stalin's demands at Potsdam for a base on the Dardanelles (control of the Straits had been a major aim of nineteenth-century Russian foreign policy). A Red Tsar seemed to want much the same things as his White predecessors. Yet if Soviet policy-makers were convinced that a future world communism depended on the Soviet Union and that the revolutionary struggle for socialism was synonymous with the security and advance of Soviet power, the ideology and the traditional great power aims of Russia could go hand in hand.

If it would be wrong, even ridiculous, to see the kaleidoscopic changes in Soviet policies and rhetoric between 1939 and 1948 as led by Marxist-Leninist ideology, it would be a mistake to see the hermeneutics that justified policy changes as so much window dressing. It was always possible, by diligent searching in the books of the socialist sages, to find a theoretical justification for any policy, but it *was* significant that such a justification had to be found.

Exercise   Consider the following three descriptions of World War II by Stalin:

(a)   'a struggle of predatory imperialist nations over the control of world markets' (20 June 1941)

(b)   'a great patriotic war of freedom-loving actions against fascism' (3 July 1941)

(c)   'an inevitable result of the development of world economic and political forces on the basis of modern monopoly capitalism' (9 February 1946)

Now answer the following questions:

1   What do you think might explain the difference between (a) and (b)?

2   What distinguishes descriptions (a) and (c) from (b)? ■

Specimen answers   1   On 22 June 1941 Germany attacked Russia.
and discussion
2   Essentially (a) and (c) identify the war in terms of laying stress on its supposed economic origins. They both to some extent impart blame on two sides, the first directly and the second implicitly, for if monopoly capitalism was responsible, then the USA and Britain as leading capitalist states were presumably impugned. We can clearly distinguish (a) and (c) from (b), which talks of freedom-loving nations, presumably Britain and the Soviet Union, engaged in a war against fascism. □

The war can thus be seen from the Soviet Union's point of view as involving an opportune and temporary alliance with what was perhaps regarded in the long term as the major enemy, the Western capitalist powers, against Germany and fascism. Once that conflict was over, fundamental antagonisms based on a Marxist reading of historical development reasserted themselves.

We may well ask how important fascism was in all this. Was it a full-blown ideology in its own right? Was there a triangle of the three 'isms', so that when two corners had drawn together to destroy the third, the conflict between the remaining two was resumed? Was fascism instead a late freak of world capitalism? It can, of course, alternatively be seen from a liberal capitalist viewpoint as, with its corporatism and elevation of the state over civil society, a socialist heresy which replaces the struggle of classes with the struggle of nations. There can be little doubt, however, that by the time of Stalin's speech of February 1946 the Soviet analysis of fascism had swung back to the dicta that had prevailed before Hitler's invasion of Russia. Hugh Thomas has described Stalin's remarks as signifying 'the view that capitalism and Nazism were at the same "last stage of capitalism" as Communists had conceived them to be in the early 1950s' (*Armed Truce: The Beginnings of the Cold War 1945–46*, 1986, p.38).

Stalin's and the Soviet Union's change in attitude and policy was sudden and harsh. During the war Marxist-Leninism had given way to Russian nationalism as a means of encouraging or cajoling the Soviet population. The *Internationale* was replaced as the national anthem by a hymn glorifying Russia. Old Tsarist heroes once more became national icons. Eisenstein's film *Alexander Nevsky* had been made as a warning to the Germans at the end of the 1930s; it celebrated the achievements of its eponymous hero, the Prince of Muscovy, who had defeated the Teutonic Knights in 1242. Stalin kept portraits of Nevsky and the great generals of the French Revolutionary and Napoleonic Wars, Suvorov and Kutuzov, on the walls of his study. Little was heard of the Party, of communism or of the class struggle, but a great deal was heard of Russia, the motherland and patriotism. Even the leaders of the Orthodox Church were wheeled out to help fan Russian resistance. Britain and then the USA were for the duration not capitalist or imperialist predators, but 'freedom-loving nations' and allies in a common struggle. The reversal of these policies began to be discernible early in 1945, and Stalin's speech of February 1946 marked their final burial.

For the reasons behind the shifts in policy we have to look at the Soviet internal situation, as well as the burgeoning dissension with the Western Allies. The Soviet Union adopted the stance of the patriotic war in the circumstances of a German invasion which was not only at first worryingly successful in military terms but shook the Soviet system of government. Vast areas of the state (about 4 million square miles and about 65 million people) were for some years under German occupation. Had the Germans, who in some areas were greeted with relief, been prepared to win over the subject population and play on the separatist desires of many of the non-White Russian regions, then they might have found valuable allies. Even in purely Russian regions there was no great enthusiasm for a war for communism; hence the appeal to Russian patriotism. Nor should we imagine that in the circumstances of a relaxation of doctrine there was any parallel relaxation of the state's grip on the populace, for the police state tightened its grip, especially as it encountered difficulty in restoring order in former occupied territories (Ukrainian nationalists, for instance, were to mount a partisan struggle until 1947). Once the war was clearly won, there was not only the problem of reinstating the state's control over all its territory but the necessity of reinstating the Party's control over the state. During the war the Party had kept a low profile and the power of generals and industrial managers had grown apace. With victory the Party became once more ubiquitous. The role of the generals was quickly downgraded and the great heroes of the victory parade of 24 June 1945, Zhukov and Rokossovsky, were soon sent to quite junior commands. 'Our victory means', said Stalin in his speech of February 1946, 'that our Soviet system has won': not, Hugh Thomas comments, Russia; nor the Allies (*Armed Truce*, p.38).

The harder line towards the Western Allies and the increased emphasis on their capitalist and anti-Soviet natures thus coincided with, and was to some extent part of, the same process by which Stalin and the Communist Party sought to overcome internal problems and redirect Soviet society along Marxist-Leninist lines. The Soviet Union desired security for its borders, which meant control of all adjacent, strategically sensitive areas. That desire by itself was increasingly creating tensions with the West, but it also desired security for its system, a system that would be imperilled by too close a co-operation with its erstwhile allies and could wither in any world system dominated by American economic might. If Soviet policy was straightforward in regard to exercising a strict hegemony over areas under the control of the Red Army which controlled North Korea as well as East Central Europe, it was more pragmatic elsewhere, in the Mediterranean and in Western Europe. In the former, as we shall see, it was for a while prepared for a British sphere of influence, while in Western Europe, if communist parties were seen as arms of Soviet influence under tight control from Moscow, Moscow's orders until the founding of the Cominform in 1947 were that they should co-operate with 'bourgeois' forces and assist with national recoveries rather than act as a force for overthrowing capitalism. Here Stalin was concerned to support almost any elements in Western Europe, even indigenous capitalists, who appeared independent of US influence.

The role of ideology in US policy was in many ways more ubiquitous than it was in Soviet policy. As we have seen, some historians (see, for instance, Joyce and Gabriel Kolko, *The Limits of Power: the World and United States Foreign Policy 1945–54*, 1972) have seen US policy as inspired by the aim of world-wide economic domination, but if this is so, it seems odd that the Cold War originated primarily in East Central Europe, an area of limited economic interest to the United States. On the whole the missionary rather than the Machiavellian view of US policy seems to make most sense. There was an altruistic urge to reform the old world in the image of the new; the resemblance between Roosevelt and Woodrow Wilson is striking, while President Truman was a convinced Wilsonian who at first followed the main outlines of Roosevelt's policies. If the Atlantic Charter, the United Nations Organization, and the plans for a new economic order agreed at Bretton Woods added up to a blueprint for a liberal world, the American isolationist impulse that destroyed Wilson was still strong. Roosevelt's announcement that American troops would be withdrawn from Europe within two years of the end of the war compounded the mistakes of Yalta. A Wilsonian stance was not only attractive to Roosevelt and Truman in its own right, but was probably essential for US domestic consumption. US politicians could not gain domestic support for a war with realistic aims but only for a war for 'one world' with liberal democratic principles. Yet the only realistic policy, given the nature of the USA's Soviet ally, lay in the acceptance of a Soviet sphere of influence in which liberal principles would not hold. Yalta and Potsdam saw the gap, between the foreign policy for domestic consumption and the necessary compromises with the USSR if the alliance was to continue, grow wider. As the gap became more obvious, it became imperative that the USA should either seek to make the rhetoric of its policies fit the practical policies or change the practical policies in line with the rhetoric. Faced with the difficulty of changing an imperfect world after World War I, the USA had moved towards isolation; but in 1945 America was far more conscious of its military and economic might. Ideology *was* in the final analysis a central factor in the slide towards the Cold War, but it was a factor more determinant of US policy, responsible to an idealistic electorate, than of Soviet policy. United States policy was to a considerable extent *led* by ideology, by liberal democratic principles, while Soviet policy tended to be *justified* by ideology.

You should note that sections 3, 4 and 5 are written by Clive Emsley.

3 BRITAIN AND FRANCE: 'GREAT POWER' STATUS AND US AID

World War II had left two genuinely 'great powers', the USA and the USSR, on the flanks of Europe. Yet there were two other powers, Britain and France, both on the winning side in the war, both with a tradition of being 'great powers', and both keen to maintain this position.

Exercise   Using common sense and your recollection of material from earlier in the course, answer the following questions:

1   How do you suppose British and French politicians could justify their country's claims to 'great power' status? What, if any, was the difference between their respective claims, given the situation in 1945?

2   Given the experience of the previous six years, what problems do you suppose impeded these great power aspirations?

3   What factors made it most unlikely that they could seriously challenge the dominance of the USA and the USSR? ■

Specimen answers   1   The British had the better claim to continuing great power status; they had, after all, been the most consistent enemy of Hitler since 1939, whereas France had been occupied and, even if de Gaulle and the 'Free French' had continued fighting, the government of the Third Republic had surrendered in June 1940 and the new Vichy regime had been created. The claim to being a great power rested partly on tradition – Britain and France were the only European powers to have survived two world wars more or less intact and with regimes not greatly different from those of 1914. It rested also on the fact that they were on the winning side in 1945, and that they still had empires spread across the globe; the British Empire was still the largest in the world, and the French Empire was the second largest.

2   Both countries had been severely weakened economically by the war. France had the greater problems as it had been plundered during the German occupation and had been a battlefield for several months following the Allied landings in June 1944. Britain had not been fought over by land armies, but had suffered from aerial bombardment and, in spite of US aid and the lend-lease agreement, had been compelled to spend enormous sums on armaments and campaigns.

3   Britain and France had neither the manpower nor the economic resources to challenge the two enormous powers on the flanks of Europe. Of course, it was possible that the USA would opt for isolation as it had done at the end of World War I, thus enabling Britain and France to fill something of a vacuum; but Russia in 1945 was in a very different situation from that in which it had found itself during the negotiations at Brest-Litovsk and Versailles. Russia had suffered enormous losses of men and material in the war against Nazi Germany, but there was no reason to suppose that it would now opt for isolation. □

Discussion   I hope that you found it possible to make a stab at those questions, and to get somewhere near my specimen answers. If not, think about the answers in the light of the questions. I want to move on now to develop the answers with some more detailed information.

The war had affected the colonies as much as the metropolis. In Asia many of the British colonies and all of the French colonies had been overrun by the Japanese, something which struck a devastating blow at the image of the white man's superiority. The war had brought a new infrastructure to those colonies and dependencies that had been battlegrounds or close to battlegrounds; modern war required roads, railways, airfields, port facilities, and so forth. It also brought economic development in areas encouraged to produce foodstuffs, raw materials, or even military equipment for wartime needs. When Malaya fell to the Japanese, for example, British West Africa became a centre for rubber production, and in India the British Raj began encouraging native entrepreneurs in the production of chemicals and light tanks rather than just consumer articles. All of this, in turn, contributed to the development of nationalist consciousness, notably among those educated members of the indigenous communities, many of whom had looked to the colonial bureaucracies for employment, but who now saw their living standards eroded by wartime inflation and the profits acquired by native landowners and businessmen.

When the Labour government came to power in Britain in 1945 it was already prepared to negotiate some kind of withdrawal from India, partly for ideological reasons and partly because of increasing difficulties with the nationalists; Indian independence was granted in 1947. In the following year, unable to solve the problem of a Jewish demand for a homeland in a land claimed by Arabs, Britain gave up its mandate in Palestine. But Britain's Labour government had no intention of a complete withdrawal from empire, and considered that overseas development, especially in Africa, would be a means of helping the sterling area in general and the British economy in particular. The French, similarly, had no intention of any withdrawal from empire. They were keen to get back into Indo-China, hoping to play off Ho Chi Minh's communist guerrillas (who, though largely confined to the north-east of the country and few in numbers, could claim to have been fighting the Japanese since 1941) against other factions. Before 1946 was over this policy had embroiled the French in the opening skirmishes of the first of their savage wars of colonial independence. The French reluctantly recognized that there would be no restoration of their mandated territories in the Middle East, but they did not yield claims to their colonies in equatorial Africa, Madagascar, Morocco and Tunisia. Algeria, with its one million white settlers, was considered a part of metropolitan France.

These continuing imperial roles may have been the marks of great powers in the eyes of the governments of Britain and France, and in the eyes of many in their populations, but in terms of production, gross national product and share of world trade, neither country was any longer in the first rank, and great power adventures and postures were expensive. In addition to their imperial role the British were also prepared to take on other international tasks to check what were perceived as threats to the peace of Europe. Both Britain and France maintained armies of occupation in defeated Germany, and in March 1947 they signed the Dunkirk Treaty, promising mutual support in the event of renewed aggression by Germany – something which still worried the French, but which the British Foreign Office described as 'rather academic', increasingly perceiving the real threat to Europe as coming from the Soviet Union. The demands of empire, occupying Germany, and sometimes playing world policemen meant that, for the first time ever, the British used military conscription in peacetime, and thousands of young national servicemen found themselves deployed in distant garrisons, sometimes being shot at.

It was believed that the shortage of manpower, given the imperial and international commitments, could be partially made up by building an atomic bomb, but there were also other reasons for this. British scientists had been involved in developing the weapon with the Americans during the war; the Labour government was furious when the Americans elbowed them out of the research and development of these weapons and determined to build their own. Moreover, Labour ministers reasoned, what better mark of great power status could there be than possession of this weapon. In the mid 1950s, a French government under Pierre Mendès-France followed similar lines of reasoning: an atom bomb would demonstrate that France was still a great power and it would help to compensate for its lack of manpower. The idea was taken up with even more enthusiasm by de Gaulle when he became the first president of the Fifth Republic in 1958. But imperial and international roles, which involved the deployment and maintenance of troops around the world, and the development of atom bombs and their delivery systems, cost vast amounts of money, and this was in short supply even among the victorious European powers.

The war had cost both Britain and France enormous sums, and as armaments became more and more sophisticated, and more and more dependent on complex, changing technologies, so they were becoming more and more costly to develop and then to produce. It was not just the new, nuclear technology that was expensive; so too, for example, were radar and electronics, both of which had been extensively developed and deployed in World War II. In 1945 there was the need to replace destroyed, damaged or worn-out production equipment, as well as roads, railways, bridges, and so on. The French transport system had completely broken down at the end of the war. Imports and exports were non-existent. There was no stock of foreign currency, and the franc was weak: in 1944 the official exchange rate was 50 francs to $1, but on the black market a dollar could fetch four times that sum. At the end of 1945 the franc was officially devalued by almost 60 per cent, to $1 to 116 francs, and a further devaluation followed in 1949.

Britain had fought the war by increasing taxes (taxation, both direct and indirect, rose from £1,007 million in 1938–9 to £3,411 million in 1945–6), by disinvestment abroad which raised some £4,198 million, and by leaning on the burgeoning US economy. As a result of the war, Britain's internal debt rose from £7,247 million to £23,372 million. Britain was not prepared for peace when it came; it had anticipated the struggle against the Japanese continuing into 1946, and perhaps into 1947, and was relying on lend-lease continuing during this period, which, it was hoped, would enable some restructuring for peace. But when, following the attacks on Hiroshima and Nagasaki, the Japanese surrendered in September 1945, so lend-lease also came to an end. Already, in July, the Labour government had received a memorandum from John Maynard Keynes warning of a 'financial Dunkirk' and stating starkly that, without help, 'a greater degree of austerity would be necessary than we have experienced at any time during the war'. Remember too that this Labour government wished to finance a new welfare state as well as maintain Britain's international role as an imperial and a 'great' power. Keynes negotiated a long-term loan from the United States of $3,750 million, but during 1946 this began to be spent at an alarming rate, far faster than anyone had anticipated. The situation was aggravated by a determination to prove that nothing had changed with respect to the British economy and financial system, and this led to the British exchange rate being set, ridiculously, at the 1939 level of $4 to £1; not until 1949 was the more realistic rate of $2.8 to £1 established.

The crunch came in 1947. The winter of 1946–7 was terrible; in both Britain and France the bitter cold was aggravated by fuel shortages, factories were forced to close, and the beginnings of a European economic recovery that had appeared in 1946 disintegrated. On 21 February 1947 the United States government received two *aides-mémoires* from its British ally. These are printed as documents II.33 and II.34 in *Documents 2*.

Exercise   Read the documents now and then answer the following questions:

1   What are the problems identified by the two *aides-mémoires*?

2   What remedy is proposed by the British government? ■

Specimen answers   1   The *aides-mémoires* describe internal problems in both Greece and Turkey: the former has acute economic difficulties and a military emergency caused by 'bandits'; the latter is not able to finance its necessary military reorganization or any extensive programme of economic development. The key problem highlighted in these documents, however, is that the British government feels itself incapable of continuing, let alone increasing, its financial assistance to Greece and Turkey.

2   The solution to these problems in the eyes of the British government is for the United States to take over the British role. □

Discussion   The specific problems of Greece and Turkey will be addressed later in the unit; the financial difficulties of the British government outlined in the *aides-mémoires* and its decision to end its aid to Greece and Turkey led, as it had hoped and suggested, to the United States taking over these tasks. Just three weeks after the receipt of these documents President Truman outlined to a joint session of Congress what has become known as 'the Truman Doctrine':

> To ensure the peaceful development of nations, free from coercion, the United States has taken a leading part in establishing the United Nations. The United Nations is designed to make possible lasting freedom and independence for all its members. We shall not realise our objectives, however, unless we are willing to help free peoples to maintain their free institutions and their national integrity against aggressive movements that seek to impose upon them totalitarian regimes. This is no more than a frank recognition that totalitarian regimes imposed upon free peoples, by direct or indirect aggression, undermine the foundations of international peace and hence the security of the United States. (Quoted in Joseph M. Siracusa, *The American Diplomatic Revolution*, 1978, p.227)

Exercise   Turn now to document II.35, a memorandum by William L. Clayton, the US Under Secretary of State for Economic Affairs, and to document II.36, the extract from a speech made by General George C. Marshall, the US Secretary of State. Read the two documents, and answer the following questions.

1   What are the problems and dangers outlined in these documents?

2   What are the remedies? ■

Specimen answers   1   The problem identified by both Clayton and Marshall is the destruction and disruption of the European economy that had been caused by war and the preparation for war. Clayton suggests that if the situation deteriorates much more, then there could be revolution; Marshall foresees the possibilities of 'disturbances', but also believes that the problems might have a demoralizing effect on the whole world.

2   The remedy is seen as coming from large-scale American aid over the next three years or so. □

Discussion   Planning for the economic recovery of Europe by means of American aid began in both Europe and the United States almost immediately after Marshall's speech. Britain took the initiative in Europe, where representatives from a dozen different countries came together in the Committee for European Economic Co-operation (CEEC, later the Organisation for European Economic Co-operation, OEEC). In December 1947 the CEEC presented a report to the United States recommending a four-year programme of aid. A series of committees studying the matter for the United States government presented similar reports at roughly the same time. In

April 1948 Congress ratified the European Recovery Program Bill, still more commonly known as Marshall Aid, and from June 1948 until June 1952 some $13,150 million in American aid was given to Europe. The largest amounts were forwarded to Britain ($3,176 million) and to France ($2,706 million); then came Italy ($1,474 million), West Germany ($1,389 million), The Netherlands ($1,079 million) and a dozen other smaller nations. Most of the money was spent in the United States itself, providing, at first, food, animal feed and fertilizers for the immediate problems, and then raw materials and semi-finished products, together with fuel, machinery and vehicles. By the end of the aid programme agricultural output in Western Europe was 10 per cent above its pre-war level and industrial output was 35 per cent above (though the outbreak of the Korean War in 1950 also had some impact in boosting European industrial production, particularly then related to military needs).

Exercise   1   From what I have said in the preceding paragraphs, does Marshall Aid appear to you to have been directed at any particular part of Europe; if so, which part?

2   Is there anything in the two documents by Clayton and Marshall that expressly denies aid to the Soviet Union or those states within its sphere of influence?

3   Can you think of any reason why the Soviet Union might reject the kind of aid offered under the Marshall Plan? ■

Specimen answers   1   The countries noted in my list of those receiving aid are all in Western Europe.

2   There is nothing in Clayton's memorandum or in Marshall's speech which specifically says that aid should be confined to the west of Europe. Neither differentiates between an Eastern and Western Europe, and whilst the only countries mentioned by Clayton are in the West and he is concerned about 'revolution', he also writes about the need to save Europe 'from starvation and chaos (*not* from the Russians)'.

3   Given the increasing ideological split between the Soviet Union and the United States, it was unlikely that the former would be keen to open up to investment by the latter. This might weaken Russia's increasing hold on Eastern Europe, but it would also be boosting the very capitalism that the Soviet system was out to replace. □

Discussion   President Truman saw Marshall Aid as part and parcel of the ideological struggle and as fulfilling the promise of support for free people outlined in the Truman Doctrine. Initially American aid was promised for all those European states prepared to participate in the programme. Shortly after Marshall's speech a meeting was held in Paris involving the foreign ministers of Britain, France and the USSR to discuss the proposal. The talks rapidly broke down, and the Russian delegation left. In some ways, given the points raised in specimen answer 3 above, the Russian walk-out was predictable; but this is not the whole story. It seems likely that the Western powers expected that the Russians would refuse the offered aid; and there was some justification for fearing that, if the Russians accepted it, then the strongly Republican Congress would, in the context of the increasing ideological split, refuse to ratify an aid Bill. Ernest Bevin, the British Foreign Secretary, and Georges Bidault, his French opposite number, also presented Viacheslav Molotov with a blueprint for the integration of the European economies which he would have had great difficulty in accepting, since it proposed that each nation should produce what it currently produced best; this suggested to Molotov that Easten Europe was to be maintained as a relatively backward area providing food for the industrial West.

4   *GERMANY DIVIDED*

At first glance Germany might appear to offer proof of both the statement that Europe divided where the Allied armies halted in May 1945, and Stalin's oft-quoted remark, made at the end of the war: 'whoever occupies a territory imposes on it his own social system'. As always, such statements need qualification. Parts of the zone of Germany placed under Soviet control in 1945 had been overrun by British and United States armies; they were handed over to the Russians as part of the occupation agreement (see map 12 in the *Maps Booklet*). Furthermore, as I hope to show below, the Soviets did not set out with the intention of creating a clone Stalinist state in East Germany.

Inevitably, the problem of what to do about Germany had loomed large in the Allies' wartime discussions.

Exercise   Look at the maps of Germany in 1914, 1920 and 1942 in your *Maps Booklet* (maps 1, 6 and 8) and note down what you think must have been a principal problem in the Allies' discussions about the future shape of the country. ■

Specimen answer   The central core of Germany remains the same on all of the maps, but the frontiers are fluid. A key problem for the Allies, therefore, was where to draw the post-war frontiers. □

Discussion   You will remember from Unit 21 and the discussion of geopolitical consequences in Units 22–25 that large areas of pre-war Germany were given to Poland in recompense for the losses of Polish lands to the USSR. Areas seized by Hitler during the 1930s, like the Sudetenland, were returned to their former owner, though the *Sudetendeutschen* were expelled; Austria was made an independent state once again. A few small readjustments were made to Germany's western borders, in favour of The Netherlands, Belgium and Luxemburg. There were also demands for a realignment of the Danish frontier, notably, it appears, from Germans who thought that incorporation into Denmark would bring about a more rapid improvement in their living conditions; these demands were resisted by both the Danish government and the British occupation authorities responsible for this frontier area, and the agitation gradually petered out in the early 1950s.

During the war there were some who argued for the dismemberment of Germany. After the invasion of Europe in 1944, for example, the British chiefs of staff advocated such a policy on several grounds: it would prevent a revival of German militarism; it would ensure that the Western Allies had possession of the economic resources of western Germany should a future conflict break out against the Soviet Union, and at the same time it would deny as much as possible of Germany to the Russians. Dismemberment was prominent on the Allies' discussion agendas early in 1945. Among the 'big three', the Russians were probably the most favourable to the idea. The British government increasingly got cold feet, believing that dismemberment would render Germany's ability to make reparations virtually impossible; perhaps more important, they recognized that a divided Germany would impose intolerable costs on the British because their zone was predominantly industrial and would require the importation of large quantities of food. At Yalta the Allies determined on the temporary control of Germany, with Britain, France, the United States and the Soviet Union each supervising a separate zone, and the whole being co-ordinated in Berlin by a Control Council made up of representatives of the four powers. The Potsdam Conference adopted a series of principles which, according to President Harry Truman:

> seek to rid Germany of the forces which have now brought her to complete disaster. They are intended to eliminate Nazism, armaments, war industries, the German General Staff and all its military tradition. They seek to rebuild democracy by control of German education, by reorganising local government and the judiciary, by encouraging free speech, free press, freedom of religion, and the right of labor to organise. (Quoted in Joseph M. Siracusa, *The American Diplomatic Revolution*, p.139)

Exercise   Given the different ideologies of the victorious Allies, can you see any problems resulting from the attempts to act in accordance with these principles listed by Truman? ■

Specimen answer   Naturally there was agreement among the Allies about the evils of Nazism and German militarism; however, Truman talked about rebuilding democracy, something which had a very different meaning for Stalin. Once the Allies set about the 'control of German education' and 'reorganising local government', there were bound to be marked differences between the different Allied zones. □

Discussion   Even if the different direction of the respective zones was bound to have an influence on their internal development, it would be wrong to assume that the four zones were completely blank sheets on which the Allies could write what they wished. Germany was devastated at the end of the war, yet there remained, at the very least, a memory of political traditions, while the economic structure continued to depend on the availability of resources and expertise. The American zone (see map 12 in the *Maps Booklet*) was composed of states with a long history of self-government. The largest single unit there was Bavaria, which had preserved much of its separate administrative structure during the Weimar and Nazi periods; the Americans were able to build on this to get life going again relatively easily. The Soviet zone, in contrast, was composed of the old Kingdom of Saxony and those provinces of east Prussia left after the westward advance of the Polish frontier. There was little experience of self-government in the latter, while the industrialized districts of the former had been a socialist stronghold; arguably both of these elements contributed to the way in which the Soviet zone developed.

Zones of military occupation do not automatically have to have a political function. It would have been possible, though possibly difficult, for a united Germany to be re-established with the four occupying armies on its soil. Indeed, following the discussions among the 'big three' at Yalta and then at the Potsdam Conference, this was the intention. The problem came as a result of the decision to establish a fourth, French zone. General Charles de Gaulle, the leader of the Free French, was furious at being excluded from the conferences; he considered the exclusion as a personal slight, and a slight on the honour of France. De Gaulle and many other Frenchmen were keen to see Germany divided and weakened; this was the old strategy of the 1920s, and a way of maintaining France's image as a great power. These attitudes and aspirations led de Gaulle to veto the creation of the executive offices which the Potsdam Conference intended as a channel for the decisions of the Control Council in Berlin to reach the local authorities that were being reconstituted throughout Germany. The direct result of the veto was that the military commanders of the occupation zones became the only links between the Control Council and the indigenous local authorities.

The Russians brought back to their zone communists who had found asylum in the Soviet Union during the Nazi period, notably Wilhelm Pieck and Walther Ulbricht. Yet these communists were the prisoners of an ideology which maintained that, before there could be a proletarian revolution, there had to be a completed bourgeois one. Their intention was to develop the Popular Front model of the 1930s: the working class was to ally itself with progressive, anti-fascist bourgeois groups. In its programme of June 1945 the KPD (Communist Party) declared that 'it would be wrong to impose a Soviet system', and it talked of establishing a 'parliamentary democratic republic with all democratic rights and freedoms for the people'. On the other hand, Pieck, Ulbricht and their followers were determined to put their stamp on the reformed system of government that emerged in the Soviet zone, and while they allowed the development of 'bourgeois' parties (Liberals and Christian Democrats), they were determined to keep control of government, and they interpreted and carried out de-Nazification as part and parcel of the class struggle. The KPD considered that the true beneficiaries of Nazism had been the economic and social elites who were the class enemies of the proletariat; de-Nazification therefore meant the removal of the social groups that made up such elites from access to economic and political power, and an immediate, if partial, nationalization of industrial concerns. In the zones run by the Western powers, in contrast, de-Nazification meant careful legal enquiries so as to identify and punish individuals. Obviously this meant the removal of such people from positions of authority, but it did not mean the emasculation of social and economic groups – though it could be argued, of course, that the Western powers were keen to establish a liberal, capitalist Germany and were therefore intent on limiting the power of those who opposed this.

Germany was devastated at the end of the war; towns had been flattened by aerial bombardment and by fighting between land armies. The loss of territories in the east, and the loss of Austria, deprived the country of many of the areas that had experienced economic investment and development during the Nazi period: 17 per cent of the coal, 40 per cent of the lead, and 75 per cent of the zinc produced in Germany in 1939, for example, had been produced in areas now in Poland. Germany could no longer be the economic unit that it had been before the war; the question was, would it be a single economic unit in the future? The resolution of this question was to make a significant impact on Germany's political future.

The Allies had promised to introduce land reform; they were determined also to exact reparations. However, the introduction of the former and the interpretation of the latter varied. The agricultural pattern of Germany varied. The north of the Soviet zone was principally agricultural, and the agriculture here was dominated by large estates; in September 1945 estates of more than 100 hectares were confiscated without compensation, as were some 4,000 smaller holdings belonging to Nazis and 'war criminals'. In total 2.1 million hectares were redistributed among former agricultural labourers and refugees from the east; the pattern of land ownership was radically altered, and the potential for the old Junker elite to reassert itself was destroyed. In the western zones, in contrast, there were far more small family farms in the first place, and the much more limited land reforms introduced here in 1947 made little fundamental difference. The Soviets interpreted the reparations agreement as allowing them rigorously to strip their zone of economic assets: the Moscow underground benefited from the arrival of the Berlin rolling stock, two synthetic rubber plants were rebuilt in Siberia, the Zeiss works of Jena were moved east, and so on. The Soviets also claimed 10 per cent of the industrial capacity of the western zones. However, the asset-stripping in the east was not a great success, since even if plants were removed in their entirety (and if they were not, Soviet machinery was not always compatible) they usually required skilled German labour to make them function. In the west, the Americans and the British considered that the Russians were going too far, and they became increasingly concerned that dismantling plant for reparations was slowing the restoration of the entire European economy.

The British zone, which included the heavily industrialized Ruhr, had been particularly badly hit by the strategic bombing campaign. Before the war, in an integrated German economy, many of the products of the Ruhr had been utilized in the east of the country, and the agricultural surplus of the east had fed the Ruhr. The Russians sent some of the agricultural produce of their zone to the west, but the food situation in the west was appalling in the years immediately following the war. At the end of 1945 only 12 per cent of German children had the normal weight for their age; the average adult male in the American zone weighed only about 51 kilograms (about 8 stone). The situation appears to have been worst in the devastated British zone: the Allied occupation government had taken 2,700 calories as the target for the distribution of food rations to individuals in Germany. In spite of strict rationing and control, the authorities in the British zone found themselves compelled to cut this first to 1,550 and then 1,050 calories; many people received below this target. The mortality rate, particularly among the very young and very old, reached catastrophic levels. In January 1947, in the midst of a bitterly cold winter, the American and British zones were fused into a Combined Economic Area (Bizone) to facilitate economic development and rehabilitation. Somewhat reluctantly the French joined in August 1948, thus making the Trizone; the French, thanks to the common frontier, had already integrated much of the economy of their zone, notably the Saar region, into their own national economy. In 1948 the three western zones also began to benefit from Marshall Aid and from the currency reform of June, whereby the greatly devalued Reichsmark was replaced by the Deutschmark.

Already different political structures were beginning to crystallize in the east and the west; the currency reform completed the economic division of Germany, and intensified the political division. There had been agreement among the occupying powers that some form of currency reform was necessary for Germany. No one had any faith in the old currency, indeed cigarettes were increasingly displacing the Reichsmark – German cigarettes fetched 4 RM, English or American 6.50 RM. The occasion of the breakdown in the talks over the new currency was the question of where the new notes should be printed: the Russians wanted them printed in their zone, the Americans insisted that they be printed outside the country. The Russians appear to have been concerned that currency reform would push the whole of Germany towards the west, and that was certainly a part of their argument with reference to the western zones when the

Deutschmark was introduced. According to Soviet Military Administration Order No.111,

> The American, British and French occupation authorities have carried out this separate currency reform in defiance of the interests of the German people, and in deference to the wishes of the American, British and French monopolies, which are working to dismember and weaken Germany and enthrall her economically. The separate currency reform in Western Germany is also designed to strengthen the position of the big German capitalists and Junkers, who ensured the advent of Fascism to power and who paved the way for and unleashed the Second World War, and who are now helping to bind West Germany in bondage to the foreign imperialists. (Quoted in Beate Ruhm von Oppen, *Documents on Germany under Occupation 1945–1954*, 1955, p.295)

The Soviets countered with their own currency reform for their zone. Since Berlin, although administered by the four occupying powers, lay in the Soviet zone, the Russians insisted that east German currency be used in the city. The Americans, British and French refused; the Russians cut off gas and electricity supplies to the three western sectors of the city, and then closed all of the supply routes to the city from the three western zones. From the beginning of April 1948 until May 1949, when the Soviets lifted the restrictions, the western sectors of Berlin were supplied by air; in fact, because of concern that the Soviets might cut the supply routes again, the airlift continued until September 1949. During the period of the airlift the western sectors of the city developed their own municipal government, and this continued in existence when the restrictions were lifted. Berlin was now a divided city with separate local government in the east and the west. 1949 also witnessed the formal creation of two separate German states.

The prospect of a united Germany had begun to look bleak at least as early as June 1947. During that month a conference had been held in Munich of the prime ministers of the different *Länder* (states). Suspicion and profound political differences between those from the east and those from the west were such that they could not even agree on the conference agenda. The SED (*Sozialistische Einheitspartei Deutschlands*, Socialist Unity Party of Germany, formed in April 1946 by a forced union of the KPD and the SPD in the Soviet zone) sought to appear the champion of a united Germany and launched a propaganda exercise aimed, the party maintained, at mobilizing the masses across Germany. The result was a first German People's Congress, with some delegates from the west, meeting towards the end of 1947, with a second meeting in June 1948. The Congress proclaimed itself the 'authorized representative for all Germany' and began drafting a constitution based on that of Weimar. The origins of this Congress, and the political climate created by the situation in Berlin, did not endear it to politicians in the western zones. The concerns of these west German politicians were heightened by the direction that politics in the east appeared to be taking. Elections had been held in the east in 1946, and the Liberals and Christian Democrats had done unexpectedly well. However, by the middle of 1948, these Liberals and Christian Democrats were finding themselves under increasing pressure to conform to the kinds of policies advocated by the SED, and the SED itself was beginning publicly to espouse a Soviet model for development. Leaders of the Liberals and Christian Democrats, who refused to go along with these policies, were forced to move to the west. In May 1949, the very month that the Soviets lifted the blockade of

Berlin, most of the *Länder* in the west (Bavaria was the temporary odd man out) agreed the Bonn Basic Law, a provisional constitution for their federation with a representative government (*Bundestag*), a president, a chancellor, and a constitutional court to rule on and interpret the Basic Law. In August the people of the west went to the polls to elect the *Bundestag*, and the Federal Republic came into being still with its provisional constitution. The response in the east was rapid. A third German People's Congress was elected in May 1949 on the basis of a single 'unity' list; this established a German People's Council, which, following the election of the *Bundestag* in the west, transformed itself into the Provisional People's Chamber. On 7 October 1949 the Provisional People's Chamber proclaimed the foundation of the German Democratic Republic.

5 A 'RED MENACE' IN THE WEST?

It was noted in Unit 21 that communists throughout Europe played an influential role in the resistance movements during World War II. The largest and most significant partisan armies may have been in the east, but once, following the Nazi invasion of Russia, the communists began to participate in resistance movements in the west, so these movements became stronger and more effective.

Exercise   What do you suppose the communist resistance fighters hoped to achieve in Western Europe following the defeat of Fascist Italy and Nazi Germany? ■

Specimen answer   If not socialist revolution, at least the communist resistance fighters hoped for significant economic, political and social change. □

Exercise   Bearing in mind the military situation in Western Europe at the end of World War II, can you think of any physical restraints on, for example, Belgian, French or Italian communists in carrying out a socialist revolution in 1945? ■

Specimen answer   Each of these countries contained large numbers of British and American troops, and it is doubtful whether these troops would have stood aside and let such revolutions happen – recall that Unit 21 describes the British action against the communists in Greece in December 1944. Moreover, the countries of Western Europe did not have common borders with the Soviet Union, and the Russian army was too far away to offer much assistance even had it wanted to. □

Exercise   Looking back to the preceding section on Germany, what sort of advice do you suppose the leaders of the communist parties in the West received from Moscow? ■

Specimen answer   Pieck and Ulbricht returned to Germany convinced that they must work with progressive, anti-fascist groups to complete the bourgeois revolution before any proletarian revolution could be attempted. There is no reason to suppose that the leadership of communist parties in the West should have been given any different advice, especially since, unlike Pieck and Ulbricht, they did not have the presence of the Soviet army to give them support if necessary. □

Discussion   Like Germany, both France and Italy witnessed the return of communist party leaders from the Soviet Union as the countries were liberated. Maurice Thorez and Palmiro Togliatti each acted as restraining influences on rank-and-file party members who had fought in the resistance and who wanted immediate and significant changes.

To the men on the ground who helped liberate their locality, the power of the resistance, and of their faction within the resistance, probably seemed considerable. In northern Italy around 230,000 people were engaged in some form of partisan activity at different times following the overthrow of Mussolini; it was partisan units which, in the spring of 1945, liberated some of the great towns of the north (admittedly helped by the progressive German collapse, and by the advance of Allied troops); and it was partisans who captured and shot the *Duce* himself. There was less fighting by resistance units in France; often all that French armed resisters had to do in the summer of 1944 was to enter a town, as the Germans pulled out, and declare it liberated. But in both countries the resistance liberators established their own organizing committees, their own local administrations, and often their own system of justice. These could be seen as the model for the new society; they posed a threat to the authority of the new central governments, and they were viewed with suspicion by the British and the Americans. If revolution, or at least the potential for armed insurrection, was to be prevented, then the central governments had to disarm these groups and dismantle their local power structures. In Belgium the Communist Party objected to the disarming of the resistance and resigned from the coalition government in protest. In France and Italy, in contrast, where the communist parties were proportionately much larger, both Thorez and Togliatti supported the disarming of the resistance and the re-establishment of the power of central government.

In Belgium, France and Italy there was a feeling that the unity of the struggle against Nazism and Fascism should be reflected in the governments established at the time of liberation. In consequence the new governments were coalitions that embraced all of the anti-fascist parties, including the communists; even though it walked out of government when the resistance was disarmed in December 1944, the Belgian Communist Party was happy to rejoin in the following February. The influence and popularity of the communists in all three countries were manifested by their successes in the elections of the immediate post-war years. In France the communists won the largest number of seats in the Constituent Assembly in the election of October 1945, but not an overall majority. In February 1946 the Belgian communists secured just under 13 per cent of the vote and won 11 per cent of the seats in the Chamber of Representatives. In Italy, the following June, the communists secured about one-fifth of the vote and one-fifth of the seats. In each election the communists sought an alliance with the socialists, and in each case this gave the two parties around half of the total seats in the respective assemblies. In no instance did the communists and the socialists form a government on their own, but they both continued to hold ministries in different coalitions. While they did not satisfy the aspirations of the extreme rank-and-file militants, these governments, with their communist membership, supervised significant reforms and political and economic change. In all three countries women were granted the vote. New constitutions were drafted for both France and Italy, and in Italy a popular referendum voted away the monarchy. France particularly experienced a massive extension of state ownership during 1945 and early 1946: railways, coal-mines, gas and electricity, leading financial institutions and some large manufacturing concerns were all taken into public ownership.

By the spring of 1947 the strains in successive coalition governments were beginning to show. Initially the French communists had revealed themselves almost as concerned as General de Gaulle about France's standing as a great power. However, in the early months of 1947 communist deputies criticized the behaviour of French troops in suppressing nationalist disorder in Madagascar, and voted against credits for the war in Indo-China; communist ministers abstained in the vote. In May 1947 communist ministers went so far as to vote against the government on the issue of a strike over the rising cost of living by workers at the recently nationalized Renault works. They were sacked from the government and, in spite of their continuing popularity at the polls, they were never to return in the lifetime of the Fourth Republic. In Belgium and Italy the internal differences between the coalition partners were, of course, different, but the effects were the same, and by the early summer of 1947 the communist parties were no longer in government.

Exercise What events in international affairs do you think may have made the positions of the Western communist parties even more difficult in the spring and early summer of 1947? ■

Specimen answer The worsening relations between East and West, manifested particularly by the Berlin blockade, the Czechoslovakian crisis, and the declaration of the Truman Doctrine. There was also the problem of how to respond to the offer of Marshall Aid, since, although it would obviously be of benefit to the recipients, the Soviet Union was critical of it. □

Discussion The Americans had been growing increasingly suspicious of communists in Western governments during 1946 and early 1947. Less than a week after the Americans received the British *aides-mémoires* on Greece and Turkey, Dean Acheson, the Under Secretary of State, was warning congressional leaders of Soviet attempts to encircle Germany by infiltration and subversion:

> In France, with four Communists in the Cabinet, one of them Minister of Defense, with Communists controlling the largest trade union (the CGT) and infiltrating government offices, factories and the armed services, with nearly a third of the electorate voting Communist, and with the economic conditions worsening, the Russians could pull the plug at any time they chose. In Italy a similar if less dangerous situation existed, but it was growing worse. (Quoted in Joseph M. Jones, *The Fifteen Weeks (February 21–June 4 1947)*, 1955, p.140)

This actually says rather more about American paranoia than Soviet intentions, since it appears that in the early months of 1947 the Western communists were receiving little direction from Moscow. For several months, for example, they received no advice on how they should respond to Marshall Aid. The French communists went so far as to welcome the offer, provided that it was administered by a United Nations agency. The Party's central committee restated its positive approach to the aid programme in the first week of September 1947. Within a month, however, it was forced to adopt a different position.

In May 1943 the Communist International (Comintern) had been dissolved on the grounds that it no longer served the interests of the working class in the different countries; at that moment the principal aim of all communist parties was the defeat of fascism. In September 1947 the Soviet leadership summoned the communist party leaders from both Eastern and Western Europe to a meeting in

Poland. The gathering heard a keynote address from Andrei Zhdanov, then Stalin's chief theoretician, and the meeting resulted in the formation of the Communist Information Bureau (Cominform).

Exercise   Document II.37 in *Documents 2* is an extract from Zhdanov's address. Read it now and then answer the following questions:

1   How does Zhdanov represent the developing world situation?

2   How does the Marshall Plan fit in with Zhdanov's interpretation?

3   How does Zhdanov's view of the international situation compare with that of Truman and his advisers?

4   According to Zhdanov, what did the dissolution of Comintern demonstrate, and what has experience subsequently shown?

5   What do you suppose the creation of Cominform meant for the communist parties of Western Europe, particularly with reference to the Marshall Plan? ■

Specimen answers   1   Zhdanov sees the world developing into two armed blocs: on the one hand the USSR, 'the stronghold of anti-imperialist and anti-fascist policy', with its supporters in 'the new democracies'; and on the other Britain and, especially, the United States, uniting 'all the enemies of the working class without exception'.

2   The Marshall Plan is simply a part of the American attempt to create a bloc of states bound to the United States and in opposition to the USSR.

3   Zhdanov's interpretation of developments, however much one may query some of his facts, is, to my mind, the mirror image of the Truman view of the 'free world' under threat from international communism.

4   The dissolution of the Comintern demonstrated that Moscow was not interfering in the internal politics of other countries and giving directions to their respective communist parties. However, experience has demonstrated that the isolation of communist parties is 'unnatural'.

5   The implication at the end of this document is that the communist parties of Europe (and elsewhere) will start receiving directions from Moscow once again (this time via Cominform), and that they will be expected to criticize and condemn the Marshall Plan as part of the American imperialist conspiracy. □

Discussion   Zhdanov's address was followed by criticism of the French and Italian parties for 'unrevolutionary' behaviour. The Yugoslav delegates to the conference, Edvard Kardelj and Milovan Djilas, led the attack, declaring that by opportunism, the pursuit of bourgeois democratic policies, and retaining government portfolios, the French and Italian parties had missed the chance of power that was offered in 1945. It mattered little that Moscow had favoured their working within their bourgeois democratic systems at that time, and that a theoretical justification had been found for this. From now on the communist parties were to encourage strikes and disorder which, it was hoped, would make the Marshall Plan unworkable and bring about the elimination of independent socialist, labour and peasant parties. The wave of strikes that began in France and Italy towards the end of 1947 had traditional economic causes, but they were seized upon and encouraged by the two communist parties. The division of Europe and the Cold War thus became as much an expression of internal as international politics.

You should note that sections 6 and 7 are written by Bill Purdue.

6 EAST CENTRAL EUROPE

Interpretations of Yalta which suggest that Stalin's solemn undertaking to permit free elections in East Central Europe were believed by Churchill and Roosevelt are naive. All parties knew that the agreement meant a sphere of influence for the Soviet Union and that it was up to Stalin to determine what happened in Poland, Hungary, Romania, Bulgaria and Czechoslovakia. Churchill and Roosevelt could simply not admit that they knew this.

However, there is still some room for debate as to what the Western Allies and even Stalin understood by a Soviet sphere of influence or expected it to be like. Was the eventual 'satellite' status of East Central Europe, involving a compulsory socialism, a mirroring of Soviet institutions, and total control by communist parties, inevitable and foreshadowed at Yalta? Was it not possible in 1945 to believe that the Soviet Union might be content with something short of people's republics and socialist systems, provided foreign policies were aligned to Soviet wishes? After all, the Soviet Union was just emerging from the period when communism had been played down and the war of 'patriotic and freedom-loving forces' had been paid lip service. Had Stalin himself not said that to impose communism on Poland would be like 'putting a saddle on a cow'? Could it not be hoped at least that Stalin might observe a little decorum and preserve a superficial façade of democracy and civil liberties while he ensured that pro-Soviet governments emerged?

Perhaps Stalin did indeed observe a little decorum according to his lights. It was at least theoretically possible that he might have incorporated the states of East Central Europe into the Soviet Union and acceded to a unanimous appeal by puppet governments for entry into the socialist motherland; the Baltic States' entry into the USSR in 1939 would have provided a model. A façade of coalition governments was maintained for some time, while the Bulgarian monarchy was not abolished until 1946 and the Romanian until 1947. Some historians have argued that Stalin only imposed complete uniformity on the states concerned amidst the burgeoning Cold War, that it was the rhetoric of Truman – who was no more prepared to use force than Roosevelt in order to prevent the Soviet domination of East Central Europe but complained more loudly about it – that led to the destruction of the last vestiges of pluralism (see, for instance, Theodore Draper, 'Neo-conservative history', in David Carlton and Herbert M. Levine, *The Cold War Debated*, 1988).

Yet there are good reasons for believing that Stalin was determined to go beyond a traditional idea of spheres of influence towards complete political control in the countries that had been 'liberated' by the Soviet army. As he explained to the Yugoslav communist, Milovan Djilas: 'This war is not as in the past; whoever occupies a territory also imposes his own system as far as his army can reach; it cannot be otherwise' (Rupnik, *The Other Europe*, p.72). This is not to allege that Stalin was inflexible (a communist leader who demanded the mandate for a former Italian colony, Libya, cannot be accused of that) but that he *was* inflexible in the areas where Soviet forces were firmly in control. According to Wilfred Loth,

> Within the sphere of influence of the Red Army, Soviet post-war policy evolved from the tradition of pre-revolutionary imperial Russia, both in the endeavour to reverse the ceding of territories that had been compelled by

the weakness of the young Soviet state in connection with the peace treaties concluded in Brest-Litovsk in 1918 and in Riga in 1921, and in the attempt to ensure the hegemony of the Soviet Union over the East European regime. (*The Division of the World 1941–1955*, 1988, p.39)

Elsewhere Stalin was prepared to probe or retreat, to compromise and even to order communist parties to support existing regimes, or, as in Germany, to continue a limited co-operation with the Western powers.

Exercise   Can you think of a significant exception, of a failure by the Soviet Union to regain territory at the end of World War II? ■

Specimen answer   Although the Soviet Union took territory from Finland, the country was allowed to remain independent provided its foreign policy was favourable to the Soviet Union. Finland was not just neutralized but 'Finlandized', for its situation was and is unique. Its situation can be compared to that of Austria, which became independent on condition of permanent neutrality after 1955, but Finland is more than simply neutral. By the 1948 Finno-Soviet Pact of Friendship, Co-operation and Mutual Assistance, Finland enjoys a qualified independence.

It was by no means obvious in 1945 that Finland, which had fought two wars against the Soviet Union, would be allowed to enjoy such independence. Perhaps the main reason Finland did not become a people's republic or become re-incorporated in Russia was that the country was not occupied by the Red Army. □

Exercise   Can you think of a country that was occupied by the Red Army but which was allowed to continue as an independent and non-communist country? ■

Specimen answer   Part of Austria was occupied by the Red Army, and indeed this occupation of Austria closely mirrored that of Germany with its separate allied zones and the joint occupation of Vienna (see map 12 in the *Maps Booklet*). It was only after the death of Stalin in 1953 that negotiations between the Soviet Union and the Western powers allowed the Allied occupation to end, and the country was allowed to move towards independence in 1955. □

Austria was probably too small to have been divided into east and west states along the lines of the German divide, but what was probably just as important was the vitality of the Austrian Socialist Party and the People's Party, which had a continuity with inter-war politics, and the poor showing of the communists in the first post-war elections.

To incorporate such diverse states as Poland, Bulgaria, Czechoslovakia, Romania and Hungary into what by late 1948 was a uniform group of people's republics was a considerable task. By 1948 Yugoslavia and Albania were also people's republics, but they had not been 'liberated' by the Red Army, though Russian troops did occupy much of Yugoslavia, and indigenous communist Partisans had done much of the fighting there (they will be discussed under South-Eastern Europe). What Poland, Bulgaria, Czechoslovakia, Romania and Hungary had in common was occupation by the Red Army, and after the cession of Ruthenia to the Soviet Union by Czechoslovakia they all had frontiers with the Soviet Union. But there were many differences between them.

Exercise   What major differences can you distinguish between these East Central European states in 1945? ■

Specimen answer   1   Some had fought alongside Germany. Hungary, Romania and Bulgaria had been allied with Germany, although Bulgaria had not declared war on the Soviet Union. Poland and Czechoslovakia, by contrast, were nominal partners in the alliance against Germany.

2   Some were by tradition and inclination pro-Russian in their outlook (Bulgaria and Czechoslovakia), while others (Poland and Hungary) were anti-Russian. Romania was not moulded by history to be anti-Russian, but Russia had territorial disputes with Romania.

3   Poland, Hungary and Czechoslovakia were mainly Catholic, and in Poland and Hungary in particular the church was a powerful force, socially and politically.

4   Romania and Bulgaria were both monarchies (so in a legal sense was Hungary, though it had no king) while Czechoslovakia and Poland were republics.

5   The pre-war regimes had varied between outright autocracies or semi-dictatorships and democracies, though only Czechoslovakia had a continuous history of democracy in the inter-war period.

6   The economies varied between the largely peasant agrarian economies of Bulgaria and Romania at one extreme and the industrialized economy of Czechoslovakia at the other. □

In its task of ensuring its hegemony over these states and in ensuring the emergence of sympathetic regimes, the Soviet Union was aided enormously by the fact that the political and indeed social structures of all the states had collapsed as a result of the war. Nazi Germany, and in the cases of Hungary and Romania indigenous fascist parties, had done much of the Soviet Union's work for it. The USSR with its often minuscule surrogates, the East European communist parties, was able to move into a power vacuum. The Red Army had rampaged through each country, committing atrocities as bad as those committed by the Germans, though this was largely ignored by the Western media of the day; this too had contributed to the final blow to the existing political and social structures. The fact that the pre-war regimes, whether democratic or authoritarian, no longer existed and that the political and intellectual elites had been destroyed, paved the way for the imposition of communism.

Hugh Seton-Watson, in *The East European Revolution*, identifies three phases in the communist seizure of power:

1   genuine coalitions: several political parties committed themselves to the joint programmes of National Fronts; there was limited freedom of the press and of association; the key ministries of defence and the interior were reserved for communists;

2   larger coalitions: non-communists were still in government, but they were selected because of their subservience to the communists (some of them were secretly communists); peasant and 'bourgeois' parties were driven into opposition;

3   the establishment of monolithic communist regimes: all opposition was suppressed; the social democrats were purged and merged with the communists; opposition representatives were arrested or forced into exile.

This broad pattern remains convincing, but in each country the timetable differed, as did the duration of the phases. Poland moved straight to stage 2, while stage 1 lasted only a few months in Bulgaria and Romania. In Hungary stage 1 lasted until 1947 and in Czechoslovakia until 1948; indeed, the February coup in Czechoslovakia, which completed the communist takeover in East Central Europe, saw that country move straight from stage 1 to stage 3.

It is noticeable that no distinction was drawn between countries that had fought alongside Germany and those that were supposedly allies of the Soviet Union. Hungary had been Hitler's last ally, but a relatively free society was allowed to last until 1947, while Poland was subjugated immediately; indeed, one might say that the Soviets took up again in Poland in 1945 what they had begun in 1939. As Jacques Rupnik comments, 'all in all the "victorious allies" received from the Soviets as a "reward" what others received as a punishment' (*The Other Europe*, p.76).

We began this unit by pointing to the importance of Poland. It was Poland that had been the most powerful of the East Central European powers between the wars, that had been the victor in the war with the Soviet Union in 1921, that was the traditional route to an invasion of Russia, and that was implacably anti-Russian by virtue of its history and Catholic religion and culture. Poland was the first of the nations to be clearly seen as under total Soviet control when in January 1945 the Lublin Committee was formally recognized by the Soviet Union as the provisional Polish government. Poland had been the main issue at Yalta. From the Soviet Union's point of view the problem with Poland was that it was almost impossible to conceive of a Polish government with popular support that would not be anti-Russian. This led to the conclusion that only a communist regime would be reliable, and thus the phase of genuine coalition government was absent from the Polish experience.

To the sympathetic eye, and there were plenty of sympathetic or self-deluding eyes in Britain and America at the time, the Polish government established in 1945 could appear a genuine coalition. The Lublin government was expanded to include ostensibly non-communist elements, but the only man of real independence in the government was Stanislaw Mikolajczyk, a former member of the government in exile in London and leader of the new Polish Peasant Party, who became a Vice Premier. The pre-war National Democrat Party was not allowed to reform and had to function as an underground organization. Splits had appeared in the old socialist and peasant parties, which had divided between those prepared to collaborate with the communists and those who wished to maintain independence; clearly it was the former who were largely invited to join the government. At the end of 1945 the new Peasant Party or PSL, founded by Mikolajczyk in August, was weakened when its Secretary General, Boleslaw Scibiorek, was murdered in Lodz by security police. The communists were firmly in control. The President, Boleslaw Bierut, and the Minister for Public Security had been in Moscow during the war, while Vice Premier Wladyslaw Gomulka was one of the few communists who had played an active part in resistance to the Germans. By controlling the key ministries of defence, public security, the western territories (the new territory gained from Germany), industry and foreign affairs, the communists, or Polish Workers' Party (PPR) as the communist party was called, had at their disposal a vast patronage system which gave them the power to distribute farms and jobs and gain political support in return.

The back-drop to the communist takeover was a civil war in the countryside.

Despite Katyn and the way the Soviet Union had allowed the Germans to put down the Warsaw Rising, there was still something left of the Polish Home Army. It was clear from the way in which the sixteen Polish leaders, including the last commander of the Home Army, General Okulicki, had been kidnapped by the Red Army while negotiating and then imprisoned in June 1945, that there could be no accommodation between the Home Army and the new regime (*The Times* described the terms of imprisonment handed out as examples of Soviet 'forbearance', which is illustrative of the lengths to which pro-Soviet well-wishers were prepared to go in 1945). Although the Home Army was formally disbanded on General Okulicki's orders, the Association of Freedom and Independence (WIN) was founded from its ranks, and it and two other organizations, the National Armed Forces (NSZ) and the Ukrainian Insurrectionary Army (VPA), carried out operations against the government forces until 1947. Norman Davies has argued that the Soviet security forces,

> by demanding total submission . . . provoked armed resistance from thousands of Poles who might otherwise have contemplated some form of practical co-operation. By branding their opponents indiscriminately as 'terrorists', 'bandits', or 'fascists', they gave rise to the impossible situation in which Communist leaders were calling for a consolidated 'democratic front' whilst the security forces were killing, arresting and deporting the very people who were supposed to co-operate. (*God's Playground*, p.560).

The existence of the civil war was convenient for the communists, as it gave them time to postpone elections until they had tightened their grip on the country, to strengthen the security forces and to allege that their main political rivals, Mikolajczyk's Peasant Party (PSL), were connected with the resistance groups. When Mikolajczyk refused to take his PSL into the communist-dominated 'democratic bloc' of political parties, intimidation of PSL members was stepped up, the circulation of PSL newspapers restricted, and local government officials belonging to the party dismissed. A new electoral law was passed in September 1946 which left the authorities scope for considerable manipulation. Before the elections of January 1947 about a million voters were disenfranchised, and many PSL candidates were struck off the ballot lists, while after the election the counting of the votes was highly irregular. The results were predictable: some 80 per cent for the 'democratic bloc' and only 10 per cent for the PSL. The first half of 1947 saw both the final liquidation of the anti-communist resistance, ending a civil war during which about 30,000 Poles and 1,000 Soviet soldiers had lost their lives, and the end of the PSL. In October 1947 Mikolajczyk escaped from Poland.

Poland, it can be argued, with its Home Army and long-established hostility to the Soviet Union, was *sui generis*. The situation in Bulgaria, Romania and Hungary in 1945 was initially somewhat different. There the Soviet Union, after its initial plundering, permitted a wider spectrum of political activity in the search for economic stabilization, and it hoped that a redistribution of land would gain support for the communist parties. Opposition to the regimes may well have been encouraged by American rhetoric, which raised false hopes of Western support and resulted in a tightening of communist control backed by the Soviet occupation forces. Seton-Watson's stage 3 had been reached by the autumn of 1946 in Bulgaria and Romania and by 1947 in Hungary: the imposition of monolithic communist regimes had begun.

If Poland was a special case, so in a different way was Czechoslovakia. As Jacques Rupnik has put it:

> The contrast between the Polish and Czechoslovak roads reveals the spectrum of Sovietisation in East Central Europe. The Poles, with Katyn on their minds, remained resolutely anti-Soviet, whereas the Czechs, with Munich on their minds, tried to accommodate the Soviet dictators. Both earned, for opposite reasons, the displeasure of the west. After the war Poland was promptly Sovietised while Czechoslovakia toyed for nearly three years with a closely watched experiment in self-limiting democracy. The Polish case came to be regarded by the west as the touchstone of Soviet behaviour and, as such, became the cause of the Cold War. In contrast, the Communist takeover in Czechoslovakia was rather the consequence of Europe's slide into Cold War. (*The Other Europe*, pp.106–7)

Post-war Czechoslovakia positively jumped into the Soviet sphere of influence. The die had already been cast by the time Soviet troops occupied Czechoslovakian territory. Although the government in exile was based in London, Edward Benes, its president, had determined that the future of a united Czechoslovakia must be based on friendship with the Soviet Union. Munich had convinced him and many Czechs that the West could not be trusted as the protector of Czechoslovakia and had given the Czech Communist Party the reputation of a patriotic party (this reputation could only be sustained if one ignored the willingness of the communists to sacrifice the concept of a united Czechoslovak state during the period of the Nazi-Soviet Pact, when the Soviet Union had recognized the separate Slovak state). A Treaty of Friendship and Co-operation was signed between Czechoslovakia and the Soviet Union in December 1943 when Benes visited Moscow. Stalin must have been delighted with his guest who, determined to take revenge on those who had been responsible for or had participated in Czechoslovakia's downfall in 1938–39, asked the Soviet leader for help in certain tasks. Would the Soviet Union help Benes expel the Sudeten Germans? Would the Soviet government put pressure on the Czechs to punish Slovaks who collaborated with the Germans? Would the Soviets ensure that the Red Army rather than Anglo-American forces occupied Hungary? Could Stalin help to turn Czechoslovak trade away from the West and towards the East? Stalin would be sure to see that the 'aristocratic and feudal caste' in Poland was destroyed. Benes, as Wilfred Loth puts it,

> proved himself to be such a stalwart supporter of Soviet interests that Stalin did not even remotely consider replacing his government with a satellite regime. The fact that the Czech and Slovak Communists were able to obtain a disproportionate number of cabinet posts in the definite formation of the 'National Front' government in March 1945 in Moscow was by no means the result of Soviet pressure but rather of the astonishing negligence of Benes. (*The Division of the World*, p.44)

The 'democracy' that Czechoslovakia experienced between 1945 and 1948 was at best a much watered-down and attenuated version of that political system. The National Front, in which the Communists had the leading role, was a coalition of democratically elected parties, but the system did not allow for a real opposition. The political spectrum was curtailed, as the pre-war political parties, the Czech Agrarian Party and the Slovak People's Party, were banned. In a sense all political views were allowed free expression provided they were left-wing and uncritical of the Soviet Union. The communists did not have a political monopoly, but Benes had permitted them to hold the key positions of power, particularly in the army and the security forces which they reshaped on Soviet lines.

This is not to deny the general shift to the left in Czechoslovakian opinion during the immediate post-war period; rather it is to suggest that the circumstances in which that shift occurred ruled out any future reversal. The Communist Party in Czechoslovakia had far more real and long-established support than any other East European communist party, and its 38 per cent of the vote in the 1946 election testified to its appeal. It is true that the elections did not permit the expression of all shades of political opinion and that the communist Minister of Agriculture was in charge of distributing confiscated German lands, but the communists benefited from the general popularity of the Soviet Union, a popularity partly born of a vague Pan-Slavism and partly based on the Soviet Union's reputation as the liberator. Yet the control by the Communist Party of the levers of power, particularly the police and army, meant that when in 1947 a general fall in living standards seemed likely to lead to a loss of communist votes in the elections set for the spring of 1947, the party tightened its grip on the state apparatus and began a systematic programme of intimidation. When the Minister of the Interior replaced the non-communist police chief with a communist minister, the Catholic, Democratic and People's Socialist ministers resigned, hoping to topple the government. Benes, never a man to make a stand against the communists and impressed by the orchestrated demonstrations and the ordering of a general strike by the communist leadership, accepted the resignation of the non-communists on 29 February 1948. The communists went on to win the long-postponed elections in which the lists of candidates were drawn up by them. The end of this period of semi- or limited democracy is often said to have been symbolized by the death of Jan Masaryk, the Foreign Minister and son of the founder of the Republic, who fell from the window of his room at the Foreign Office on 10 March 1948. The non-communist parties were dissolved.

The major question remains whether, granted that Stalin was determined to impose a general hegemony over the states of East Central Europe, the uniformity of communist governments that had come about by 1948 fulfilled his original intentions. If not, did the situation in each country have a dynamic of its own by which a desire by the Soviets to have pliable governments led to communist-controlled governments and inevitably to communist regimes? Or was it rather that the timetable of communization was set by the worsening relations between the Soviet Union and the West, and that as American and British criticism of the Soviet Union increased, as the Truman Doctrine was propounded and as the Marshall Plan was unveiled, the increasingly defensive Soviet government reacted by tightening its and the communist parties' grip on East Central Europe?

The answer would seem to lie in an interaction between developments in the countries of East Central Europe and the increased tension between the Soviet Union and the West. On the one hand there was an internal dynamic which impelled the communist parties of the East Central European states to tighten their grip. Once the Soviet Union had gone further than demanding a mere alignment of foreign policies from the states and had insisted upon a leading role for communist parties within them, the internal politics became a matter of being for or against the policies of communist-dominated 'National Fronts' and therefore for or against the Soviet Union. Soviet policy could not contemplate reverses for its surrogates, and the surrogates were impelled to take more and more power to guard against reverses. Yet the process of communization was also reactive to criticism by the West and support from Britain and America for forces within the states opposed to the increasing communist monopoly of power: each step by which communist rule was imposed resulted in further criticism by the West, which often encouraged anti-communist opposition in the states; this in turn was followed by a further tightening of the screw to silence such opposition.

It is the view of the new left school of American historians that it was the articulation of the Truman Doctrine and the announcement of the Marshall Plan that led to exclusive communist rule in East Central Europe, a legitimate response to America's schemes of military and economic encirclement. This ignores the internal dynamic and the fact that the process of communization was well advanced by 1947. The combined effect of the Truman Doctrine and the Marshall Plan was to put the Soviet Union on the defensive, and one effect of the Cominform policy of September 1947 was a process of consolidation in East Central Europe which meant a greater uniformity as the common model of people's republics was adopted.

The Marshall Plan hit the Soviet Union at its most vulnerable point, its inability to compete economically with the West. The Soviet government was severely shaken by the initial positive reaction of the East Central European states towards the prospect of Marshall Aid. It was the inefficiency of socialist economics that led to the creation of an autarchic Eastern bloc in which trade with the West, which had been growing, was discouraged and the production of the region was geared to the needs of the Soviet Union. Economic direction from Moscow was added to the existing political direction and, as part of this process, political uniformity was imposed upon what became full satellite states.

East Central Europe was where World War I and World War II began; it was where the Cold War developed. Already by May 1945 Churchill was talking of 'an iron curtain, drawn along the line Lübeck–Trieste–Corfu'. (The image of an 'iron curtain' had been used by Goebbels in March 1945 in an article in *Das Reich* in which he warned of the dangers if the Germans surrendered – see Hugh Thomas, *Armed Truce*, p.699). By the time Churchill used the image again in his famous speech at Fulton, Missouri in 1946, when he talked of the iron curtain that had descended across the continent 'from Stettin in the Baltic, to Trieste in the Adriatic', the division of Europe had been drawn more firmly. By the end of 1948 there was indeed an iron curtain, on the eastern side of which were states with uniform systems bound together economically and politically under Soviet control. The US diplomat George Kennan commented in 1948, prior to the Czech coup:

> As long as Communist political power was advancing in Europe, it was
> advantageous to the Russians to allow the Czechs the outer appearances of
> freedom. In this way Czechoslovakia was able to serve as a bait for actions
> farther west. Now that there is a danger of a political movement
> proceeding in the other direction the Russians can no longer afford this
> luxury. (Quoted in Rupnik, *The Other Europe*, p.107)

The bleak uniformity that descended on East Central Europe was soon to be buttressed by the Warsaw Pact and Comecon and to take on an appearance of permanence and imperviousness. Events such as those in Hungary in 1956 and Czechoslovakia in 1968 may have been evidence of opposition to the political and economic systems, but the impotence of the Western powers revealed that the essence of Yalta still stood. Just as important was the misleading impression that the ideological divide was all that mattered, that the national and religious rivalries of East Central Europe that had made the region so unstable belonged to the past. In 1990 we can see more clearly that the Cold War and Marxist-Leninism may have frozen national and religious rivalries in East Central Europe for a generation, but that in the late twentieth century they are a profound influence. National movements make the unity of the USSR seem as fragile as in the aftermath of the Treaty of Brest-Litovsk. The national aspirations of the Hungarian minority were a factor in the overthrow of the Ceausescu government in Romania, while the overthrow encourages the desire for reunification of Romanians in the Moldavian SSR with Romania. Religion is linked to nationalism as a major source of identity. It is clear that Catholicism in Poland is a central element in cultural and national consciousness, while throughout East Central Europe the old religious divides between Catholics (or Uniates) and Orthodox and, further east, between the Orthodox Church and Islam are reasserting this importance, not least in Bulgaria and Yugoslavia. As I argued in Book II, Units 8–10, nationalism is a force that has been continuously undervalued by Western historians in the analysis of modern Europe. It should not be undervalued now when what seemed to many to be history becomes current affairs and when old maps may have more relevance than those published yesterday.

7 SOUTH-EAST EUROPE

As we saw in section 3, Britain in the immediate post-war world was still a great power but was finding it difficult to maintain that position. A searching appraisal would have revealed that Britain's commitments extended beyond its resources, that its armed forces were overstretched, and that its financial affairs were in a sorry state. Yet, though it was obvious that Britain was no longer in the same league as the United States and the Soviet Union, few, at least until 1947, drew the conclusion that Britain could not maintain its great power role for much longer. The Americans, who were in the best position to judge the strength of their ally, came to no such conclusions. This was why the message delivered in late February 1947 by the British Ambassador to Washington, Lord Inverchapel, to General Marshall, the Secretary of State, came as a shock. The news that Britain could no longer be responsible for economic aid to Greece and Turkey had the most profound complications for American foreign policy.

Britain's continued military and political role as a great power had enabled Washington to avoid full acceptance of the consequences and responsibilities of its new status as the world's greatest power. The delusion that American troops could be brought home from Europe at the end of World War II had stemmed from the conviction that Britain would be there. Such hopes had waned, but although Roosevelt and Truman had had a certain feeling of moral superiority over Britain, had disapproved of the British Empire, and had been prepared to bully their ally and act against its interests, they had relied on Britain to shoulder responsibility for many strategically important areas and to take on tasks that might be unpopular with American public opinion or that they were too squeamish or too irresolute to take on themselves. South-Eastern Europe and the Mediterranean were, in particular, areas that had been regarded as a British sphere of influence.

Roosevelt had written in a memorandum of 21 February 1944: 'I do not want the United States to have the post-war burden of reconstituting France, Italy and the Balkans. This is not our actual task at a distance of 3,500 miles or more. It is definitely a British task in which the British are far more vitally interested than we are'. He went on to say: 'our principal task is not to take part in the internal problems in southern Europe'. Between 1944 and 1948 the USA was to find itself increasingly driven to take on responsibilities and commitments that it had at first balked at. But until 1947 the problems of Yugoslavia, Greece and Turkey were largely a British concern.

Exercise Why do you think South-East Europe and the Mediterranean should have seemed naturally a British sphere of interest? ■

Specimen answer 1 Britain had traditionally always given priority to the East Mediterranean as the route to India.

2 Partly for that reason Britain had always taken a close interest in Turkey and the Black Sea straits.

3 As a great naval power Britain had sought to ensure its naval supremacy in the Mediterranean.

4 The British colonies of Gibraltar, Malta and Cyprus supported a British military presence in the Mediterranean.

5 Britain had given a guarantee to Greece in 1939 and had tried to honour that guarantee in 1940.

6 The possibilities offered by the Italian campaign in terms of pressing on into Eastern Europe had always appealed more to the British than the Americans.

7 Support for the Yugoslavian resistance had largely come from Britain.

Although by 1945 the route to India seemed likely to become a less important British preoccupation, British plans to consolidate its interests in the Middle East, because of the increasing importance of the oilfields, pointed to a continued interest in the Mediterranean. □

Churchill's agreement with Stalin in October 1944 as to spheres of influence had recognized Britain's special interest in South-East Europe, so that Britain was given a putative 50 per cent influence in Yugoslavia and a 90 per cent interest in Greece. That agreement, as we have seen, had been the outcome of Churchill's frustration with Roosevelt's refusal to look beyond the end of the war with Germany and was essentially an attempt at damage limitation. Harold Macmillan, Britain's peripatetic Minister in the Mediterranean area, and by November 1944 Acting President of the Allied Commission in Italy and in practice the adminis-trator of Italy, found himself also heavily involved with British policy in Yugo-slavia and Greece. He noted in January 1945 that he could count less and less on American assistance: 'the Americans want to "liquidate" as soon as possible the whole situation arising from the war in Europe' (Alistair Horne, *Macmillan*, vol.1, *1894–1956*, 1988, p.244).

Macmillan's position and that of General Alexander, Commander-in-Chief in Italy and Supreme Allied Commander, Mediterranean, underlined the major responsibility of Britain in the region. British policy under Churchill's direction was to support and re-establish the monarchies of Italy, Greece, Albania and Yugoslavia. American pressure, influenced by the Republican sympathies of New York Italians, was against the Italian monarchy, and only in Greece was Britain to be successful in implementing a monarchical restoration.

Yugoslavia

In the last years of the war Britain directed support to the Yugoslavian resistance from Italy. The war in Yugoslavia was both extremely nasty and extremely complex. The German and Italian forces, aided by the fascist Ustashi in Croatia, had ranged against them two resistance movements, the communist Partisans led by 'Marshal' Tito and the Chetnik royalists under General Mihailovich (Minister of War in the royal government based in London); these two armies fought each other with as much enthusiasm as they fought the Germans and with considerable brutality and cruelty (recall Clive Emsley's discussion of partisan warfare in section 4 of Unit 21).

Considering that the policy of the British government was to restore the royal government, the switch of British support from Mihailovich to Tito late in 1943 seems odd. It is explained largely by the strange enthusiasm for Tito demonstrated by the largely Conservative British intelligence and liaison officers who had contact with the Partisans. Tito had an expansive personality and convinced Brigadier Maclean in particular that, not only were the communists bearing the brunt of the fighting against the Germans, but that their success would help produce 'a strong, democratic and independent Yugoslavia' (he was to be proved right about the independence in the long run, but wrong from the beginning about the democracy). British support for Tito helped ensure that the communists emerged as the most powerful force in Yugoslavia, though the Soviet occupation of parts of the country in September 1944 also played a part. The Titoists were able to make a convincing claim to have been the force that liberated Yugoslavia, though in fact no one liberated Yugoslavia: the Germans withdrew because they had been defeated elsewhere.

British policy was thus ambivalent: while on the one hand it sought to support the royal government based in London, on the other it provided arms for the opponents of the government. The compromise of December 1944, by which members of the all-party assembly AVNOJ (Anti-Fascist Council of National Liberation) and six representatives of the government in exile were admitted to the communist-dominated government, was largely cosmetic. There was never a genuine coalition and never any real opportunity for anti-communist associations to organize. In November 1945 this government felt secure enough, having terrorized the population and killed or intimidated much of the opposition, to hold elections in which the communists gained 81 per cent of the vote. The consequences of the election were the abolition of the monarchy and the end of the pretence of pluralism.

In the closing stages of the war Tito's Partisans moved into Austrian and Italian territory, into Klagenfurt and Austrian Carinthia and into Trieste and other parts of north-east Italy. A considerable responsibility was then thrown upon General Alexander and Harold Macmillan. Should they make a firm stand against the Yugoslavian communist Partisans with forces already depleted by the demands of Greece and with American support in doubt? Macmillan wrote on 9 May 1944:

> I feel that we must be very careful. Neither British nor American troops will care for a new campaign in order to save Trieste for the 'Eyeties'. On the other hand to give in completely may be a sort of slav Munich. (Horne, *Macmillan*, vol. 1, p.247)

Though Alexander and Macmillan at first found it difficult to get clear orders from London or indications of American support, they stood firm, gaining Churchill's and eventually Truman's support. Tito was told that unless Yugoslavian forces withdrew, Alexander would be asked to take matters into his own hands. Tito conceded on 9 June and began to withdraw. It was against this background that perhaps the most shameful episode of Britain's conduct of the war took place, the forcible repatriation of Cossacks and other members of Axis military units to the Soviet Union and of refugees from Yugoslavia to the Titoists. The fact that Alexander's army was overstretched and might at any moment find itself at war with the Yugoslav communists goes some way to explaining, if not excusing, the repatriation. British firmness against the Yugoslavs in both Italy and Austria had a considerable impact on Italian public opinion and played a part in increasing support for the Western powers in Italy. Clearly, however, it also reduced any remaining British influence on Yugoslavia. Yet Tito was by no means getting unequivocal support from the Soviet Union at this time.

Tito's achievement was to demonstrate that Stalinism could exist without Stalin, and this did not endear him to the Soviet dictator. The Yugoslav communists had already imposed their own administration and security apparatus on two-thirds of the country by the time the Red Army arrived, and Soviet attempts to penetrate these instruments of control were one of the main reasons for Stalin's eventual break with Tito. It may well have been that Stalin would have preferred to satisfy Churchill and allow King Peter to return. Certainly Stalin showed little enthusiasm for Yugoslavian ambitions in Austria and Italy. But by 1946 relations between Stalin and Tito were already strained as the Soviet representatives attempted to recruit Yugoslavs for their own security services, while Soviet propaganda which exaggerated the role of Soviet forces in the war in Yugoslavia was unwelcome to the Yugoslav communists. The main reason for the split that was to occur in 1948 was the independence of Tito and the Yugoslav Communist Party – an independence which, as we have seen, had already been noted by Fitzroy Maclean.

Albania

As in Yugoslavia, the partisan forces that opposed the Italian and German occupations were split between monarchists and communists. Enver Hoxha and the communists emerged as the victorious force in 1945. As with Yugoslavia, more British arms seem to have gone to the communists there than to the supporters of King Zog, though this may have had more to do with the infiltration of the Special Operations Executive by the communist agent James Klugman than to London's intentions. Subsequent attempts by the British from 1946 on to take advantage of Albania's long coastline and establish a guerrilla movement within the country seem to have been successively betrayed by communists within the secret services. By 1946 Albania was a people's republic and effective resistance was stamped out.

Greece

In the long run British intervention in 1944 was to ensure the survival of the monarchy and the failure of the Greek Communist Party's bid for power. But it was to prove a long and costly battle. There was an essential continuity of policy towards Greece between the Churchill government and the succeeding Labour administration. Churchill had been steadfast in his support for the Greek monarchy and had committed Britain to maintaining in power a succession of unstable coalition governments. British forces were largely instrumental in crushing the rising by the Greek communist partisans ELAS in December 1944, and in maintaining the government's position when ELAS resumed the civil war in 1946.

Churchill went so far as to make a personal visit to Greece, flying to Athens in late December 1944 and helping to establish a government under Archbishop Damaskinos. Churchill wrote:

> When three million men were fighting on either side in the Western Front and vast American forces were deployed against Japan in the Pacific the spasms of Greece may seem petty, but nevertheless they stood at the nerve centre of power, law and freedom of the western world. (Churchill, *The Second World War*, vol. VI, 1986, p.269)

Ernest Bevin was strongly committed to maintaining British resistance to the Greek government until the threat from ELAS, the armed wing of the Communist Party, was over. During the winter of 1945–46 there were 40,000 British troops in the country. Hugh Thomas describes the British as

> not only the most influential foreign power but, in effect, the rulers of the country appointing and dismissing prime ministers, dictating all departments of state from defence to employment plus arranging for the Secretary General of the British Trade Union Congress, Sir Walter Citrine (fresh from similar lectures in Germany) to suggest how to revive the Greek unions (*Armed Truce*, p.545)

It was indeed suggested by the Australian-born British Ambassador to Greece, Sir Reginald Leeper, that Greece should join the British Commonwealth as a dominion.

The agreement between Stalin and Churchill over Britain's 90 per cent influence in Greece remained intact until the end of the war. There was no Soviet support for the Greek communist uprising in late 1944, and the Yugoslav communists, who had supported the rising to begin with, withdrew, probably on Moscow's insistence. By 1946, however, the Soviet Union was supporting ELAS.

Bevin's declared intention was to promote the establishment of a broad-based coalition in Greece, to provide for free elections, and to withdraw British troops. Nothing, however, polarizes opinion better than a bloody civil war, and the series of governments supported by the British were for the most part governments of the right. They were able to control the towns, but the mountains remained mostly in the hands of ELAS.

There was opposition to the British government's policy in Greece from the left wing of the Labour Party, but the most effective opposition came from Hugh Dalton, the Chancellor of the Exchequer, and was based on economic rather than political grounds. Could Britain afford its Greek policy? Until January 1947 Bevin beat off Dalton's complaints, but then, as Britain's financial problems became overwhelming, gave in. On 30 January Bevin endorsed Dalton's view that Britain should cut its losses in Greece, abandon a commitment which was costed at an additional £50 million, and withdraw British forces.

Turkey

In giving Turkey support against a threat from Russia, Britain was fulfilling the familiar role that had characterized its nineteenth-century foreign policy. Turkey had been persuaded to declare war on Germany in 1945 but had in fact been fairly pro-German and anti-Russian during the greater part of the war. In March 1945 the Soviet Union announced that it was not going to renew the Turko-Soviet Treaty of Friendship signed in 1925 and, later in June, Molotov demanded the revision of the Treaty of Montreux, which gave Turkey control over the Straits, a Russian base in the Dardanelles, and territorial concessions from Turkey to the Soviet republics of Georgia and Armenia. These demands demonstrate an impressive continuity with Tsarist policy towards Turkey; indeed, one of Molotov's complaints concerning British opposition was to wonder why Britain refused to allow the Soviet Union to have that access to the Straits which it had been prepared to give to the Tsar in the secret Treaty of London of 1915. Ernest Bevin was, if anything, firmer than Churchill in his support for Turkey (Churchill at Potsdam had been prepared to accept a division of Montreux in the Soviet Union's favour): 'I do not want', he said to the House of Commons in 1946, 'Turkey converted into a satellite state'.

British support for and aid to Turkey in 1945 and 1946 was important for the future. It linked Turkey securely to the West. Since the 1920s the country had been a one-party state, but now it sought to align its political system to that of the Western powers, allowing the opposition Democratic Party to be formed. In the post-war world Turkey would need to maintain a large army to confront the obvious Russian designs on its territory, and it would need allies. Turkey's role in NATO was foreshadowed. Indeed, British policy in this period did much to tie two strategically important but mutually antagonistic partners, Turkey and Greece, to the future Western alliance.

The last *Pax Britannica*

British interest and involvement in South-East Europe and the Mediterranean in 1947 was not, any more than it had been in the nineteenth century, for the sake of that area alone. In the past British concern had centred on controlling the route to India. It was now the Middle East that was Britain's main concern. Bevin, fully appreciative of the importance of the Middle East oilfields and the vulnerability of Iran and the Arab world to Soviet penetration, saw the importance of the Mediterranean in terms of maintaining Britain's position in the Middle East (Britain, the United States and the Soviet Union all had troops in Persia/Iran in 1945, and it was there that the Soviet Union made its only move to seize new territory when it attempted to detach Persian Azerbaijan). A British sphere of influence thus stretched through the Mediterranean to the Middle East. It was a heavy commitment for the medium-sized power that Britain had in reality become.

Richard Mayne has succinctly summarized Britain's position:

> Living on rapidly dwindling credit, Britain was at the same time bearing heavy overseas burdens. Not only Greece and Turkey, but a number of other countries, were dependent on her aid. In 1946 she had spent 60 million dollars on feeding the German people, however inadequately; in the first quarter of 1947 she was to spend 60 million dollars more. Around the globe . . . British soldiers were still acting as policemen – against Communists in Greece, against the Zionist *Irgun Zvei Leumi* in Palestine, between Hindus and Muslims in India. Nearly two years after the end of World War II there were still a million and a half men in the services, while at home the available manpower was 630,000 short of Britain's needs. (Mayne, *The Recovery of Europe*, 1970, pp.97–8)

The announcement that military and economic aid to Greece and Turkey would have to be suspended forthwith marked Britain's withdrawal from great power status. The implication for the United States was that, if the Soviet Union and communism were going to be contained, they could not rely upon Britain to be in the front line. The atavistic reaction of the United States at the end of the war was to retreat from European commitment; lend-lease was terminated, it was hoped to bring the troops home, and in 1946 a Republican majority in Congress called for cuts in taxes and military expenditure. Such actions, rather like Britain's commitments, were echoes of the past. The USA's giant economic strength had inevitably to be translated into political and military muscle if it was to further its foreign policy aims and ideological preferences outside the American continent. The chimera of Britain's continued great power status had helped to enable US policy-makers to avoid, at least in public, the full consequences of its foreign policy aims. No doubt the essentials of what became the Truman Doctrine were already implicit in the reality of US policy, but that doctrine, enunciated under the pressure of threatened British withdrawal from Greece, made explicit that the USA was now a power with world-wide responsibilities. It also heightened the ideological dimension of the divisions that had taken place in Europe since 1945; it was not possible to convince American public opinion of the necessity for US spheres of influence, but it was possible to enthuse it for a world-wide conflict between expansionist communism and Western free democracy. The Truman Doctrine proclaimed on 11 March 1947 was to the effect that the United States would henceforth take over the burden of military aid to Greece, Turkey and other potential victims of Soviet aggression. In fact a British military presence was maintained in Greece until 1950, but it was clear from March 1947 that, not only had the line between two Europes been firmly drawn, but the containment of Soviet expansion was to be underwritten by the United States.

References

Churchill, W. S. (1986) *The Second World War*, 6 vols, Harmondsworth, Penguin.

Davies, N. (1981) *God's Playground: A History of Poland*, 2 vols, London, Oxford University Press.

Dockrill, M. (1988) *The Cold War 1945–1963*, London, Macmillan.

Draper, T. (1988) 'Neo-conservative history', in D. Carlton and H. M. Levine, *The Cold War Debated*, New York, McGraw-Hill.

Horne, A. (1988) *Macmillan, vol.1, 1894–1956: The Making of a Prime Minister*, London, Macmillan.

Jones, J. M. (1955) *The Fifteen Weeks (February 21–June 4 1947)*, New York, Viking.

Kennedy, P. (1988) *The Rise and Fall of the Great Powers*, London, Unwin Hyman.

Kolko, J. and Kolko, G. (1972) *The Limits of Power: The World and United States Foreign Policy 1945–54*, New York, Harper and Row.

Loth, W. (1988) *The Division of the World 1941–1955*, trans. C. Krojzlova, London, Routledge and Kegan Paul.

Mayne, R. (1970) *The Recovery of Europe. From Devastation to Unity*, New York, Harper and Row.

Oppen, B. Ruhm von (1955) *Documents on Germany under Occupation 1945–54*, London, Oxford University Press.

Rupnik, J. (1988) *The Other Europe*, London, Weidenfeld and Nicolson.

Seton-Watson, H. (1984) *The East European Revolution*, Glencoe, Ill., Westview Press.

Siracusa, J. M. (ed.) (1978) *The American Diplomatic Revolution*, Milton Keynes, Open University Press.

Thomas, H. (1986) *Armed Truce: The Beginnings of the Cold War 1945–46*, London, Hamish Hamilton.

Zamoyski, A. (1987) *The Polish Way: A Thousand Year History of the Poles and Their Culture*, London, John Murray.

UNIT 27 SOCIAL CHANGE 1945–55

Introduction and sections 1 and 2 by Arthur Marwick; section 3 by Tony Aldgate

Open University students will need to refer to:

Documents 2: 1925–1959, eds Arthur Marwick and Wendy Simpson, Open University Press, 1990

Course Reader: *War, Peace and Social Change in Twentieth-Century Europe*, eds Clive Emsley, Arthur Marwick and Wendy Simpson, Open University Press, 1990

INTRODUCTION

You have just been reading about the single most salient geopolitical fact concerning Europe in the post-war years, the divide between the communist East, and the liberal democratic West. Other important themes in the general history of the period immediately single themselves out:

1   Wartime developments greatly weakened Western colonialism (it resulted in severe loss of prestige for the Japanese, and gave opportunities for wartime participation by nationalist leadership groups, particularly in Africa).

2   The movement towards West European unity (the Second World War had brought home the disastrous consequences of continuing disunity).

3   (Contrary to all expectations) there was steady economic growth, noticeable from the late 1940s onwards.

4   It was a period of significant social and cultural change, to which various labels have been applied (there is much room for discussion and counter-argument here): the welfare state; mass society; modernization; Americanization.

In beginning my book *British Society since 1945* (1982) I remarked: 'Nobody has ever said precisely how many ways there are of skinning a cat. Probably there are about the same number of ways of writing a Social History of Britain since 1945.' The same sort of remark could be made about the task of writing about social change in Europe since 1945. However, by this stage in the course you will have become familiar with two major contrasting ways of approaching the topic (first introduced in Book I, Unit 1, and also discussed in the Introduction to the Course Reader): the approach which looks at changing structures of power, 'ideal types' (Weber's phrase for conceptual abstractions defining a category of phenomena, the *category* not necessarily coinciding with any one individual phenomenon), and which makes much use of such terms as 'corporatism', 'stabilization', or 'revolution of modernity'; and the approach which prefers to concentrate on a detailed list of overlapping areas of social change. We have also discovered that an interesting way of analysing some of the most important social developments is to consider the notion of the emergence of what can be defined as 'mass society'. This brief discussion provides the key to the tripartite structure of this unit (the three ways chosen, if you like, to skin the cat). In the first section I examine two slightly different approaches from within the 'nomothetic' perspective: one a continuation of the ideas of Charles Maier extended to incorporate the post World War II period, the other a discussion of the historical problem of 'the two Germanys' by one of today's most distinguished sociologists, Ralf Dahrendorf, who is known in particular for the way in which he has updated Weber to apply to developments in class since World War II.

1 SOCIAL CHANGE: TWO NOMOTHETIC PERSPECTIVES

Charles S. Maier: 'The two post-war eras and the conditions for stability in twentieth-century Western Europe'

This paper, originally delivered to a meeting of the American Historical Association, was printed in an occasional *Forum* section published by the famous American historical journal, *American Historical Review*, in April 1981 (vol.86, no.2, April 1981, pp.327–52). Maier's paper is followed by comments and criticisms by Professor A. Stephen Schuker and Charles P. Kindleberger, and is rounded off with a final reply from Maier. The entire forum provides an excellent example of historical controversy conducted at the highest level.

Maier begins his main article by quoting from the radio broadcast given by A. J. P. Taylor in November 1945, in which Taylor claimed that in the aftermath of war private enterprise was now dead. Maier says he wishes to raise the question of why, in Western Europe at least, 'there was less transformation than he [Taylor] envisaged.' Maier, in fact, is again raising exactly the kind of question you encountered in the extracts from his *Recasting Bourgeois Europe* in the Course Reader: 'how did Western Europe achieve political and social stability by the mid-twentieth century after two great, destructive wars and the intervening upheaval?' Characteristically, Maier declares: 'stabilization is as challenging a historical problem as revolution' (these quotations are all from p.327 of the article).

Exercise I am now going to give you a number of extracts from the article. I want you to write down your own comments on these, saying what you find particularly helpful and what, if anything, you feel is open to question. Take this exercise in a very relaxed way: where you feel it is relevant (if at all) bring in material from the discussions of Maier's ideas in the Course Reader and in Book III, Units 14 and 15. Comment on the style, phrasing, etc. Start off by discussing what answer Maier is giving to the question, 'was there significant social change in the years after World War II?' I shall try to be as open-ended as possible in my discussion, in which I shall also introduce some of the main points made by Schuker and Kindleberger, ending up with Maier's own reply to these two commentators.

I have numbered the separate extracts merely to make identification of your (and my) comments easier.

The first extract I quote follows immediately upon Maier's statement that 'stabilization is as challenging a historical problem as revolution':

> 1   Stabilization, moreover, does not preclude significant social and political change but often requires it. Certainly the two World Wars broadened democracy in Britain and stimulated economic transformation in France. World War II finally removed the contradictions between modernity and reaction in Germany, thereby facilitating a meritocratic pluralism. Yet, despite the transformations, earlier Liberal and élitist arrangements that governed the distribution of wealth and power either persisted or were resumed after authoritarian intervals. And at least until the end of the 1960s the societies of Western Europe seemed more cohesive, humdrum, and routine than either those who feared change or those who longed for it would have predicted. (p.327)

2   Stabilization meant not so much preserving liberal procedures as re-establishing the overlapping hierarchies of power, wealth, and status that can be loosely termed as 'capitalist'. (p.333)

3   Repression, co-optation, and the success of the managerial mystique with its vogue of productivity had reconsolidated the bureaucratic organization of industrial work in the 1920s. The economic accomplishments of the period after 1948 completed the second half of the stabilization assignment. They seemed to eliminate the vulnerability of economic life and enhanced legitimacy with output and growth. Despite the tragic waste of the Great Depression, the immense destructiveness of two World Wars, and the countless lives scattered like dry autumn leaves throughout Europe, Western leaders recovered more of their prosperity and liberalism, retained more of their privileges and prerogatives, than they would have dared predict. (p.347)

4   Fully to comprehend the period from 1918 to 1950 as a search for stabilization on the part of the old upper and middle classes, now augmented by a reformist working-class leadership, requires looking at the international architecture as well as domestic structure. (p.348)

5   . . . the international corollary of the era of domestic stabilization may be viewed as a German-American (or perhaps a trilateral German-American-Japanese) association achieved only after two world wars. Success for this policy was registered not by the rubble of Berlin but by the frustration of such postwar German leaders as Jakob Kaiser of the CDU and Kurt Schumacher of the SPD, both of whom sought unsuccessfully to maintain under democratic auspices a less capitalist and less exclusively Western-oriented German society. Their very setbacks testified to the triumph of stabilization in West Germany, Western Europe, and the noncommunist countries as a whole. Just as the end of the Second War against Germany resolved the international issues left undecided after the close of the first, so the strengthening of Western pluralism after the second war completed the European domestic institutional restructuring begun after the first. Stabilization meant an end to the German problem. It likewise meant winning the adherence of a large enough segment of the working classes to preserve the scope for private economic power and hierarchy that defined liberal capitalism. The achievement was not simply restorative, for the new, very real guarantees of social welfare and social-democratic political participation contributed change even as they purchased continuity.

6   This suggests that the major socio-political assignment of the twentieth century paralleled that of the nineteenth, which saw the incorporation of the middle classes and European bourgeoisie into the political community . . . The institutional device for the nineteenth century was parliamentary representation; the institutional foci for the twentieth-century achievement included trade unions, ambitious state economic agencies, and bureaucratized pressure groups – the components of what I have termed elsewhere 'corporate pluralism.' (Both paragraphs 5 and 6 run continuously on p.351) ■

Discussion   Maier is saying that there was no change on the scale longed for by socialists or feared by conservatives; private enterprise, despite A. J. P. Taylor, was not dead. The old elitist arrangements governing the distribution of wealth and power, the old 'capitalist' hierarchies, were re-established. The old leadership recovered their prosperity and operated in the old 'liberal' (that is, non-socialist) framework.

Aided admittedly by 'a reformist working-class leadership' the old upper and middle classes remained in charge. However, within that broad picture of absence of change within structures of power (the main concern of the sort of approach Maier espouses) significant social and political change was not precluded: there was change (I will discuss this in detail in a moment) in Britain, France and Germany. Economic growth and rises in output removed 'the vulnerability of economic life' for the masses. There was a new place for the reformist working-class leadership.

One could indeed say that Maier rather brilliantly summarizes the social change that did take place in the West (and it is undoubtedly true that older hierarchies and elites were not utterly overthrown, and reconstituted in a new manner, as they were in the East). The crucial question, with regard to the different approaches to social change, is, 'what sort of social change is it reasonable to expect?' Maier's insistence that 'stabilization is as challenging a historical problem as revolution' is central to his way of seeing things. His, at heart, is the traditional conflict model of society (postulated, in slightly different ways, by both Marx and Weber): conflict, the overthrow and replacement of classes, hierarchies or elites, is to be expected. Stabilization therefore requires explanation. Yet one could argue that in Western Europe stability has been far more in evidence than revolution, and that it is only because Maier's basic assumptions lead him to expect revolution, that he places so much emphasis on stabilization. You may very properly feel that assumptions about the possibilities of revolution, or at least about crises or power relationships in society, are sensible ones, or that this criticism of Maier can be pushed too far and that Maier is being perfectly realistic when he talks of 'two great destructive wars and the intervening upheaval' and of 'the tragic waste of the Great Depression, the immense destructiveness of two World Wars'. In the end, support for, or criticism of, Maier reduces to a question of the extent to which one supports his broad, conceptualizing approach, which presents the same classes or elites as being in existence over most of the century. Professor Kindleberger specifically criticized: '(1) the concept of power elites that make "efforts" over two continents and half a century, and (2) the notion that the two post-war periods form part of the same effort' (p.358).

Professor Schuker was critical of Maier's 'strategy' as he saw it:

> One begins with a governing hypothesis and then surveys the literature selectively to find substantiation for it. If the hypothesis is shrewdly chosen, the outcome may suggest an enlightening way to organize information within a plausible explanatory structure. That strategy, however, also harbors dangers. It provides little incentive to avoid the use of unrepresentative data. And it can tempt a writer into employing abstract terms in order to obscure the discrepancies between an arresting hypothesis and inconvenient facts. (p.353)

Now, you may feel that without some hypothesis it is impossible to bring any kind of order or organization to the infinite masses of historical information. Personally, I have great sympathy for Maier's attempt. My point would be more that he has perhaps not got hold of the right hypothesis, that the assumptions which lead him to look for revolutionary change mean that he possibly undervalues the real change that did take place.

Let us look at the individual extracts.

1   As already noted, there are valuable points here. You will remember the arguments about how far the position of the working class in Britain did change, how significant the welfare state was, and so on, but 'broadened democracy' seems a not inaccurate phrase: one could cite François Bédarida in support of the notion of economic transformation in France. The bit about Germany is perhaps more puzzling. The idea of 'contradictions between modernity and reaction' has its origins in such writers as Dahrendorf (whom we shall be looking at in a moment) and, along with a phrase like 'meritocratic pluralism', is very much in keeping with this kind of 'sociological' or 'nomothetic' historical writing. 'Modernity' here implies democratic voting rights, freedom of speech, welfare policies, and so on. The argument (a form of which we encountered in the chapter by Gerald Feldman in the Course Reader) is that even after World War I reactionary elements in Germany were able to resist this modernity; only the destruction and defeat of World War II, and the 'year zero' or 'new start' which followed it, made possible the kind of liberal democratic society in which there is no rigid state control and in which individuals can advance by merit. The next sentence, of course, is making Maier's fundamental point, though the phrase 'after authoritarian intervals' is perhaps puzzling. He seems here to be referring to the Labour government in Britain, and to the Resistance-dominated governments that were only briefly in office in France and Italy: these governments, he seems to be suggesting, tried in 'authoritarian' ways to alter the structures of power and wealth, but did not last long. I, on the contrary, have suggested that some (though admittedly limited) changes came about because of the war experience itself and could not be reversed. Our course ends in 1955, and it may well be right to say that Western European societies at that time were 'cohesive, humdrum and routine'. All in all, one might comment, this is not a bad thing for societies to be, so that the question again arises of why look for anything more radical or revolutionary? Still, Maier does have a valid point in challenging popular, over-coloured versions of recent history which suggest that European societies were totally transformed by World War II.

2   If 'liberal procedures' means democratic voting rights, freedom of speech, etc., one may ask why there would be any suggestion as to their not being 'preserved'. The main point, however, is that this is the kernel of Maier's argument, the re-establishment after World War II of capitalist hierarchies. Schuker, it may be noted, challenged the use of the word 'capitalist', suggesting as an alternative, 'bourgeois', which is not, in my view, necessarily an advance. The real issue is whether or not (and one can legitimately answer the question either way) such blanket terms as 'capitalist' (or, for that matter, 'bourgeois') obscure important detailed changes that do take place.

3   The first sentence is a summary of some of Maier's main arguments in the extracts from the *Recasting of Bourgeois Europe* that you have already studied. As you know, they are open to debate. Again, Maier makes important points about economic achievement after 1945. The final sentence is another summary of Maier's essential position. It may be that he rather overworks this idea of changes not being as great as the elite themselves feared: (a) was it the *same* elites who were doing well in the later parts of the post-war period?; (b) there were elite figures in all West European countries after the war who *complained* about their loss of privilege, as they saw it. A major source of criticism in this paragraph, however, is

the use of the phrase 'the stabilization assignment'. You may have noticed that a similar phrase crops up in paragraph 6. You may not have thought much about this, but it is in fact typical of Maier's type of approach that he postulates that certain social agents, the 'bourgeoisie' or the 'power elite' have 'assignments', rather as you, working your way through this course, have had 'assignments'. I want to come back to this again at the end when I return to one of Professor Schuker's major comments, but I will just say here that some historians would feel that it is rather dubious, or even dangerous, to write history in this way.

4   As already noted, this brief sentence contains suggestions of both non-change (maintenance of their position by the old upper and middle classes) and change (a joining with them of the reformist working-class leadership). Its main point in the development of Maier's article is to direct attention to the significance of international as well as domestic development (as so often, Maier turns a nice phrase here).

5   In referring to associations between the Germans, the Americans and the Japanese, Maier is, of course, looking into the 1950s and beyond; however, certainly the economic revival of Germany, and the USA's association with it, fall well within our course material. Kaiser and Schumacher scarcely belong to the 'authoritarian intervals' mentioned in paragraph 1, but Maier is making the point that leaders of their socialist and neutralist outlook could not compete against the resurgence of capitalist and pro-Western forces. Possibly that verdict would seem a sound one in 1955, though personally I would think it wrong to ignore the strong elements of social democracy to be found, particularly in some local and state governments in West Germany. Maier's notion of stabilization is perhaps slightly dubious throughout, and seems particularly so when he seems, in the next sentence, to be posing an antithesis between the notions of social democracy and stabilization, which he really seems to be regarding as analogous to the triumph of conservatism. How far it is really true, with a divided Germany, that World War II 'resolved the international issues left undecided after the close' of the First World War, must be open to question: even more open to question, as I have already suggested, is the notion that there was now a completion of a deliberate institutional restructuring begun after World War I. It now begins to seem that Maier is so proud of his discovery of 'stabilization' that he is making it a central explanatory factor, both for, as he sees it, the ending of the German problem and for re-established liberal capitalism. But again he does point to two important social changes: the incorporation of a segment at least of the working class in the new social structure, and genuine guarantees of social welfare. The final sentence of this paragraph is a fine example of Maier's style at its brilliant best. All I would say is that this to me sounds like an intelligent and desirable change; I can't quite see why it is necessary to spend so much time 'explaining' the victory of stabilization over some imagined more radical upheaval. But, once more, if you find Maier persuasive don't allow me in any way to put you off.

6   Here we have the quintessence of the Maier style, postulating that centuries have 'major socio-political assignments'. If there is a problem of how 'the middle classes and European bourgeoisie' rose to, and continued, their dominance, then Maier deals with it brilliantly. What one can question is whether there is a problem of exactly that nature, and whether the terms used are the correct ones (as distinct, say, from discussing the way in which individual classes themselves change, along with the relationships between the several classes). In his earlier work, you

will remember, Maier spoke about the rise of 'corporatism'. Interestingly, he subsequently moderated the phrase, as repeated here, to 'corporate pluralism'. This is an improvement in so far as it recognizes that corporatism was not quite the central, rigid development he earlier implied, but one might continue to have doubts about the validity of the concept in whatever form.

Now let me quote Professor Schuker's second major general comment:

> Professor Charles Maier evokes a historical universe in which idealism still holds sway. History had 'tasks', centuries receive 'socio-political assignments', and governments are 'called upon' by unnamed powers to maintain economic growth and high unemployment at specified levels of income. (p.358)

By 'idealism', it should be explained, Schuker means that type of historical (or philosophical) thinking which conceptualizes agents and forces, envisages history as a process with certain definite 'purposes', and, of course, employs 'ideal types'.

As I said way back in Book I, Unit 1, the answers one gives to questions about war's effects on social change depend in part on one's general approach to historical study. In his reply to Schuker and Kindelberger, Maier recognized (p.367) that he does believe in the value of employing 'ideal types' in historical analysis. The conclusion to his reply is witty and impressive. Note in it Maier's admission that his approach might be (interesting adjective!) 'over structured'; here he is responding to a very interesting comment made earlier by Professor J. H. Hexter (an extremely conservative American historian, utterly opposed to anything suggesting Marx, Weber, structures, or ideal types).

> When I presented the paper at the American Historical Association meeting of December 1978, Professor J. H. Hexter admitted sympathetically that it had been stimulating but wondered if, after all, the real reason for stability following World War II did not derive from the simple fact that people were tired of despotism. The observation was sobering in its implication that my account might be over structured. Let me respond two years later that people rarely want despotism, or war, or idle factories, or worthless money. But they sometimes get them. Here I have tried to outline the circumstances that let at least some of them translate yearnings for normalcy into the liberal capitalist efflorescence that followed the great wars of our century.

Ralf Dahrendorf: 'The two Germanys'

Maier, we have seen, sometimes speaks of classes (upper and middle classes, bourgeoisie, working classes) and sometimes of 'elites'. There are arguments, as we have seen, over what exactly constitutes a class. However, there is agreement that a class, whether seen (as I would have it) as an aggregation of actual families or as an agent in historical processes, is in formation and, more important, in existence over a considerable period of time – generations if not centuries. Elites, by contrast, are groups possessed of particular powers and particular privileges, possibly over short periods of time: thus sociologists have spoken of 'business elites', 'political elites', 'cultural elites', 'labour elites', etc. Those who envisage the most important elites as being closely intertwined with each other, have spoken of 'power elites' or 'strategic elites'. One of the most influential books on the subject has been *Beyond the Ruling Class: Strategic Elites in Modern Society* (1963) by the American sociologist Suzanne Keller. The difference between 'elite' and 'social class' is well incapsulated in her statement: 'For elite recruitment as a whole social class will be a variable rather than a constant element' (p.205). In other words, elites *may* be recruited from several different social classes.

One possible way of describing how social structure has changed in the twentieth century (and particularly in the aftermath of World War II) is to say that in what Maier has described as 'pluralistic meritocracies', dominance by class (the upper class, the bourgeoisie, etc.) has given way to dominance by elites, which may be recruited from several classes. Certainly, in Eastern Europe new political elites have been created, many of whose members are drawn from the former working class. This is certainly an argument you should consider in any further reading you may do; personally I have argued for the continuing significance of class (though not defined quite as Marx or Weber defined it – see my *Class: Image and Reality in Britain, France and the USA since 1930*, 1980, and *Class in the Twentieth Century*, 1986). Another thesis that has been advanced is that while there continues to be a ruling bourgeoisie, this is supported by an educated 'service class'. That is another view (also challenged by me in the books I have just mentioned) to look out for in your reading. The most recent variant is Harold Perkin's notion of 'the triumph of the professional class' (*The Rise of Professional Society: England since 1880* – by 'England' Perkin means 'Britain' – but he does not, of course, deal with developments on the European continent). Incidentally, when, referring in advance to the review I had written for the *English Historical Review*, I told Perkin that I disagreed with his book, his reply was: 'But if you didn't, Arthur, there would have been no point in writing the book!' – a rather neat way of making the important point that if historians simply wrote books repeating, and agreeing with, each other, the subject would very quickly die.

The main part of this sub-section is devoted to discussing the key ideas in the final two chapters of Ralf Dahrendorf's *Society and Democracy in Germany* (1968). These chapters are entitled respectively: 'The Two Germanys: The German Democratic Republic', and 'The Two Germanys: The German Federal Republic'. Though written by a sociologist, this book is concerned with problems that we would recognize as being essentially historical. Three conceptualizations are central to the parts of Dahrendorf's arguments we are concerned with: (a) what he terms the 'German Question' – briefly touched on by Maier, and explained at the beginning of the extracts from Dahrendorf's book which are printed below; (b) what he calls 'The Revolution of Modernity' – some of the main elements of this I have touched on, but Dahrendorf sees modernity as paradoxical, 'good' in aspiring to equality for all citizens, 'bad' in that it always carries the risks of what Dahrendorf calls totalitarianism; (c) in the tradition of Marx and Weber, Dahrendorf envisages conflict between classes or groups as endemic and indeed 'natural' in society.

Exercise   Below are printed extracts from chapters 26 and 27 of Dahrendorf's *Society and Democracy in Germany*. To facilitate discussion I have again numbered the extracts, though note that there are sizeable omissions. Again I want you to take a very relaxed attitude, writing down comments on how persuasive you find the arguments, on what you find particularly helpful, and on the style and phrasing.

Chapter 26

1   Why did the constitutions of liberty fare so badly in German society? If this is the German Question, modern German history may be understood as a chain of diverse answers to this question, all of which refer to defeats in the social infrastructure of politics.

. . . Imperial Germany brought about hitherto unknown faults of industrial and pre-industrial structures which are impermissible to the present day by the standards of all accepted theories; as a result, an authoritarian political constitution managed to assimilate the new conditions of an industrial civilization. The Republic of Weimar had lost the authority that belongs to this constitution; at the same time, it delayed the revolution that might have opened its society to more liberal patterns. The achievement was not unlike that of Sisyphus, for it did not prevent the rock from rolling; in the end, revolution came after all. But the revolution now showed its ugliest face; modernity entered Germany in its totalitarian dress and thus forbade the constitution of liberty once again. This was the most costly answer of German society so far to its ever more pressing question: eventually, it led to the challenges of total defeat in May 1945. (p.419)

2   This is the starting point of a development that makes it even more interesting for the sociologist, but even more painful for the people involved, to follow Germany's postwar history: the division of the country. After 1945, German society gave not one, but two answers to the challenges of defeat. (p.420)

3   Around the turn of the years 1945/1946 it was evident to nearly everyone living in the then Soviet zone of occupation that the brief interval in which the reins of power had been held more loosely was to be followed by a development that, for many people, differed little from the National Socialist past.

If anything, this development documented how incomplete the National Socialist revolution of modernity had remained. The East German revolution went further. It attacked the same survivals of a closed past; but it did not stop short of any one of them. This time, the last farm, the last family, the last church community was drawn into the process. (p.421)

4   By contrast to National Socialist Germany, there are hardly any islands of tradition left in the DDR. But then, the social revolution of National Socialism was continued quite deliberately here. Already its result may be described as the total modernization of the country, that is, the general transformation of social positions that used to be quasi-ascribed into positions that the individual may in principle acquire for himself. (p.422)

5   De facto, there is no universal, equal, free, and secret suffrage, no liberty of the person and of political activity, no equality before the law; but there is a society that would enable its members to make effective use of these liberties, if only they had them. Once again modernity shows its Janus face.

It is a fact of great importance that the inclusive process of social co-ordination in East Germany has involved the realization of that equality that is a precondition of effective citizenship rights; all the more since it probably constitutes the hard core of East German social changes, which can never be undone . . .

If one interprets modernity as we have done throughout, the society of the DDR is the first modern society on German soil. In it the French Revolution has been led to its horrid extreme . . . Whoever wants the constitution of liberty must want modernity, even if he acquires with it the very immediate danger of totalitarianism. (pp.422–4)

6   Social conflict is a reality that does not bow to the dictate of even the most powerful state party. In fact, the history of the DDR may be a history of internal conflicts seeking modes of expression. Where the open clash of solidary groups is forbidden, the missing energies of opposition find their expression in other ways . . . The fever curve of refugees from the DDR since its establishment in September 1949 is an impressive document of the failure of totalitarian rule . . . It suffices to call to mind the revolts of June 17, 1953. (pp.424–5)

7   . . . unification of the political elite was merely the first stage in a process that eventually brought about a new political class in the DDR . . . Nationalization of the economy and its administration by state functionaries, politicization of the new army, reconstruction of the entire educational system, the legal system, the administration were some of the stages on this road . . .

The result is a leading stratum whose properties and values today determine the picture of society in the DDR. In its social composition and orientation, the stratum has almost nothing in common with its historical predecessors or with the previous political class of the Federal Republic. Almost without exception it consists of new people. (p.427)

Chapter 27

8   Differences began with the way in which the two parts of Germany reacted to the social revolution of National Socialism. While in the East this revolution was confirmed and, if anything, accelerated and radicalized, certain developments in West Germany might be described as counterrevolutionary in this respect. As a reaction to the National Socialist revolution, but probably also as part of the search for reliable fixed points of social structure, West German society had chosen, in quite a few areas, the return to premodern structures. The narrowness and integrity of family ties was promoted by the state, even anchored in constitutions in the form of parental prerogative. The Länder re-emerged and were equipped with greater rights than they had in the past; indeed a strong emphasis on the regional ties of man including the social acceptability of dialects is noticeable in the Federal Republic. Church membership with all its social implications found the interested support of many public agencies, so that a general tendency toward secularization was countered by a German tendency toward denominalization. (pp.435–6)

9   In the Federal Republic, the realization of the equal basic status of all men stands in sharp contrast to the DDR. While in the East the social conditions of the role are present, but its legal and political potential is minimal, the Federal Republic recognizes the legal status of the citizen in the full range, but many of the social preconditions of its effective realization are lacking. (p.436)

10   . . . social changes . . . proceed extremely slowly in the Federal Republic . . . Government policies in the fields of subsidies and social services are designed here to lay an effective basis for citizenship rights rather than to bring about a welfare state in the traditional sense. (p.437)

11   Although, therefore, the picture of civic equality is by no means as unidimensional for West Germany as it is for East Germany . . . the tendency toward development is equally clear. It means the slow completion of modernity. This is the background before which the most significant single event for West German social development has to be

seen, the economic miracle. While the DDR is shaped in its social reality by the process of the planned formation of a uniform, monopolistic elite dominated by its more narrowly political elements, the explosive development of its economy is the dominant and determinant feature of the short history of the German Federal Republic. (p.438)

[Dahrendorf now states (p.439) that a liberal market naturally means conflict.]

12   Recognizable traces of a new style of conflict have entered into the traditional authoritarian system of industrial relations . . . parliamentary democracy in the Federal Republic comes very much closer to the idea of government by conflict than the Weimar Republic ever did.

However, by and large the social effects of the economic miracle were least pronounced in the field of conflict regulation. The consequences of the liberal dynamics of West German economic development are much more striking in respect to the composition of elites. To begin with, the economic elites themselves differ considerably in their composition from their historical predecessors. Apart from the leaders of political parties, West German business leaders are the only upwardly mobile group in the political class of the Federal Republic.

There are many new men in this group who have acquired office and fortune since the war. Furthermore – and since this is harder to measure it must remain an assertion here – the weight of business leaders among the elites has greatly increased. (p.440) ■

Discussion   The German question is explained right at the beginning as being that of why liberty fared so badly in German society. As a result of the apparently peculiar development of Imperial Germany, the new conditions of an industrial civilization existed within an authoritarian political constitution. This, you may well have felt, is an illuminating comment, though you may also have felt, as I do, that there is something deterministic, and indeed not very well expressed, in the phrase 'hitherto unknown faults of industrial and pre-industrial structures which are impermissible to the present day by the standards of all accepted theories'. (I am not sure that a historian can accept that developments which actually took place can be described as 'impermissible', nor that there are 'standards of all accepted theories' by which one can make judgements.) The next sentence expresses an interpretation which, in slightly different words, we have encountered in both Feldman's and Maier's Reader chapters: we have the old question of whether there really was a possible or practicable revolution which Weimar 'delayed' (you should have your own views on that by now). The metaphor of Sisyphus (in classical mythology hopelessly pushing the rock up the hill) suggests that Dahrendorf regards revolution of some sort as inevitable: the revolution, in the event, was that of Hitler. Are these sweeping generalizations justified? The last sentence, rather in the style of Maier, postulates that it is legitimate to talk of societies (again, as if they were students!) giving answers to questions: this is the 'idealism' criticized by Schuker. Nazi revolution led (this seems fair enough) to the 'challenges of total defeat'; this marks the starting point for Dahrendorf's two final chapters.

In extract 2, in what may seem a reasonable summary of a major historical development, we again have this notion of society as some kind of coherent historical agency, giving 'answers'.

Perhaps the change of perception in the Soviet zone had come by the end of 1945, possibly it took a little longer. The crucial points are the notions that

National Socialism involved a 'revolution of modernity', and that under Soviet rule this revolution was continued and extended, with farm, family, and church being fully drawn in, and (extract 4) practically all islands of tradition being obliterated. Dahrendorf says that the social revolution of National Socialism was 'deliberately' continued, which seems not to allow for (one would think) the very different ideologies of National Socialism and communism. By 1955 much of East Germany seemed undeveloped and archaic, fixed in the 1930s, compared with rapidly developing West Germany. Yet Dahrendorf speaks of 'total modernization', though he is speaking purely of political rights – in traditional societies people are born into their positions, they are 'quasi-ascribed', whereas in principle at least the DDR stands for equal rights for all.

In extract 5 Dahrendorf goes on to expand the paradox: actually there are no liberties, no equality before the law, but if there were, there is the social and economic provision to enable people (in contrast to other societies, such as Weimar Germany) to make effective use of them. What East Germany has established, Dahrendorf is saying, is equality, and he believes that is a social change which will never be undone. Whether this is really true seems to me highly dubious. Dahrendorf gets rid of the paradox, or the inconsistency, by speaking of the 'Janus face' of modernity. Perhaps you find this a persuasive explanation. I would prefer a full statement of the facts as they actually are in East Germany, and then one could do without this rather contorted conception of modernity. Next there is the contention that the DDR is the first modern society on German soil, the French Revolution 'brought to its horrid extreme'. The core of Dahrendorf's thought here is in the last sentence of this extract, that liberty requires modernity – that is to say, the destruction of traditional strongholds of power and privilege, which interfere with equality – but that this necessary destruction involves the danger of totalitarianism. Again, you may feel that Dahrendorf is right: it really depends on whether one accepts Dahrendorf's implication (unstated at this point) that the attempts at liberty in Western democratic countries are incomplete because of the persistence of economic inequality.

With extract 6 we come to another of Dahrendorf's central contentions, concerning social conflict. Dahrendorf gives two examples which he claims demonstrate the necessary continuance of social conflict. Personally, I would simply attribute the rising number of refugees, and the East Berlin revolts of 1953, to intense and justified dissatisfaction with the regime (which I see as a totally different matter from the alleged inevitable existence of social conflict).

Extract 7 is particularly useful as a description, and explanation, of the transformation of social structure in the DDR (a transformation on a scale completely lacking, as Maier was at pains to point out, in the West).

With extract 8 we move on to the chapter on West Germany. We have here a most arresting and thought-provoking thesis: that the revolution of modernity initiated by National Socialism was continued in the East, whereas in the West there was a 'counter-revolutionary' attempt to return to premodern structures. I am sure you found the detail here fascinating and worth very careful attention. Whether the overall thesis is sustainable is a different matter.

In extract 9 we are back to the fundamental, though somewhat paradoxical, contrast which we have already encountered. The DDR has the social but not the actual conditions of liberty; the Federal Republic genuinely has the legal conditions, but not all of the social preconditions. It is for you to decide in the light of further reading how far this is an adequate summary.

Whether or not you agree with what is said in extract 10 depends on how you approach the phrase 'a welfare state in the traditional sense': is the welfare state in essence something new and liberating, introduced after 1945, or is it a traditional device for maintaining the existing unequal social hierarchy? That is the sort of thought I hope you noted down.

Personally, I find extract 11 rather puzzling. The failure of understanding is probably mine, and if you have done better than me, then my heartiest congratulations. To me there seems to be something of a contradiction of earlier arguments. It is now stated openly that the DDR has a monopolistic elite dominated by its more narrowly political elements, while in the West, after all, there is a tendency towards the slow completion of modernity. Perhaps Dahrendorf's purpose is to identify the explanation for the latter (though it cannot explain the former), the German 'economic miracle'. At any rate, he is surely right to give it this amount of prominence.

Finally, we come back to the question of the inevitability of conflict. Dahrendorf gives the Federal Republic some credit for finding progressive new ways of institutionalizing conflict. But the more striking consequences have been with respect to the composition of elites. Dahrendorf here is making a strong case for there having been important changes in social structure since the war. However, note that it is not a question of transformation in class structure, but simply in the way in which elites are recruited, and the way in which business leaders have become more important.

I am sure you found Dahrendorf's analysis stimulating. What he says about elites in both Germanys, about the destruction of surviving islands of tradition in the East, and about certain tendencies towards traditionalism in the West, are all worthy of the fullest consideration. But this is, intentionally, a very schematic account. Many of his generalizations need to be checked against details of the realities of life in the two Germanys.

2 *SOCIAL CHANGE: IDIOGRAPHIC PERSPECTIVES*

I do not propose here to work through the ten overlapping areas of social change which formed the basis of the discussion of the social impact of World War II in Units 22–25. However, do keep these ten headings firmly in mind as a useful framework against which to evaluate the information provided throughout this unit. Geopolitical changes have, of course, been explored in Unit 26.

There is not a great deal to add to what was said in Units 22–25 with regard to social geography. Most important are the new industrial centres developed to the east in the Soviet Union; the new commercial centres of Western Germany (particularly Frankfurt and Stuttgart); the movement of population, which continued in the post-war years in the form of a steady leakage of population from Eastern Europe to the West, and West Germany in particular; and also the surprising upward movement in the birth rate in the post-war years.

In the realm of economic theory (the first part of the second area of social change) the important developments are in (a) the internationalization of the world economy under the sponsorship of the United States, thus breaking with the narrow and debilitating economic nationalism of the inter-war years, and (b) the growth of a new pragmatic managed capitalism involving, most notably in France and Italy, indicative state planning, but also the encouragement, within an organized framework, of private enterprise and market economics (Britain, arguably, was less successful in getting the balance right). With regard to economic performance, the crucial element was economic growth, apparent in all the Western countries from the late 1940s onwards. This was most apparent in the 'economic miracle' of, first, West Germany in the early 1950s (assisted by the currency reform of 1948), and then, following closely, in Italy. France underwent intensive growth in its industrial and commercial sectors, with the consequence of a drastic reduction in the 1950s in its agricultural sector. Economic growth was apparent in East Germany from the early 1950s. Russia and Poland, of course, had the desperate devastations of the war to recover from. On the whole, economic policy and achievement in the Eastern bloc was still very unsatisfactory at the end point of our course, 1955. Note, incidentally, that while other countries outside the Soviet sphere of influence were undergoing economic miracles, Greece was undergoing the civil war which drastically set back any prospects of recovery there. The most thorough study of the first half of the period under consideration here is Alan Milward's *The Reconstruction of Western Europe 1945–51* (1984), which stresses that reconstruction was not simply from the devastation of World War II, but from a catastrophe which went back earlier in time. He sums up his main argument thus:

> Western Europe was reconstructed, not from the destructive consequences of the Second World War only, but from those of the catastrophic economic collapse of 1929–32 and, in so far as that collapse itself was attributable to the First World War, from the consequences of the First World War too. (p.463).

Once again you see how complicated the interrelationships are between war and peace, and peace and war, and how difficult it is to attribute consequences in a simple and direct way to any single war. Among points that can be made associating the economic boom of the post-war years with the war itself, are the following:

1   the idea of a new beginning, breaking away from the disastrous economic policies of the inter-war years (part of Milward's point);

2   the creation of new capacity, particularly technological capacity, to meet the special needs of war;

3   the readiness of certain countries (partly because of the destruction brought by war) to re-equip their factories, and rebuild their infrastructures, using the most efficient technologies;

4   the high level of demand in the post-war years because of the destruction of resources during the war;

5   the willingness in defeated or occupied countries to concentrate all energies on economic growth rather than the satisfying of consumer needs.

It has already been noted that European states as they were redefined after the war were more ethnically homogeneous than they had ever been before, though many ethnic problems remained (in Belgium as well as Russia, for instance) that were eventually to surface after the end of our period. Units 22–25 gave you a good deal of material on social welfare and class, to which more has been added in the first section of this unit. In the primary sources to be studied in this section, look out particularly for issues relating to material conditions, customs and behaviour, women and the family, high and popular culture, and political institutions and values. (As regards material conditions, always bear in mind the forces of contingency, and particularly questions of climate and pestilence; the winter of 1945/46 was the coldest of the century, worse than that of 1941/42, and in Russia, for instance, thousands starved to death.)

I now want to take up again the discussion of the two Germanys initiated through the extracts from Ralf Dahrendorf.

The two Germanys

The series of exercises on documents in this sub-section are intended both to develop your skills in the interpretation of documents, and, through the additional information that I provide in my discussions, to develop your knowledge of social change in the two Germanys.

Exercise   Turn to document II.38 in *Documents 2*, the speech by Konrad Adenauer.

1   Say what this document is and set it in its historical context.

2   Adenauer says, 'a new chapter of German history in the postwar years begins.' What is he referring to?

3   He also says, 'We do not, of course, possess as yet complete freedom'. What is he referring to?

4   Identify the main social problem discussed in paragraph 2, and discuss its significance.

5   What international development does Adenauer refer to?

6   What new international development does he propose?

7   In connection with explaining these international developments, what oblique reference does he make to the war?

8   Where do we find a reference which suggests Adenauer's own political affiliation? ∎

Specimen answers and discussion   1   It is always a delicate question knowing exactly how much historical context to give. Just to make sure you are familiar with the main developments relating to political institutions and values, let me recall (and this would be important for setting the context in an examination) that as relationships between the Soviets and the Western powers deteriorated, the western occupation zones were amalgamated into first the Bizone and then the Trizone, which formed the basis of the German Federal Republic recognized by the Allies on 8 April 1949, when the Allied Military Governors were replaced by Civilian High Commissioners. That the arrangement was not seen as a permanent one is illustrated by the fact that instead of a fundamental Constitution, the new Republic simply had a 'Basic Law' enacted in May 1949. First elections took place in August 1949, with the first session of the new parliament meeting on 7 September. Konrad Adenauer had been 'dug out' by the Allies as an experienced politician (of conservative cast, but as a native of the Rhineland looking to Germany's Western associations, rather than to its Prussian traditions). He became leader of the new German Christian

Democracy, and now emerged as Chancellor of the new Republic. It is in this capacity that he is here addressing the Civilian High Commissioners. Obviously Adenauer would not be able to say anything that would offend them; at the same time he had to appeal to his own German voters. In fact, Adenauer was an extremely shrewd politician, and this speech exemplifies the careful path he always trod. (You may not have included anything like these last remarks; however, as you know, it is important always to say something about the author of any historical document.)

2   The new chapter involves the convening of the German Federal Assembly, the election of a President, the choosing of a Chancellor (Adenauer), and the appointment of a cabinet.

3   'Complete freedom' is impinged upon by the Occupation Statute and the existence of the High Commission.

4   The social problem is that of the refugees. Obviously it was a problem that called for action by the government. At the same time, the flood of refugees furnished West Germany with an abundance of willing, and relatively cheap, labour.

5   The international developments are European co-operation and the Marshall Plan.

6   Adenauer proposes, with reference to international control over the Ruhr, that such international exploitation should be extended to the industrial areas of other countries.

7   The oblique reference is to the way in which the independent European nationalisms led to 'the splintering of life in Europe', which appears to be a euphemism for the war.

8   When Adenauer refers to 'the sources of European civilization, born of Christianity' this reminds one that he himself is a Christian Democrat. □

Exercise   Now turn to document II.39, 'Law for Safeguarding the Freedom of the Press'. Now, apart from noting that this document has the same date as the previous one (*always* consider the date of a historical document), so that much of the same context applies, you will not know much, if anything, of the detailed background to this law. Let me therefore tell you that the Basic Law of May 1949, in keeping with the intention of encouraging the fundamental political values of Western democracy, had guaranteed the freedom of the press. However, the High Commission was still concerned that nothing hostile to its own position should be published, and continued to exercise overall censorship and control, basically by means of a system under which all newspapers, publishers, broadcasting companies, etc., had to secure a licence from the Commission. This particular requirement was ended by Law No.5 of 21 September 1949, though ex-Nazis were still prohibited from owning any of these agencies (John Sandford, *The Mass Media of the German-speaking Countries*, 1976, p.27). The general tenor of this law, elaborating on issues of freedom and restriction of the press, can be taken as demonstrating that the Basic Law was itself considered temporary.

It seems to me that three major issues, relating on the one hand to the general development of society, behaviour and culture, and on the other to the relationship between the Allies and the German Federal Republic, emerge from this document: what do you think they are? ■

Specimen answers and discussion   The points that struck me are:

1   The document demonstrates the continuing power of the Allied High Commission over the new Republic – this emerges in articles I, II (paragraphs 1 and 2), III, IV, V and VI.

2   The document demonstrates the significance of 'press, radio and other information media', characteristics, one could say, of 'mass society' – this emerges particularly in articles III, IV and VI.

3   The Allies are quite prepared to apply techniques of control and censorship, which have certainly not disappeared now the war is over – this is particularly apparent in articles VI and VII. □

Exercise   Turn to document II.40, the announcement by the German Economic Commission of the Soviet High Commission.

1   Which one of the documents you have already studied does this parallel?

2   I have noted three significant ways in which it differs from that document: what do you think these are?

3   How genuine is the appearance of democracy presented in the document? (You will probably only be able to answer this in general; I shall add some details in my answer and discussion.)

4   Is this document more of a propagandist tissue than the Adenauer speech? (I shall answer that after you have dealt with the next document.) ■

Specimen answers and discussion   1   This parallels document II.38, in that it is referring to the setting up of the German Democratic Republic. In parallel with the West, the Soviet Military Administration in Germany had been replaced by a Soviet High Commission.

2   This is a statement from the occupying Commission, not a German politician. It refers to an impending development – the actual date of the setting up of the German Democratic Republic being 11 October 1949. While the Adenauer document refers to the Allied occupying powers, there is no mention of Russia in this document.

3   The reference to the strongest fraction in the People's Chamber is not completely phoney, since three parties were still permitted to exist in the Russian zone: the Socialist Unity Party (the product, however, of a forced union of the Socialists and the Communists in April 1946), the Christian Democrats, and the Liberal Democrats. However, the actual popular vote had been limited in that only a single list of candidates (drawn from the three parties) was presented to the voters – the only choice they had was to vote 'no', and actually one-third did do this. Mention is made of representatives of the *Länder*; as you may recall from Dahrendorf, there was a deliberate policy of diminishing the powers of the *Länder*. □

Exercise   Read carefully document II.41, the Resolution of the Central Committee of the Socialist Unity Party on formalism in art.

1   Does the regime regard culture as important? Can you make any comparisons with Western attitudes to culture?

2   Does the document maintain that cultural achievements in East Germany have been high? Do you have any comments on this view?

3   What thesis with regard to Americanization does this document support?

4   What is the attitude of the Resolution towards modernism in the arts? What label does it apply to modernism?

5   What political arguments does it make about modernism?

6   What art does it support?

7   Where is the model for this kind of art to be found?

8   How do you find the general tone of the Resolution? ∎

Specimen answers and discussion

First of all, I want to answer question 4 from the previous exercise:

4   Not altogether, would be my reaction. Adenauer's speech is not without its own propagandist elements, though I would have to say that it does seem closer to what was really happening than does Document II.40.

1   Clearly culture is regarded as very important, since it is seen as informing all other attitudes and activities (political, social, etc.) – this is typical of the attitude of one-party dictatorships. State subsidy of the arts had increased greatly in Britain as a consequence of the war experience and the setting up of the Arts Council. The other Western countries generally subsidized such high cultural activities as opera, drama and music either on a local or national level. While there isn't the same instrumental vision of the inter-relationship between culture and ideology, it was part of the progressive, optimistic, psychological consequences of the war that the state should support the arts, as well as social welfare. (You wouldn't need to say all of that in commenting on this document; however, any comparisons and contrasts that you can make are always to be welcomed.)

2   The Resolution is very critical of East German cultural achievements. If you happen to be aware that the distinguished Marxist playwright Bertolt Brecht had returned to East Germany in October 1948, along with many other talented though internationally lesser known figures, you might feel that this was a puzzling judgement.

3   The Resolution supports the thesis that with American economic and political power has come the Americanization of Western culture.

4   The Resolution is very hostile to modernism, which it labels 'formalism'.

5   The political argument is that formalism equals cosmopolitanism which equals American imperialism.

6   The Resolution supports realism in art.

7   The model is provided by the USSR.

8   I can only say that I find the tone that of hectoring, ludicrous propaganda. It is certainly true that one could find pronouncements as daft and as hysterical among extreme right-wingers in the West, but I for one find it amazing that apparently intelligent people should expect their purposes to be served by this kind of unpersuasive rubbish. If you can muster arguments to take up a different view, then all credit to you. □

Exercise   Turn to document II.42, the two statements by the government of the GDR.

1   What is the historical context of these documents?

2   Who are these two government statements blaming?

3   How would you define the wider historical significance of these documents for the study of war, peace and social change? ∎

Specimen answers and discussion

1   The immediate context is obviously disquiet in East Germany, and the riots that have broken out in consequence. Here is a little more detail. Under the East German Five-Year Plan, while wages were squeezed, there was also a concentration on industry, and therefore an attack on farmers; in turn, there were constant shortages of food. Thus there was already a good deal of sullen discontent when on 5 March 1953 Stalin died. On 9 June the 'New Course' was announced from Moscow, which resulted in many of the most severe measures of the East German Five-Year Plan being cancelled on 11 June. However, this principally meant the mitigation of the attacks on farmers and intellectuals, and did not directly benefit the working class, especially since the decree of 28 May 1953 calling for at least a 10 per cent rise in productivity norms was not rescinded. On 16 June a strike and demonstration were mounted by construction workers on the *Stalinallee* in East Berlin. On 17 June there were strikes and demonstrations involving over 300,000 workers, about 5 per cent of the total labour force. The Soviet Army immediately declared a state of emergency and cleared the streets. However, demonstrations continued on 18 June in Halle-Merseburg and Magdeburg. The ruling Socialist Unity Party seemed to have lost control; 21 demonstrators were killed. The workers' demands were both for higher wages and lower productivity norms, and for political liberalization. In the restoration of stability, the economic demands were conceded, but not the political ones. By 1955, just to complete the story, the three-party system still existed, but control was now back as firmly as ever in the hands of the Socialist Unity Party (see David Childs, *The GDR: Moscow's German Ally*, 1988, pp.31–3). Both of these documents are therefore immediate reactions to the rioting on 17 June.

2   The blame is placed on the fascist agents of foreign powers, West German capitalist monopolists, and so on (that concessions were made indicates that recognition that there were real grievances could not be avoided).

3   This document relates to the defeat and occupation of Germany as a result of World War II and more specifically to the way in which East Germany lay under Soviet dominance. The documents themselves are clear evidence of discontent within East Germany, and of the public attitude of the government there which was to blame foreign capitalism, etc. You might wish to relate the document to Dahrendorf's theories about a continuing revolution of modernity in East Germany, and the continuing persistence of conflict. For myself, I would be content to use the document to point up the contrasts between East and West Germany in the aftermath of war. □

For further information on the two Germanys you could consult David Childs and Geoffrey Johnson, *West Germany: Politics and Society*, 1981; J. Krejci, *Social Structure in Divided Germany*, 1976; and Martin McCauley, *The German Democratic Republic since 1945*, 1983. McCauley, just to round off this sub-section, argues (p.78) that by 1955 the class structure of the GDR was very similar to that of the USSR (and this model could probably be taken as accurate for all of the East European countries). He divides society into two large classes, the working class and the collective farmers. Then there are two 'strata' – the intelligentsia and the ruling stratum, 60.5 per cent of whom, he reckons, originally came from the working class, and which in total comprise about 10 per cent of the population.

Life in an average French town in 1950

Exercise   I want you now to turn to document II.43, 'An average French town in 1950'. Just note for your own general information, with regard to changes in class structure, the social composition given at the beginning. Then read the rest of the document carefully. I want you to note down what it tells you about such questions as Americanization and the effects, or lack of them, of World War II, and about social distinctions and social snobbishness. I suggest you just note down your comments as you work your way through the document: that is the way I am going to give my comments in the specimen answer below, rather than structuring them into an organized commentary. Then I'd like you to speculate a bit as to how representative this document would be for the rest of France, and then for other parts of Europe. ■

Specimen answer   After the table, the very first sentence makes the comment that people's leisure
and discussion   activities are differentiated by social class (or 'social strata' as the authors put it). The next two sentences are equally positive: the cinema takes first place. Is this just the normal development of modernization, or mass society, or is it a result of the war experience, or of Americanization? There are arguments that in difficult wartime conditions people tended to take refuge in, and therefore developed a taste for, the cinema. On the other hand, we do know that the cinema was already growing rapidly in popularity before the war. At this point, the document does not provide any definitive answers. What the next paragraph repeats is that people from different social backgrounds go to different cinemas. Most interesting are the comments on the *Select*. The religious influence is clear in that the cinema was built by a Monsignor in the Catholic church, and it is part of a chain directed by the organization 'Familia' in Paris. All this seems to date back to pre-war times, though it is noteworthy that the cinema was reconstructed in 1948. We do then get an answer to the Americanization question: according to this document the public favour French films, while success for American films, it is said, depends on their being shown in conjunction with publicity in the film journals. (Note the detail of preferences, which may well be useful to you in answering other questions; they do not relate to the specific questions I have asked.)

The argument for the war having popularized radio is probably stronger than that for the war popularizing film, though again the document does not make the connection. The figures are certainly worth noting.

Now we learn that reading in fact shares first place with film-going. The origins of this activity clearly go back well before the war. Yet the jump in books borrowed as between 1939 and 1945 is quite considerable: it can be argued that in the restricted conditions of wartime, people do turn to reading (this is certainly demonstrable in Britain). Again we find some class distinctions in reading habits. Detective stories are widely popular, and, on the evidence from bookshops, translations from English. Now whether this indicates a growing popularity for American-style crime novels is impossible to say. It is known from other sources that British books were quite popular (this matter is also discussed in Unit 15 of the Open University course A324 *Liberation and Reconstruction*). Thus there is no positive support for the Americanization thesis. Does one, in any case, think of the Americans as rating reading among their top two leisure activities?

It is significant that the Auxerre Stadium was built in 1942, since this would suggest a link with Vichy policies of encouraging sport. Again we must note the influence of the same Monsignor, which this time goes back even before the First World War. Football, if anything, betrays a British influence, but perhaps basketball betrays an American one. In general, I hope you agree, this is an interesting document with a fascinating range of information.

Now, before speculating on how far it is representative of the rest of France, or the rest of Europe, one really ought (as a basic first question) to have asked how reliable it is for Auxerre itself. If you look at the end of the document, you will see that what we have here is a social survey. It has been carried out, though you would not know this, by two distinguished academics; so although there may have been room for the expression of some slightly snobbish opinions, we can on the whole take it as being as reliable as such a survey could be in 1950. (One could reasonably argue, incidentally, that the idea of systematic social surveys was very much a product of American universities.)

What other areas of France are there? Well, there are big cities and there are purely agricultural areas. In so far as this comes, as it were, 'in the middle', it might be considered as representative as any single document could be. One could reasonably speculate that the biggest variations would come in Paris, but perhaps also Lyon and Marseilles.

As for the rest of Europe, this is probably going to be more typical of the West than the East, though perhaps the activities specified would not be all that different: great emphasis will certainly be given to sports and to youth in the Eastern countries. No document can possibly be representative, and certainly not over a wide range of regions and countries, but I feel that this gives you as good a single insight as you could get. Maybe what strikes us most today is the relative lack of sophistication of the activities and attitudes listed. Whatever changes the war may have brought, there were still many other transformations to come, with the further advances of modernization, mass society and, above all, the advent of consumer affluence. □

The role and status of women

It is in this realm of social change that some of the bitterest arguments over the effects of war have raged: generally, feminists have argued that wars have had no significant effects in improving the position of women. Simone de Beauvoir's massive *The Second Sex*, published in France in 1949, has become the bible of feminism. It is worth noting what she wrote in the historical chapter of that book, entitled 'Since the French Revolution: the job and the vote'; she has just been describing the activities of the British suffragettes:

> The war intervened. English women got the vote with restrictions in 1918, and the unrestricted vote in 1928. Their success was in large part due to the service they rendered during the war. (*The Second Sex*, 1988 edition, p.155)

I propose to conclude the discussion of this topic by looking at some extracts from *The Second Sex* (there is a more thorough discussion in A324, *Liberation and Reconstruction*, Unit 13). How, if at all, does this book relate to the study of war, peace and social change? To speak of the book as a 'consequence' of the war would, of course, be absurd. However, de Beauvoir does rank with the group of Liberation writers who achieved popularity with the reading public in the post-war years. In the words of Maurice Crouzet:

the literature that found most favour with a public disappointed in the conventional variety was that of the liberation, whose most impressive representatives or interpreters were Albert Camus, Jean-Paul Sartre, Simone de Beauvoir and Maurice Merleau-Ponty. It was these philosophers and writers who, inspired by the ideas of Heidegger, Jaspers and Husserl, made existentialism fashionable. Their works offered the pessimistic picture of an artificial, absurd, incomprehensible and useless world in which man feels frustrated and cheated, for 'It is a suspended death' and 'every society creates its own hell'. (*The European Renaissance since 1945*, 1970, p.139).

Simone de Beauvoir, to put matters as concisely as possible, was part of an intellectual and literary movement which was itself part of the concluding phase of the war in France. *The Second Sex* is not an existentialist work, but a very powerful analysis of the position of women in contemporary society, drawing upon Hegel's concept of self and other, and upon anthropology, sociology, biology and psychoanalysis. Clearly it relates to European society as it was in the immediate post-war years, but references to World War II, direct or indirect, are very rare. Quite obviously the book owes most to de Beauvoir's own experience and intellect: in the philosophy degree she took at the Sorbonne in 1929, she came second to Jean-Paul Sartre, who was to be her life-long companion. But the book is of central relevance to war, peace and social change in that it both offers evidence for the status of women in the aftermath of World War II, and is a key text in the modern feminist movement, given that the old question of the relationship of war to the changing status of women and to feminism remains a legitimate subject for discussion and debate. In so far as *The Second Sex* persuasively and convincingly identifies the disabilities still affecting women, it is evidence that whatever changes have been brought about by two world wars must have been quite limited in character; but then the manner in which de Beauvoir identifies the nature of these disabilities, and the remedies which she proposes, may well suggest that there could be no possibility that the sort of experiences which wars bring could affect these disabilities.

These points are offered as guidance on how you can relate the extracts from *The Second Sex* printed as document II.44 in *Documents 2* to the major themes of this course (and it is along these lines that I shall be setting the questions in the exercise that follows shortly). We have printed less than half a dozen pages from a book which runs to two volumes each of about 400 pages, but even these few pages are immensely rich, and may well provoke very individual responses from different readers. As a primary source this is obviously very different from the ones we studied earlier in this unit.

Both de Beauvoir and Sartre, it is useful to know, were supporters of the French Communist Party. In estimating the significance of *The Second Sex*, it is also helpful to know that the original French edition of 1949 was translated for American publication in 1953 and, later the same year, British publication. The book has been continuously in print in both French and English (and many other languages) ever since, with the latest British paperback edition coming out in 1988. Extract (a) comes from the historical chapter early in Book One, shortly after the comment I have just quoted on British women and the First World War. Extract (b) comes from the last main chapter in Book Two, in Part VII, which has the general title 'Towards Liberation', while the chapter itself is entitled 'The Independent Woman'. Extract (c) is from the Conclusion.

Exercise   Now read the extracts from *The Second Sex* printed as document II.44. You may well wish to note down other points that particularly strike you, but I want you to note down answers to the following questions:

1   What indications are there that women *have* recently made considerable advances?

2   What indications, if any, are there that these are in any way directly or indirectly related to the Second World War?

3   What are the basic disabilities that women still suffer from?

4   How does de Beauvoir propose that these be removed? Are wars relevant, or irrelevant, to such proposals?

5   Extract (c) presents an idea, related to one of the approaches to history that I discussed in Book I, Unit 1, and perhaps also to de Beauvoir's politics, which has been central to most feminist writing since. Identify, discuss, and critically evaluate this idea. ■

Specimen answers   1   Extract (a) seems to end very optimistically with its reference to the United
and discussion   Nations Commission on the status of women: 'the game is won'; 'The future can only lead to a more profound assimilation of woman into our once masculine society.' Of course, this quotation recognizes that this assimilation is far from having taken place at the time de Beauvoir is writing (in fact, the remainder of this chapter goes on to qualify the optimism). Soviet women, who anyway are 'in a singular [or exceptional] condition', having made great advances, have now suffered set-backs. French women, in theory at least, now have the main civil liberties. Today, according to extract (b), it is less difficult for a woman to assert herself.

2   De Beauvoir refers to the 'masculine' and, indeed, 'military' activities of Russian women in World War II. Perhaps there is an implicit connection here with the aspects of the status of Russian women de Beauvoir admires, but certainly no explicit connection is made. The major reference, really, is to the United Nations Commission, if we follow the train of thought that the United Nations, and the various commissions associated with it dealing with economic, cultural and social matters, were products of the war. I would certainly see the United Nations Commission on the Status of Women as representing both the 'psychological' desire for a new beginning engendered by war, and also the recognition of women's participation in the war effort; but that is not an argument that would command universal support. The connection is not made explicitly, but you would certainly be expected to be able to comment in an exam that the French woman's right to vote only came in the concluding stage of the war. On the whole I think one has to conclude that de Beauvoir does not provide very powerful testimony in support of the thesis about the connection between advances in the status of women and war.

3   Women's biological role in the family was clearly what lay at the heart of the set-backs in Soviet Russia. But the main point made at the beginning of extract (b) is women's lack of economic independence. However, as extract (c) makes clear, although the economic factor is the basic one, there remains the fundamental problem of the way in which society socializes females into being different from males.

4   The emphasis throughout is on positive, interventionist or 'guided' action by the state. In the first extract it is clear that de Beauvoir greatly admires the interventionist action on behalf of women taken by Lenin. In the last extract she refers to changes in laws, institutions, customs, public opinion, and the whole social context, and goes on to indicate the necessity for a total transformation in the way in which children are brought up and educated. Individual initiatives will be no good: 'The forest must be planted all at once' – that is, complete and comprehensive reforms must be enacted. De Beauvoir's emphasis, it seems to me, is very much on positive, intentional action, which is rather different from the unintended consequences of war that I have been discussing from time to time throughout this course. On the other hand, I would argue that the necessities of war sometimes did entail the near obliteration of gender differences. Possibly this is implied in the references to the Russian experience in extract (a); on the whole, however, de Beauvoir's text does not lend great support to this line of argument.

Comprehensive, deliberately planned change would seem to be what her arguments point to. As I have said, this text is particularly open to a wide range of personal responses. The critical thing is to consider the document in the context of its relationships to the major issues this course is concerned with, even if you feel that these relationships are tenuous or negative.

5   I wonder what you made of this difficult question. This time there definitely is a 'right' answer, but to get it you probably either have to be acquainted with recent feminist writings, or, like me, very interested in those approaches to academic study and life in general which in Book I, Unit 1, I described as 'Marxist/ sociological/linguistic' and which are most evident in contemporary cultural theory. If you are in tune with all that, then you will have identified the critical phrase as: 'in human society nothing is natural and . . . woman, like much else, is a product elaborated by civilization.' Woman, in other words, is not made by biology, but is made by society. It is out of this theory that the word 'gender' was created to replace the old word 'sex'; using the word 'gender' implies that the differences between men and women, once believed to be fundamentally sexual, are no more than what is decreed by society. De Beauvoir (like many other feminists, of course) does not go as far as this, recognizing elsewhere in her book characteristics, biological and physiological, particular to women. But the notion of woman as 'a product elaborated by civilization' has been an enormously influential and liberating one.

Now, I asked you to evaluate this idea critically. With respect to historical significance, which is what this course is about, it has undoubtedly had great influence on the development of the general movement of feminism (though after 1955, rather than before – I shall return to this). To discuss whether it is 'correct' or not would take us right back into the conflict over approaches to academic study, which I discussed in Book I, Unit 1. For myself, I shall simply say that I find nothing to quarrel with in Simone de Beauvoir's magnificently rich and complex development of this fundamental idea. I do happen to believe that it has, in some quarters, been pushed to absurd extremes. Think about it, and decide for yourself (the way one looks at this issue will affect the way one looks at historical issues in general). I would put it like this: because the roles and attributes of men and women manifestly are *influenced* by society (or civilization), that does not mean that they are *determined* by society. There is, in my view, a balance between social and biological factors. As I say, in this question is encompassed a whole debate about how one should look at society and history. □

The Limits of 1955

In getting into the little dispute above, so reminiscent of the discussion of academic approaches in which I was embroiled in Unit 1, I was actually thinking ahead to what I now have to tell you about our cut-off date of 1955. In the world of the ordinary British university teacher or student the problem scarcely existed in 1955. The basic principle of feminism which we have just identified only began to be developed and taken to a wider audience at the end of the 1960s and into the 1970s. Here, then, a salutary word of caution: this course ends with the working out of the consequences, or the *alleged* consequences, or the *possible* consequences, of World War II; it does not include those radical transformations which only began to become clear well into the 1960s. If one is to argue at all about war having effects on social change, then one must not simply concentrate on the period of the war itself; one must look for longer-term consequences, or, indeed, prepare oneself to recognize that whatever may appear to have changed during the war was in fact restored to 'normalcy' after the war. Thus it is necessary to go up to 1955, in order to pose such questions as: did wartime changes last that long, or did things go back to the way they were in the 1930s? Even given that things did not go back to the way they were in the 1930s (which they did not – though Maier, among others, is arguing that the basic patterns of power remained the same), was this really because of the war, or was it not because of, on the one hand, long-term structural and ideological forces, and, on the other, short-term political ones? What we do in a course such as this is to force you to reflect on serious questions; we try also to furnish you with the ideas, information, and reading to help you find some answers: in the end the answers should be yours.

To indicate how one might begin to arrive at such answers, I am going finally to look at the country which, as I write this unit, is the focus for my own specialist researches into the nature of contemporary society (if you want to look at *one* way of examining the complex but pervasive influence of World War II on British society, you could consult my *British Society since 1945*). First, however, I want to repeat my warning about the dangers of reflecting what happened in the 1960s and afterwards back into the post-war era prior to 1955. A great deal has happened since 1955: as you and other students read this course in the 1990s, you are as far from people in 1955 as people in 1955 were from people who had just experienced the First World War. In various of my writings I have spoken of a 'Cultural Revolution in Britain'; I see that as covering the 1960s, and originating only in the late 1950s. The contemporary feminist movement (thinking back to the de Beauvoir text we have just studied) in many ways began as a reaction to the 'male liberation' of this 'Cultural Revolution'. Martin Clark, whose excellent textbook *Modern Italy* we have used throughout this course, picked up the phrase: his chapter 18 is titled 'The Great Cultural Revolution: Italy in the 1970s'. Note the second half of the title. The lesson is clear: this course certainly includes the beginnings of the 'economic miracles'; it does not include the 'cultural revolutions'.

I turn, therefore, to Italy in the post-war years. In 1943, much of Italy was in turmoil and upheaval; as and where they had the opportunity, peasants took over the land by force (Clark, p.354). Clark makes the general comment, it not being very clear which precise months and years he is referring to, that: 'Governments were faced by rural revolt and, as usual, bought it off.' A temporary effect of war? Absolutely not: in 1950 a series of laws was passed setting up state land reform agencies which could take over land, improve it, and then sell it to peasants on long, low-cost mortgages, often also providing necessary services for the development and cultivation of the land. Generous loan facilities were provided by the state-sponsored bank for the south, *Cassa per il Mezzogiorno*. Even earlier, over the period 1945–46, a positive state-directed programme, aided by the wartime technological discovery of DDT, had wiped out malaria in the south: that is the kind of change on which there is no going back.

Social geography was one of our ten topics within the subject of social change: in Italy, well before 1955, there was a very marked migration to the great northern cities, both from the south in general and from the agricultural areas in central and northern Italy; to quote Clark again, 'Migration and urbanization were by far the most dramatic features of post-war population history.' At the same time, as elsewhere in Europe, death rates and birth rates were falling. These are not *directly* consequences of the war, but they are related to the major economic transformations, which in turn are *related* to war in the manner indicated in my earlier quotation from Milward.

Before 1955 some of the special new features of Italian society which were to have international implications were apparent: the development of the contemporary expresso coffee machine (a machine of a sort was at least as old as the Futurist movement), motor scooters, distinctive design in domestic interiors and motor cars, and theatrical and operatic presentations. Were these related to the war? All I can say is *perhaps* they were related to the *release* of the war (I am thinking of a release from the narrow restrictiveness of Italian society, apparent in the days of Giolitti and accentuated under Mussolini, I disagree with Dahrendorf's equation of 'totalitarianism' with 'modernity'). But it is difficult to go further. Clark speaks of speedy 'modernization' in the post-war years. His concluding chapters are full of statements like: 'A "mass", "lay" society was gradually forming; no-one had anticipated it, and few intellectuals welcomed it'; 'Italy in 1950 was a country of bicycles; in 1960, of motor-scooters; in 1970, of cars'; the south between 1950 and 1970 'had gone straight from an agrarian to a "post-industrial" society, without the intervening stage of industrialization'. But how far had things gone by 1955? Clearly, 1955 lies somewhere in the middle. Some courses encourage you to let your work spill on ever forwards to the present. This course concentrates on the two world wars; 1955 may be rather an artificial terminal point, but what we are asking you to concentrate on is developments related to, or at least *arguably* related to, World War II.

Look around the Europe of 1955 and you will find most Western countries governed by shifting, unsatisfactory coalitions, with, in Britain, a Conservative government still adjusting to wartime, and post-war, changes. Despite the death of Stalin in 1953, Eastern Europe was still very much in its post-war ice age: the big rebellions were still to come (and to be crushed) in Hungary and Poland in 1956; the Berlin Wall was not yet built. Much of what has most affected our world today – the Beatles, militant feminism, colour television, Japanese economic supremacy, *glasnost* in Eastern Europe – was still in the future.

You should note that the following section is written by Tony Aldgate.

3 SOCIAL CHANGE: THE QUESTION OF MASS SOCIETY

At the outset of my discussion of mass society in Book III, Unit 19, I looked at some questions arising from Michael Biddiss's book *The Age of the Masses* (1977). To conclude the topic, I should like to do the same. The following extracts come from his final chapter on 'Ideas and society in post-war Europe'. Consider, first, what he marks out as the distinguishing features of East European culture in the aftermath of the war:

> In the Soviet bloc the development of ideas over the whole period since 1945 has been greatly affected by the Kremlin's fluctuating assessment of how much freedom of expression it is prudent to tolerate. The nature of the alliance against Hitler had raised some expectations that henceforth the USSR might sustain a more relaxed and less isolationist policy regarding communication with the West. Yet the fact that great numbers of Russian soldiers had been in contact, however temporary and imperfect, with alien influence actually made Stalin all the more determined to minimize such exposure during peacetime. This further tightening of state control over all aspects of intellectual and cultural life was supervised by Andrei Zhdanov, until his death in 1948. Under his direction the scholar or creative artist in search of audience and livelihood was ever more strictly compelled to operate within an appropriate craft organization policed by the party bureaucracy. Officialdom dictated to painters not merely the style but often also the subject of their work; the products of the Russian cinema declined in quantity and quality alike; even a composer of Shostakovich's eminence could be reprimanded for writing music insufficiently concordant with mass taste . . . Stalin certainly proved himself the enemy of cultural diversity both amongst the non-Russian populations within the USSR itself and amongst the various nationalities of the new 'satellite' states beyond.
> (*The Age of the Masses*, pp.316–17)

Now read what Biddiss has to say about West European culture:

> During the first years of peace a whole spate of impressive creative work became public. Much of this was suffused by the Resistance spirit, and was embodied in items that could not be properly presented, or completed, or even begun while Fascism flourished. Only after this initial outburst did it become plain just how heavy was the toll that the war had levied on the creative spirit and just how rare would be works of lasting worth. While Eastern European literary and artistic life suffered from the excessive uniformity of state-inspired realism, imaginative effort in non-communist countries was complicated by a dearth of agreed deadlines. Amongst most westerners there was certainly some similarity of mood. The overthrow of Fascism prompted a shared sense of relief; and soon there developed, more soberingly, an equally widespread awareness of the depth to which Europe had been materially and morally wounded and of the gravity of dilemmas and threats ahead. Even so, there was far less consensus about appropriate modes of response to these problems and perils. Traditional lines of demarcation between genres were often blurred, and styles were adopted and discarded with great rapidity. Such variety and fluidity were sometimes stimulating, but more often they were merely confusing.

> Political messages were still quite common, yet they became generally harder to interpret. Much avant-garde culture, in particular, seemed more than ever remote from both the concerns and indeed from comprehension of a mass public. (*The Age of the Masses*, pp.325–6)

The passages are rather dense and complex, especially the second one where Biddiss is attempting the difficult task of comparing East with West, and surveying the Western cultural context. But I trust you will be familiar with some of the issues he is raising from your reading on the post-war period thus far.

Clearly, Arthur Marwick, for instance, would agree with Biddiss's initial summary of Eastern Europe under Soviet hegemony. He has, after all, just described it as an 'ice age'. Earlier, you may recall, he pointed out how the theories gradually monopolizing cultural life in the Soviet zone of Germany were based on models formulated in the Soviet Union. Cultural conformity was sought from new satellite states like the German Democratic Republic by means of Soviet-inspired resolutions calling for greater 'realism in art'; this in turn meant uniform socialist realism of the Soviet variety, which, as we have seen, had evolved during the 1930s. It is noticeable also that many of the interminable party debates on culture in the Soviet zone of Germany simply reworked the Soviet concerns of that era. They were based upon 'dogmas articulated and implemented during the 1930s', as David Pike puts it, 'and these were little more than the norms associated with socialist realism in the Soviet Union during the same decade' ('Cultural politics in Soviet-occupied Germany, 1945–46', *Journal of Contemporary History*, vol.24, no.1, January 1989, p.105). There was, indeed, much that was repressive, regressive and stultifying in the Stalinist cultural policies imposed on post-war Eastern Europe. But their effects are difficult to ascertain. Arthur Marwick, you may remember, was distinctly sceptical about the 'hectoring, ludicrous propaganda' of the East German SUP's resolutions on art, which he dismissed as 'unpersuasive rubbish'. That may well have been the sort of response it engendered in its day. Perhaps in 1989, especially, with the remarkable events in Eastern Europe and the demands for autonomy on the part of several of the Soviet satellite states, we have witnessed the legacy of the high Stalinist period and its hostility towards cultural diversity and pluralism in all forms.

When it comes to post-war Western culture, by contrast, Biddiss and Marwick plainly agree, once again, that there was an initial phase of impressive creative work and cultural regeneration. Here, too, realism was the dominant aesthetic induced by the war, but it was artistically rich and imbued with the resistance spirit. Yet for Biddiss in particular this was a short-lived phenomenon. The traditional divide between the cultural elites and the mass public soon reappeared.

Let us examine, first, the nature of the cultural elite's response to post-war reconstruction, which contributed to this divide. I want you to look at an extract from one of Roberto Rossellini's films. Rossellini is often considered the founding father and a leading exponent of the Italian neo-realist cinema which emerged at the end of the war. In such films as *Roma Citta Aperta* (1945) and *Paisa* (1946) he explored the nature of the Italian reaction to the wartime experience (these films are discussed in considerable detail in A324 *Liberation and Reconstruction*, where the whole question of neo-realism and its impact on post-war Italian culture is broached). For the third film in his war trilogy, *Germania Anno Zero* (*Germany Year Zero*, 1947), Rossellini concentrated on Germany at the moment of defeat.

Exercise   Set in 1945, *Germany Year Zero* chronicles the experience of a twelve year old boy among the rubble and ruins of bombed-out Berlin. His father is ill, his brother, an ex-soldier, is in hiding from the authorities, and his sister is compelled to drink with Allied soldiers for cigarettes which can then be bartered for food to eke out the family's precarious existence. Falling under the influence of his former schoolteacher, an unrepentant Nazi who dutifully trots out such catchphrases as 'The weak are always eliminated by the strong', the boy administers poison to his ailing father. The extract you are about to watch comes from the very end of the film.

Watch item 20 on video-cassette 2 now, bearing in mind the following questions:

1   What does this film convey?

2   Why do you think the film turned out to be a commercial failure? ■

Specimen answers and discussion   1   It conveys the extent of the destruction and devastation of Berlin at the end of the war. The city is destroyed and so too are its people, with the family unit disintegrating under the pressures of everyday survival. It is a bleak picture with an added note of personal despair. The boy is lost, alienated and defenceless. Christianity can offer no solace (the symbolic meaning, surely, of the scene by the roofless church), and the only guidance he has been given comes from the warped mentality of a former member of the Nazi educational establishment. Death is now a commonplace in the city (notice the casual loading of his father's coffin on to a lorry already heaped with coffins). The boy is oblivious to the calls of his sister, who seems remote as he looks down from a vantage point in the ruined buildings opposite, and the only way out is suicide. There is a lot of critical debate, as you can imagine, about the meaning of the boy's suicide. Rossellini maintained the intention was to show that the 'flame of morality is not extinguished in him'. He commits suicide to escape the 'malaise and contradiction' of 'an erroneous education', 'the false morality which is the very essence of Nazism', and which leads the child 'to perpetrate a crime while he believes himself to be carrying out an heroic act'. Whatever moral dilemmas the film may highlight, to my mind it reveals an essentially nihilistic vision of the world.

2   Though, of course, any answer to this question must be largely speculative, I cannot help but think that the film failed simply because it was too bleak and too pessimistic. People did not want to see this sort of thing. German cinemagoers were no more inclined to watch their own film-makers' rendition of the problems that beset them. Wolfgang Staudte's *Die Mörder Sind Unter Uns* (*The Murderers Are Among Us*, 1946, produced in East Berlin) and Helmut Kautner's *In Jenen Tagen* (*In Those Days*, 1947, made in West Germany) are often cited as examples of the native 'Trummer' (rubble) films, the German efforts that most closely parallel the concerns of the Italian neo-realists. Yet they too did badly at the German box office. The British film of *The Wicked Lady* (1945), a costume melodrama starring James Mason and Margaret Lockwood, epitomizes the sort of film that did well in Germany, West and East alike, in the immediate aftermath of the war. Escapism was, unsurprisingly, very much the order of the day. The audience for neo-realist films throughout most of Europe was generally confined to the realms of elite art-house cinemas. Even in Italy, neo-realism proved a short-lived movement whose concerns and forms were increasingly seen as being far removed from the interest of the masses. □

Stills from classic neo-realist films: (top left) Germania Anno Zero *(dir. Roberto Rossellini, 1947);* (top right) Riso Amaro *(dir. Giuseppe de Santis, 1948);* (bottom) Roma Citta Aperta *(dir. Roberto Rossellini, 1945) (all courtesy British Film Institute)*

Stills from the neo-realist film Paisa *(dir. Roberto Rossellini, 1946) (courtesy British Film Institute)*

Having looked, however briefly, at the relationship between the cultural elites and the mass public, let us now examine the political elite's perceptions of the masses. As you know from your reading earlier in this unit, Charles Maier argues that the European political elites, appreciating the impact of World War II and its proletarianizing results, devised strategies of reconstruction and restoration that were designed to re-establish the old order. How well did these strategies work?

Exercise   Documents II.45–II.47 in *Documents 2* are the transcripts of commentaries to four official government films. The first is an American documentary made late in 1944 and shown from April 1945, just before the end of war in Europe. The second is a British Crown Film Unit documentary made in the summer of 1945 and released at the outset of 1946. The third and fourth are from the Anglo-American newsreel, *Welt im Film*, which was compulsorily screened in Germany between 1945 and 1950. Read them now, and then answer the following questions:

1   Who were these films aimed at?

2   What points of emphasis do you detect and what were the intentions?

3   What would you say they generally reveal? ■

Specimen answers and discussion   1   The first was clearly an indoctrination exercise intended for American troops in Germany. The second explains the government of the British zone of occupation and was obviously meant for domestic audiences in Britain. The third and fourth were plainly examples of newsreel stories primarily intended for exhibition to the occupied German population.

2   The American film is somewhat vindictive in tone and urges vigilance as the troops embark on full-scale occupation. After a potted history of German militarism, it emphasizes the collective guilt of the German people for the war and cites this as a reason for non-fraternization. While equally intent on conveying the message of collective German guilt, the British film is really more concerned with showing how some of the principles agreed among the Allies for the reconstruction of Germany – de-Nazification, democratization and re-education – are being put into practice. The 'get tough' attitude advocated before war's end had noticeably softened into a more conciliatory note once the actual process of reconstruction got underway and the sheer size of the problems was revealed. (The extent to which there was genuine disagreement among the Allies over their approach to reconstruction has already been outlined in Unit 26. The Potsdam agreement essentially settled on the so-called 'Four Ds' – demilitarization, de-Nazification, democratization and de-industrialization – though not without considerable debate, as you have seen. Nicholas Pronay has argued, however, that Britain saw re-education as the paramount issue throughout and central to all objectives, plans and propaganda on the matter. See his introduction in N. Pronay and K. Wilson, *The Political Re-Education of Germany and Her Allies*, 1985.)

The first *Welt im Film* newsreel from June 1945 shows much the same sort of emphasis on the complexity of reconstruction, with stories on returning prisoners of war, the recovery of stolen artworks, the rebuilding of democracy through the restoration of a free press and the establishment of a new education system (under Allied control and supervision, of course), and the investigation and execution of war criminals. It concentrates, predictably, on the German defeat and Allied power, with some space reserved, you will note, for an item stressing the efforts of

Russian and American forces alike in the liberation of Czechoslovakia. By June 1948, however, *Welt im Film* has clearly become a mouthpiece for the Western Allies alone. Now the Soviet Union is the enemy and Berlin 'the symbol of the new democratic order in a Germany that hungers after peace'. The Cold War is engaged and the Americans, British, French and Germans are working together to break the Soviet blockade of the city which 'serves only to intensify the determination of democratic peoples everywhere'.

3   Perhaps the most obvious feature about these items is the extent to which they reveal, once again, a belief in the power of propaganda and the malleability of the subjects chosen as its target. In the event, little of this official propaganda appears to have achieved its desired effect. *Your Job in Germany*, for instance, argued a policy which, as David Culbert has pointed out, was 'abandoned well before the film completed its original run' (see his essay, 'American film policy in the re-education of Germany', in Pronay and Wilson, p.180). Non-fraternization proved, as Culbert states, 'a totally unenforceable regulation'. Similarly, the policy stressing collective German guilt was soon abandoned. 'The futility of such feelings became apparent', Culbert notes, when occupation forces discovered that 'The physical destruction of so much of the country . . . meant that practical matters relating to food and housing obviously took precedence' (p.175). Indeed, if anything, official films like *Your Job in Germany* could prove counter-productive to the urgent task of reconstruction when given a general release to civilian audiences. 'While everyone directing occupation policy in the American zone turned to the practical matter of feeding a starving German populace', Culbert concludes, 'groups in America learned emotional responses to oppose such largesse' (p.190).

Audience reaction to the British Crown Film Unit's *A Defeated People* was always likely to be similar: why help a people we have spent so long trying to overcome? (Hence, perhaps, the attempt to offset such questions with its obvious *vox populi* introduction.) The Crown Film Unit was disbanded in 1951. The endless stream of commercial feature films made between 1946 and 1958, which gloried in the war and evoked traditional stereotypes of the enemy, might provide a more accurate picture of the way in which the British preferred to view their former foe. □

Welt im Film fared little better, it appears, when it came to the considerable task of re-educating German cinemagoers. Official surveys reveal some measure of animosity towards these Allied newsreels. Their impact can be judged from anecdotal and impressionistic sources. One German schoolboy, for instance, remembers that the tune which accompanied the newsreel titles was invariably greeted by a chorus of young voices singing a home-made verse:

Haut sie 'raus, den Tommy	(Chuck 'em out, the Tommies
Haut sie 'raus, den Ami	Chuck 'em out, the Americans
Haut sie 'raus, den Russki	Chuck 'em out, the Russians
Haut sie 'raus, das allierte Pack	Chuck 'em out, the Allied rabble)

(Quoted in Roger Smither, *Welt im Film 1945–1950*, Microfiche Film Catalogue No.1, Imperial War Museum, 1981)

The official surveys highlighted certain salient, if unsurprising, features – not least the finding that 'The Germans have been filled to overflowing with propaganda, and will reject in disgust any output which tastes even faintly of an attempt to propagandise'. Little wonder, then, that the re-education policy proved difficult to implement, especially given that the wartime ideals on which it was based – the ideals that had been marshalled to inspire the British and Americans to fight 'the Good War', 'the Justified War', 'the Necessary War' – were hardly likely to recommend themselves to a nation imbued with its own ideology but now defeated and on the receiving end. Inevitably, the successful reconstruction of Germany owed less to Allied propaganda espousing the cause of re-education, albeit highly-minded and laudable, than it did to the provision of such essentials as economic help and support. By contrast, when it came to 'selling' the Marshall Plan, more sensible and pragmatic opinions prevailed about the wartime prop-agandist ideals. 'These ideas all revolved round the notion of *raising living standards everywhere*, of economic well-being as the key to social and political stability', David Ellwood states, 'of Fascism and Communism as roughly the mirror image of each other, produced by backwardness, underdevelopment and misery'. Thus, the operating principles applied to Italy, as elsewhere, agreed that:

> ERP is a unique chance offered to European nations toward reconstructing their economy, raising the standard of living among the masses, and attaining by the year 1952 an economic stability which is the foundation of political independence . . . Every worker, every citizen is bound up in their rebirth. The future and the peace of Italy and Europe, the general well-being of all, depend on the will and the work of each single one of us. (Ellwood, 'From "re-education" to the selling of the Marshall Plan in Italy', in Pronay and Wilson, p.232)

Thereafter, the campaign set out to 'Carry the message of the Marshall Plan to the people. Carry it to them directly – it won't permeate down. And give it to them so that they can understand it' (p.229). The people could hardly fail to get the message when the Marshall Plan Freedom Train bore the slogan 'Prosperity makes you free' while distributing gifts, aid and comfort. 'This was the meaning of the Marshall Plan', Ellwood concludes, 'a vision of consensus and prosperity conveyed by a programme of action which brought material aid and propaganda together as never before' (p.220).

Conclusion

If you were to go to the cinema in Britain during 1955, there was a considerable amount of choice. Fancy a musical? Take your pick from *Carousel*, *Guys and Dolls*, *High Society*, *The King and I* or *Oklahoma*. It was a particularly good year for musicals, but they were all American, of course. American war films and westerns did well, too. Of the latter, you made your selection from John Ford's *The Searchers*, starring John Wayne, or two films directed by Anthony Mann, *The Far Country* and *The Man From Laramie*, both starring James Stewart, among the many others available. When it came to war films, there was Jeff Chandler in *Away All Boats* and Van Heflin in *Battle Cry*. If you insisted on a British film you did not fare badly. War films predominated, it must be said, what with *The Colditz Story*, *The Dam Busters*, *The Sea Shall Not Have Them*, *The Man Who Never Was*, *Cockleshell Heroes* and *Ill Met By Moonlight*, with *Reach for the Sky* just around the corner. But then we were, after all, 'retreating from Empire', and life at the time was nothing if not insular, even parochial. Hence also the Ealing comedies such as *The Ladykillers*. British radio was little different. *Family Favourites* and *Children's Hour* were just two of the regular and popular attractions. As far as BBC television was concerned, the coronation had set the standard there.

For Britain in 1955, as indeed for much of the rest of Western Europe, the 'cultural revolution' was yet to come. Yet one minor 'revolution' did occur in Britain in that year, or so it was construed at the time. In September 1955, new regionally based television companies started broadcasting in competition with the BBC. Commercial television had arrived. For many this was, indeed, a momentous event. Lord Reith, who had long advocated the principle that British broadcasting should provide 'the best of everything', spoke of it in scathing terms. His opponents in a significant House of Lords debate in May 1952 argued in favour of 'giving the public what it wants' – 'Trust the people' was the Lord Chancellor's motto. What, though, had really changed? As you read the extract from Reith's speech in the Lords (document II.48 in *Documents 2*), consider also the following summary of the events, what it tells you about the values that informed the debate and about the way in which the elite construed the masses:

> In 1946 when television broadcasting was resumed, the BBC's popularity at home and prestige abroad were even greater than before, largely because of the wartime experience. Yet barely a decade later the BBC's monopoly of the air waves was destroyed. Television and subsequently radio were placed on a new competitive footing. More than anything else, this has shaped the aims, structure and output of all television programming over the last quarter of a century.
>
> The change was not brought about by public pressure but by a small group within the ruling Conservative Party. It was opposed by bishops, vice-chancellors, peers, trade unions, the Labour Party and most national newspapers. Reith compared the introduction of commercial broadcasting into England with that of dog racing, smallpox and bubonic plague. The objections to commercial broadcasting were diverse, but most were anti-American, and opposed the encouragement of crude materialist desires. Criticisms of this kind were particularly vehement on the left . . .
>
> The commercial lobby fought a hard and frequently unscrupulous battle. It was successful because important members of the government, including the Prime Minister, Churchill, were not prepared to defend the BBC. Significantly, the campaign also had the active support of Lord Woolton. He had modernised the Conservative Party organisation before the 1951 election and brought a new kind of candidate into Parliament. This group represented industry and advertising rather than law or hereditary wealth.
>
> Woolton wanted free enterprise to dominate the 'new age of postwar prosperity'. 'Our individual lives today', he complained in a broadcast, 'are hemmed in by no less than 25,000 controls.' He wanted to associate the party with the long-term material aspirations of the people and believed that commercial television would help to do this.
>
> The opposition to commercial television was organised by the National Television Council with Christopher Mayhew as its secretary. Support came from surprising quarters. 'The establishment', wrote Henry Fairlie, 'came as near as it has ever done to organising a conspiracy against the government of the day – a Conservative Government.' This group objected to the cultural consequences of commercial television – it would 'vulgarise, bowdlerise, and coarsen', wrote one critic.
>
> The argument became more fierce when it was learnt that in America the Coronation had been shown interspersed with NCB's television chimp,

J. Fred Muggs, selling tea. A deodorant had been advertised just before the ritual anointment. Horrified MPs suggested that if a commercial system were started here, royal tours would be interrupted by commercial breaks extolling the makers of the Queen's chairs and carpets.

Nevertheless the Act introducing commercial television was passed in 1954 because most Tories believed that in some way it would promote industry, commerce and the free market. The new service was named by some genius of euphemism, 'Independent Television'. (James Curran and Jean Seaton, *Power without Responsibility*, 1981, pp.205, 207–8)

Thus the advent of commercial television in Britain did not reveal much greater 'trust' being placed in 'the people', as some advocates claimed, any more than it did elsewhere in Western Europe. The arguments about its introduction and the victory it represented were redolent, most of all, of traditional elitist perceptions of the people as passive, gullible and manipulable individuals or of the greater mass audience as a crude and materialistic open market. It is not surprising, perhaps, that one commentator has been prompted to observe of contemporary Europe: 'One of the characteristics of the mass society of which radio and television have become the principal structuring machinery is the sense of powerlessness, the feeling on the part of individuals that there no longer exists any part of the overpowering mechanism of society in which they can intervene' (Anthony Smith, *The Shadow in the Cave*, 1976, p.273). Clearly, World War II did something to change the nature of the relationship between the masses and the elites. How far, though, did the post-war period see a restoration of the old elitist arrangement of society?

Selected bibliography (note: works referred to in the text are listed in the references)

Addison, P. (1985) *Now the War is Over. A Social History of Britain 1945–1951*, London, BBC and Jonathan Cape.

Armes, R. (1971) *Patterns of Realism*, London, Tantivy Press.

Briggs, A. (1979) *The History of Broadcasting in the United Kingdom*, vol.IV, *Sound and Vision*, London, Oxford University Press.

Ellwood, D. (1985) *Italy 1943–1945*, Leicester, Leicester University Press.

Forgacs, D. (ed.) (1986) *Rethinking Italian Fascism, Capitalism, Populism and Culture*, London, Lawrence and Wishart.

Gerner, K. (1986) *The Soviet Union and Central Europe in the Post-War Era*, London, Gower.

Guess, G. M. (1987) *The Politics of United States Foreign Aid*, London, Croom Helm.

Harper, J. L. (1987) *America and the Reconstruction of Italy 1945–1948*, Cambridge, Cambridge University Press.

Pollard, R. A. (1986) *Economic Security and the Origins of the Cold War 1945–1950*, New York, Columbia University Press.

Short, K. R. M. (ed.) (1976) *Western Broadcasting over the Iron Curtain*, London, Croom Helm.

Smith, A. (ed.) (1974) *British Broadcasting*, Newton Abbot, David and Charles.

Smith, A. (1978) *The Politics of Information. Problems of Policy in Modern Media*, London, Macmillan.

Smith, A. (ed.) (1979) *Television and Political Life. Studies in Six European Countries*, London, Macmillan.

Thomas, R. (1976) *Broadcasting and Democracy in France*, London, Bradford University Press/Crosby Lockwood Staples.

Tunstall, J. (1977) *The Media are American: Anglo-American Media in the World*, London, Constable.

Williams, A. (1976) *Broadcasting and Democracy in West Germany*, London, Bradford University Press/Crosby Lockwood Staples.

References

Biddiss, M. (1977) *The Age of the Masses. Ideas and Society in Europe since 1870*, Harmondsworth, Penguin.

Childs, D. (1988) *The GDR: Moscow's German Ally*, London, Unwin Hyman.

Childs, D. and Johnson, G. (1981) *West Germany: Politics and Society*, London, Croom Helm.

Clark, M. (1985) *Modern Italy 1871–1982*, London, Longman.

Crouzet, M. (1970) *The European Renaissance since 1945*, trans. S. Baron, New York, Harcourt, Brace, Jovanovich.

Culbert, D. (1985) 'American film policy in the re-education of Germany', in Pronay and Wilson (eds).

Curran, J. and Seaton, J. (1981) *Power without Responsibility: The Press and Broadcasting in Britain*, London, Fontana.

Dahrendorf, R. (1968) *Society and Democracy in Germany*, London, Weidenfeld and Nicolson.

Ellwood, D. (1985) 'From "re-education" to the selling of the Marshall Plan in Italy', in Pronay and Wilson (eds).

Keller, S. (1963) *Beyond the Ruling Class: Strategic Elites in Modern Society*, New York, Random House.

Krejci, J. (1976) *Social Structure in Divided Germany*, London, Croom Helm.

McCauley, M. (1983) *The German Democratic Republic since 1945*, London, Macmillan.

Maier, C. S. (1981) 'The two post-war eras and the conditions for stability in twentieth-century Western Europe', *American Historical Review Forum*, vol.86, no.2, April.

Maier, C. S. (1975) *Recasting Bourgeois Europe: Stabilization in the Decade after World War I*, Princeton, Princeton University Press.

Marwick, A. (1980) *Class, Image and Reality in Britain, France and the USA since 1930*, revised edn 1990, London, Oxford University Press.

Marwick, A. (1982) *British Society since 1945*, revised edn 1990, Harmondsworth, Penguin.

Marwick, A. (1986) *Class in the Twentieth Century*, Brighton, Harvester Press.

Milward, A. (1984) *The Reconstruction of Western Europe 1945–51*, London, Methuen.

Perkin, H. (1989) *The Rise of Professional Society: England since 1880*, London, Routledge and Kegan Paul.

Pike, D. (1989) 'Cultural politics in Soviet-occupied Germany 1945–46', *Journal of Contemporary History*, vol.24, no.1, January.

Pronay, N. and Wilson, K. (eds) (1985) *The Political Re-education of Germany and Her Allies after World War II*, London, Croom Helm.

Sandford, J. (1976) *The Mass Media of the German-speaking Countries*, London, Oswald Wolff.

Smith, A. (1976) *The Shadow in the Cave*, London, Quartet.

Smither, R. (1981) *Welt im Film 1945–1950*, Microfiche Film Catalogue No.1, London, Imperial War Museum.

INDEX